CINEMA AND COMMUNITY

CONTEMPORARY APPROACHES TO FILM AND TELEVISION SERIES

A complete listing of the books in this series can be found online at wsupress.wayne.edu

General Editor
Barry Keith Grant
Brock University

Advisory Editors
Robert J. Burgoyne
University of St. Andrews

Caren J. Deming
University of Arizona

Patricia B. Erens
School of the Art Institute of Chicago

Peter X. Feng
University of Delaware

Lucy Fischer
University of Pittsburgh

Frances Gateward
California State University, Northridge

Tom Gunning
University of Chicago

Thomas Leitch
University of Delaware

Walter Metz
Southern Illinois University

CINEMA AND COMMUNITY

Progressivism, Exhibition, and Film Culture in Chicago, 1907–1917

Moya Luckett

WAYNE STATE UNIVERSITY PRESS   DETROIT

© 2014 by Wayne State University Press, Detroit, Michigan 48201. All rights reserved. No part of this book may be reproduced without formal permission.

18 17 16 15 14   5 4 3 2 1

Library of Congress Cataloging-in-Publication Data

Luckett, Moya.
   Cinema and community : progressivism, exhibition, and film culture in Chicago, 1907–1917 / Moya Luckett.
       pages cm.— (Contemporary approaches to film and media series)
   Includes bibliographical references and index.
   ISBN 978-0-8143-3725-7 (pbk. : alk. paper) — ISBN 978-0-8143-3726-4 (ebook)
   1. Progressivism (United States politics) in motion pictures. 2. Motion pictures—Political aspects—United States—History—20th century. 3. Motion picture audiences—Illinois—Chicago—History—20th century. I. Title.

PN1995.9.P755L83 2013
791.43'6581—dc23

2013000150

For Mum and Dad, with all my love.

CONTENTS

Acknowledgments ix

Introduction: Progressivism, Modernity, and Transitional Cinema 1

1. From Crowds to Communities: Progressive Era Spectatorship Theories 26

2. Progressivism and Early Feature Films: Textuality, Oversight, Uplift 50

3. Celebrity, Self-Awareness, and the Consciousness of Self 93

4. Private Pleasures and Public Space: Community Culture and the Dominance of Neighborhood Theaters 130

5. Oversight and Regulation: Film Censorship, Local Government, and Social Reform 169

6. Citizenship and Black Cinema 206

7. Patriotism and Patronage: Regional and National Identity in Chicago's Theaters during World War I 253

Conclusion 294
Notes 299
Index 399

ACKNOWLEDGMENTS

As befits a book that took such a long while to write and research, I owe many thanks to all those involved in the process. My dissertation advisor, Don Crafton, and my committee members, Tino Balio, Lea Jacobs, and David Hayman, helped me start the process of mapping this area of early cinema. Tino Balio first opened my eyes to the significance of film history while Tom Gunning, Vance Kepley, and Lynn Spigel's classes and counsel inspired me to explore the interfaces of media history, theory, and criticism. I was fortunate to study with a supportive and stimulating group of grad students, including Steve Classen, Sean Feeney, Kevin Glynn, Antonette Goroch, Mike Quinn, Greg Smith, Jeff Smith, and Pam Wilson. Particular thanks go to my dearest Madison friends who always continue to inspire me: Lisa Parks, Jenny Thomas, Alyssa Goldberg, Shari Goldin, Aniko Bodroghozy, Jeff Sconce, and Jan Levine Thal.

My students at the University of Houston were a constant delight and helped make my short spell in Texas very special, especially the time spent with Marcy Basile, Jesse Handy, Erik Ribeiro, Shannon Harrison, and Bruce Abbate. At the University of Pittsburgh, my greatest thanks go to Jane Feuer and Kathie Ferraro (and their cats Cyd and Phoebe) for their kindness, fierce intelligence, sharp wit, love, friendship, wisdom, strong counsel, and amazing hospitality. They will forever be part of my family. I was very fortunate to have such supportive and inspiring colleagues as Jane, Lucy Fischer, David Bartholomae, Nancy Glazener, and Neepa Majumdar. Particular thanks go to my graduate students and my teaching assistants, David Sidore, Daniel Wild, Barry Howell, and Hugh Manon, as well as Amanda Klein, who offered sage advise on the book, particularly its introduction, and along with Al-

ACKNOWLEDGMENTS

lyson Wuerth and Coral Ruppert truly enriched my life in Pittsburgh and beyond. John Kikrilis, Patrick Sutton, and Tiffany Habay helped me to see another side of Pittsburgh before we explored New York life together, while Chris Androlia and Shawna Sullivan became the dearest of friends with whom I've shared Madonna and Spice Girls concerts, shopping, cat shows, and much laughter. Special thanks go to Daniel Wild, Susan, and Angela DiGeronimo for their kindness and support.

I thank the staff at the archives and libraries who helped me locate the resources necessary to write this book, particularly Charles Silver at the Museum of Modern Art Film Library, the staff at the interlibrary loan departments at New York University and the University of Pittsburgh, the archivists at the University of Illinois–Chicago special collections, and the staff at the Chicago Historical Society and Chicago Public Library.

This book would not have been possible without support from Anna McCarthy and Rick Maxwell. I am most grateful to Pamela Church Gibson for all her help, advice, and friendship. Special thanks go to my colleagues and students at NYU, particularly Richard Allen, Antonia Lant, Chris Straayer, Jonathan Kahana, Patricia Lennox, Ken Sweeney, Melanie Daly, Cathy Holter, Dana Gravesen, Rebecca Bachman, and the students in my early cinema, historiography, and women's picture courses. Thanks also go to my wonderful Gallatin students, particularly Colby Jordan, Laura Kraisinger, Blair Lancer, and Emily Levine. At Queens College, special thanks go to Amy Herzog, Julian Cornell, Karen Mandoukos, Nelson Torres, and so many of my undergraduates.

My friends in New York have helped me both with the book and with much needed down time. Everybody should have a friend as good, as loyal, as funny, smart, and kind as Alyssa Goldberg. Noah Tsika and Sue Collins read countless drafts of the manuscript and provided first-rate critical feedback as well as firm friendship and support. Ben Horner has been the perfect dinner, desert, movie, and TV companion and I am fortunate to have him as a friend. Brynn White, Ashley Swinnerton, Brittan Dunham, and Taso Georgakis are remarkable people who have shared their film knowledge and DVD collections with me. Cindy Im, Monica Pelaez-McGinley, and Caroline Sinders helped make fashion even more fun, along with ex–New Yorker in Portland, Marti

ACKNOWLEDGMENTS

Zimlin. In Brooklyn I was lucky enough to have the best neighbors ever in Deborah Berman and Warren Shaw and wish they were still just a few feet away.

Evan Cooper deserves special thanks for his role helping this book come to fruition, for his encouragement in gently steering me to work and reminding me when to stop. He has made my life better, easier, more fun, and more, and is a very special person and great father-to-be. Thanks go to our adorable cats, Peeps, Blue, and Remy, for being their very lovely and very silly selves, the ideal distractions and perfect cuddlers. I thank Evan's wonderful family—Tobey and Syd Meistrich, Alison, Eddie, Jesse, Rebecca, and Aliza Phillips—for welcoming me into their homes and lives. I love every minute I spend in their company.

Most of all, I want to thank my family and friends in the UK. Nothing could have ever happened without the support of the best parents ever—Mum and Dad if I can do a fraction of the job you did and continue to do, I'd be very happy. My wonderful brother, Giles, and his amazing wife, Carol, have offered peerless hospitality and support throughout all my crazy adventures, for which no thanks could ever be adequate. I thank them and their lovely daughter, Molly; Dominic; Cara; and my gorgeous niece, Charlie, for the precious time we spend together. Sarah Broyden has been the sister I never had and is a stunning inspiration, making me push myself to greater successes. Harry Aubrey is the truest, most loyal friend and the sweetest person I've ever met. Tim, Sue, Max, and Sadie Juby are the best friends anybody could ever have and their kindness and generosity is peerless. Thanks also go to my other friends from Kent, particularly Clare, Gabriel, and Anna Furey and Graham Hitchin and Jenny Hammerton. Margo Boye-Anawoma has been one of my dearest friends for well over half my life, and I thank her and her husband, Martin Soorjoo, for their generosity and kindness. Thanks also go to Pat and Derek Cox Maurice and the late Sue Broyden, Clifford and Ruth Walters, Jane, Rachel, and the late Sten Laue-Knudsen. And last, but far from least, my high school friends, Christiane Groom, Sue Framington, Debsy Fletcher, and Sarah Mitchell. I just wish I could spend more Thursday mornings at Caffe Nero in King's Lynn with all of you, walk around the town laughing at gold groovers, and see you more often. It's friendships like the ones we share that inspire me and ground my next book.

ACKNOWLEDGMENTS

Special thanks go to series editor, Barry Keith Grant, and the anonymous readers for their invaluable feedback and suggestions. Annie Martin has been the most supportive editor and I thank her so much for her help at all stages of this process. Thanks go to the other staff at WSUP, including Kristin Harpster and Maya Whelan, and freelancer Dawn Hall, who have made this process remarkably smooth and enjoyable.

Introduction
Progressivism, Modernity, and Transitional Cinema

Caught between the seemingly protoclassical emergence of features and the older model of the short film program, the 1910s have typically posed a problem for studies of early American film. Our understanding of this cinema's institutional and textual developments is limited, partly because we lack a coherent conceptual framework to contextualize its operations. In the following work, I fill some of these gaps by looking at the period's social and cultural climate: American Progressivism. In the process I move away from the problematic idea of decades, looking at 1907–17 to get a better sense of this period, its defining characteristics and distinctive features. Much as the Cold War influenced the 1950s, Progressivism shaped this period's cinema, culture, and social life. As is typical of Progressivism more generally, constant change marked this period of film history, witnessing the rise of stars, serials, features, and the stabilization of exhibition around the neighborhood theater.[1] As Charlie Keil and Ben Singer note: "If the movies were indeed representative of American modernity during this decade, it was arguably the ever-changing nature of motion pictures and the rapid transfiguration of the industry creating them that capture most vividly the representative quality."[2] Rather than winnowing down options in favor of the all-dominant feature-length film, this period needs to be seen as one of increased diversity.

Exploring this cinema from the vantage point of Progressivism reveals important continuities between American film and society that highlight the industry's debates, concerns, and goals. Cinema was a typically Progressive institution, attesting to the period's investment in leisure, its more public lifestyle, and its fascination with celebrity. Significantly, Progressivism structured multiple ways of seeing, visual modes that informed cinema's formal discernible structures and modes of address while also defining its characteristic conceptual space, bridging public and private. The industry generally participated in Progressive culture, as seen in exhibitors' emphasis on community, leadership, and its more general emphasis on uplift, a trend that marked much film production—from pictures on matters of public interest to those based on literary classics and theatrical adaptations. Indeed, many of cinema's defining characteristics during this period, such as its community, oversight, self-awareness, uplift, and national identity, were quintessentially Progressive.

Considering this cinema in terms of Progressivism raises issues of periodization. Despite substantial changes, there was still much continuity between 1907 and 1917, particularly in terms of exhibition. Throughout these years, the movies were deeply invested in more collective forms of spectatorship and reception, as seen in the industry's focus on the community-centered neighborhood theater. Even though many important producers and distributors (like Paramount, Lasky, World, Mutual, and Triangle) were formed during the 1910s, most pioneer Trust companies remained in business until 1917–18. Despite marked differences, films from 1907 and 1917 shared distinctive aesthetic properties, frequently evoking the continuities between motion pictures and society. Often formally open, these films flirted with the culture and its values while variously locating themselves in the context of the spectators' imagination, the theater auditorium, within a community of moviegoers, in the context of myriad new writings about cinema as well as the broader climate of public recreation.

Historically, Progressivism predates the era of cinema under consideration, raising questions about the separation of this cinema from the period of attractions, a period marked by self-conscious cinematic display and exhibitionism that lasted from the medium's inception to 1907–8. As the Progressive Era is usually dated from around 1890 to 1917, it encompasses the earliest films and even forms of precinema. Although these first movies exhibit some of this period's key traits, I do not consider them fully part of Progressive Era cinema—not simply because they were nascent and underdeveloped novelties. Indeed, attractions owe much to Progressivism. They blur the lines between public and private and foster spectatorial self-awareness through their use of display and exhibitionist address. Along with the period's other new media, such as tinfoil sound recordings, and its new recreations, such as professional sports and amusement parks, they demonstrate the rise and expansion of leisure as central to American life. Novelties abounded in Progressive society and were part of its ongoing process of change. But even as the public thrilled at these sensations, Progressive Era culture was more invested in taming and rationalizing these forms. As historian Sean Dennis Cashman states, Progressivism was invested in the "desire for reason, order, efficiency," goals linked to its overriding attempts to temper modernity's attractions into more disciplined cultural ideals.[3] After 1907, motion pictures would follow what historians Steven J. Diner and Jackson Lears consider a quintessentially Progressive path: their novelties were industrialized, integrated into big business, and were attracting mass audiences with developed and systematic forms of circulation, promotion, and address.[4] For these reasons I exclude prerental system, prenickelodeon cinema from consideration, positioning this later post-1907 cinema as more Progressive because it participates in the broader mandate of stabilizing continual change. Nonetheless, the relationship between sensations/attractions and the later, more integrated cinema is important as it attests to the kind of dialectical tensions at the heart of Progressivism.

Progressive Era cinema emerges, then, as motion pictures become big business, a characteristic that historians like John Whiteclay Chambers II, Steven J. Diner, Richard Hofstadter, Jackson Lears, and Daniel Earl Saros all see as central to Progressivism.[5] The formation of a trade press was important in establishing cinema as a developed, modern industry, replete with its own discourse and institutional ideals. First published in 1907, the period's most important trade, the *Moving Picture World*, testifies to a major shift in cinema's status, self-presentation, aspirations, and institutional status. Upholding such Progressive ideals as uplift (moral, cultural, social, and educational improvement) and community, the *World* distanced itself and its putatively more reputable readers (primarily distributors and exhibitors) from sensational cheap amusements. Besides testifying to cinema's reinvention along Progressive lines, the *World* marks a movement away from modernity's seemingly random shocks and sensations.[6] Although the relationship between Progressivism and modernity demands further examination, I first want to outline Progressivism's most important conceptual features, its quintessential ways of seeing and distinctive understanding of public life and modern subjectivity. Together, these provided the framework for this cinema—aesthetically, institutionally, and in terms of its reception.

Conceptualizing Progressivism: A Specific Way of Seeing

Unlike the Victorianism it displaced, Progressivism was specifically American, imbued with ideas of progress and change even as it struggled to balance novelty and order. More than a period of American history, Progressivism represented a new way of seeing that emerged during the transition to a more complex, modern, industrialized, and consumer-oriented society. It is not easy to define though, partly because it was rooted in debate and in pragmatic action.[7] As social historian Rivka Shpak Lissak notes, Progressivism may not possess a singular or consistent ideology but it had "a general common ideological denominator."[8] It was not without its own distinctive cultural vantage point, however, one that called for a new and improved social order. John Whiteclay Chambers II summarizes this process:

> The Progressive Era holds particular significance because it represents America's first full-scale attempt to come to terms with the rapidly emerging multicultural, urban, industrial society. Western "modernization," which has been described as a process of change in which social institutions have been altered to adapt to mechanization and rising economic productivity, touched virtually every aspect of American life. . . . Furthermore, significant ambivalence permeated this transitional era, tensions between seeking change—the idea of progress was, after all,

part of the American creed—and wanting to preserve traditional ways of life, especially traditional values concerning individual liberty and opportunity, personal and traditional morality, and pride in the Republic.[9]

Despite tensions between old and new, debates over the role of government, individual liberties, and the growth of big business, Progressive Era concerns centered on a set of identifiable issues. As Chambers suggests, the period's overarching priority was managing modernity's now waning shocks and sensations into a new coherent culture—an agenda that was perhaps too ambitious in an era of rapid transformations. Other important concerns involved upholding community, uplifting culture, and making society more transparent so that its workings could be made visible, monitored, and thereby improved—stabilizing a new American national identity in the process. This stronger American citizenry would presumably be able to resist social dangers like crime, vice, and the debased pleasures linked to cheap entertainment and urban anonymity—all phenomena linked to the period's industrialization and modernity.

Chambers isolates four dimensions of Progressive reform: curbing big business to make it accountable to the public and American values, reforming government to eradicate corruption, helping "exploited workers and the urban poor," and "a coercive effort by old-stock Americans to impose a uniform culture based on their values."[10] The first two authorized intervention in the name of the public good, while the latter pair licensed middle-and upper-class intrusions into more private spaces and ways of life. Soon, all American culture appeared subject to oversight and regulation, from workplaces to businesses, cities, homes, cheap amusements, and even fashion. Still, many Progressive policies were widely beneficial, despite the substantial attention given to quasi-Victorian forms of "charitable" intervention, incarnated in the archetypal meddling reformers of D. W. Griffith's films and the seemingly disruptive operations of early film censorship.[11] In her study of American literary naturalism, June Howard calls attention to Progressivism's often liberal and altruistic undercurrents, as it prioritized tackling crime, cleaning up urban politics, and protecting the poor.[12]

Such a complex society could not reach its goals without guidance and monitoring, however, hence the increased authority granted all levels of government. Progressivism was therefore unusual in American history, giving the state powers to reform business and modern culture, using legislation to tame "the mayhem of unchecked modernization," including the rise of large corporations, mass immigration, widespread urbanization, and the growth of cheap amusements and consumer culture.[13] Although a variety of agencies and professionals, including charities, social workers, trade unions, and universities, helped in regulatory efforts, the federal government was the only institution with the authority to take on trusts, price-fixing, oligopolies, and other combinations that consolidated power among major corporations.[14] The most famous of these laws was 1890's Sherman Antitrust Act, a foundational piece of Progressive Era legislation. While these expanded government powers were an interim strategy to improve American life and maintain national identity, they represented a major and not uncontroversial shift in American thought.[15]

Nevertheless, pragmatic considerations motivated much Progressive Era reform. Rapid urban expansion challenged the private sector's capacities by the 1880s, duplicating some services (like railroads) while almost entirely abandoning others (like city planning, and health and social services for the new urban poor).[16] As Richard Hofstadter observes, these interventions foregrounded the inadequacies of America's fabled free markets: "The Progressive movement . . . may be looked upon as an attempt to develop the moral will, the intellectual insight, and the political and administrative agencies to remedy the accumulated evils and negligence of a period of industrial growth. Since the Progressives were not revolutionists, it was also an attempt to work out a strategy for orderly social change."[17] Such "evils and negligence" were most often found in modern cities like Chicago and New York. Besides housing new corporations, banks, factories, and stockyards, these metropolises had rapidly expanded upward and outward, making urban geography opaque. Complex institutions in their own right, these cities appeared increasingly unmanageable, leading city councils, police, social workers, and reformers to develop strategies to monitor their residents (particularly the poor) at work and at play. Vice of all kind could be hidden here, often under the guise of cafés, saloons, and cheap amusements, while rampant poverty threatened the physical health of many residents, including large numbers of immigrants.

Metaphors of vision abounded in period discussions of cities and large corporations, further pointing to the need for reform, with the idea of pure oversight linked to the restoration of a neoclassical social order. Such a gaze structures famed architect and city planner Daniel Burnham's unimplemented 1909 Chicago City Plan and marked the City Beautiful movement more generally, linking beauty and cleanliness to moral uplift, physical health, and greater order. Associations between vision and order are important as they helped define one of the era's characteristic looks—oversight or monitoring, a gaze that licensed public intervention into otherwise private elements of everyday life to combat broader social problems. This gaze marked two of the period's signature professions—social work and investigative journalism. Both endorsed scrutiny of private life for the greater public and individual good, as seen in muckraking journalism and novels like Upton Sinclair's *The Jungle* (1906). In drawing attention to these "watchdogs of Progressivism," Cashman highlights the structural role of this forceful monitoring gaze and its capacity to improve life (workplace legislation, shorter working weeks, educational reform, improved housing) as well as its less welcome interventions into areas like recreation and immigrant culture.[18]

Besides caring for the urban poor, Progressive reformers turned their attention toward immigrants, hoping to assimilate them into a more polite society closer to their own values and away from ghettoes and cheap entertainments.[19] Such interventions were often unwelcome, leading to the period's Americanization movements and its broader anxieties over national identity.[20] With many immigrants arriving together from small towns and villages, they preserved communities and rituals to the chagrin of many reformers and assorted urban onlookers.[21] As Chambers observes: "Without restriction or purposeful social direction, industrialization, urbanization and immigration seemed to threaten American traditions of individualism, competition and opportunity and the ideal of a democratic relatively classless society of independent producers."[22] Concerns about national identity consequently became central to Progressivism, with immigrant and urban masses together exacerbating period fears about modernity's capacity to erase American individuality and destabilize culture and order.

INTRODUCTION

Community seemed to be a panacea for the anonymity and dangers of the modern city. Historian Daniel Eli Burnstein describes how this Progressive Era model of community combined traditional American individuality with civic responsibility, merging "individual fulfillment . . . and individual responsibility to others."[23] Steven J. Diner further links community to the all-important idea of progress, something that "could be measured by the extent to which individuals in a society worked together for the common good, since it was achieved collectively, not individually. Individual fulfillment came only through society."[24] Community became central to a Progressive Era sense of order, variously incarnated in the period's settlement houses, black and ethnic theaters, churches, YMCAs, neighborhood movie theaters, local athletic leagues, and the urban clean-up campaigns Burnstein discusses. Representing an ideal to which individuals and institutions could both aspire, community became associated with uplift, the Progressive ideal of moral, intellectual, and social improvement often linked to the arts, physical recreation, and more edifying entertainments.

As American society looked closely at itself, monitoring its institutions and the private behavior of its citizens via the period's reform, muckraking, and leisure surveys, it became increasing self-aware and self-conscious. This self-monitoring would be replicated on a more individualistic scale in the period's personality culture with its self-awareness and "consciousness of self."[25] It also went hand in hand with the Progressive Era's more public, leisure-centered lifestyle and its diminution of truly private space. Functions formerly associated with the Victorian home, like restoration and moral rejuvenations, were increasingly associated with commercial recreations, prompting calls for moral reform and ever-tighter municipal regulations. Such tendencies produced a new understanding of social spheres, emphasizing the multiple and expanded functions of public life in an era in which the public increasingly eclipsed the private. Yet efforts to monitor public space testified to its greater openness—women, children, and immigrants all had greater access to urban life. For all its regulations, then, Progressive Era culture was more inclusive than Victorian society in terms of social life and access to public space.

The rapid rise in commercial amusements during the Progressive Era led to the reconceptualization of leisure as its own separate sphere:

in 1915, famed reformer and professor of social work Edward Alsworth Ross announced, "The three master forces fixing the mundane welfare of human beings are Work, Living Conditions, and Recreation. Students of society learned to appreciate the first two of these three before they noticed the third."[26] Now seeing play as essential, social scientists, domestic writers, and medical and religious professionals endorsed "healthy" recreation as necessary for a strong, well-balanced, and patriotic population.[27] They did not believe that this kind of recreation could be achieved in many urban homes, particularly in poorer districts, at least not without their intervention. As public recreation (be it in parks, saloons, movie theaters, or amusement parks) took on the restorative functions of the Victorian home, then, it became subject to increased scrutiny from film censors, municipal regulators, reformers, social workers, and the new professionals in this field who established journals like *The Playground*. Neighborhood theaters subsequently tried to offset such concerns, offering the comforts of an idealized home that most patrons would never otherwise experience—child care; comfortable furniture; clean, well-stocked restrooms; spacious lobbies; even ornate staircases. By adopting a quasi-domestic address, cinema further undermined the Victorian separation of public and private in true Progressive fashion.

Progressivism was more than the repressive and paternalistic force behind reform and censorship or the uplift movements motivating film education and groups like the National Board of Review.[28] It is more accurately seen as a complex and pervasive social climate that tried to manage modernity's ongoing cultural and technological changes. Cinema constituted this culture's emblematic entertainment and displayed its somewhat contradictory ways of seeing—uplift, distraction, oversight, and leadership. It was caught up in Progressivism's sociocultural battles as the film industry attempted to align the medium with values like uplift, community, and national identity while regulators sought to contain it through other Progressive mechanisms like censorship and regulation.

In what is probably the best known study of Progressivism and cinema, Lary May analyzes how 1910's film content mirrors a Progressivism that he defines as a constellation of uplift, censorship, and vice crusades.[29] But he also hints at a more nuanced understanding of the era's defining characteristics, gesturing to Progressivism's concern with the relationship between individuality, social order, and increased government power and its increased government interventions to "'order' the new."[30] He also acknowledges Progressivism's validation of public leisure and its anxieties about the consequences of improperly managed entertainments.[31] Although underdeveloped, these insights trace key elements of the conceptual framework that shaped this society and period film form, regulation, and exhibition.

More recent work returns to Progressivism, positioning this social context as a significant conceptual framework for 1910s cinema. For example, Charlie Keil positions Progressivism as integral to the industry's transformations, part of a context invested in change that produced new trends—picture palaces, film stars, features, and more widespread motion picture advertising.[32] Constance Balides considers the period's rise in public leisure in relation to workers' need to recuperate from increasingly routine and monotonous labor, a development that politicized recreation, sanctioning various state and charitable interventions.[33] She is particularly interested in the relationship among gender, class, and work, pointing to efforts to educate the increased number of women in the workplace about better forms of consumption. Crucially, Progressivism's new consumer economy necessarily displaced the nineteenth-century virtue of thrift, as society depended upon individual spending, even from the poor.[34] The more secular and somewhat bureaucratized morality that characterized Progressivism thus drew on education, surveillance, and theories of scientific management to manage the temptations of this increasingly consumer- and leisure-centered industrial economy even as it recognized their cultural importance and necessity. This ideological shift produced a series of anxieties about leadership and authority that marked the period's film censorship, exhibition, and its theories of spectatorship and left their mark on motion picture narratives, textuality, and its star/celebrity culture.

Progressivism and Motion Pictures

Progressivism structured cinema in significant ways beyond regulation and censorship. Its core traits are particularly important here—its deep concern with collective forms of self, its uplift, its reconsideration of public and private spheres, its heightened self-awareness, and its investment in stabilizing American national identity. Many of these characteristics were simultaneously linked to a somewhat nostalgic desire for community and were annexed to plans for a new, improved, and efficient American life. In struggling to manage modernity, then, Progressive culture was Janus-faced, simultaneously evoking the old and the new. Investments in community and fears of the crowd demonstrate this ambivalence, as the former evoked an idealized folk culture restored amid the flux of modernity, migration, and consumerism while the latter articulated increasingly paranoid visions of the changed modern subject. Yet both terms pointed to a recognizably different modern self, a socially and psychically collective subject potentially riven by individualistic yet mass-marketed consumer desires.

The film industry's efforts to negotiate such conflicting parameters marked the neighborhood theater, the period's dominant form of exhibition. As early as 1907–8, these spaces were associated with community, partly to placate critics, distance their entertainment from crowd consciousness, and offset regulation. But their enormous success was not the result of these forces. It instead signified how this community address enhanced cinema, particularly in fostering a more intimate relationship with the medium. Neighborhood theaters also provide insight into Progressivism's redefinition of public and private life, offering private pleasures in public spaces while locating recuperation outside the home.

Neighborhood theaters were developed with an idea of the audience—real or putative—in mind, and this practice was particularly Progressive. Audience study was part of a widespread effort to make sense of popular amusements and the new leisure culture, a practice that also had links to crowd theory.[35] Municipal, academic, and reform interests in recreation and spectatorship testify to Progressive Era society's self-monitoring, a practice that heightened public self-consciousness. Cinema and print media further compounded such self-awareness, encouraging the public to eavesdrop into other people's real or fictional lives, watching unseen from the shadows. These practices translated into film form and narrative, participating in Progressivism's more self-conscious and self-analytical culture. Print coverage increasingly tutored film audiences to think about their constructions of self in relation to identities performed on screen, and in the reported off-screen lives of their favorite players. This self-aware culture, with its emphasis on oversight, helped produce an inward-looking society in thrall with itself, fascinated with its own machinations. Such self-consciousness further encouraged audiences to think about the construction of self, testifying to the need to produce a unique identity and separate oneself from the crowd.[36]

Although contemporary spectatorship theory owes little to Progressive theories or social concerns, these earlier interventions laid important groundwork while simultaneously refining cinematic etiquette, reception practices, and regulation. Progressivism witnessed the earliest efforts to theorize spectatorship—arguably developing the very concept—sometimes in specifically cinematic terms, as in Hugo Münsterberg's, *The Photoplay: A Psychological Study* (1916), sometimes in terms of audiences more generally, as with Gideon H. Diall's *The Psychology of the Aggregate Mind of an Audience* (1897).[37] Most works positioned spectatorship as collective and psychosocial, not individualistic and text-centered, with this very model influencing film regulation, censorship, and building ordinances as well as exhibition practices.

Progressivism also influenced cinema in more straightforward ways. In highlighting *uplift*—a term used to refer to intellectual, moral, and spiritual improvement—it shaped trade press discourse, exhibition practices, and production trends like epics, instructional/educational films, feature-length documentaries, and prestige pictures. By the mid-1910s, the industry's increased efforts to position the medium as a national cinema participated in broader efforts to stabilize American identity. Censorship was another peculiarly Progressive phenomenon, combining uplift, monitoring, and oversight with an investment in establishing community standards. Other Progressive characteristics influenced the very fabric of cinema with the era's celebrity culture producing the social conditions that led to the rise of the film star.

Progressivism and Transitional Cinema: Rethinking the "Modernity Thesis"

As previously noted, this period has been termed "transitional cinema," a term Charlie Keil and Shelley Stamp apply to the years between 1907 and 1917.³⁸ Perhaps deliberately, this concept lacks an overriding structure, something Keil acknowledges: "Debates on the efficacy of the phrase 'transitional period' to identify the years when narrative cinema began to hold sway will continue unabated for some time, a strong indication that we are still working through the historiographical implications of periodizing the pre-Classical era."³⁹ Nonetheless, the concept is useful in challenging notions of 1910s films as either a "late" form of early cinema or proto-Classical constructions, instead placing them in the complex dynamic of their own time.⁴⁰ Rather than looking for sudden and irrevocable change—around the emergence of the feature film or the rise of picture palaces—transitional cinema rightly considers the period's innovations in terms of diversity, an important and significant historical development. Seen in this light, transitional cinema *expanded* the medium rather than marking progress toward a new standard, displacing ideas of an incipient classicism—a periodization that acknowledges the coexistence of multiple film paradigms, revealing an elastic and flexible industry.⁴¹ This textual diversity coexisted, however, with relative stability in film form, exhibition, and industrial organization. Furthermore, during this period the medium's social functions were limited, particularly "the uses to which it might be put, and thus effectively about what it could or would be," making movies "harmless entertainment" and restricting their diversity as film lost its First Amendment rights.⁴²

Although Progressivism and transitional cinema have much in common, they are *not* conceptually equivalent. Both carve out a near-identical period, suggesting commonalities that earlier work overlooks while indicating something distinctive about this cinema. Their differences are significant: Progressivism is specifically American, whereas transitional cinema is more global/international/comparative. Furthermore, Progressivism offers a conceptual framework and provides a methodological specificity missing from transitional cinema. As such, it provides an answer to Keil and Stamp's question: "is there anything distinctive about this period beyond its end point signaling the arrival of a 'mature' classical cinema associated with the studio era?"⁴³

Progressivism also addresses another problem Keil raises: the blanket use of "modernity" to explain early cinema's form, reception, and meaning. He coined the term "transitional cinema" partly to decenter

INTRODUCTION

what he and David Bordwell term the "modernity thesis," something they rightly find too broad and insensitive to stylistic and institutional changes.[44] Keil asks, "if modernity so perfectly encapsulated the form and content of early cinema, why did film form change?[45] Rather than dispensing with the concept of modernity, I want to nuance it: it is clear that modernity—in its various forms—*did* influence early cinema. Progressivism does not displace modernity but instead recognizes that it is dynamic, marked by its own distinct periods and different tensions between old and new, shock and integration. Progressivism can be seen as a later phase of modernity, one in which novelties exist but where the prevailing tendency is to integrate them, revealing the dialectical sensibility typical of this age. Progressivism is thus more specific, more rooted in concrete institutional and social changes than some of the broader uses of modernity Keil critiques. As a response to modernity's somewhat fading novelties and an effort to restore stability and coherence, Progressivism addresses Keil's complaints without abandoning modernity completely. It is compatible, for example, with his critique that many vaunted modernist responses to cinema, particularly from after 1910, can easily be countered with observations from "numerous contemporaneous writers who approach cinema with matter-of-fact acceptance as a fairly conventional narrative medium. . . . Rarely do these writers suggest that cinema reflects a fast-paced urban environment or a technology-ridden culture dependent on endless sensorial shocks. In fact, trade press writers tend to suggest the opposite."[46] As he notes, there is little evidence at this time to suggest that watching film "was tantamount to a crash course in perceptual realignment," especially after movies became part of mainstream culture.[47] Still, his critique does not necessitate a wholesale abandonment of modernity. Indeed, Progressive Era cinema engaged with changes in modernity, particularly in terms of its broader cultural move toward integration, showcasing how sensations and attractions could be assimilated into narrative, efforts that were ongoing. Progressivism thus reasserts the period's prevailing social context while acknowledging modernity's flux and the new tensions this produced, including those that were responsible for transformations in cinema and film form.

But this period was not only about change: Progressivism and transitional cinema both highlight the *stability* of many institutions and practices, including exhibition. This is particularly important when considering feature films, which represent another aspect of the period's cinematic diversity, not the start of a new era: "Understanding film production, distribution and exhibition everywhere in the 1910s is impossible unless it is realized that one phase of cinema, that of the one-reel film, co-existed with another, that of the feature, at the same time that it was giving way to it."[48] Indeed, the feature and the short program were more intertwined, not merely "parallel institutions," with an implied fundamental separation of production, distribution, exhibition, and reception.[49] There is still dissent on this point, however. Most notably, Tom Gunning argues that the arrival of features in 1913 marked the end of an era, but this assertion is problematic.[50] As Jennifer Bean and Ben Singer have shown, features did not eclipse short film production until far later than generally assumed, with short film production, distribution, and exhibition dominating the industry throughout mid-1910s—their numbers even increasing between 1913 and 1915, the earliest years of regular American feature film production.[51] Singer's calculations show that "in 1914, shorts composed no less than 94 percent of all titles produced by the American film industry," although he adds that this "does not take into account who saw these films, their box office and their social impact. Nor does it account for imports."[52] While features (four or more reels long) were available as early as 1912, programs of mixed one- and two-reelers dominated the American market at least through 1914.[53] The film service—the dominant distribution/exhibition model whereby short films were packaged together and rented to exhibitors, often as a complete program—was based on variety. It was thus relatively easy for features to join a bill comprised of an assortment of split-reel comedies, one-reel dramas, two- and three-reelers, and serials, even if exhibitors had to rent longer films separately. The much-quoted 1914 statement made by Chicago-based film producer William Selig, himself an important feature pioneer, highlights the film service's strength and longevity: "That the single reel photo-drama is the keystone of the motion-picture industry becomes more apparent daily. . . . Patrons of the film drama want their programs as diversified as possible."[54] Selig's comments do not reveal an out-of-touch Trust company but speak to the state of the industry at this time, with features not yet threatening the popularity of the one-reelers on which the service was based.[55]

Rather than overlooking the feature film, or marginalizing its importance, Progressivism and transitional cinema do the opposite. Seeing features as something other than monumentally transformative lets us study them on their own terms, exploring their formal, institutional, and cultural links to other forms of cinema (like the short program) rather than looking at them as something other (artistic, theatrical) or focusing on their links to Classical form. Feature films are so important that I devote a chapter to them, exploring their diversity, their specific formal properties, and their links to Progressive culture. Still, they did not change the industry for some time. For at least four years (1912–16), features coexisted with serials and shorts, with neither tethered to a single (or double) tier of exhibition or reception. If anything, economics, not class or taste, finally limited this diversity, exacerbated by the rise of the star system (and the resultant increase in salaries), war in Europe, and 1917's box-office collapse. Features likely became dominant because it was easier and more profitable to rationalize production and programming around a weekly rather than a daily change, especially as the cost of real estate and the proliferation of theaters demanded a product that could support admissions higher than a nickel. In urban areas, competition (and the prevalence of low income patrons) produced strong resistance to price increases until war taxes led to higher admissions, causing many theaters to close.[56] Such changes effectively marked the end of an era, not the appearance of features several years earlier.

Local History: Cinema in Chicago

Richard Abel has argued that variations in pre-1920s film reception make it difficult to understand its reception outside of local studies, partly because regional variations in operating hours, ticket prices, censorship, theater size, demographics, and programming practices (daily or weekly changes, features or short programs) resist generalization.[57] An essentially local practice throughout the Progressive Era, particularly given its community pleasures, moviegoing still negotiated cinema's national (and transnational) provenance and the illusory "reel" world of stars and stardom that alternately intersected with this broader world and evoked its own specific and often fantasmatic space. I deal with these oscillations, considering the regionally specific and the more broadly national, focusing on specific details of film exhibition and regulation and the more general concepts and practices (spectatorship, features, celebrity) central to cinema at this time.

I focus on Chicago, the city reputed to have the nation's highest rate of film attendance and the one often considered the nation's most Progressive. New York is still the city most closely associated with early cinema and perhaps disproportionately affects our knowledge of urban exhibition—its nickelodeons, movie theaters, and other cheap amusements have been the subject of detailed studies by Robert C. Allen, Kathy Peiss, and Ben Singer.[58] Even Lauren Rabinovitz's study of pre-1908 cinema in Chicago discusses New York nearly as much as Chicago.[59] This emphasis reveals the availability of archival materials, the city's significant role in film production and distribution, even the prevailing New York focus of much of the (Chicago-based) trade press. But New York was exceptional, both for its close industry ties and its status as the nation's largest and most established market. By the early 1910s, major producers like Vitagraph and Paramount owned large first-run theaters in the city's theater district, offsetting their costs as marketing expenses. Chicago's downtown theaters were independently owned, making the city somewhat more representative of general exhibition trends, even though it was far from typical (if any city could be).[60] To a lesser extent, it was an industry town, being the nation's distribution center, home to *Photoplay*, the *Motion Picture News*, *Motography*, and two major producers, Selig and Essanay.[61] As the hub of the nation's rail network, it was the customary resting point for stars traveling cross country in the 1910s, making it convenient for industry conventions and leading stars to make more personal appearances here than in most cities.

Reputedly the most Progressive of all American cities, as well as the place where the short-lived Progressive Party was formed in 1912, Chicago was a center of urban reform.[62] It was also the birthplace of sociology, a particularly Progressive discipline concerned with analyzing and improving everyday modern life.[63] The city's history reputedly produced its Progressive outlook: University of Chicago political science professor Charles Edward Merriam claimed its swift regeneration after the devastating 1871 fire was responsible for its quintessentially Progressive orientation: "Within less than a century it was necessary to build and rebuild the physical structure of the city, establish and develop its industrial position, reconcile a maze of conflicting racial elements, contrive measures for communication, health, safety, comfort, and culture, weave the web of governmental understandings, ideals, and achievements without which a city cannot be."[64] This unprecedented rapid, uncontrolled development had created enclaves of poverty and not-so-hidden crime and vice districts. The city's extremes of riches and poverty, its rampant crime, police corruption, gambling, and prostitution were all attributed to this laissez-faire attitude and associated with a similarly unchecked individualism.[65] Two strategies were developed to counter these problems, one practical, one academic. The former consisted of a program of public works encompassing everything from city planning to film censorship; the latter involved sociological observation and the development of new theories about contemporary urban life. Both influenced each other and would play a foundational role in Progressive thought and activities nationwide.

The University of Chicago (founded in 1892) was another seminal Progressive institution. Besides pioneering modern American sociology and emphasizing observation of poor inner-city neighborhoods, it trained social workers and had close ties to urban reform and settlement houses (like Hull House).[66] Its faculty included such noted reformers as Sophonisba P. Breckenridge (School of Civics and Philanthropy, established 1903); Edith Abbott (sociology); John Dewey; George H. Mead (philosophy); Allan Hoben (theology); and Graham Taylor (social economics and theology), founder of the Chicago Commons Settlement and possibly the nation's most respected reformer.[67] Together they produced numerous studies into urban life and recreation, work with clear consequences for cinema, not least through their influence over the Chicago censorship board. These academics pioneered methods of observation and reform that further contributed to Progressivism's heightened self-awareness and self-consciousness.

Movies were well established in Chicago by 1907, with the city challenging Pittsburgh's claims as the nickelodeon's birthplace. In 1914, Robert Grau reported "Big Bill" Steiner's claim that he had been the first to run a film-only theater in Chicago in 1902, although he believed such places existed as early as 1895.[68] More recently, Lee Grieveson has suggested, "The first nickel theater opened in Chicago in mid-1905. There were a handful in operation by January 1906, and theaters multiplied quickly thereafter, primarily along the main thoroughfares of immigrant neighborhoods."[69] Chicago's nickelodeons quickly grew in size: although still predominantly storefronts, they averaged under two hundred seats by 1907, with additional standing room available.[70] By late 1907, Chicago reputedly had more picture theaters than any other American city and the nation's largest film audience.[71] The city would soon be renowned for its neighborhood houses—some of the nation's largest and finest—and for its emerging movie theater chains, reportedly the first in America. Both were definitively local enterprises, catering to a more general neighborhood sensibility that could accommodate specific ethnic and racial needs, both in their general address and through their supporting entertainment (like song slides and live performances). Chicago's censorship board—the nation's first—also attracted national attention. As the distribution center for the western and central states, the city wielded significant influence, and its censors therefore tried to establish cinema's moral tone for the much of the nation.[72] Many of Chicago's elites, including reformers and sociologists, resented New York's hegemony over urban morals, customs, and culture, an animosity dating from the earliest days of the city's boosterism when speculators predicted it would overthrow New York as the nation's largest and most influential city.[73] Film censorship allowed these Chicagoans to assert their values over the world's most influential entertainment, although their efforts would ultimately be unsuccessful. Besides pointing to the limitations of local efforts to regulate an increasingly global industry (albeit one increasingly centered on American films), the board demonstrably failed to articulate community standards in Chicago and was increasingly mocked in the local press, ignored by exhibitors, and critiqued for giving Chicago a bad name.

Before turning to my chapter breakdown, I briefly want to consider sources. Few primary documents about film exhibition in Chicago have survived. Although some censorship materials are available at Northeastern Illinois University, few forms of theater publicity survive: the Chicago Historical Society has just four theater programs and one door-knob flyer from the period in its collection. No movie theater records exist, making the city's daily newspapers and the trade press the best source of information. The *Lakeside Classified*, the city's largest business directory, lists movie theaters citywide but generally by proprietor, not theater name or address. I therefore relied heavily on the trade press and local newspapers, particularly the *Chicago Herald*, a paper that was briefly so invested in cinema that it advertised its services in the *Moving Picture World*. Local papers only feature regular motion picture coverage from 1913 to 1914, however, and predominantly focus on major downtown and larger neighborhood houses. They are still an important resource as they cover exhibition, theater construction, and describe theater interiors as well as offering film reviews, star coverage, and movie contests. Neighborhood papers gave even more space to the daily rituals of smaller theaters in the area, but very few survive. The Chicago Historical Society holds an incomplete run (1912–13) of the *Daily Calumet*, serving South Chicago, but no other title exists. None of these sources are definitive, and some of my conclusions must remain provisional. There are always problems inherent in studying exhibition and reception in neighborhood theaters because they are not exceptional, received less press coverage, and left behind few records or traces of their existence.

Reformers often visited movie houses to investigate the conditions of exhibition and reception, yet, frustratingly, their published works and unpublished papers reveal little about what they found. Many books and pamphlets reprint the same findings, often verbatim, as in Louise de Koven Bowen's three studies, *Five and Ten Cent Theaters: Two Investigations* (1911), *Safeguards for City Youth at Work and at Play* (1914), and *Some Legislative Needs in Illinois* (1914).[74] Although Bowen led the Juvenile Protective Association on many research missions to local movie houses between 1909 and 1914, she does not record any details about the actual places she visited, their location, or the conditions she found. This is characteristic of most reformers who offer unsupported social criticism and frequently note: "conditions were as bad as expected."[75] These omissions display their lack of interest in cinema and cast further doubts on their conclusions, which appear preformed, suggesting that they were not the careful or "scientific" observers they claimed to be.

INTRODUCTION

I start this book with some foundational work on Progressivism, looking at its more general influence, period theories of spectatorship and popular culture, and its structural influence on feature films and the era's celebrity culture. Chapter 1 outlines how theories of film spectatorship as a collective experience both influenced journalistic accounts of cinema and its audiences and informed the period's social reform, including regulations levied on Chicago's movie theaters. Most of this work draws on crowd theory, a combination of sociology, psychology, and social paranoia popularized in Gustave Le Bon's best seller *The Crowd: A Study of the Popular Mind* (1895).[76] Le Bon believed that modern civilization, particularly in the new densely populated cities, suffered from what he called "crowd consciousness" or a loss of individuality. Characterized by extreme passivity, a highly suggestive, semihypnotic mental state and an inability to distinguish between fiction and reality, this condition was often linked to film spectatorship. I analyze these theories, looking at how the negative connotations of crowd psychology, particularly its links to hypnotism and psychological regression, were associated with cinema well after its novelty phase.[77]

At a fundamental level, crowd theory rendered identification with the screen problematic, posing problems for more integrated narrative films that emerged from producers' efforts at uplift, as these increased the likelihood of absorption in the film. While transformations in content—away from crime and toward chaster, morally upright, and educational topics—offset some criticism, questions about films' powerful illusions and their relationship to regression remained. These theories influenced exhibition and production, balancing absorption and detachment (through programming as well as production) to ensure polite contemplation and a "healthy" distance from the screen. These strategies continued throughout this era, influencing the heterogeneous address of feature films, particularly the tendency toward multiple diegesis I discuss in chapter 2, as well as the continued importance of physical surroundings in both neighborhood and Loop houses.

The next two chapters explore how Progressivism influenced film form and audience address, producing films that were far more diverse and less self-contained than usually assumed. Chapter 2 examines three principal formal characteristics of early feature films—their use of prologues, multiple diegesis, and oversight—exploring how they manifested Progressive Era investments in self-awareness/self-analysis and uplift. I consider how these texts oscillated between directly acknowledging the work of the audience and more closed, self-effacing narrative forms. This formal diversity associated features with the short film program and acknowledged audience's desires to see themselves inscribed on screen, even if only through gestures that recognized them as a presence in the auditorium. Other distinctive features of early feature films, like the use of multiple diegesis, linked cinema to allegory, universal language, religion and "art," while still producing easily understood popular entertainment.

Chapter 3 explores the period's cinema in the light of its celebrity culture, another product of Progressivism's oversight, self-analysis, and self-awareness. Celebrity authorized inquiries into modern individuality, social mobility, and the construction of the new public self. Motion pictures were an ideal vehicle for this cultural self-examination, even before the rise of movie stars. In turn, film stardom was an important manifestation of Progressivism's rampant celebrity culture, one that necessarily evoked the off-screen knowledge that increasingly mediated film consumption in an era of film journalism and extensive publicity campaigns. Stardom relied on this audience knowledge, gleaned from other films, fan magazines, newspaper columns, and even the trades, opening up the text, albeit in ways quite different from earlier cinema. Just as attractions were central to cinema's earliest articulations of modernity, I argue that film stardom was pivotal for the Progressive Era. The attraction of celebrity was more than a spectator sport, however. As movies increasingly became a vehicle for fame, fans aspired to a screen career. I discuss how Chicago's newspapers (in conjunction with leading companies like Essanay and Universal) capitalized on these desires, while annexing celebrity to local community ideals and social spaces.

The following chapters consider Chicago-specific developments, such as exhibition, reception, censorship, citizenship, and local identity, developing an understanding of Progressivism's more local operations. Chapter 4 examines exhibition, focusing on Chicago's neighborhood theaters while also considering the other tiers of exhibition: neighborhood theaters, first-run Loop houses, and theaters in entertainment districts. More than location, neighborhood theaters were distinguished by their evocation of community and their distinctive reworking of public and private spheres. Far more important than usually presumed, these theaters quickly eclipsed the nickelodeon, which was short-lived in Chicago, at least. As early as 1912–13, the city's largest movie theaters were predominantly found in residential neighborhoods, areas valued for their community ties and their ability to withstand urban alienation. Following the advice of trade press pundits, exhibitors emphasized the neighborhood cinema's civic duties, particularly its capacity to bring residents together in an otherwise atomized city. Attending neighborhood theaters gave audiences a new identity—that of a patron—distinguishing the pleasures of neighborhood spectatorship from more anonymous and often itinerant experience of attending downtown theaters.

The growth of theater chains, another area that Chicago reputedly pioneered, also testified to the strength of neighborhood houses as well as the growth of big business typical of this period. Neighborhood houses were also prime sites for feature film exhibition as local audiences had the time to watch a longer film, unlike spectators downtown, who were primarily there for business or other activities. While the industry needed these more centrally located theaters to showcase increasingly expensive feature releases (and to differentiate each film as the market became more crowded and competitive), the cost of Loop exhibition was not subsidized as it was in New York, where many producers owned first-run theaters. As downtown exhibition became increasingly uneconomical, exhibitors invested even more in neighborhood houses, establishing them as the backbone of the industry.

Although (or maybe because) Progressive society recognized the importance of leisure as one of three structuring principles of modern life, it also sought to rein in its influence. Chapter 5 explores the formation of Chicago's censorship board in November 1907 in the context of efforts by city government, social reformers, and even the local press to establish community standards for cinema. A perfectly Progressive institution, censorship invested power in local government, endorsed oversight, and monitored public actions and taste—all while asserting the need for uplift. Censorship waxed and waned under different mayors (and was particularly tough under Carter Harrison II) whose actions responded to the pressures of their own favored political constituencies. As movies became more popular with the middle classes by the mid-1910s, they were held to tougher standards, partly because they threatened established authorities, like the press and local reformers. By 1914 the development of different forms of motion pictures increasingly tested the city's attempts to formulate coherent community standards, especially after the advent of prestige pictures. The sometimes destructive tendencies of government and reformers attested to larger battles in Progressive society about who (or what) should have the kind of authority and power motion pictures now possessed, an issue that shaped different mayors' treatment of censorship and marked broader debates over the medium's power and cultural influence.

The final two chapters explore how cinema's community appeal was increasingly used to address questions of citizenship and national identity, a project complicated by the nation's diverse, fractured, and sometimes antagonistic allegiances. Chapter 6 focuses on race and cinema, particularly African American calls for full citizenship that were manifested in two ways: through the production of black films and the far more widespread consumption of white films in black theaters. As more black movie theaters opened on South State Street at the heart of the city's African American entertainment district between 1911 and 1914, preferences for distinct stars and genres emerged. These investments in mainstream motion pictures attest to American cinema's success in establishing itself as a national cinema—something that necessarily evokes belonging but was more problematic for black audiences still seeking recognition as full citizens. African American fondness for these films did not come without struggles or recuperation, as evidenced in exhibition and promotional strategies used in black theaters. Black film production operated from a different perspective, pointing to the potential alienation of African Americans from the screen and its relationship to a vision of nation that omitted black experience, achievements, and culture. Chicago is an important site for such analysis, as seen in the work of Jacqueline Najuma Stewart and Mary Carbine. Besides being a key early site for the black migration north, Chicago-pioneered black film production began, starting with William Foster's Foster Film Company and the Peter P. Jones Photoplay Company. Each asserted black citizenship in its own way, using history, newsreels, and dramatic reconstruction or opting for comedies of everyday life and the possibility of black film stardom.

Chapter 7 continues investigating the intersection between national identity and community, this time in relation to World War I. This chapter explores how Chicago's movie theaters supported multiple conflicting definitions of national identity during wartime, responding to the city's particular ethnic mix. After the outbreak of war in Europe, local loyalties fragmented as Chicago residents failed to maintain consensus not just on international policy but on the very definitions of national identity itself. As in Europe, for Americans World War I was a war about nations, nationalism, and the redefinition of boundaries, although in America its stakes and consequences were very different. I analyze its implications for the competing definitions of national identity then operating *within* the United States. The persistence of strong pro-German/anti-British sentiments in Chicago reveals how concepts like national identity, America, and patriotism were open to multiple definitions based on the citizen's own biography and ancestry. These beliefs were deeply held, and not easily swayed by world events or by national cinema. As over half Chicago's adult citizens were born overseas, even the most local community was often created out of transnational allegiances.

World War I is doubly significant as it led to cultural changes that effectively displaced Progressivism's key tenets, even as it initially emphasized its concerns with forging a unified national identity. In foregrounding differences in local definitions of nation, the war struck a temporary blow to the ideals of a unified and coherent American identity. It also solved one of Progressivism's key problems, demonstrating how modernity could be integrated into American culture. Cinema played an important role, both in supporting the war effort and in providing a valuable distraction from its stresses, helping maintain order and morale at home. Seemingly resolving Progressivism's pivotal issues or rendering them irrelevant, the war marked the end of an era. It also produced changes that profoundly affected the film industry. As admissions fell and increased war taxes plagued movie theaters throughout 1917, production declined, leading to widespread industry consolidation that changed movies forever.

ONE

From Crowds to Communities
Progressive Era Spectatorship Theories

One of Progressivism's characteristic features was its fascination with studying society in the hopes of stabilizing and managing modern life, a practice seen in its inward gaze and tendency toward self-analysis. As modernity's transformations were widely believed to have altered the very manifestations of subjectivity, quasi-scientific theories were formulated to account for new forms of self. One oft-noted change was the perception that the individual had been lost to the crowd, a quintessentially modern form of subjectivity believed to link minds together, often through the powerful force of mass culture. While Victorian in origin, these theories constituted an important part of Progressivism's conceptual framework, participating in its efforts to account for and even arrest the process of continual change. These forms of consciousness purportedly reduced intelligence, increasing impulsiveness and lowering resistance to criminal activities, threatening both individuality and social order. By 1907 movies were charged with producing this collective consciousness, with crowd theory used to justify tighter regulations on movie theaters, film content, and the length of film screenings. As its influence grew, crowd theory shaped reception protocols, exhibition practices, and even textual forms.

From Crowds to Communities

Efforts to explain spectatorship, like much of Progressivism, were part of a broader effort to understand and manage modern life. An assault on modernity couched in the language of a pseudoscience, crowd theory focused on the new forms of consciousness arising out of urbanization and mass culture. Resulting from the technologies that gathered people physically together and those that produced psychic publics, the crowd seemingly bound individuals together in shared altered states (like film identification). Essentially an irrational and regressive force, crowd consciousness caused individuals to lose reason and become unthinking, reactive masses. These sensations often lingered, causing crowds to imitate what they had seen, act on thoughtless impulses, and wreak havoc. As crowd consciousness was supposedly contagious, these theories testified to continued anxieties about the influence of modern culture.

Attesting to Progressive society's self-fascination and motion pictures' emerging cultural influence, crowd theory revealed the period's markedly different understanding of spectatorship as a collective social and psychic phenomenon.[1] While other accounts certainly existed, including the film industry's own models (spectatorship as uplift, as community formation, as universal language), the version derived from crowd theory was particularly influential despite being rooted in prejudice and paranoia rather than concrete social evidence. Significantly, cinema's relationship to crowd consciousness was most strongly felt in the years immediately following the nickelodeon boom when the medium's power and influence expanded, increasing fears about its capacity to wreak social and psychic havoc, particularly among working classes, women, immigrants, and children. Like other paternalistic concerns, these anxieties attested to fears about changing authority—away from social elites and toward movies, a canned, popular medium with immense and expanding influence.

The growth of narrative films exacerbated these anxieties as movies reached more people and took on forms that increased identification and narrative absorption. Such shifts in spectatorship were linked to "suggestion"—the hypnotic force that was believed to draw individuals together into crowd consciousness—revealing more ambivalence about this later narrative cinema than is usually acknowledged. Partly to counter this threat, the uplift-minded film industry reconfigured cinema's collective aspects—like its large audiences, its propensity to invite identification, and its growing fan culture—in terms of community, something highly prized in Progressive culture. Although efforts were made to individualize spectatorship, these usually existed dialectically, in tandem with movies' larger community address, indicating widespread acceptance that spectatorship was a collective process. Reception was consequently framed in terms of one of Progressivism's major dilemmas: would collective consciousness lead to a more civic-minded society or would it amalgamate consciousness and destroy individuality?

Despite lacking rigor and sometimes flirting with hysteria, the period's crowd theories constitute an important context for Progressive Era cinema as they influenced regulatory discourses and shaped exhibition practices (discussed further in chapters 4 and 5). Now seen as a relic at best, crowd theory had widespread influence, even inspiring major scholars like Freud. A broadly accepted response to modernity, crowd theory was first popularized in the 1890s via international best sellers like Gustave Le Bon's *The Crowd*. Its influence continued into the 1910s: 1913's best-selling book was Gerald Stanley Lee's *Crowds: A Moving-Picture of Democracy*, in which the author (a minister and professor) asserted that "the fundamental principle of this present age [was] the crowd principle."[2] Often pessimistic, even antidemocratic, crowd theory usually placed cinema into a preexisting conservative (yet still Progressive) framework that condemned the massification of modern society, seeing modern culture, its innovations and sensations, as preeminently "suggestive." As P. David Marshall has shown, "late nineteenth- and early-twentieth century crowd theories allow some insight into how the collective was being reconceptualized in an era of both increased democracy and entrenchment of capitalism. Often the interests of the writers coincided with those of a conservative elite."[3]

Le Bon's work centered on the individual's response to modernity, arguing that its new range of powerful stimuli dissolved individual consciousness, creating an easily swayed aggregate mind with limited intelligence—reactive, emotional, and in search of immediate gratification. With its capacity for rational thought eclipsed, along with other traces of individuality and higher-level thought processes, the crowd was particularly open to suggestion. He believed that crowds could be produced in several ways. Large groups gathered closely together could share emotions and visceral impulses, as seen in modern cities. Powerful forces—like rousing speakers and mass-produced images—were especially dangerous as they produced this crowd-mind without the masses being physically present:

> Thousands of isolated individuals may acquire at certain moments, and under the influence of certain violent emotions—such, for example, as a great national event—the characteristics of a psychological crowd. . . . At certain moments, half a dozen men might constitute a psychological crowd, which might not happen in the case of hundreds of men gathered together by accident. On the other hand, an entire nation, though there may be no visible agglomeration, may become a crowd under the action of certain influences.[4]

It is easy to see why these ideas were attractive, particularly in accounting for the lure of motion pictures whose influence had fast extended beyond the screen. Lee Grieveson points out that Le Bon was writing "just before the Lumière brothers unveiled the cinematographe . . . [and he would] later go so far as to suggest that the cinema should be placed in the hands of the government."[5] His work appealed to those who wanted to understand, regulate, or even eliminate cinema, especially as the medium's power to transform and mesmerize audiences became more evident. Indeed, segments from his work, like the following, supported those who interpreted film spectatorship in these terms:

> A crowd thinks in images, and the image itself immediately calls up a series of other images, having no logical connection with the first. . . . Our reason shows us the incoherence there is in these images, but a crowd is often blind to this truth and confuses with the real event what the deforming action of his imagination has superimposed thereon. A crowd . . . accepts as real the images evoked in its mind, though they often have only a very distant relation with the observed fact.[6]

Le Bon argued that this imaginative, highly emotional state made crowds into ideal theater—and later movie—audiences. Crowd theory was soon applied to film audiences, baseball spectators, and customers of other cheap urban amusements, revealing fears about social changes, particularly those that might empower the working classes.

Crowd theory influenced efforts to understand cinema during the Progressive Era, leading many to see spectatorship as essentially collective. Drawing on the uncanny similarity between motion pictures and descriptions of the formation and operation of the crowd mind, most of these accounts feature little detail, arguing largely through analogies supported by suspicions and bigotry. At one level, these limitations are not relevant. My purpose is not to prove that spectatorship was collective, nor to argue for crowd theory's insights, rigor, or consistency. Instead, I want to foreground its significance as a discursive context influencing exhibition, reception, textuality, regulation, and spectatorship practices, particularly between 1907 and 1915. While not the only available account of spectatorship, crowd theories are important because they were so dominant, offering increasingly familiar—and often lazy—explanations of cinema's psychological affects. Often politically expedient, these accounts supported calls for regulation that attested to the medium's growing power, an influence that threatened existing authorities like the press, reformers, or local government.

It is not surprising that cinema was subject to such scrutiny given its increasing prominence and its capacity to produce emotional and cognitive changes in audiences. Reformers who visited movie theaters during the late 1900s and early 1910s to monitor conduct inside theaters, observe building conditions, and analyze the films themselves noticed these very transformations.[7] As Gregory Waller suggests, these texts reveal "anxiety concerning impressionability and the perils of watching [that] found its corollary in the fear of the audience as a commingled, dangerous crowd."[8] Disappointingly, these accounts are often superficial, but they nevertheless reveal crowd theory's influence, particularly through their use of key terms like *suggestion*. While crowd theory offered a convincing and quasi-scientific explanation for predominantly upper-class writers who rarely attended movies and were confounded by their appeal, its influence not surprisingly faded after 1914–15 as the medium broadened its class base.[9] Powerful at the time because these writers often lobbied for regulation or influenced censors, these accounts have value today as discourses on reception.

Tellingly, crowd theory even shaped more positive and more serious accounts of spectatorship, like those of Vachel Lindsay, Hugo Münsterberg, and Gerald Stanley Lee. Important early works like Lindsay's *The Art of the Moving Picture* (1915) and Münsterberg's 1916 *The Photoplay: A Psychological Study* positioned cinema as a social leader, presented a collective spectator, and debated whether audiences were communities or crowds—all concepts central to crowd theory. Lee's *Crowds: A Moving Picture of Democracy* went further, focusing on cinema's capacity to help citizens communicate with one another. His work revealed the ubiquity of crowd rhetoric, as he argued: "A crowd civilization produces, as a matter of course, crowd art and art for crowded conditions. This fact is at once the glory and the weakness of the kind of art a democracy is bound to have."[10] In passages later echoed by Lindsay, he found characteristics of crowd society in "crowd art"—motion pictures, large, dense novels, "several hundred pages of crowded people in crowded sentences," the telegraph, photographs, and lithography.[11] Although Le Bon influenced both Lindsay and Lee, their work *celebrates* the crowd, democracy, and cinema, here linking cinema's collective spectator to community, a characteristic central to period exhibition practices.

Spectatorship was widely upheld as collective, then, both in terms of the pessimistic crowd theories and in the more positive community-based models. Unlike more contemporary film theory, which associates increased identification with a more individualistic address, crowd theory maintained the opposite, stoking fears about longer story-based films' power over audiences. In strengthening identification with the screen, these pictures increased the medium's suggestive force. Many councils and reformers, including those in Chicago, responded by trying to restrict cinema's power, shortening shows, increasing theater lighting, and imposing breaks between reels. Although the industry typically tried to offset these concerns by positing cinema as a communal and therefore healthy pleasure, some producers flirted with the idea of suggestion, featuring representations of hypnotism and other such forces to offer another kind of thrill linked to intense identification with motion pictures.

CHAPTER 1

"Spectatoritis": Crowd Theories and the Collective Spectator

Crowd theory responded to a rapidly transformed everyday life where overoccupied apartments, congested city streets, and packed public amusements minimized physical and social distances between individuals. As Patrick Brantlinger observes, the period's urban mass culture appeared to be on the verge of eclipsing social order: "The masses . . . threatened upper-class hegemony through revolution . . . threatened class distinctions through entropy and apathy, overwhelming social boundaries by sheer numbers."[12] This combination of physical proximity and the new mass culture led to widespread concern about individuals who lacked the resources to separate themselves from the crowd, particularly the immigrants and urban working classes who flocked to movies and other cheap amusements like vaudeville, arcades, and amusement parks.[13] Mass culture was charged with limiting difference (through movies, fashion, and other popular trends) and blamed for making public life more homogeneous despite an influx of new immigrants and the increased presence of women. Crowd theory's pseudoscientific accounts of a changed subjectivity therefore suggest widespread recognition that the Progressive Era's more public lifestyle had fundamental and transformative implications.

Le Bon's influence on period social thought produced a range of writings on cinema whose conclusions were seemingly determined in advance and repeatedly outlined resemblances between suggestion and identification. Most of these works added little to these core assumptions other than developing different classifications of audiences or asserting how suggestion led to crime or other forms of degeneration. As such they reinforce Marshall's observation that Le Bon's writings were not important because of their accuracy or theoretical insights, but because of "their status as both popular and influential texts," applied to all aspects of modern life, including civil engineering, town planning, social theory, psychology, business studies, and analyses of motion picture audiences.[14] He influenced thinkers as diverse as Hitler and the Frankfurt School, providing "a theoretical position that was . . . critical for understanding the twentieth century."[15] Le Bon believed the crowd was the dominant force behind universal suffrage, labor unions, mass production, consumption, and the desire for a "classless"—and therefore disorganized—society. While his old-fashioned, antidemocratic impulses structured a work that feared "the divine right of the masses . . . replacing the divine right of kings," they still struck a chord in the United States.[16] Large American cities generally developed later and grew even faster than their European counterparts, with Chicago representing the newest and fastest-growing metropolis. Le Bon's work offered a persuasive account of the changes involved in urbanization and modernity, particularly for those who longed for the return of tradition and saw urban life in terms of crime and disorder.

Le Bon's work articulated and legitimated existing social fears about increasing urbanization and the growing popularity of new forms of mass culture. As early as 1841, English lawyer Charles Mackay had linked increased urban growth imitation, suggestibility, mass consciousness, and crime with decreased individuality—three decades before respected French psychologists and sociologists like Gabriel Tarde and Auguste Comte.[17] Like these later, more serious thinkers, Mackay believed popular trends (songs, slang, and the like) created unthinking mobs. His crowd was solely working class, unlike that of later theorists, transmitting its fads through direct contact, containing its influence in ways not possible with later mass culture.[18] If crowd consciousness was contagious, as Le Bon believed, it was a greater threat in cities and other places where vast groups of people gathered—in streets, at professional sports, political rallies, cheap amusements, and, later, movie theaters.

Although Le Bon's work was vague, paranoid, and supported by limited evidence, it shared characteristics with more serious modernist thought, signifying broader consensus about the problems of individuality in modern society. In his 1903 essay, "The Metropolis and Mental Life," Georg Simmel argues that the "deepest problems of modern life flow from the individual's efforts to preserve his singularity against society against the weight of the historical heritage and the external culture and technique of life."[19] Like other critics of modernity, Simmel believed that the shocks, stimuli, and speed of the new metropolis produced a depersonalized mind that erased the individuality produced by centuries of social evolution. The city was particularly dangerous because it transcended individual power and could survive without even its most formidable subjects, "outgrowing every personal element."[20] Simmel attributed the modern urbanite's characteristically cold attitude to her/his desperate attempts to maintain distance from "the dense crowds of the metropolis [where] . . . bodily closeness and the lack of space make intellectual distance really perceivable for the first time."[21] Echoing Le Bon, he maintained that urban fads led residents to renounce individuality and transfer "action from ourselves to another."[22] He found this tendency most pronounced in disempowered groups, such as women, who adopted a "superficial" individuality (like following fashion) to compensate for what he considered their innate inability to lift themselves out of the crowd.

Le Bon also influenced social reformers, many of whom were drawn from the nation's highest social classes, and conservative academics like the University of Wisconsin's famed sociologist (and bestselling writer) Edward Alsworth Ross. Ross believed modernity's new media and new forms of social organization threatened American life, agreeing with Le Bon that the admission of "poorly educated" classes into public life would destroy civilization. As these groups were most likely to fall prey to crowd culture, Le Bon believed that their irrational minds were not suited to a cultured, autonomous existence:

> Crowds are only powerful for destruction. A civilisation involves fixed rules, discipline, a passing from the instinctive to the rational state, forethought for the future, an elevated degree of culture—all of them conditions that crowds, left to themselves, have invariably shown themselves incapable of realising.[23]

The University of Chicago's pioneer sociologist Robert Park (a former student of Simmel's) was similarly concerned with collective behavior, particularly in the city, seeing the crowd as a sign of disruption and instability:

> Precisely because the crowd proves to be a social power whose effect is always more or less disruptive or revolutionary, it seldom arises where there is social stability and where customs have deep roots. In contrast, where social bonds are removed and old institutions weakened, crowd movements develop more easily and forcefully.[24]

From Crowds to Communities

Like his colleagues, Park studied the city, a place where there were few "deep roots" given its numerous immigrants and rapid expansion: Chicago's population had reached 1,893,219 in 1904 from 334,270 in 1871 and would grow to 2,464,189 by 1915.[25] It was a perfect laboratory to study the consequences of modernity with its proliferation of modern commercial amusements, railroads, manufacturing, crime, vice districts, urban ghettoes, and racial diversity. This crowded and chaotic space seemingly validated collective psychology, as many inhabitants appeared to display the crowd's collective instincts. Without strong roots and stable social institutions, these citizens gathered in more ad hoc ways, often in public amusements. There were plenty of opportunities: a 1910 article in the *Review of Reviews* calculated that Chicago (population two million) had 310 movie theaters seating an estimated ninety-three thousand patrons.[26] In September 1913, Walter Prichard Eaton estimated that national daily attendance at movie theaters was probably "closer to twenty million than the five million estimated by the proprietors. . . . This means that more than one-fifth of our entire population are patrons of the movies every day."[27] By 1914 the *Dial* reported that "the patronage of the moving picture theaters in Chicago numbered three-quarters of a million persons every twenty four hours," adding that most of these theaters attracted their predominantly working-class audiences by "ministering to vulgar and deprived tastes."[28]

Park believed "psychic interaction" produced the crowd through reciprocal communication between separate minds, often while their attention was channeled toward a single goal. His language strikingly evoked cinema—echoing the terms of its apparatus, its use of projection, its suggestive influence, and its capacity to gather hundreds of people together and focus their attention on a single stimulus. (Although Park did not link cinema and the crowd, others drew such conclusions.) His use of the term *psychic interaction* revealed the influence of social psychologist Gabriel Tarde, another theorist who believed that sociology should be concerned with "those aspects of the psyche that are transmitted between minds."[29] Park believed:

> Crowd behavior is characterized above all by a concentration of attention on a single object. The immediate consequence of this heightened

collective attentiveness is an inhibition of customary impulses and associations that result in increased suggestibility. Through social attentiveness in the crowd, customs and stable forms of intercourse are loosened and finally dissolved.[30]

All these statements resonated with those seeking explanations for cinema's effects on audiences. As late as 1915, the *Literary Digest* cited one Dr. Seth Bishop, who analyzed spectatorship in terms that echoed Le Bon, Park, and others. He claimed that the movies' suggestive force was very much like hypnosis, muting agency and rationality as it lured audiences into a sleeplike state:

> The drowsiness that comes over some of the [motion picture] audience is so complete as to induce a loss of consciousness in sleep for short periods of time in spite of every effort to keep awake, even in well-ventilated theaters. This is comparable to the effect of gazing fixidly at a bright object, which is employed by hypnotists to tire the muscles of the eye until a hypnotic state is brought on.[31]

Besides seeing spectatorship as a near-hypnotic trance, crowd theory also addressed concerns about the anonymity of cheap amusements and movie patrons' rowdy and thoughtless interactions, particularly after they left the show. Between 1906 and 1913 a glut of sometimes-absurd newspaper stories associated movies with crime, using Le Bon's work to connect cinema with crowd consciousness.[32] Younger and more "vulnerable" audiences were believed to be most at risk, as they appeared to be unable to distinguish between reality and fiction, leading them to imitate what they saw on screen. In 1914, the *New York Sun* tried to explain this process:

> Within the province of the moving pictures lies a dangerous power for evil. . . . A written story of crime and human frailty may pass from memory, but a sordid delineation is apt to remain. Take a serial picture of sordid crime, like those that illustrate the shocking features of white slavery, drug depravity, and gunmen gangs. What good purpose can any normal person expect them to serve? To the rough and weak and ignorant it is like throwing more fuel upon a fire already hard to control.[33]

Fearing the influence of movies and seeing them as a threat, the press jumped on stories linking films to crime, no matter how fragile the connection: in 1910, the *Review of Reviews* observed that most newspaper files were full of stories about tragedies resulting from audiences imitating the movies.[34] In January 1913, for example, papers nationwide reported on ten-year-old Katherine Gregg, the leader of a gang of four middle-class Sunday-school girls convicted of house robbery, reputedly inspired by motion pictures. Sentencing them to reform school, famed juvenile judge Ben B. Lindsey stated: "This is the worst case of immorality among children I ever had come before me. . . . It is another case of the depraving influence which motion pictures or any suggestive action of such a nature can have upon the childish mind."[35] As Grieveson has shown, stories about young boys who killed or girls who ran away from home after seeing films were also common.[36] Many period reports argued that motion pictures were a greater threat than the most sordid and sensational dime fiction because the apparatus had the power to brand images on minds already placed in a heightened state of suggestion.

The first American spectatorship theories similarly posited a collective spectator. In one of the earliest such accounts (an essay published in 1912), George Elliott Howard, professor of social psychology at the University of Nebraska, argued that movies contributed to the formation of the audience's aggregate mind. Nevertheless, he found their influence secondary to the conscious and unconscious interactions among audience members, a not-uncommon belief that testified to the continuing significance of the exhibition context.[37] He claimed that this state stimulated the audience's emotions and produced pleasure:

> A game of football, a drama, or a motion-picture [*sic*], however stirring, would hardly carry the solitary spectator "off his feet" . . . the result of bodily contagion in the spectator crowd . . . increase[s] the effects of "multiple suggestion." Every emotion, every psychic manifestation called out by the stimulating spectacle is intensified. The emotional conductibility of the mass is very great. Nor must it be forgotten that pleasurable sensations or emotions, even if morbid, take the most enduring hold of the conscious or the subconscious self. They well up readily in

associative memory. How vast, then, for good or ill, must be the emotional discharge in the theater-crowd. For almost every social situation, almost every moral crisis or emotional conflict, almost every desire, passion or ideal is presented to consciousness.[38]

Howard believed that motion pictures merely primed spectators' minds for these mental transformations, acting very much like hypnotists' optical devices. Films were still a problem, but not one that producers could solve by altering content or form. Instead, change had to come from exhibition, reception, or municipal regulation.

Like many of his contemporaries, Howard believed that cinema's suggestive force could be dangerous. Audiences might be lured back to a primitive state connected to a series of communally held archaic memories and instincts, disregarding social laws and their individual conscience, a phenomenon that accounted for the bad or criminal behavior some patrons exhibited after watching films. He dubbed this characteristic "spectatoritis"—a term that caught on during the teens to describe excessive absorption in / identification with motion pictures. Because the aggregate mind was so open, spectatoritis was extremely contagious. As sociologist Richard Henry Edwards observed:

> *Spectatoritis*, like the professional [entertainer] who spreads it, depends upon crowds and crowd contagion. Our study of amusements has shown the crowd spirit at work in almost every phase of the problem. This means that great masses of people meeting in the highly suggestible state of crowd consciousness are daily exposed to the professional entertainer, the expert crowd stimulator who has unique power for the contagion of virtues and vices, in the epidemic of degrading or uplifting suggestions.[39]

"Contagion" was an attractive metaphor that justified regulation in terms of public health, just like many of the period's recreation studies. Suggestion was a matter of foremost concern, as it was held responsible for crowd consciousness and the unruly actions of those so afflicted.

Howard dubbed suggestion the "sine qua non" of social psychology, adding that Edward Alsworth Ross "has virtually restricted the field of social psychology to the various aspects of suggestion."[40] A term borrowed from studies of hypnotism, *suggestion* referred to the powerful force that created an aggregate mind and caused the excited but passive state of the crowd.[41] As Grieveson has shown, early film spectatorship was often described in terms of hypnosis and suggestion:

> The early reports on nickel theaters and juvenile spectatorship posited a model of spectatorship akin to hypnosis. This model was deeply affected by debates over crowd psychology, sociology and the emerging field of social psychology. For Le Bon and Tarde, individuals were suggestible—capable of being influenced by others—via a process of transference that was heightened in relation to images.[42]

Usually the most "vulnerable" groups were considered more susceptible: women, children, immigrants who were seen as more easily led and open to criminality. Others saw suggestion in less pessimistic terms. Münsterberg believed cinema effectively replicated the workings of the human mind, communicating through suggestion and the related play of associations, giving the medium its incredible social and psychic power.[43] While warning, "The possibilities of psychical infection and destruction [from salacious and violent films] cannot be overlooked," he balanced such caution against "the wholesome influence emanating from the photoplay [which] must have an incomparable power for the remolding and upbuilding of the national soul," a fundamentally community-oriented endeavor.[44] His position on suggestion was unusual, however, with most period commentators and critics seeing it as one of modernity's more feared phenomena, something that could not be annexed to community, empathy, or uplift.

Suggestion was alternately described through electrical, telepathic, or photographic metaphors or in terms of sickness and contagion. While the former linked it to modernity, the latter positioned it as a harmful to the social body. For example, Le Bon claimed that once a crowd was aroused, "suggestion . . . implants itself immediately by a process of contagion in the brains of all assembled, and the identical bent of the sentiments of the crowd is immediately an accomplished fact."[45] Alfred Binet, another leading crowd psychologist, believed suggestion modified consciousness, allowing thoughts to move impercep-

CHAPTER I

tibly from brain to brain.⁴⁶ He described it as a preeminently *visual* force: once it struck, it produced visions and hallucinations that, in turn, communicated with others in the crowd.⁴⁷ Tarde's belief that imitation was at was at the heart of all social relations corresponded closely with ideas about suggestion. He called imitation "a quasi-photographic reproduction of a cerebral image upon the sensitive plate of another brain," a process that was believed, in turn, to occur during the act of watching a film.⁴⁸ These descriptions offered a perhaps too perfect analogy for cinema's power and its links to crime, with major figures like Tarde and Park working extensively in criminology.⁴⁹ In 1909, for example, Jane Addams reported that one of Chicago's doctors had a number of child patients "whose emotional natures have been so over-wrought by the crude appeal to which they had been so constantly subjected in the [movie] theater, that they have become victims of hallucinations and mental disorders."⁵⁰

Two forms of suggestibility dominate descriptions of the earliest forms of "spectatorship." The largely apocryphal stories of early audiences fleeing from images of oncoming trains depicted the most fundamental expression of spectators' unthinking reactions.⁵¹ A later, more popular, form associated with later narrative films emphasized their power to place audiences in a trance, implanting ideas and controlling their thoughts. Such accounts increased around 1910–11 as one-reel films dominated the market and more seamless editing produced longer periods of this more dangerous spectatorial absorption.⁵² Mary Heaton Vorse's much cited, if more sympathetic, 1911 description of movie audiences in the Lower East Side provides two examples of the reactions associated with cinema's suggestive power—the extremely vocal and active hypnotized spectator and her more passive mute counterpart. One woman was evidently "so rapt and entranced . . . with what was happening on the stage that her voice accompanied all that happened. . . . It was the voice of a person unconscious. . . . She was there in a fabled land full of painted savages." At another performance, she saw a "little girl of ten or eleven" who was "so spellbound, that she couldn't laugh, couldn't clap her hands with others."⁵³ Observing that spectators had shed their individuality, she describes them as "little pallid ovals" transfixed by the movies and oblivious to the world.⁵⁴ In 1913, Olivia Dunbar commented on the trancelike state of such spectators:

"Are these pleasure seekers . . . half-asleep? . . . There is not so much as a change of its expression, much less a sign of applause, as companies of shadow-soldiers are assembled and drilled; parades of a dozen kinds trail their blurred length across the curtain; foreign cities flash out glimpses of their characteristic scenes."[55] While Vorse and Dunbar never refer to crowd psychology, their observations are shaped by its tenets—hypnotized masses, devoid of individuality, all in thrall to a suggestive force. Still, neither woman was unsympathetic to movies or their audiences.

As I suggest in chapter 5, it was not coincidental that demands for tighter censorship corresponded with the influx of more narrativized films around 1907 and again resumed around 1913–14 with the emergence of features and multireel films. Some critics clearly believed the more emotional, hypnotic states induced by narrative films destroyed viewers' ability to distinguish between fiction and reality, immersing them in a surface world of synthetic relationships. From the perspective of crowd theory, this mode of spectatorship was far more dangerous than that associated with the cinema of attractions, as it amplified suggestion, threatening the viewers' sense of self, producing imitation and leading to social chaos outside the theater. As late as 1915, Francis Hackett would call cinema "the greatest instrument of popular suggestion that has ever been devised. Capable of pouring the most diverse material into the brain, it is limited only by mental capacity."[56]

From the perspective of crowd theory, the well-made, thematically unified features (or even the likes of Griffith's one-reel Biograph melodramas) were potentially more suggestive, more hypnotic than their predecessors, making them more problematic. Although some of these films were considered more reputable, bourgeois, even "literary," their increased prestige only compounded tensions over cinema. Among more conservative reformers, the fear of cinema's suggestive power was more powerful *after* the development of longer films, more closed narratives, and more seamless textuality. Even the practice of surrounding features with thematically unified supporting material (like poems, overtures, and acted prologues) played with contradictory expectations—if film was to be more artistic, it had to display greater dramatic unities, hence the dissemination of its narrative and subject matter over the entire auditorium (which was also something that

CHAPTER I

could aid audience understanding). Other times these different media and their different sensory appeals evoked a variety aesthetic to moderate the dangers of absorption and suggestion.

Municipal Regulation and Industry Actions

Responding to these pressures, Chicago's city council attacked cinema's supposedly suggestive effects with regulations targeting the length of film shows, theater lighting, and other facets of programming. A 1910 ordinance compelled exhibitors to light their auditoriums "brightly enough to allow patrons to read a newspaper throughout the show," responding to habitual complaints that theaters' dark interiors encouraged unruly behavior while simultaneously moderating the medium's suggestive force.[57] For some time after this, the *Moving Picture World* lamented that many theaters were "remarkably light, even to the detriment of the pictures, as the lights are allowed to shine directly on the screen . . . all detail is lost in the shadows of the picture . . . [which] has a tendency to become merely a white silhouette."[58] While new projectors and screens evidently improved the image, the city's theaters were relatively bright into the 1910s.[59] Exhibitors and the trade press barely complained, presumably because they believed increased lighting would reveal that audiences were not misbehaving while further maintaining order and preserving their property.[60] It would also showcase their theaters' increasingly elaborate interiors.

Exhibitors protested other regulations, including a March 1910 law prohibiting them from keeping over three thousand feet of film in the booth during a performance—an assault that would necessarily shorten shows. Violators would be fined "not less than $5 and not more than $100," with each day counted as a separate offense.[61] *Billboard* claimed this was regressive, as most theaters screened at least three reels:

> In other words, if a theater should attempt to run more than three reels or even keep or store it in its operating room . . . they will have violated this ordinance and be subject to a fine. It is a well-known fact that twenty per cent of the picture theatres of Chicago have from five to six thousand feet of film at all times, during a show, and are exposing from three to five thousand feet at each show. Under this ordinance,

they would not be permitted to do so and would run the hazard of having their licenses revoked and their show closed.[62]

Responding to these complaints, the city extended the limit to five thousand feet in August 1911, although this was soon insufficient.[63] Although the law seems not to have been enforced, these regulations clearly targeted longer shows—and longer films—that encouraged more prolonged identification.

Subsequent actions reveal continued concerns about longer films' influence on spectators. In February 1914, the city announced they would enforce a five-minute break between reels, a proposal that coincided with neighborhood theaters screening subsequent-run features on a routine basis. Exhibitors immediately complained that these breaks would "mean at least one show less a night and a discontented audience, which will either have to look at a blank screen or a vaudeville act."[64] While this law did not pass, it is nonetheless important as it indicates that the prolonged spectatorship associated with features was *not* at first universally welcomed as a sign of cinema's higher cultural standing. Instead, features disturbed those observers who believed that identification threatened individuality and caused regression, revealing crowd theory's continuing influence.

Between 1909 and 1915, the industry responded to fears about suggestion by emphasizing a balanced program that included multiple short films of different genres or paired short films and features. Of course, the balanced program also offered variety, accommodating diverse tastes and offsetting boredom. Some of the earliest film programs were arguably deliberately disjointed, as many commentators pointed out, possibly to offset mesmerism (considered by some a persistent danger thanks to the nature of the apparatus and the use of projection).[65] A 1910 article in the *Review of Reviews* suggests that the disjunction between reels did not entirely rupture the illusion, focusing on the difference between a "mesmerizing" new Film D'Art release and the action-filled comedy that followed: "The delicacy and reverence of *The Kiss of Judas* is without a single false note of the theatrical. I first saw it following a helter-skelter comedy that had kept the house in a ripple of laughter. When it was over, silence continued—until a woman laughed shrilly, half-hysterically, and the spell was broken."[66] In trying to moderate cinema's suggestive effects, such programming allied film to vaudeville's shocks and sensations, not the unities of more established arts. Still, the medium's power was not so easily muted. In 1913 Dunbar was amazed that neither the discrepancies between films nor the frequent use of inappropriate music altered spectators' hypnotic response.[67]

The balanced program revealed the tensions that existed between the need to offset suggestion and the urge to upgrade production according to the seamless model of the nineteenth-century novel or legitimate drama. Combining different genres of increasingly hermetic one-reel dramas thereby fostered the dialectic of illusion/distraction/absorption that structured much programming until at least World War I. Significantly, distraction bred individuality as it broke the spell that produced collective consciousness.[68] Even the De Luxe feature presentations discussed in chapter 4 appealed to different senses (including the smell of perfume and burning incense) to ensure viewers' attention was not always focused on the image; indeed, elaborate frames around the screen arguably invited eyes to wander. Such screenings evoked the diversity of reception and the complexities of spectatorship, its dispersal across the body and the senses. Given that identification was linked to suggestion and seen as a collective process, such "distractions" were likely designed to produce a more singular spectator by puncturing the spell that bound viewers to one another, bringing people back into their own body and pulling them out of crowd consciousness. This was most apparent in the shouts and arias that often pierced first-run features, emanating from singers hidden in the wings. These unexpected noises would shock audiences back into awareness of their own individuality, tempering any illusion spun on screen or by the apparatus. Rather than distractions characterizing the more collective engagement with film that Miriam Hansen advances, by the early 1910s, they arguably promoted forms of individuality, breaking the spell and limiting the influence of any single motion picture.[69]

Anxieties about cinema's suggestibility persisted into the feature era, particularly in high-culture circles. In 1915 the *New Republic*'s Francis Hackett noted that the trend toward "improved" movies (feature length literary and theatrical adaptations) transfixed, rather than enlightened audiences. To resolve this problem, awaken passive spectators, and break down crowd consciousness, he advocated changes in film form—changes he admits were as yet unknown—to transform cinema into something more "aesthetic."[70] In a sense, his distaste anticipated post–World War I modernist movements and the development of avant-garde cinemas. Still, criticism of film's suggestive effects faded by the mid-1910s possibly because the writers for such elite journals as the *Dial*, *Outlook*, *Harper's Weekly*, and *New Republic* were no longer immune to the movies' pleasures and better understood the responses they once analyzed. Even if they still dismissed cinema as kitsch, as mass produced entertainment (unsuccessfully) seeking the veneer of art, they were less likely to impugn it given its widespread middle-class address.

Suggestion as Attraction

Such was the influence of crowd theory and suggestion that the film industry played with these tropes in narratives that offered audiences the frisson of dangerous (over)identification. Scenes featuring hypnotism tantalized audiences with the possibilities of even stronger absorption, flaunting the movies' power while playing with links among suggestion, crowd consciousness, and cinema. For example, Selig's November 1911 release, *The Inner Mind*, featured a hypnotist detective, Professor Locksley, whose powers were so convincing that the *Moving Picture World* speculated that they might be real, noting that the film "grips the spectator in a peculiar way, but grips him strongly."[71] Several feature films had plots dealing with hypnosis, perhaps most famously *Trilby* (Maurice Tourneur, Equitable-World, 1915), which reportedly so "affected a spectator at a New York theater . . . that when the night watchman went the rounds, he found a woman in a trance. It became known when a physician at a nearby hospital restored her to consciousness, that she lost her senses after Svengali did the hypnotizing stuff."[72] Whether or not this was a publicist's fabrication (as seems likely), the point was clear: such films capitalized on suggestion's danger, daring audiences to experience these thrills for themselves.

A glut of hypnotism titles produced around 1915–17 gestured to these issues while exploring the thrilling possibilities of suggestion in a form increasingly marked by prolonged identification. Examples in-

CHAPTER I

cluded *The Case of Becky* (Frank Reicher, Jesse L. Lasky Feature Play Company–Paramount, 1915), based on a Belasco play in which a young girl is hypnotized and it is discovered that she has a split personality; *The Ruling Passion* (James C. McKay, Fox Film Corporation, 1916), an Indian-set story of hypnotism and revolution; and *The Witch* (Frank Powell, Fox Film Corporation, 1916), another exotic hypnotism drama, this time set in Mexico. Dramas blending hypnotism and murder were even more common and included *The Green Cloak* (Walter Edwin, George Kleine-Kleine-Edison Feature Service, 1915); *The Romantic Journey* (George Fitzmaurice, Astra-Pathé, 1916); *Infidelity* (Ashley Miller, Erbograph-Art Dramas, 1917); and *The Stolen Play* (Harry Harvey, Falcon Features-GFC, 1917). Hypnotism also enabled baroque variations on stock plots, as seen in the five-reel *Her Temptation* (Richard Stanton, Fox Film Corporation, 1917), which centered on a physician with extraordinary hypnotic powers and his equally talented rival, who hypnotizes the doctor's sweetheart and marries her. This film was clearly a lowbrow affair, as the *Moving Picture World* noted that the spectator needed "a belief in powers of hypnotism that are nothing short of marvelous and a readiness to accept the author's explanations at any and all times."[73] Hypnotism was even used in lighter forms like comedy: the Ella Hall vehicle, *The Love Girl* (Robert Z. Leonard, Universal, 1916), in which a young girl falls under a Swami's influence.[74] It also provided timely and lurid material for serials like *The Crimson Stain Mystery* (T. Hayes Hunter, Consolidated-Metro, 1916), whose second and third episodes, "In the Demon's Power" and "The Broken Spell," showed heroine Florence Montrose (Ethel Grandin) being hypnotized by Pierre La Rue, leader of the Crimson Stain gang. The spell was broken without La Rue's presence in a manner the *Moving Picture World* claimed to be particularly authentic (likely relying on the producer's own promotions):

> The method of breaking the hypnotic spell is in absolute accord with the laws of hypnotism. At the time that Albert Payson Terhune wrote the story, he experienced great difficulty in discovering a way to bring the heroine out of her trance. After consulting the best authorities on hypnotism and reading more than a dozen books on the subject, Mr. Terhune discovered the method which he has incorporated in the third episode of "The Crimson Stain Mystery."[75]

Community

Although many crowd theorists were pessimistic, some believed the phenomenon was more benign. In 1917, British neurosurgeon Wilfred Trotter dubbed it a fourth instinct, called "gregariousness." He argued it complemented Freud's already discovered "self-preservation, nutrition, and sex" drives, observing the human tendency to live in social groups. He believed that suggestion was merely a component of gregariousness, linked to the human need to bond and communicate with others:[76]

> Man's suggestibility is not the abnormal causal phenomenon[, it is] a normal instinct present in every individual . . . the only medium in which man's mind can function satisfactorily is the herd, which therefore is the source of his opinions, his credulities, his disbeliefs, and his weaknesses, but of his *altruism, his charity, his enthusiasms, and his power.* (My emphasis)[77]

Trotter was not alone in his acceptance of, even enthusiasm for, this collective way of life. One of its specific forms—community—represented a social ideal in Progressive America: according to historian Rivka Shpak Lissak, "community, communication, and consensus were 'the sacred trinity' upon which Jane Addams and John Dewey's democracy was based."[78] Following from Gabriel Tarde, communities were perceived as rational publics, operating *cognitively*, not emotionally, distinguishing them from the thoughtless, irrational, and destructive crowd. Leading Progressive intellectuals, like Dewey, and their followers, including Jane Addams, believed community could stabilize and organize contemporary society.[79] They believed that poverty was the problem, *distorting* gregariousness into the crowd and producing the slums' weakened communities. Such deprivation also produced toxic and antisocial forms of individuality, making crowd culture a symptom, not a cause of social malaise.[80]

Building on Progressivism's respect for community, exhibitors tried to reposition the collective force of spectatorship away from the crowd and present cinema as a more disciplined, elevating, humanistic form.[81] From around 1907–8, the trades encouraged exhibitors to present their businesses as the hub of local communities, as discussed in chapter 4. These developments were most pronounced in the urban neighborhood theaters that played a key role in establishing cinema as a respectable form of entertainment, moderating anxieties about the crowd by associating cinema with community.

This tactic is significant because it reveals that the film industry also saw spectatorship in largely collective terms. At their most optimistic, ideas of community-oriented spectatorship were linked to a utopian vision of a society without boundaries, where cinema enabled people to transcend their differences. The most famous example was the universal language theory that associated movies with culture and order while offsetting fears of crowd contamination.[82] Its proponents, like D. W. Griffith and poet Vachel Lindsay, touted the medium's ready legibility, its educational potential, and its capacity to unite and enlighten humanity. Lindsay emphasized motion pictures' ability to strengthen the links between individuals, thus celebrating both (Christian) fellowship and (American) democracy: he also recommended Lee's *Crowds: A Moving Picture of Democracy* to his readers as a potentially rich source of future film scenarios that would "make world voters of us all."[83] Describing movies and their spectators in collective terms, Lindsay lauded cinema's "crowd-appeal," arguing that it represented the medium's democratic potential, its ability to represent and unify humanity.[84] He even divided films into "genres" using crowd theory, praising one of his favorites, the "picture of crowd splendor," for representing monumental events and "eternal truths." He considered this the "most noble" form because it stimulated the greatest passion in audiences.[85] One of his favorite films, *The Birth of A Nation*, was "a Crowd Picture in a triple sense. On the films [sic], as in the audience, it turns the crowd into a mob that is either for or against the Reverend Thomas Dixon's poisonous hatred of the negro."[86]

Lindsay's work may have been idiosyncratic, but it further testifies to Progressivism's emphasis on the collective nature of spectatorship. This concept contrasts with more recent theories about individualized spectators, revealing key differences in the ways spectatorship was theorized, disciplined, and performed—as Lesley Brill has argued, film theory "largely addresses itself to viewers as collections of individuals," ignoring the audience's relationship to crowds, including the safety and desire to belong these might offer.[87] Using another definition of collective spectatorship, based more on the Frankfurt School's theories and the work of British cultural studies, Miriam Hansen has argued that this phenomenon was short-lived, fading out between 1907 and 1911 with the eclipse of the cinema of attractions and the emergence of more narrativized films with an increasingly closed diegesis.[88] According to Hansen, this "singular, unified, but potentially universal category, the commodity form of reception" emerged as exhibitors adopted a predominantly film program, eliminating distractions (including non-film entertainments). She argues that this process coincided with the development of more "proto-classical" forms of representation that invited a voyeuristic, noncorporeal mode of reception that displaced older forms of collective engagement based on display. It reached an apotheosis with the hegemony of the feature film, whose singular diegesis absorbed the individual into the text.[89] This trajectory was not so clean-cut, however, and does not account for the prevailing sense that an inherently social and collective spectatorship continued well into the early feature film era, albeit through the dialectical relationship with the individual that was an important characteristic of Progressivism.[90]

These assumptions about transformations in spectatorship rely on a set of conceptions about the feature film. The shift away from sociocultural collective audiences to textually determined individualized spectatorship was by no means as abrupt as Hansen and others have suggested—as seen in the continued importance exhibitors attached to communities well into the feature film era as well as the lingering fears about crowd consciousness and suggestion that haunted film censorship into the mid-1910s. Indeed, early features were often marked by a somewhat open textuality that played with and gestured to spectators' knowledge and self-awareness while flirting with the social world outside the screen. In the process, they established a social-textual dynamic that played to Progressivism's individual/community dialectic. As a form, then, the early feature was more diverse and less hermetic than usually assumed, with attendant consequences for spectatorship, issues I discuss at more length in the following chapter.

TWO

Progressivism and Early Feature Films
Textuality, Oversight, Uplift

Although Progressivism was a cultural and social movement, many of its features also structured film form and narrative. Warren Susman has detailed how Progressivism shaped an aesthetic and cultural climate based on transformation, abundance, and new forms of communication, but other key features shaped American film practice.[1] I examine some of these here, exploring how such Progressive tendencies as uplift, self-awareness, and oversight marked early features' formal and narrative properties. Although many of these characteristics mark shorter films, I focus on early American features (1913–17). It would be impossible to survey all forms of cinema from 1907 to 1917, ten years that span significant and unprecedented changes. I chose early feature films as they are a transitional and a far from stable form that clearly evinced Progressivism's broader ethos of trying to integrate modernity's more disruptive aspects into something more cohesive—both textually and institutionally. This integration had significant limitations, however. The star system, the era's celebrity culture, and the success of superfeatures reveal that the feature film did not solely lend itself to efficient rationalization but opened up possibilities for different kinds of address.

Progressivism and Early Feature Films

Early features are often mischaracterized, as I discuss below. Exploring them within their institutional context and that of Progressivism reveals their distinctive textual features. Despite borrowing elements from one-reelers, they had formal and narrative characteristics infrequently seen in post–World War I films. These features were not completely self-contained, nor were they designed to foster a spectatorial regime centered purely on an illusory individuality; instead, they actively engaged with other films, promotions, forms of amusements, and cultural trends. Features did not solely fuel the growth in inner-city picture palaces, elevate cinema's cultural standing, or produce a spectator who was largely a product of its textual effects as is often claimed.[2] Furthermore, these complex transformations were not necessarily integrated: the move to larger theaters and the rise of the star system were somewhat unrelated developments that responded to other Progressive Era trends. As I point out in chapter 4, features did not play as well in downtown first-run theaters. Additionally, stars and features were often alternative, competing attractions, especially before 1915.

Jennifer Bean, Ben Brewster, and Ben Singer are among those who have demonstrated that features did not displace short programs but instead added to this diverse cinema's range—much like television several decades later, this was a medium that did not rely on a single form.[3] The very term *feature film* evokes this diversity, initially referring not to a longer film but a featured attraction, like a vaudeville headliner.[4] As Michael Quinn observes, it *required* the presence of other films or amusements, as the term "was not associated exclusively, or even primarily, with any particular production trend, but instead with *differentiation*" (my emphasis).[5] The different categories of feature film production/distribution discussed here foreground this diversity, which was also evidenced at a formal level, particularly through motion pictures' use of multiple diegesis. Multiple diegesis included prologues and epilogues; the juxtaposition of different temporalities, fantasies, and allegorical scenes; as well as portmanteau films containing several different stories. While *Intolerance* (D. W. Griffith, Triangle-Wark, 1916) is the most famous, it had several predecessors, including Griffith's earlier effort, *Home, Sweet Home* (Majestic-Reliance, 1914), which again juxtaposed several separate story worlds. Almost by definition, multiple diegesis films are not classical or closed texts. Many tended toward allegory, another popular period trend that showcased film as art. Allegory was particularly associated with films that aspired to national cinema, producing a style that evoked the monumentality of the American enterprise.

Still, early features had their own distinguishing characteristics, although these were obviously not found in all films. The period's very limited rate of film survival complicates analysis, as does the loss of many of its most important films like *The Battle Cry of Peace* (J. Stuart Blackton, Vitagraph VLSE, 1915); *Cleopatra* (J. Gordon Edwards, Fox Film Corporation, 1917); *Daughter of the Gods* (Herbert Brenon, Fox Film Corporation, 1916); and *Neptune's Daughter* (Herbert Brenon, Universal, 1914). Many extant films are missing footage, entire reels, or only survive in abridged versions intended for 1920s home viewing. But the rate of feature production was so high—around one thousand films a year by the mid-1910s—that enough titles survive to make analysis possible.

While early features were part of the industry's efforts to improve its artistic and cultural reputation, this was more typical during 1911–13, before they became widely available. Features were still uncommon in 1913 and were largely shown in legitimate theaters in large cities during that year, primarily addressed to more upmarket and better-educated audiences. Possibly the most significant and widely seen early feature, the Italian epic *Quo Vadis?* (Enrico Guazzoni, Cines-Kleine, 1912), typified the form: an imported work, screened in specially rented legitimate theaters during the summer off-season, and handled by a specialist distributor (Chicago's George Kleine). Still, these early features did not threaten cinema's real base—and real growth—in neighborhood houses. Despite its success, *Quo Vadis?*, like the other European imports, was not a template for the features that followed. Besides, features took several years to dominate the market, partly because the industry—and its stars—was centered on the short film program, which remained popular for several years.

Economics, not class or taste, finally limited cinema's diversity, exacerbated by the war in Europe and the nationwide depression of the mid- to late 1910s that accelerated the short film program's demise. Companies like Selig, Kalem, and Essanay thrived as both feature and short film producers, collapsing in 1918 as overproduction, increased star salaries, war taxes, and diminished exhibition profits led to a new institutional model.[6] Likewise, many important early feature film producers and distributors only lasted between 1914 and 1917, with Triangle failing in 1918 and Goldwyn absorbing World in 1920.[7] Many pioneer producers were still important players (especially Selig) until just before their collapse, suggesting broader systematic changes that marked the end of an era, not small-scale mismanagement. Indeed, short film programs were still viable until 1916, a year that saw the emergence and demise of the Unicorn Film Service, which tried (and failed) to compete with the GFC for the short film market. Its existence testifies to the widespread belief that the short program had been unduly neglected, reflecting continued demand, most likely from rural theaters.

While it is beyond the scope of this chapter to provide a comprehensive history of early American features, I will explore how these films' history, institutions, and textuality responded to the Progressive zeitgeist, looking at various tiers of feature film production, its adaptation of the film service program model, and its signature formal and aesthetic properties. Through their use of prologues and epilogues, multiple diegesis film and editing strategies, these films emphasize Progressivism's overseeing gaze and its play with public and private space. While some of these characteristics are associated more with big-budget superfeatures, they were also found in the five-reel film, the industry's basic commodity by 1916. Throughout this period, early feature films developed a characteristically self-aware style, gesturing outside textual boundaries and toward the broader culture of film consumption and reception—a practice with significant consequences for spectatorship.

Early Features, Diversity, and the Film Program Model

Early feature film distribution reveals that features were understood as part of a subscription-based variety program, not as a singular commodity. No real distribution or exhibition network existed for the earliest features (circa 1909–13), making it difficult to screen them in neighborhood theaters. Paramount and Warner's Features devised a solution based on the program system that quickly led to the former's dominance.⁸ Triangle, VLSE (Vitagraph Lubin Selig Essanay), KESE (Kleine Edison Selig Essanay), and other major feature distributors all followed, eschewing the alternative of open booking, where each film was sold separately.⁹ Under this program model, exhibitors signed up for a set number of films changed a certain number of times a week. Like their short film counterparts (most of which included some features by 1914), these services represented several different companies except in the case of Triangle.¹⁰ Exhibitors often contracted with multiple services, including those specializing in short films, changing programs more frequently than one service might allow.

By 1915, most major producers had stratified feature production into several distinct tiers. Besides the five-reel programmer, they offered superfeatures of eight to twelve reels and the three- to four-reelers included in some short program services. For instance, Chicago's Selig-Polyscope—a major and overlooked pioneer feature producer—produced short films for the GFC program and offered a variety of feature-length productions: "Spectacular Specials," "Diamond Specials" (named after the firm's Diamond-S logo), and "Red Seal Plays." Production of Spectacular Specials commenced in fall 1914, with the first film released in February 1915. Mainly shot in Chicago, these star-studded features were usually well over five reels long; based on stage successes, famous novels, or original exotic scenarios; and usually featured specially signed theater luminaries (like Tyrone Power) alongside players from the Chicago stock company. These films were typically road-showed and distributed through states rights.¹¹ Diamond Specials were cheaper, shorter (approximately three-reel) features. Often adaptations of novels and plays, they were distributed through the GFC's Special Feature Service (they were *not* available on their own). Most Diamond Specials were popular fare, including Tom Mix westerns, wild animal exotica, thrillers, and melodrama.¹²

With the organization of feature distributor VLSE in 1915 and then KESE in 1916 to distribute each company's midrange features, all the member companies shifted even more resources into feature films. After the formation of VLSE, for example, Selig announced a new brand: Red Seal plays, which averaged five reels, fell somewhere between Spectacular Specials and Diamond Specials, and were largely shot in Chicago under T. N. Heffron, Midwest head of production.¹³ Reportedly consistently strong draws, their production was wound down in favor of Selig's trademark blockbuster spectaculars, a policy that led to the company's demise in 1919 in a market oversaturated with prestige pictures with limited popularity in the depressed entertainment economy of World War I and its immediate aftermath.[14]

Chicago's other big producer, Essanay, had a different approach to features, one that revealed continued uncertainty around the form's definition. In late 1915, co-owner and president George Spoor engaged stage stars to appear in dramatic adaptations and announced the diversion of resources away from one-reelers and toward multireel films.[15] Only the relatively expensive one-reel westerns starring his business partner "Broncho" Billy Anderson would be exempt, with Spoor describing these as "so satisfactory that no change is contemplated." Claiming it was only in the market for "stories and books of well-known authors [with] an intrinsic worth," Essanay formed a production unit specializing in feature-length theatrical adaptations, possibly the most visible and expensive (but not necessarily popular) trend of the mid-1910s.[16] A month later, Spoor announced an increase in feature production, but this claim was deceptive, largely accomplished through a new investment in predominantly three-reel programmers. Within a few months, he reasserted the importance of shorter films—one- to three-reelers—shuffling resources back to these films.[17] This uncertainty marked Essanay's approach toward feature production until the company's 1918 demise.

Spoor's subsequent policy statements revive the older meaning of the term *feature* as a headlining attraction in a vaudeville show or a program of mixed shorts as seen in his December 1916 announcement of two new feature brands. Each was a series, consisting of thirty-three-minute-long films featuring Essanay stars in popular stories from everyday life.[18] The first, Black Cat features, would run for two years, with each of its one hundred self-contained stories adapted from thrillers published in *Black Cat* magazine.[19] The second, *Is Marriage Sacred?*, was initially envisioned as twelve films (released through GFC) but was so popular that five more titles were added in February 1917 and its run indefinitely extended.[20] A spin-off, *Do Children Count?*, was added in March 1917—this time released through KESE, Essanay's feature distributor suggesting its greater economic, aesthetic, and social importance.²¹ Featuring twelve thirty-minute episodes, it proved hugely popular, as did its six-year-old child star, Little Mary McAlister.²² By July 1917, *Do Children Count?* was a featured attraction in big Loop houses, breaking records in theaters like the Ziegfeld and Pastime that had not run two-reelers for years in any capacity.²³ These films reveal one of Essanay's key release strategies: the use of brands to market short features, a format that straddled the series and the discrete feature, as these were often related but self-contained narratives (sometimes sharing casts in completely unrelated stories).

Other Essanay production units revealed a more conventional understanding of the term *feature*. In December 1917, the company announced plans for "superfeatures," star-laden literary adaptations. Over six reels long, released through George Kleine's new subsidiary, Perfection Pictures, and marketed as specials, the first two "Ultra Pictures" were *Uneasy Money* (Laurence C. Windom, Perfection Pictures–Essanay, Kleine, 1918), a film based on the P. G. Wodehouse story, starring the stage performer Taylor Holmes, and Mary McLane's *Men Who Have Made Love to Me* (Arthur Bethelet, Perfection Pictures–Essanay, Kleine, 1918).²⁴ Although McLane's film was well received, neither was as popular as Essanay's war vehicles, like 1917's Bryant Washburn film, *The Man Who Was Afraid* (Fred E. Wright, Essanay-KESE, 1917); its wartime comedies that successfully diverted an anxious nation; or, of course, *Do Children Count?*²⁵

Selig and Essanay were not alone in constructing different tiers of feature film releases—as Quinn suggests, this was an industry-wide tactic whereby these pictures would be handled and priced differently, made available from different distributors, and given varying degrees of individual handling. A Black Cat feature was identified through its relationship with other films in the series, whereas a superfeature like *Beware of Strangers* (Colin Campbell, Selig Polyscope, 1917) was distributed through states rights and treated as an event. These practices demonstrate that feature films did not bring about standardization, either institutionally or textually.

Formal Strategies of the Early American Feature Film, 1913–17

Eileen Bowser has pointed out that "The coming of the feature film brought changes in film form again. The longer film created problems similar in some ways to, if not as extreme as, the narrative crisis of the nickelodeon days."[26] There were many approaches to this challenge. One solution was to borrow a theatrical model, another was to join together "a series of one-reel units," organizing material around reel breaks so that these early features could be shown in theaters with one projector or shown over a number of different days.[27] By 1913, Ben Brewster sees signs of change away from this one-reel model, evinced both in *Traffic in Souls'* construction and in articles written by Louis Reeves Harrison in the *Moving Picture World*.[28] Calling it "the miraculous birth of an entirely new kind of cinema," he maintains the film defies the then available models: the one- and two-reel American film and European import.[29]

An idiosyncratic film rather than a model for later releases, *Traffic* still includes elements that characterized many mid-1910s features, including a prologue and epilogue. Another of *Traffic*'s structural properties typical of Progressive Era features (although not one of particular interest to Brewster) is its organization around what I call the overseeing gaze—a structure where a character's look motivates cuts to other spaces or actions. This character usually goes unseen by those (s)he watches, but it is clear that the viewer is looking at something witnessed by another person, an aesthetic that embodies the oversight so central to Progressivism. This device links scenes and provides rudimentary scene dissection, motivating cuts to a different angle or a change in camera set-up (there is not much intrascene editing in early features, as I discuss below). As such, it speaks to the Progressive Era's changed relationships between public and private while articulating this culture's self-fascination, something discussed in more detail in the next chapter. Bowser suggests that this look was one of the most significant ways to motivate scene dissection, although she collapses it in with other shots from a character's point of view, editing that can include scene inserts as well as point of view sequences proper.[30] Although it does not really appear in *Traffic*, Brewster also mentions another technique found in mid-1910s American features—the use of multiple diegesis. Together, prologues, the overseeing gaze, and multiple diegesis would constitute the key textual and narrative characteristics of early features.

Scene dissection remains limited in most early features. Many of these films were made quickly, particularly the increasingly important five-reelers, with their form, editing, and set-ups often resembling the single-reel films from 1912–13 Charlie Keil analyzes in *Early American Cinema in Transition*. They use extensive cutting from space to space (often maintaining one camera set-up for each location), alternating editing and some point of view cutting. Shot/reverse shot is relatively rare as camera set-ups rarely change within a space. Instead, editing abridges scenes and creates spatial relationships along axes of vision and proximity like the earlier films Keil discusses.[31] Repeated set-ups imbue spaces with specific connotations, allowing narratives to draw on their earlier meanings to increase pathos, melodrama, or irony. For example, *Old Heidelberg* (John Emerson, Fine Arts-Triangle, 1915) often shows Kathie (Dorothy Gish) standing on the steps to the right of the beer garden looking on as her love interest, Prince Karl (Wallace Reid) drinks with his fellow military cadets. After Karl is compelled to marry another princess to prevent war, the repetition of these familiar spaces and set-ups underscores the characters' sadness and sacrifice. Kathie is seen on the steps in the same medium long shot (MLS) as before, looking at the cadets drinking in the beer garden, but whereas she had formerly been dressed in white and worn her hair loose, she now wears black, her hair pinned up. The repetition of these earlier set-ups connotes unhappiness, acceptance, and maturity and hints at the permanence of her loss. This style marks many early features, spanning different studios, directors, years, budgets, and genres.[32] Such set-ups and framings economically narrativized space while facilitating rapid production (necessary given the quick turnaround the five-reel feature demanded), allowing space to accrue meaning throughout a film, helping build irony and pathos and establish moral discourses.

A combination of the kind of depth staging often associated with Vitagraph one-reelers and the room-to-room / space-to-space cutting Griffith pioneered constituted the staple way of organizing interior space by 1914. Sets are constructed to provide several planes of action. Most commonly, there will be a desk, a chair, a table, a piece of furniture or some other divider in the foreground where the characters can sit or interact—or even be framed in isolation—with deeper space behind them, establishing several planes that can be used to stage different actions and reactions. Typically, the most important action remains at the front of the frame, with actors shot in medium or even medium long shot. Action could therefore unfold without editing, establishing a variety of shot scales as actors moved back or forward, while allowing audiences to make meaning across different planes of narrative action.

The Overseeing Gaze

This formal strategy internalized Progressivism's concerns with monitoring the public.[33] Oversight encouraged all members of society to look at themselves more closely and to be aware of how they presented themselves in public, knowing that others may be watching. The overseeing gaze enacts this emphasis on supervising other people's lives, making it both an important formal strategy and a commentary on period culture. Many period features used this strategy to critique Progressive Era conditions, evoking concerns about law and order, efforts to stabilize society, the erosion of privacy, and urban overcrowding and its consequences for the broader community. The device also exists on its own, revealing these films as a product of their times, capturing one of the period's fundamental ways of seeing that was not unrelated to the new possibilities opened up by modern technologies.

Drawing on then-current concerns about white slavery, *Traffic In Souls* focuses on two sisters, one (Lorna) lured away from her job as a store clerk by a member of a white slavery gang, while the other (Mary) investigates, unmasking her boss, Trubus, as the group's mastermind, helped by her police officer boyfriend who brings the group to justice. Structured around an overseeing gaze that motivates the film's narrative progression and its movement from space to space, *Traffic* engages with Progressivism's broader reform project through its investigation of the white slave gang. This look is most strongly emphasized during the investigation of the film's villain, Trubus, and embodied in the surveillance technologies used to catch his white slave gang. Significantly, the story proper starts after approximately thirty minutes documenting police investigating vice, looking around corners and overseeing criminal actions. Something like a prologue, this first act establishes the film's theme, preparing us for the story proper while reinforcing the formal and thematic significance of oversight. After Lorna (Ethel Grandin) is abducted, a key change occurs, there are fewer shots of cops around every corner, highlighting the loss of social control and producing a sense of danger. The film remedies this by restoring oversight, suggesting its close association with a stable and moral society, in the process endorsing Progressive methods of social control.

Traffic's narrative relies on oversight, overhearing, and the use of technologies to survey otherwise discrete places. Mary (Jane Gail) uses a Dictaphone invented by her father to listen in on the gang and record their incriminating conversations. She also looks through windows to spy on her employer, Trubus, who is in league with the slavers. The use of telephones, Dictaphones, cameras, telescopes, and other technologies permitting characters to overhear, oversee, or somehow permeate space are, of course, constants of early cinema.[34] Their role in structuring narrative and framing images not only attests to the Progressive fascination with oversight/overhearing, but also makes a statement about the "correct" use of modern technology. In *Traffic*, such inventions preserve morality, save young women, prevent crime, and bring culprits to justice. But similar technologies are also linked to criminality. Even as the Dictaphone helps stabilize society, Trubus uses a similar invention, the dictagraph, to read the notes his henchman writes on an electronic pad in another office.[35] He also monitors conversations through headphones linked to a device in the criminals' office. Here technology is harnessed to disruption—albeit not the disruption of shocks and sensation, but a more profoundly antisocial form: criminality. The narrative ultimately pivots these two forms of technology, these two forms of oversight, against each other. Not only does the good win the day, but the newer technology also triumphs, suggesting a perfect Progressive solution.

Traffic in Souls is saturated with references to both modernity and Progressivism, linking surveillance to the era's new ways of seeing. Vital communications are carried through electronic intermediaries like the telegraph and telephone, while technologies that transcend space and time are used both to contain and commit crimes. In setting up parallels between the ways good and evil forces survey and manage the city—the police, the press, and the Dictaphone on the one hand,

and the criminal gang, Trubus, and his dictagraph on the other—the film explores the paradoxes of Progressivism, like the charity woman whose husband is a white slaver, again calling for even greater oversight.

Trubus is ultimately undermined by his attempts to balance a life of crime with one of reform. His wife's morality and charitable works lead him to dismiss his old secretary (after Mrs. Trubus oversees her kissing a man at work), installing Mary, her favorite candy store clerk, in her place. Discovering the dictagraph and a hidden speaker, Mary listens in, hears the voice of the man who abducted her sister, and then follows the wires linking Trubus's office to the slaver's headquarters downstairs. After climbing down the fire escape, she realizes the truth—tellingly, through another instance of the overseeing gaze—as she looks in the window and sees Trubus with the gang. As she returns to her desk and calls her boyfriend, Officer Burke, the juxtaposition of both sides and their technologies of oversight are manifested through a rapid alternation between Mary, Burke—both in separate spaces on the phone to each other—and Trubus, listening in on his headphones while monitoring his dictagraph. As the film reaches its climax, we see all the leads either looking in or eavesdropping on one another. Burke is on patrol outside Trubus's office building, keeping a protective eye out for Mary while spying on Trubus and the gang. Meanwhile Mary records Trubus's incriminating conversations as he listens in to his gang's meetings. Although the police are highly organized, the criminals are not, a structure that links disorder to self-interest and the absence of community spirit. Unsurprisingly, the crooks scatter once they realize they are being watched, while the police officers engage in a series of almost military-style drills that result in the villains' capture. This careful planning culminates in a successful raid on the brothel, where Lorna is held, that begins as one officer's perfectly timed hand gesture sends his colleagues into the building—just in time to stop her being whipped.

Traffic suggests that oversight could be used for good or malevolent ends (and points to the role of management across a range of institutions), just like other aspects of modernity or Progressive culture. Other films take a more defined stance, commenting on a world where characters often watch other's private moments or survey the more public aspects of their lives. As such, at formal and narrative levels, they

CHAPTER 2

evoke the Progressive Era's reconfiguration of public/private life, affirming the difficulty of achieving privacy, particularly for the working classes. For example, the oversight that opens *A Fool There Was* associates this look with foreboding as the vampire surveys her prey, the Schuyler family. Her gaze attests to its implications for privacy, invading domestic intimacy and foreshadowing her role its dissolution.

Not surprisingly, many period films use the overseeing gaze to comment on the dynamics of social reform and its potential encroachment on personal freedom. For example, *Where Are My Children?* (Lois Weber, Universal, 1916) expresses distaste for reform that oversteps its boundaries, intruding on intimate decisions. Dr. Homer, a birth control evangelist on trial for distributing contraceptive literature, visits a series of impoverished tenements unbeknownst to their occupants. In the first, he watches over a young mother who despairs about the size of her growing family. Shortly afterward, he witnesses someone jumping off a bridge (possibly the young mother). Then he looks in on another struggling family: this time, a husband and wife fight after he returns home drunk while three small children sleep in the sole bed in their one-room tenement. As a group of neighbors gather outside to watch, the husband and wife reject Homer's offers of help, attack him, and throw him out. Homer is subsequently found guilty of distributing harmful literature, suggesting that it is immoral to intervene in the intimate lives of others, worthy intentions notwithstanding.

Oversight also testifies to aspects of the contemporary urban condition, particularly the dissolution of privacy and the changed role of family associated with overcrowded tenement life. *Regeneration* (Raoul Walsh, Fox, 1915) constitutes this space as one that exists amid a nexus of gazes from reformers, criminals, wary citizens, law enforcement—even the "tourist" gaze of more upper-class onlookers. Oversight also points to the shifting power relations between characters. Its two protagonists—gang leader, Owen, and settlement worker, Marie—both have powerful gazes that are frequently emphasized (through performance, lighting, framing, and editing), and both have occupations that depend on oversight.

The overseeing gaze structures *Regeneration*, constituting its central narrative and formal feature. The first two scenes establish Owen's early life—as a young boy and a seventeen-year-old man—focusing textually

Progressivism and Early Feature Films

and thematically on oversight and foregrounding its implications. As the film starts, Owen's mother has just died, leaving him orphaned in a tenement. His neighbor overhears him playing his harmonica, opens his door, and looks in. After seeing that he is alone, she returns to her drunken husband, announces that she is bringing the boy to live with them, grabs him, and forces him to work for her. Owen soon acts as her "sentry," in the words of the intertitles, watching out for her husband and reporting back when he is drunk. Here, the overseeing gaze evokes the loss of privacy, the fragility of family, and the diminution of intimacy in urban slums, as well as pointing to the need to capitalize on anything that might give some small advantage in life (using Owen to help around the home before someone else uses him). The latter is linked to a form of work—spying on others—that suggests the breakdown of community loyalties and the social contract they imply.

As the film cuts to Owen's young adulthood, other forms of oversight testify to this gaze's narrative and formal complexity and its centrality for the period's culture. Now a strapping seventeen-year-old, Owen works at the Manhattan docks breaking ice. After a small hunchbacked man's coat is thrown in the river, Owen looks up, presenting the scene from his perspective. As he rushes over and attacks this assailant, we cut back to a medium close-up of the victim watching the fight. As Owen battles on, we cut to a variety of other reaction shots of onlookers, including one man with an exaggerated cauliflower nose whose face is framed within an iris, foregrounding both the act of looking and the spectacle of his bizarre appearance. As these viewers nod, smile, and take pleasure in the fight, they are positioned as an audience, transforming this brawl into a performance. The sequence features eighteen shots, equally split between the fight and the viewers. But while there is only one set-up for this battle—a long shot, used seven times, and one medium shot and one close-up—there are three set-ups of the viewers. One of these is the close shot of the hunchbacked man Owen defended; another is the irised shot of the man with the strange nose. The other two show a small group of onlookers standing outside a door, one in long shot, the other in medium close-up. Watching is thus emphasized over fighting, especially as it seems to have as much—if not more—screen time and certainly more visual interest. As such, this scene encapsulates *Regeneration*'s narrative discourse, one primarily constituted from scenes of people watching others' actions. Besides establishing Owen's innate heroism, this sequence restates that life is now lived in public, where people look on and evaluate the conduct of others. Although this scene (the only one from Owen's teen years) prefaces his rise to leader of the gang, it also establishes him as a man of some virtue, intolerant of bullying.

The first shot of Owen at twenty-five—a medium close-up of him smoking and looking out into space, surveying his terrain—underscores his power and its association with vision. By way of contrast, his subordinate, Skinny, wears an eye patch and typically looks down and to the side, his unsteady glance contrasting with Owen's penetrating gaze, here emphasized through chiaroscuro lighting. Associations between his strong look, oversight, and crime are made explicit as Owen sits in a bar and watches a customer whose hand is full of bills. A close-up shows Owen rolling his eyes as he demands the man buy drinks for everybody at his table then picks his pocket. As gang leader, he does not have to commit crimes but rather take on a quintessentially Progressive managerial role, assigning duties, watching over his men and their turf.

As in *Traffic*, *Regeneration* juxtaposes the roles of management in law enforcement and crime, intercutting the activities of Owen's gang with those of new district attorney Ames and his circle at the same club, Grogan's. Ames brought his group there after his friend, Marie Deering (Anna Q. Nilsson), a social butterfly, soon-to-be-reformer, and the film's female lead, expressed her desire to see at close quarters the gangsters who fascinate her. With its stage and vaudeville acts, Grogan's again underlines the associations between oversight and performance in Progressive culture established earlier in the fight at the docks. As Owen scans the room, examining its new arrivals, he becomes the object of Ames's group's look, a spectacle in his own right. As both groups survey each other—an exchange that embodies vision's inherent power—Ames's party decides to leave. Gangsters immediately approach their table to start a fight, as a smiling Owen remains seated, his gaze indicating his control and obviating his need to act. This inscription of power onto the look is further emphasized via Marie, who is seen in close-up looking at the fray, her large eyes registering terror. As her look meets Owen's, his glee softens into something approaching curiosity and romantic interest. Her gaze dominates, increasing its power as Owen breaks up the fight, restoring peace to her face. The strength of their looks foreshadows Owen and Marie's romance, while pointing to a shared distinguishing characteristic.

Having established the links between oversight and power, the film then explores another significant iteration of the overseeing gaze: reform. After breaking up the fight at Grogan's, Owen greets Ames and his friends, escorting them to their car as Marie pointedly looks out over the streetscape. Her look motivates a cut to a speaker preaching charity and leads to a change of heart, transforming her into a neighborhood settlement worker. Unlike some films from this time, *Regeneration* presents its reformers positively: Marie organizes events for the community (and, with Owen, saves them from a fire in a pleasure boat, caused by Skinny's careless disposal of a cigarette), teaches adults, and helps mothers.[36] Significantly, *Regeneration*'s settlement workers do not spy on neighbors or intrude into other people's business unless asked. Owen is gradually drawn to them through his attraction to Marie and is converted to their cause after the group requires his physical help to rescue a baby from an abusive father. The sequence structured where Owen renounces his previous life and returns to the settlement house is another important one, once again structured through oversight. Here, Owen looks into one of the building's windows and smiles at a mother, baby, and small child as Marie watches him from another open window. The camera tracks with him as he enters the settlement house, underscoring his epiphany formally and narratively, along with his renunciation of criminal life.

Still, Owen's redemption destabilizes the neighborhood's social order. Once again, the film uses the overseeing gaze to establish the paranoia that defines other characters' reaction to Owen's transformation. Characters spy on both leads, creating the conditions for tragedy. One of Marie's male friends tries to convince her to return to her life as a socialite, jealously watching on as Owen gives her flowers and she teaches him to write. Meanwhile, Skinny, now the gang leader, runs to Owen for help after he stabs a cop who hit him with a baton—events all seen through the gangsters' eyes. While Skinny and Marie's friend spy on him from different places inside the settlement house, Owen plays tough as a detective interviews him, trying to protect the former friend who once saved him without returning to his former life of crime. This double surveillance epitomizes the paranoia that results from too many conflicting agendas and too many characters' efforts to control the behavior of others—actions that end in disaster. The resultant conflict leads to Marie's death at Skinny's hands and a distraught Owen struggling with the dual impulses to avenge her or stay the moral course she requested on her deathbed. Finally the hunchbacked man (a character who largely looks on at the action and protects those like Marie and Owen who have helped him) shoots Skinny to protect Owen. As the gang leader falls down from a laundry line stretched between tenements—an action seen from the hunchback's point of view—it is unclear if he was shot or simply fell.

Regeneration offers an elaborate, systematic, and nuanced exploration of oversight and the way it embodies both general Progressive tenets and more specific aspects of social reform, using the device to structure its narrative and guide its scene dissection. In documenting its characters' awareness that they could be watched at all times, this film presents members of a more self-conscious public, aware of maintaining their image and invested in controlling how others might perceive them. This resultant increased self-awareness is linked to the very conditions of representation, largely through the use of the overseeing gaze. Such self-awareness marked early features in other ways, particularly through the use of prologues, one of the early feature's signature characteristics, which I examine below.

Prologues and the Self-Aware Spectator

Prologues—short introductory sequences that variously set up the story, its characters, actors, theme, moral, tone, and address—were a distinctive component of many early American features, although they were also found in some series and serials. Bowser references them in a somewhat roundabout way, noting that early features often started with some spectacle that introduced actors and clarified plots.[37] Prologues used the feature's additional length to engage directly with audience and narration, framing these as issues to be explored in their own right. Most importantly, they reveal the early feature's distinctive formal self-awareness, one that often gestured toward reception, suggesting that these films are far from self-contained. As I argue below, one consequence of this is the production—or evocation—of a self-conscious spectator, a construction that shares Progressivism's self-awareness while gesturing to the period's celebrity mania and audiences' desire to be acknowledged on the screen. Although prologues are textual features, they signify the importance of extratextual cinematic practices, highlighting the screen's role in the mediation of on- and off-screen identity.

I am interested in the ways that prologues point to the early features' difference from later films. Although some of them have affinities with the opening credit montage sequences found in early 1930s films, particularly those from Warner Bros. and RKO, they assert a markedly different diegetic space unlike these later films. As early features were formally quite diverse, it is not surprising that prologues were not universal.[38] Nonetheless, they were one of the form's more consistent features. They are found in adaptations and original stories, five-reelers and twelve-reelers, highbrow artistic films and populist fare, movies with stars and those without.

Prologues originated around 1912–13 as an exhibition strategy. Initially acted, they provided information while imbuing features with the aura of art and uplift. Such prologues prefaced the new prestige features given the De Luxe staging described in chapter 4. As some spectators were new to cinema, these prologues not only legitimated but also clarified the text, as some early features were difficult to understand, even for audiences familiar with the medium.[39] Some prologues were mini stage plays (resembling vaudeville's "tabloids") expanding or commenting on the film's narrative and its context, sometimes even delivering the full plot to audiences. This combination of film and theater may have reached its apex in *The Sign of the Rose / The Alien* (Thomas Ince/Reginald Barker, NYMP, 1915), which was not only prefaced by an abbreviated playlet in first-run exhibition but also cut back to the stage for its climax when "the screen is lifted and the players themselves tread the boards and complete for you the story of the play."[40] The film, based on George Beban's one-act vaudeville playlet, was screened in full in neighborhood houses but retained its live finale in first-run theaters in large cities.

Samuel "Roxy" Rothapfel's presentations were particularly influential here and provide insight into how prologues might function.

CHAPTER 2

His 1913 presentation of *Quo Vadis?* at Chicago's McVicker's and New York's Regent Theater began with an orchestral prelude, followed by a dramatic performance in which a little boy asked the well-known speaker, William Calhoun, what "quo vadis?" meant. In an otherwise darkened theater, spotlights focused on the boy as Calhoun entered a box on the left-hand side of the auditorium. He discussed how Henry Sienkiewicz, author of the source novel, conceived the story and then summarized its plot. As a choir started to sing, three trumpet blasts were sounded and the film's first "act" was shown. As was then standard, the film was broken into three parts, each prefaced by Calhoun's lectures on the events to follow (the feature's length was believed to pose some difficulties for the audience).[41] Separate films sometimes replaced acted prologues, although this was less widespread. A scientific filmed prologue shot by Dr. Daniel Carson prefaced Griffith's eugenics drama, *The Escape* (Griffith-Majestic-Mutual, 1914), at Chicago's Studebaker and New York's Cort theaters, showing what were reportedly the first films of "various forms of infursoria [sic] in the process of cell division."[42] This scientific film presumably underscored the educational aspects of Griffith's now lost drama, which contrasted the care animals took in selecting mates to the "haphazard" selection of human partners, focusing on the poor choices of a criminal's children.[43]

In general, stage prologues were somewhat more straightforward than their cinematic equivalents, emphasizing plot, elaborating important narrative themes, and adding prestige. Even here, however, something else appeared to be at stake as some first-run presentations of early features received an unnecessary degree of narrative support. For instance, the New York preview of *A Fool There Was* featured the complete text of Kipling's poem—the movie's source material—read to the audience before the movie started, even though the film opens with intertitles presenting the entire poem.[44] This narrative redundancy created specific spectator positions, building up potentially excessive levels of knowledge, thereby limiting suspense and even temporarily undermining patrons' absorption in the narrative. Some early feature films used prologues to similar ends.

Prologues were quickly internalized, appearing in features from 1913. These introductions often acknowledged the importance of spectators' work—as opposed to exhibitor's staging practices—positioning film consumption as an integral part of cinema. Although low rates of film survival make generalizations difficult, prologues appear to have been reasonably widespread, taking a variety of forms, most with a different temporality and address from the body of the film. Many surviving films feature some kind of prologue, and descriptions of lost films further suggest their widespread use, with the term frequently appearing in the trades, fan magazines, and film reviews and intertitles (examples include *Home, Sweet Home* and *The Spoilers* [Colin Campbell, Selig, 1914]).[45]

Prologues are quite distinctive and usually cannot be missed. Typically short, often less than three minutes, they take several forms. One is the character introduction seen in *The Spoilers*, *The Cheat* (Cecil B. DeMille, Jesse Lasky Feature Play Company–Paramount, 1915), and *The Little American* (Cecil B. DeMille, Mary Pickford Company–Paramount, 1917), which shows the actors posing, often directly acknowledging the camera and sometimes establishing key themes and images. Another kind relayed important plot information, sometimes in tandem with character introductions (as in *A Fool There Was* [Frank Powell, Fox, 1915]). Two other types acknowledge audiences more directly: one through the use of a stage or performance frame as seen in *The Wishing Ring* (Maurice Tourneur, Schubert-World, 1915) and *Snow White* (J. Searle Dawley, Famous Players–Lasky, 1916). The other focused on spectatorship as an act of reading and transformation, as in *The Italian* (Reginald Barker, NYMP-Paramount, 1915). Many films combine two or more such forms. Others start with something akin to a prologue, establishing background information before the main story starts, sometimes featuring the earlier life of a character (as in *Regeneration*) or showing similar events that predate those in the main story (as with the earlier instances of girls being trapped into white slavery in *Traffic in Souls*). I do not discuss these here as these longer introductions represent different kinds of narrative organization and do not assert a separate diegesis.[46]

Prologues are significant in making films into highly self-aware texts. They gestured to the public that they were as important as their on-screen favorite players, giving audiences their own conceptual space on screen. As such, they combine two of Progressivism's characteristic ways of seeing—self-examination and oversight—defining spectatorship in ways that draw on both forms, making them an important part of period discourses on spectatorship and reception. A contradictory device in their own right, prologues thus point to some of the tensions surrounding spectatorship during the mid-1910s. While primarily narrative devices offering information and establishing context for the story to follow, they tend toward display, sometimes reviving devices associated with the cinema of attractions, including frontality and trick effects. As such, they use the obsolete and archaic in the service of the new. In many cases, they also gesture to the spectators' awareness of themselves as viewers, positioning them as active participants in screen culture.

Prologues explored narrative, performance, context, even aspects of cinematic technique, in the service of reception protocols. In the process, they displayed another constitutive aspect of early feature textuality: multiple diegesis. Most prologues, by definition, establish another diegetic world, even if only to introduce their actors as their on- and off-screen selves. They consequently fragment any singular reality, presenting a space outside of narrative that comments on the action to follow, gesturing outside the text to audiences and their knowledge of the screen. This use of multiple diegesis sets up a self-aware narration, and while it may not last long, it mediates identification as it gestures to both the film's source (the world of production) and the act of reception. Prologues thus underscore a tension in these films as they point to extratextual knowledge and to a physical spectator, aware of themselves, their presence in the audience, and their identity as a cinema aficionado while priming viewers for a more prolonged identification with the following narrative.

Even in their most simple form—an introduction to actors and characters—prologues undermine the coherence of their story worlds, both through their own space and via their juxtaposition with the body of the film. Sometimes this is self-evident (as with a look at the camera or a gesture to the spectator), other times it occurs more subtly through temporal manipulations. For example, the prologue of *The Wishing Ring* (Maurice Tourneur, Schubert-World, 1914) plays with the narrative parameters of the story that follows. It is comprised of a series of shots of its principal characters that constructs a fusion of past-present-future narrative, something viewers will recognize as soon as

Progressivism and Early Feature Films

the story begins. This suggests the prologue's omniscience while indicating that the narrative has a fixed trajectory, so viewers know they are not following events as they unfold. Other films, like *A Fool There Was* and *The Cheat*, configure a utopian, stable, and emblematic temporality that is isolated from narrative time. Sometimes, as in *The Little American*, the prologue's discontinuous editing cues spectators that its presentation of character is separate from and thus outside narrative. Such juxtapositions indicate an important disjunction between story and prologue, establishing the latter as a space of greater knowledge.

One of the prologue's most obvious functions is to introduce characters. It was commonly used to these ends in early American and French features, responding to shifts in film practice, including the move "from the previous anonymity of players to a new emphasis on the presence of actors, often stars previously known from theatrical careers, in films."[47] But there was more at stake. Besides acting, these prologues evoke the power of celebrity (whether screen or stage), drawing on *audience knowledge* of the actor's on- and off-screen life. In players' flirtations with the camera, as well as through their codes of presentation and framing, prologues play with this knowledge, gesturing outside the screen. The importance of celebrity and audience foreknowledge marks *The Cheat*'s use of a prologue to introduce its three principal characters. First Haka Arakau, a "Burmese ivory king," is shown in a medium shot (MS) seated at a desk in the front of the frame as he examines and brands an ivory figurine, actions that typify his character and foreshadow what will happen.[48] As is typical in some prologues, the background of the shot is dark—isolating a character while minimizing the details associated with narrative space. As Arakau brands the figurine, there is a cut to a close-up (CU), highlighting the act's significance and foreshadowing key narrative developments.[49] The next title introduces Richard Hardy, who is similarly posed in MS against a black background, setting up the two men as rivals or equivalents. He sits in the foreground studying ticker tape before looking up dreamily, almost directly into the camera, and smiling. Edith, Hardy's wife (and presumably the source of his smile) appears next, framed quite differently in long shot (LS), seated against a white background with a large dog by her side, as though posing for a photograph or portrait. This longer-shot scale reveals the details of her elaborate costume (significant for the plot and central to her character, but also supporting her off-screen reputation as a clotheshorse). The camera tilts as she stands, then walks forward into a MS and smiles, as though recognizing the spectators. The narrative starts with the next title, "The Butterfly," prefacing a shot of Edith in her social milieu—complete with highly decorative sets that are missing from the first three scenes (five shots and three titles). Throughout this prologue, both men seem less aware of the camera than Edith (Arakau does not acknowledge it at all). Her recognition of the apparatus is linked to Fannie Ward's stardom—her name is above the film's title, and the intertitle that introduces her is the only one to give the performer's name first ("Fannie Ward as Edith Hardy"). Her gestures evoke (and respond to) the audience's desire to be recognized by the most famous person on screen, putting them in contact with the film's star. While Ward is presented as a celebrity, the men are introduced solely in narrative terms, as their characters. Not surprisingly, the power of this introduction ultimately hinges on Ward's seeming recognition of the viewer, privileging it above narrative.

Many prologues feature performers breaking character as actors acknowledge the camera directly, seemingly gesturing to a spectator and sharing their awareness that the following story is itself staged. This occurs in *The Spoilers*, which introduces all seven major characters, each in a single shot, after the intertitle, "Prologue." Each is in costume, framed against a black background and within picture frames labeled with the actor and character names: each vignette is literally a moving picture. The first three—William Farnum, Bessie Eyton, and Tom Santschi—look around and smile at the audience (each was well known, Farnum on the stage, Eyton and Santschi from the screen). Eyton dips her head as she smiles and looks at the camera, as though registering our applause and recognition.[50] Most prologues are far more elaborate, with character introductions constituting just one of their functions. But many of them retain the power of celebrity and the audience's desire to connect with, and be recognized by, the stars.

The Wishing Ring's prologue is one of the more complex, foregrounding its staging while flirting with our desire to see the story. It opens with a LS of four old-fashioned showgirls (the Ballet Russe) dancing on a stage. They touch its curtains several times before finally opening them to start the film, or rather, to continue the prologue. Character introductions follow.⁵¹ Each vignette comically gestures to the actors' and viewers' knowledge that this is a role, as the actors flirt with breaking the illusion. Sally poses as if for a portrait, but is bothered by an errant bow on her dress. Giles appears from behind a tree, eating one apple and clutching several more, before seeing something that startles him—the spectator?—and popping back behind the tree. Each shot is increasingly detailed, striving for a realism that is simultaneously undermined, while acknowledging how cinema depends on a progression toward trust in the image to build identification. This trust is finally lambasted with the punchline that ends the prologue, displaying the fourth "lead," Sally's dog, Gyp Williams, posed on a table inside a basket. In playing with the audience's recognition of theatrical and cinematic conventions, this prologue positions spectators as knowing, aware, and conscious of their role in receiving the film, referencing both the work of making sense of the film and the hermeneutic desire that leads patrons to the theater.

Unlike narrative frames, which primarily establish different points of view, prologues typically point to the spectator's awareness of their participation in building the fiction and their ready acceptance of different types of illusion.⁵² *The Wishing Ring* returns to this practice with its epilogue as the curtain is closed by the four members of the Ballet Russe, who also appear in the film toward the end—first admiring Sally's new dress, then meeting boys of their own, and finally appearing at her wedding to Giles. Their presentation foregrounds the film's play with multiple diegesis, gesturing to the boundaries of each narrative world while using the girls' appearance to undercut the story's illusion. Through their evocation of performance and off-camera identities, these dancers point to a fragmentation and multiplication of narrative space.

Multiple diegesis is more markedly established in prologues dealing with narration or presenting events leading up to the story that necessarily exist in a completely different world. For example, the prologue to *Tom Sawyer* (William Desmond Taylor, Morosco-Paramount, 1917) presents Mark Twain writing the book, complete with trick effects. He is seated behind a desk when a tiny boy (Tom Sawyer) appears on a pile of books, swinging his legs and tossing a ball. As Twain picks up a quill

CHAPTER 2

pen, the famous text appears at the right-hand side of the frame: "Tom Sawyer, who is not the model boy of the village." The film proper then starts with an introductory MS of Jack Pickford as John, facing his aunt's wrath. Hobart Bosworth presented similar prologues showing Jack London in his series of feature adaptations of London's work, including *The Sea Wolf* (Hobart Bosworth, Hobart Bosworth Productions, 1913), acting as "a kind of guarantee of authenticity."[53] Similarly, *Ghosts* (John Emerson, Majestic, 1915) starts with the title "HENRIK IBSEN. A life-like representation of the great poet and dramatist. Posed by Carl Formes." Formes is then shown, standing rigidly and refusing to move, in a brief and oddly archaic prologue that acknowledges its own inauthenticity.

A more developed author prologue opens *The Raven* (Charles Brabin, Essanay VLSE, 1915), focusing on the ancestry of Edgar Allan Poe, the film's protagonist and the author of the short story that inspired the film. It starts with John Poe's migration from Ireland in 1745, cuts to the revolutionary patriot David Poe in 1776, then the actors David Poe Jr. and Mrs. Hopkins, who married in 1805, are seen on stage (fittingly given the prologue's presentational tableaux style). Finally, their son, Edgar, born January 19, 1809, is introduced and is seen as an adult after a title announcing "The Characterization by HENRY B. WALTHALL." Here an irised shot of a portrait of Poe dissolves into a close-up of Walthall's face as he moves his eyes slowly around (keeping the rest of his body still), conjuring up inner torment before looking into the camera and dipping his head down. In a series of more developed scenes we see how the young Poe was orphaned, adopted by Mrs. Allan, and given the name Edgar Allan Poe. This relatively long prologue uses two emblematic shots of a disturbed Poe to move into the story. First there is the shot of Poe following the portrait, and then a strange scene in which a drunken Poe dreams that he killed himself in a drunken duel. These shots bookend the story of Poe's early life, setting the stage for a story that cuts between his stories, fantasies, and biography. As these prologues suggest, the life of an author—particularly a colorful one like Poe or widely recognized figures like London or Twain—could be maximized for its celebrity value as well as to foreground the source material's significance and give weight to its narration. In the case of *The Raven*, Poe's persona and the gothic quality of his stories further permits artistic license, freely intertwining stories and biography.

While some prologues evoke narration—often in complex ways that undermine any sense of a singular narrator—many more are concerned with consumption, either approaching it elliptically or tackling it head on. Devices associated with the cinema of attractions are often used here, as these texts display themselves to a knowing spectator, one who has likely read fan magazines and newspaper film coverage. *20,000 Leagues Under the Sea* (Stuart Paton, Universal, 1916) starts in such a way with intertitles discussing the Williamson Brothers, "who alone have solved the secret of under-the-ocean photography." The next title introduces "Ernest and George Williamson," who shot the film's submarine scenes, then cuts to a MS of them looking directly into the camera and smiling before taking off their hats and bowing.[54]

The Italian offers perhaps the best-known example of a prologue that directly addresses reception and spectatorship. George Beban (who stars as Italian immigrant Beppo and was famous for playing this role on stage) is shown reclining in a smoking jacket while reading the film's source novel. A dissolve leads us into the action, and, metaphorically, into Beban's head, presenting what follows as his visualization of the written text, a metaphor for spectators' immersion into the film. The idea of having the star transform into their character as they read a novel was used elsewhere, foregrounding the power of consumption, linking it to the realization of character and narrative and to the figure of the star. In the prologue for episode one of *The Mystery of the Double Cross* (Louis J. Gasnier, William Parke, Astra, 1917), star Mollie King receives a letter at home in Astoria (a New York district then known for its motion picture studios), inviting her to play the lead in *The Mystery of the Double Cross*. She searches her well-stocked library for the exact title and sinks into a chair to read, her excitement captured in the intertitle, "I'd love to play that!" Trick effects frame her in its pages, walking toward the camera as she becomes immersed in the fiction, then cutting to her in character. In both guises, she looks at the camera—an effect prologues used to suggest that viewers and stars were aware of the masquerade to follow. Even as King is engulfed in the book, she—like the viewer—knows its fictional status and recognizes the work involved in the film itself. As Shelley Stamp points out, such prologues are non-Classical, "continually point[ing] outside [the text] . . . and to the audience watching."⁵⁵ In the process, prologues belie claims that longer films narrowed down reception diversity in favor of a text-based absorption in an on-screen world. Their strategies of display acknowledge audiences' participation in other off-screen cinematic activities and gesture to this knowledge. In building up the significance of the spectator, prologues remind us that audiences also craved recognition, wanting their presence acknowledged on screen, even if only in terms of their proxy position as spectators.

Significantly, the provision of narrative foreknowledge does *not* motivate most prologues. While there are narrative components to the prologues for *Snow White* and *20,000 Leagues Under the Sea*, these sequences deal with well-known stories and play with audience recognition, directly acknowledging spectators' awareness of what is to come. *Snow White* opens with a completely unrelated vignette, placing the film in the context of its Christmas 1916 release (another gesture to the audiences' world outside the film), and plays with the spectator's desire to look. It starts with a long shot of Santa Claus entering a large living room from the chimney. As he points, a large Christmas tree magically appears, suspended from the center of the room. There is a cut to a medium shot from a different angle as Santa places dolls on a table in the middle of the room near the tree. A young girl's feet descend down a majestic staircase and the back of her curly head appears as she peeks over the banister, her look motivating a closer view at the elaborately costumed dolls on the table—some of them male. Cutting back to the original medium shot of the table, we see it is now covered with dolls, including a brunette in a ragged dress (Snow White) and what look like seven dwarves. An alternation follows between the little girl running down the stairs and Santa, who tiptoes off. The little girl desperately tries to keep an eye on him without being seen, briefly catching her foot in the curtain and backing up the stairs to keep herself hidden, her drive to look remaining strong throughout. After Santa walks into the large fireplace, there is a cut back to the table full of dolls, and then a slightly mismatched cut to a view slightly farther back—the cast has replaced the dolls in a second magical transformation. A second part of the prologue begins here—this time focusing on performance. The cast begins to move. Some preen themselves; Snow White stretches out her hands and the showgirls/ladies in waiting curtsey. The prince walks over to Snow White, introduces himself, takes her hand, bows, then his parents come over and everyone bows and curtseys before freezing in position as the screen fades to black. Then the first title of the film proper comes up, starting with the key words: "Once upon a time." Embedded within a child's magical Christmas adventure, the miraculous transformation of dolls, the performative conventions of a play, and the narrative conventions heralding the start of a fairy story, the film that follows is multiply mediated. Even then, as a fairy story, it makes little claim to realism and, indeed, the addition of this diegesis not only adds to its thrills but also plays with the excitement that fairy stories—and Christmas—might embody for its audience.

Prologues did not emphasize display to distance spectators, evoking a representational practice quite different from Gunning's attractions. Early features encouraged absorption into the screen world, and prologues relied on this identification, even as they also moderated cinema's hypnotic force. As noted in the previous chapter, cinema's suggestive powers had not escaped critique, and this could be a problem for feature-length narration. If, as Gunning suggests, prologues helped uplift features through linking them to established arts (like the stage), they also helped manage the medium in another way, balancing absorption and awareness. As prologues returned viewers to their conscious self, they established reading protocols that coupled textual and extratextual pleasures. They also evoked another kind of oversight: that of the film audience looking on at the screen, inculcating a self-awareness in audiences that mediated their identification. Furthermore, prologues pointed to one of the early feature's more distinctive and decidedly *not* Classical properties: the use of multiple diegesis.

Multiple Diegesis

Multiple diegesis has often been discussed in terms of a radical departure from Hollywood aesthetics. Jane Feuer positions it as the "antithesis to the 'single diegesis' of the classical narrative cinema." She refers to Peter Wollen's use of the term to discuss the radically separate story worlds found in Godard's work, foregrounding the technique's modernist tendencies, particularly its use of "dual worlds to mirror within the film the relationship of the spectator *to* the film" (emphasis in original).⁵⁶ Similarly, Catherine Fowler argues that films with multiple diegesis present heterogeneous worlds, sometimes veering into incoherence and fragmentation (like Wollen, she is interested in more avant-garde textual practices).⁵⁷ It is important not to overstate the fragmentation and radicalism of early features where multiple diegesis exists besides integrated narrative worlds—as Feuer points out in relation to the Hollywood musical, genre conventions can accommodate this practice. While many early features seem to flaunt discrepancies between their story worlds, often refusing to contain them within the text, I have found no evidence that suggests this disjunction was distracting or unusual, indicating that it was accepted and therefore conventional, part of a distinctive textual practice that departs from later, Classical ideals.

While Brewster attributes the early feature's multiple diegesis to the influence of one-reel films, his definition of multiple diegesis centers on narrative time, referring primarily to films based on memories, flashbacks, or fantasies.⁵⁸ By multiple diegesis I mean the construction of separate narrative worlds, compete with their own conception of time and space, all existing independently within a single film. There is usually no attempt made to link the two, as seen in the relationship of prologue to the body of the text in films like *20,000 Leagues Under the Sea*, *Snow White*, and *Tom Sawyer*. Other times they are solely linked through intertitles that bring different worlds together to make a broader, often allegorical, point, as in *Intolerance* (D. W. Griffith, Wark-Triangle, 1916).

Several types of multiple diegesis films exist, including some borderline cases that warrant a closer look. The first, and by far the most common, includes films with prologues and/or epilogues. Another kind is the portmanteau film that features several different narrative worlds, some intercut, as in *Intolerance*, sometimes unfolding in sequence, as in *Home, Sweet Home*. Seen in this context, *Intolerance* was not simply a bold narrative experiment but an extreme example of an established, if more "artistic," practice. Yet another form of multiple diegesis film favors one dominant narrative world but features another, sometimes as a narrative frame, as in *Joan the Woman*. This film is a borderline case, however, as its principal character, Eric Trent (Wallace Reid) experiences both worlds through divine intervention, and their relationship is at least made clear. In presenting different story worlds linked supernaturally, via religion, *Joan* supports some grander allegorical point, something also seen in *Civilization*.

Other films play with the possibilities of multiple diegesis in minor ways, cutting briefly to other story worlds for a variety of reasons, indicating that this technique was not just reserved for grand artistic statements. One example is the five-reel *Children in the House* (Chester M. and Sidney Franklin, Triangle-Fine Arts, 1916). After establishing the unhappy marriage of Cora (Norma Talmadge) and Arthur Vincent (Eugene Palette), who neglects his wife in favor of a dancer, the film introduces Cora's faithful suitor, Charles (William Hinckley). As he starts to tell her children a story, there is a cut to a fairyland, partly motivated by his tale but largely acting allegorically to establish the purity of their love. As a fairy, Talmadge flies over the landscape while her suitor (Hinckley) looks on. Recognizing his love, the Queen of Fairyland makes Cora mortal so the two can be together, and Cupid accordingly shoots her with his arrow. But another mortal, Selfish (Palette) intervenes, commanding two dwarfs to cast a spell on her, turning her love to hate, causing her to leave Hinckley's character and turning "his heart to stone." The story's presentation exceeds its diegetic motivation, commenting on Charles, Cora, and Arthur's relationship and establishing the authority for their love. In linking her marriage to Vincent's subterfuge, it prepares viewers for a happy ending where the couple is reunited, giving their love more authority through this other, allegorical space while justifying Charles's feelings for another man's wife.

Another common use of multiple diegesis was to link the secular world with Heaven, fairyland, or some kind of afterlife, rationalizing this practice as these worlds are literally separate from one another. Examples include *Where Are My Children?* and *Home, Sweet Home*. *Where Are My Children?* starts with a prologue introducing a place in Heaven where unborn souls wait to come to earth and where others are repeatedly sent back (a none-too-veiled reference to abortion). *Home, Sweet Home* is structurally more complex, using multiple diegesis to create a portmanteau film that links three different one-reel stories via a prologue and epilogue about the life of John Howard Payne, composer of its title song. Each of the three separate stories—identified in titles as episodes one, two, and three—features families and lovers on the verge of dissolution until they hear Payne's song. Its epilogue creates a spiritual space where Payne repents for his sins (in the prologue he is seen in a debtors' prison, being tempted by the Worldly Woman, and dying in Tunis).[59] While not as long as its fifteen-minute prologue, the epilogue is quite developed and entirely allegorical, featuring Payne struggling to get out of the "pit of evil" while his former sweetheart/angel (Lillian Gish suspended by wires) is superimposed on a cloudy sky, guiding him toward her even as other sinners try to pull him down. After a fade, he gets out of the pit as smoke passes over him and he smiles, arms open in supplication, and runs off front left. There is a cut to Gish, now surrounded by a group of angels who all wave at Payne, then to a long shot of her superimposed against the seashore before the image fades out. Gish is then seen again in the sky, floating down to a tombstone swathed with lilies, before the film cuts to a slightly different angle (more to the right) as Payne clambers up to join her with the help of his guardian angel who embraces him and surrounds him in white fabric. The reunited lovers/angels float in the sky before Gish leads them to heaven and the film fades out. Emphasizing the magnitude of Payne's redemption, his elaborate and relatively long epilogue makes parallels between his song and cinema's own redemptive role.[60]

Multiple diegesis was frequently used for allegories—a major tendency in 1910s cinema—partly because the technique displayed cinema's unique capacity to see more, to tell stories that brought a variety of worlds together, enabling the medium to draw grand conclusions. Period reviews and commentary suggest that several important lost films used this technique, including *The Battle Cry of Peace*; *War Brides* (Herbert Brenon, Herbert Brenon Film Corporation-Selznick, 1916); and *The Girl Philippa* (S. Rankin Drew, Vitagraph-VLSE, 1916). *Joan the Woman* demonstrates how allegory could be used to motivate audiences to accept a preparedness message, emphasizing history, lost loyalties, love, and eternal "truths" rather than contemporary issues of who was right or wrong. It begins with a series of titles outlining the story of Joan of Arc. A symbolic scene featuring a haloed Joan follows, where the film's star, opera diva Geraldine Farrar, moves her arms slowly out in supplication to Christ, her figure forming a cross connoting both her martyrdom and faith. Meanwhile an illuminated fleur-de-lis outlines her body as iconically French, representative of a sacred national sovereignty. A cut to a 1916 English trench in France follows, where officers are seeking a brave man for a suicide mission to throw a large grenade into an enemy trench. Nobody is interested. We follow one officer (Wallace Reid) back to his bunker, where he finds an old sword, formerly Joan's, hidden in his fireplace. This prompts the title "Memory," the appearance of a matted-in Joan, a fade out and a title, "Into the Past." Here Reid plays Eric Trent, a British soldier who becomes Joan's lover and then is forced to capture her, leading to her death. After Joan's death some 120 minutes later, the film fades back up onto Reid's unnamed officer later that night, contemplating the meaning of his vision. Before dawn, he volunteers for the suicide mission, which he successfully accomplishes before being fatally shot. As he lies dying in no man's land, a towering armored Joan appears, offering first her hand and then her prayers. As he dies, the vision disappears and the film fades to black. *Joan the Woman*'s political allegory is clear: the British officer's death compensates for his—or his symbolic double's—earlier failure to help Joan and save France from British conquest. If Joan can forgive, and the soldier can give his life for France, then the present cause (World War I) is somehow timeless, sanctified in its fight for national sovereignty. America should thus join this sacred war and forgive previous wrongs (here British colonialism and its other forms of military aggression), following the example of Trent, Joan, and France.

Another allegory, *Hypocrites* (Lois Weber, Bosworth-Paramount, 1915), is structured almost entirely around multiple diegesis, cutting between a heavenly space (represented through gates, a signature Weber image) and visions past and present to construct an allegory of religion and morality. It opens with a brief, two-part prologue. First its protagonists are seen sitting on a throne on a dais, in rigid and still poses as though statues in an old church. As each actor plays more than one role, their image dissolves from their major character to one of their secondary parts, with their names underneath (for example, Myrtle Stedman as The Woman). After a title, "The Gates of Truth," there is a cut to a LS of a pair of large white curved gates in a wood as a superimposed image of a young naked woman ("Truth") dances in and passes through. As the prologue ends, there is a cut to a church, revealing a disgruntled congregation and distracted choristers (one reading a newspaper) barely listening to a sermon on hypocrisy. The angle of these shots positions them as the vicar's point of view as he looks down from the pulpit, revealing he is aware of their reactions. At the end of the service, some older men praise the vicar to his face and then retreat to discuss firing him. As he retreats to his sacristy, he falls into an alternate state as his spirit leaves his body, now clad in white monk-like robes. As the screen tints green to indicate this new reality, he leads his congregation up a steep path. Some follow him, others find themselves bogged down by a child or a bag of gold and give up. Still others do not attempt the climb, while the rest fall behind. As he reaches the peak of a mountain, he sees the gates and the naked girl, Truth (again in superimposition), and asks her to come to his people, as they cannot make it to her. A transition to yet another world follows, the one of "Gabriel the Ascetic: A Legend." According to the titles, Gabriel is a medieval monk who found truth through fasting and prayer (played by the same actor, Courtenay Foote, in the same dress as the modern vicar), but his fellow monks are more worldly. He works on a sculpture of Truth, presenting it to the people at a festival, but everybody (save a devout nun and a young girl) is shocked when they see her naked female form and immediately cover her. Led by the abbot, the riotous mob attack and kill Gabriel while the nun prays and the statue disappears. A series of brief vignettes set in different places follows, each showing Gabriel/the minister accompanied by Truth trying to open corrupt moderns' eyes. The first, "Truth holds her mirror up to politics," shows a politician on stage next to a banner stating: "My Platform is Honesty." As Truth and Gabriel/the priest walk onto his stage, the image fades to an oval mask—representing Truth's mirror—that frames the politician in his office, taking bribes from a long line of reprobates. As the scene returns to his campaign speech, Truth and the minister leave, having revealed his hypocrisy. The next section, "Society," shows a group of high society men and women at play, collapsing onto chairs and chaises while a drunken girl dances, accompanied by an inebriated man. Gabriel/the priest enters and approaches a woman in the foreground who tells him "Truth is welcome if clothed in our ideas." She hands him a scarf, presumably to cover his naked companion, which he places back on her before departing. This picks up one of the film's more unusual ideas, its equation of nudity with purity, something seen in the Modesty vignette where a group of overdressed beach revelers are scared and appalled at the vision they see in Gabriel's mirror—that of them frolicking in bathing suits. After finishing their travels, the priest crosses back through the closing gates. The film cuts back to the men who were plotting to fire him as a young boy calls them into the church where the minister has been found dead.

Like many allegorical multiple diegesis films, *Hypocrites* asserts the importance of seeing everything, presenting a vision unbound by time—it spans the Medieval years to the present—or even death (the vicar's journeys seemingly happened after he died). Cinema is associated with this "improved" way of seeing, not just through its ability to reveal many different worlds but also through the trope of the mirror that allows the truth to be shown—itself a metaphor for certain uses of the medium. Movies can therefore be upheld as a technology linked to higher spiritual ways of seeing, with the power to uplift and elevate the soul—as long as viewers wish to see the truth that they present. Such an improved way of seeing again corresponds to Progressive ideals, as seen in the desired clarity of vision espoused in urban planning, the curative oversight of reform, or the cleansing gaze of the City Beautiful movement.

Intolerance represents perhaps the best-known and most notorious example of the period's multiple diegesis film. In her detailed analysis of the film, Miriam Hansen observes that critics used its failure to "legitimize the very tradition whose norms it had once called into question," that is, the tradition of the self-contained narrative film that would later develop into Classicism.[61] As she notes, *Intolerance*'s mythical status blinded historians, "blocking serious critical debate on the film."[62] This is also the case when it comes to analysis of its form. Rather than carefully explore the film in the context of the cinema of the time, its difference has been enshrined. It has not, for instance, been seen as one (possibly) extreme version of a tendency already exhibited in Griffith's work in *Home, Sweet Home* and manifested in that period's cinema more generally. In her reading of *Intolerance*, Hansen points to its inclusion of

> scenes that are diegetically unrelated to any single epoch . . . [including] a visionary epilogue of about twenty shots presenting images of

CHAPTER 2

> warfare and oppression that dissolve into images of harmony, bliss, and millennial peace, a number of intertitles that either instruct the viewer as to the organization of the plot or point out analogies between different narratives . . . recurring shots that emphasize the theme and furnish transitions between the different narratives (the title-card of the Book of Intolerance, the emblem of the Woman Who Rocks the Cradle) as well as graphically distinct title-cards for each of the three narratives.[63]

Many of these characteristics—allegory, spiritual spaces, parallel narratives, thematic emblems—were found in other early features, typically found in multiple diegesis films, including those with prologues. *Intolerance* may not be a conventional film, but it was not completely unique or unexpected given period trends.

Placing *Intolerance* in the context of multiple diegesis films—as a production trend that included serials with prologues—complicates Hansen's argument about spectatorship and its relation to film form. As discussed in the last chapter, spectatorship was primarily seen as a communal phenomenon at this time, a belief that affected exhibition practices that were not quite as individuated as Hansen suggests. Furthermore, period films were not as self-contained as she implies. Multiple diegesis "acknowledges the viewer as a potential presence (rather than as a structural absence)" more widely than she suggests, as shown in the winks and bows of actors in prologues, the shifts between diegetic worlds, and the frequent use of intertitles featuring direct address.[64] As she points out with regard to *Intolerance*, multiple diegesis films oscillate between more and less self-contained narrative, and the forms of spectatorship each evokes, but this practice was less unusual than she implies. This shift between different registers of reception also had parallels in movie theaters where incense might be burned, different lights shone on screen, even food offered, indicating that audiences were accustomed to moving between different modalities of identification and self-awareness.

Hansen's reading of *Intolerance* is instructive and insightful if extended more broadly to multiple diegesis films, particularly those that use this technique to structure the body of the text. These included films that tried to make the most profound statements on the day's major issues (the war, religion, national identity, even birth control), while simultaneously asserting the motion picture's right to speak on these topics. Arguably, they adopted forms like multiple diegesis to legitimate cinema's voice, adopting a mode that was consciously nonliterary and nontheatrical—even if the source material originated on stage, as a vaudeville playlet, or as a novel.

But more than medium specificity is involved here: multiple diegesis evoked other period discourses used to elevate film, specifically the idea of film as a universal language, something central to Hansen's discussion of *Intolerance*. Although multiple diegesis would seem to foreground the text and audience awareness in ways that seem antithetical to the "natural" flow of images the universal language myth evokes, there are still strong connections. If one aspect of multiple diegesis lies in self-awareness, another asserts cinema's ability to bring together many discrete worlds. Conceptually, this practice is affiliated with the ways that cinema itself gathers a public, gesturing to Progressivism's emphasis on communities. More specifically, it suggests the movies' all-seeing eye (something that is at the heart of *Civilization* [Reginald Barker/Thomas Ince, Ince/Triangle, 1916]), a vision that improves on all others because it can transcend space and time, bringing together completely different worlds. This is exactly what happens in many multiple diegesis films.

As Hansen points out, in *Intolerance*'s publicity, Griffith evoked Hugo Münsterberg's mental analogy in which he claimed the mind and cinema worked in similar ways. Of particular relevance here is Münsterberg's idea that the mind makes connections between past, present, and future, with its "endless interconnections" forming the "true substance of our understanding."[65] This is where the relationship between multiple diegesis and cinema as universal language comes into play. Cinema's visual roots are upheld for more than their seeming transparency and accessibility: they are linked to hieroglyphics (particularly by Vachel Lindsay) and used to ground the medium in both a broader and higher level of communication. Because each story world is easy to understand on its own, these films fulfill the accessibility mandate of the universal language ideal while their juxtapositions aspire to the highest levels of connection. For instance, *Intolerance* and *Joan the Woman* draw together different historical epochs with some kind of allegorical space—an afterlife or eternity—transforming these juxtapositions into something profound. Although possible in other forms, they would be less accessible to mass audiences, as well as less "realistic." Multiple diegesis feature films thus combine accessible form and complex structures, allowing audiences to understand what is going on just as they recognize that the film is making a complex statement. This kind of cinema would thus appear particularly suited to uplifting diverse audiences, including those without much education, giving it potentially greater social value than more abstract and difficult works of art and literature.

As with prologues, multiple diegesis films display early features' tendency to combine the old and the new. *Intolerance*, for example, revives a parallelism typical of one-reel construction, as Hansen points out, highlighting both its self-conscious narration and an overt reliance on the spectator to make meaning while undermining claims (like those made by Christian Metz[66]) that positioned *Intolerance* as a closed textual system. For Hansen, this revival of parallelism, and the (re)turn to the spectator that *Intolerance* demanded, was historically regressive, inviting "a return of early modes of spectatorship, readmitting the variability factor of empirical audiences which proponents of the classical paradigm had been striving to minimize and control."[67] Other aspects of staging and film form in the multiple diegesis film use devices typical of the cinema of attractions like superimpositions, mattes, and forms of display, particularly for representations of the afterlife or nonsecular spaces. For example, *Where Are My Children?* employs superimposition to show the Waltons' unborn (aborted) children through the years next to the childless couple seated by their hearth. *Joan the Woman* frames Joan of Arc against a blank background, using lighting changes to cast a cross and fleur-de-lis behind her figure, again placing her on display. This image recalls the metaphorical tableaux and emblematic shots used during the cinema of attractions that connoted the films' themes, sometimes suggesting closure while gesturing toward the greater moral meanings of the film. More generally, these films evoke older narrative strategies, foregrounding the obtrusive narration and direct address that both Gunning and Hansen link with earlier cinema.[68] Such forms may occur consistently or sporadically through a film—*Intolerance* is arguably a limit case as its narration is almost entirely obtrusive, whereas

Children in the House is almost entirely unobtrusive save for its juxtaposition of the fairytale world to its dominant story world. Still, all these gestures suggest the presence of a narrator who knows how the story will progress and is able to place these characters and their actions in a greater context that includes all supernatural and secular life. This structure is typical of almost all the multiple diegesis films I have seen, and it overtly marks the narrator's and spectators' knowledge as greater than that of the characters, as well as testifying to these pictures' typically open narration.

It is thus not surprising that multiple diegesis was commonly used for allegory. The presence of multiple worlds created an omniscient narrative voice that lent itself to grand statements, something further reinforced when these films referred to—and represented—higher spiritual authorities. They evoke an abstraction that is central to allegory and its efforts to assert universal truths, whether this involves the importance of having children (as in *Where Are My Children?*) or the sublime value of peace and horror of war (*Civilization*). As Hansen suggests with regard to *Intolerance*, allegory abstracts meaning from the narrative, suggesting that each story is more an illustration of a greater point, hence the turn to multiple diegesis that allows several narratives to be combined in the search for truth.[69] As she notes, the "allegorizing voice . . . interposes itself between its own creations and the spectator."[70] Through its subordination of individual narrative goals, allegory aspires to "timeless" truths, overarching rules that illuminate the otherwise incomprehensible aspects of individual situations. Structurally this resembles Progressive efforts to stabilize modernity, attempts to establish rules that might manage the chaos, upheavals, and diversity of contemporary society, or, at the very least, illuminate how all this works.

In discussing allegory, Hansen evokes Walter Benjamin, who considered it a "master trope of modernity," resembling the activity of criticism as it invited readers/spectators to analyze, fragment, and interpret a work or the world itself. Furthermore, allegory evoked a symbolic world of order, hierarchy, and stability while asserting "a cognitive device that registers the historical dissolution of that very order."[71] Here allegory exemplifies modernity's nostalgia for stability as well as its very tendencies to undermine it, something that Progressivism reorients as it tries to manage the waning shocks and sensations of the new, teasing them into a fresh, stable culture.

At the same time, multiple diegesis posits some kind of allegorical—and Progressive—solution to these very problems. It suggests that if there is little in the way of meaning—let alone truth—to be found in the contemporary maelstrom, this might be because our focus is too limited. Focusing on several worlds might bring these rules to the fore and help us make sense of what might otherwise elude us, a perspective that requires us to monitor *more* of the world, not less, essentially demanding the help of some higher force—or some new technology. This can be seen in *Joan the Woman*'s present-day scenes that focus on the Great War, a particularly vexing conflict whose causes and meanings are still under debate. In particular, the film's suicide mission is an activity that encapsulates the epistemological and existential crises this war epitomizes. Through multiple diegesis, Joan finds sense in this senselessness as it foregrounds the religious dimensions of love for one's country through the Joan of Arc story and uses a mystical time-travel plot where Joan contacts Trent, causing him to repent his earlier betrayal and seek redemption. Consequently, the stability of the universe is reasserted, even as time is presented in two contradictory ways. While Joan's afterlife is eternal, her interventions in the present suggest—and require—that history folds back in on itself, destabilizing the linear continuity the film asserts. Even though this structure does not entirely undermine the film's message, it requires it to turn away from the present in its search for meaning, locating its "truths" deep in the past and through Christianity. Joan is not alone here: *Home, Sweet Home, Where Are My Children?*, and *Civilization* similarly resort to religion and/or the past as a way to make sense of what they present as contemporary problems, indicating that allegory might be a response to modernity but not entirely modern in itself. Unlike Wollen's avant-garde multiple diegesis, then, these films do not fragment the screen world but instead work toward closure. In many cases, this comes from a perspective seen from the end of history where all has its place, a position allied to a more conservative Judeo-Christian way of seeing. Still, this very need to look elsewhere, to find another time or world to clarify the problems of the present indicates the difficulties of managing the quandaries of contemporary life.

Not all films with multiple diegesis operate in this fashion, however. Some illustrate the heterogeneity that still marked cinema, using multiple diegesis pragmatically, offering up different story worlds to keep audiences entertained, adding visual variety and offsetting boredom in spectators who may not be as fond of longer films. Here multiple diegesis reveals the residual influence of the mixed film program as features catered to an audience used to marked shifts in screen worlds, albeit here within rather than across films. Sometimes, multiple diegesis allows the inclusion of something akin to a one- or two-reel film within a feature, almost giving viewers a break before returning to the story proper. Such diversion can be seen in *The Little Princess* (Marshall Neilan, Mary Pickford Company–Artcraft-Paramount, 1917) when Sara Crewe (Pickford) entertains her fellow students with a story from the *Arabian Nights*. While directly lifted from Frances Hodgson Burnett's source novel, this scene takes on a life of its own: at around sixteen minutes (with an additional minute of shots showing the storytelling), it constitutes over 25 percent of the film's sixty-two-minute run time and lasts for longer than a one-reeler. The sequence is presented in a way analogous to cinema: as Pickford's Sara notes, "If you close your eyes, you can *see* fairy stories so much better in the dark!" This cinematic metaphor extends to the way the storytelling is staged: as Sara starts talking, the background of the room dissolves into a scene from the *Arabian Nights* as though it is a film projected on a screen. Gradually this narrative space replaces the darkened room, evoking the process of cinematic identification. Here, Pickford plays an adult woman in a mythic Orient, seemingly testing more adult possibilities for her screen self while reassuring her audience that her character is still a child.[72] Although radically different in space and time from the bulk of the film's London school setting, this sequence is arguably not a separate diegesis as it is a visualization of Sara's story. As such, it has a clear relationship to the diegetic world of the film and is not another competing reality. Unlike the story in *Children in the House*, the *Arabian Nights'* narrative does not function allegorically but simply stands on its own. As Fowler notes, "Traditionally, only one form of multiple diegesis is allowed [in more Classical cinema]—the play within a play—whereby the second, discontinuous diegetic space is embedded or bracketed within the first, making these sequences more conventional."⁷³ Still, its length and elaborate staging suggest something that is not so easily reconciled with a more closed aesthetic.

Rethinking Feature Film Specificity

More than any other development, the feature film has been linked with a diminution of textual variety at the level of genre differentiation, presentational strategies, and formal innovations. Besides closing down cinematic options, the feature has also been associated with a shift to more contained narratives, closed textuality, and the production of a more individuated mode of spectatorship based on textual identification rather than social and contextual factors. According to this argument, exhibition conditions and other contexts were relegated to a minimal role in structuring reception, particularly as the audience's engagement with the film caused patrons to lose awareness of their physical surroundings. In contrast to the ways features purportedly standardized exhibition, the program of shorts was imbued with the aura of a live performance, replete with variety and its own specificity, evoking a sense of collective presence rather than the individualization produced by identification with a (singular) text.

Miriam Hansen's account of this transformation is the most developed and influential. Although she allows for exceptions, such as the formal oddity of *Intolerance*, and the development of the star system whose social and extratextual knowledge punctured the otherwise self-contained text, she argues the introduction of features led to a more closed text and more individuated, commodity form of spectatorship. "The most effective step in minimizing awareness of the theater space—in particular the distractions attendant upon the variety format—was the introduction of the feature film (1912–13), which mandated prolonged attention and absorption."⁷⁴ She outlines this process as follows, associating features with the emergence of "a coherent diegetic space" and suggesting that their form alone—one that was more varied than she allows—shaped exhibition practices without examining other factors (social, institutional, cultural) involved in the show. Nor does she allow for the continued presence of other forms of distraction within theaters.

> Representational strategies aimed at suppressing awareness of the theater space and absorbing the spectator into the illusionistic space on screen: closer framing, centered composition, and directional lighting; continuity editing which created a coherent diegetic space unfolding itself to a ubiquitous invisible observer; and the gradual increase of film length, culminating in the introduction of the feature film.[75]

Admittedly, Hansen uses early features more as a limit around which to construct her argument rather than exploring them in detail. Still, her work assumes a clean break that rarely exists in practice and fails to engage with the diversity inherent in the period's cinema, let alone its feature films. Influenced by critical orthodoxies at the time of writing, Hansen's work represents more of a methodological intervention, one that associates features and their spectators with a more ahistorical, psychoanalytic paradigm and affiliates them with a Classicism that is more of a conceptual ideal than a reality—as seen in the way she makes *Intolerance* into more of an exception than is perhaps warranted. Earlier films are presented in terms of another tradition, permitting affiliations with other forms of criticism—from the Frankfurt School to cultural studies theories of agency and theories of modernity.

Lost within all this is a careful discussion of the early feature film, a form that needs to be examined more closely, both in terms of its varied textual practices and its signature narrative strategies. As I suggest above, early features are often curious texts, although not without their own conventions, and may not be self-contained, as seen in textual features—like prologues—that directly address audiences, puncture and fragment the diegesis, and invite self-aware spectatorship. This kind of address leads spectators to recognize themselves, evoking their desire to be on the screen, even if only as the recipients of an on-screen actor's gestures and nods of recognition. In turn, these scenes acknowledge the viewer, putting them in an imaginary off-screen space next to the diegesis. This form thus produces an address that foregrounds an illusory continuity between film and theater space, undermining claims that they were entirely self-contained.

Prologues further highlight the ways in which the multiple diegesis of mid-1910s feature films invited heterogeneous responses while encouraging more collective forms of reception. Prologues that refer to the difference between character and actor, or reference the craft of film production, address spectators as social subjects with their own knowledge of cinema and its celebrity culture gleaned from fan magazines, theater lobbies, newspaper columns, and even the trade press. As such, these films cannot be seen as completely self-contained, especially those that use multiple diegesis and encourage viewers to draw connections across different worlds. Indeed, much viewing pleasure came from ways in which early features evoked continuities among the screen world, the theater, and other social and cultural contexts, prompting spectators to think across different registers of knowledge and experience while receiving these films.

Spectatorial self-awareness also shaped exhibition strategies that made patrons conscious of the theater and their presence in it. As already mentioned, these included decor (including elaborate frames around the screen), colored lights projected onto the image, the presence of costumed ushers, and the use of incense. All were most common in first-run screenings, again suggesting that the feature was not about a radical shift in exhibition or spectatorship but had a more complex relationship with variety-based practices.

Indeed, early features exhibit many of the tensions that define Progressivism. Their reception and textuality correspond to the Progressive Era's stress on integrating different aspects of culture while maintaining diversity, a dialectic and a balancing act that shaped everything from the period's urban planning to its immigration policies and civic education. While there is much more work to be done on this topic, the early feature reveals more about its mechanisms and operations when surviving films are explored in detail and placed in their own conceptual contexts—one of which is Progressivism—rather than studied in relation to earlier paradigms or subsequent developments. The specific oscillation between identification, self-awareness, individual self-recognition, and community consciousness that characterized early feature film spectatorship and its formal encounters with oversight, multiple diegesis, and self-reflexivity can then be understood in more detail. In particular, these developments in film form and spectatorship need to be read in the contexts of the period's celebrity culture, a phenomenon that was both based on and further developed this self-awareness, matters I consider in the following chapter.

THREE

Celebrity, Self-Awareness, and the Consciousness of Self

> One of the things that make the modern world "modern" is the development of consciousness of self.
> —Warren Susman

Following the rise film of stardom and the Progressive Era's fascination with celebrity, newspapers and fan magazines began to run contests offering readers a chance at fame. In September 1915, *Photoplay* announced its first ever star-search contest: "Beauty and Brains" was open to all female readers with no prior movie experience. For the next eight months, the magazine printed pictures of contestants next to those of stars they were said to resemble. Eleven finalists selected from over ten thousand entrants received a trip to New York and met William A. Brady and Maurice Tourneur at World studios for a screen test. The winner was offered a one-year contract; the rest were told to return home. Even as the magazine espoused the winners' "morning loveliness and consecrated ambition," they consistently reminded viewers that these girls might not become stars.[1] This contest suggested a complex and ambiguous stance on stardom—possibly attainable for the price of a photo and a stamp and simultaneously difficult to achieve. As

CHAPTER 3

Photoplay pointed out, the winners of most contests did not pass their screen test; they might also have added that those who did had yet to become stars.[2] As if to reinforce these difficulties, *Photoplay* printed letters from unlucky entrants who failed to make the final eleven, noting "the generous . . . and the bitter spirit of losers." While many writers expressed disappointment, frustration, and even some surprise, most vowed to persevere. As one contestant put it, "I am only the more determined to prove that my success is to be made in the silent drama."[3] Displaying caution about the difficulty of becoming a star, yet using the magazine's pages to offer the kind of exposure synonymous with celebrity, "Beauty and Brains" captured some of the period's key tensions surrounding fame. It also revealed how widespread dreams of stardom often owed little to the desire to act, emanating instead from hopes of being transformed into the apex of screen glamour.

This contest was one of many local and national competitions to capitalize on the star mania of the 1910s, revealing how "the movie screen became a sight of fantasy [particularly] for young female fans encouraged to imagine their own image projected there."[4] Contests like Beauty and Brains—as well as those ran by the *Chicago Herald* that I discuss below—held out the promise of film fame but delivered a form of celebrity instead. Even if they did not produce real stars, these contests provided their predominantly female contestants the chance to see themselves on the screen, in papers, and in magazines. As Maria Elena Buszek points out, these competitions bore a structural resemblance to the photo machines placed in movie theaters that "allowed filmgoers to photograph themselves at the very theaters that catered to their fantasies and narcissism."[5] These photo machines allowed audiences, particularly female patrons, to fantasize that they were producing identities like those of screen stars and were part of a whole apparatus designed to let them see, imagine, and fix their image in close proximity to their screen favorites.[6] There was more than a narcissistic component involved in this form of image production: it articulated the structural conditions of self-presentation in the Progressive Era, a period defined through the awareness that one was likely to be looked at given its culture of oversight and the ubiquity of print and filmic representation. In this chapter, I trace what such contests reveal about the strong public interest in celebrity that was a defining characteristic

Celebrity, Self-Awareness, and the Consciousness of Self

of Progressive Era America. Film stardom was the apex of screen fame, but it had other manifestations, including the short-lived and often local acclaim given to film contestants who briefly attained celebrity.

There was clearly something about cinema—as an institution—that affiliated it with celebrity beyond its power to make stars. Its position on the interface of public and private, its global reach, its play with the boundaries between surface and the work that goes into creating an image—even the size of film screens with their unprecedented visibility—made cinema a particularly potent vehicle for thinking about the staging of self. The film industry fed this fascination as films and the press selectively increased public knowledge of its operations during the 1910s. As such, movies participated in the Progressive Era fascination with self-examination. While purportedly revealing the secrets behind cinema's star-making machine, texts about stardom capitalized on broader public awareness that the screen image is a construction, feeding the curiosity about what was on the other side.[7] Star-search competitions created the illusion of opportunity, compounding cinema's reputation as a medium of transformation, turning unknowns into stars, and displaying social mobility. As such, these contests resembled the serialized print stories about girls becoming stars that Stamp discusses, forming a discourse on fame that "encouraged female readers to identify with the drama of rising stardom, to envision themselves in the same role. Together with celebrity profiles . . . [these] fostered a mode of identification that allowed readers to project themselves into these persistent fantasies of self-transformation."[8] Although local contests literally presented stardom as something to be found elsewhere, a journey that would take the recipients away from home, they also stressed its community ties, emphasizing audience's role in creating stars as well as the community stars necessarily produced.

Celebrity expressed several of Progressivism's key characteristics, particularly its investment in monitoring the behavior of others, its concerns with constructing an appropriate self, and its more general investment in self-analysis. The film industry responded to and became part of this celebrity culture, building a star system to replace its more self-effacing stock company model and hiring famous people to appear in movies. Yet its relationship with celebrity was vexed as players' fame destabilized producers' control of their product and its reception. By

CHAPTER 3

1916, the industry tried to curtail stars' salaries after realizing that their newfound power was incompatible with the industry's prevailing economic model; indeed, the trades and fan magazines even claimed that stars' new prominence threatened to destroy the business.[9] As all this suggests, the factors that precipitated a move toward something like a Classical cinema—like stars appearing in feature films—hardly suggested the emergence of a mature and stable industry. For much of the 1910s, stars and features were often positioned as alternate attractions rather than complementary developments toward a new form of cinema.

Films about celebrity and period star-search contests—such as the ones I discuss here from the *Chicago Herald* and Universal—reveal much about audience's fascination with screen fame during the Progressive Era and the industry's own very different approach to the topic. Films about celebrity like *How Molly Made Good* and *Men Who Have Made Love to Me* are few and far between, yet they evidence how fascination with fame displaced the stunts and sensations associated with prior incarnations of modernity, as celebrity effectively became the Progressive Era's key attraction. Without knowledge of period celebrities, these films often make little sense, revealing their far-from-closed textuality. Star-search competitions and related publicity stunts further illustrate how cinema's increasingly close relationship to celebrity discourse encouraged audiences to make connections between the screen, the space of the theater, and social life more generally. Some local star contests even used the appeal of celebrity to forge new communities. Notably, these competitions reveal how fascination with celebrity expressed frustrations with the limited social mobility available through mainstream work, particularly for women who often believed self-display offered a means of self-advancement in a modern, visually dominated society. Increasing numbers of women worked outside the home during the Progressive Era (and, indeed, had more opportunities in education and other facets of public life), but many still faced real limitations to self-development and professional improvement. Many homemakers experienced similar frustrations with domesticity as public life took on greater allure, something further compounded by cinema, consumerism, and the role of celebrity more generally. Increasingly, movie-struck girls looked to the screen for self-advancement that was blocked

Celebrity, Self-Awareness, and the Consciousness of Self

elsewhere.[10] This desire for screen celebrity partly resulted from a sense that social mobility was foreclosed, that work was no longer enough or even relevant in an era of big business and urban anonymity.

As a period of transition for women, the Progressive Era gestured toward possibilities that were not yet fully attained. While this might be frustrating, the sense that gender roles were no longer as fixed fueled excitement and possibly optimism about the promise of new opportunities and a different, more self-oriented way of life. Factories, department stores, the screen, and stage all needed female labor, while the number of women undergoing clerical and secretarial training soared as a result of America's increased corporatization and bureaucratization. Even though a college education was still largely reserved for elite classes, female enrollments soared—by the early 1910s, Mark Whalan estimates that 15 percent of PhD degrees went to women—preparing more women for professional life, although opportunities remained limited.[11] Still, working life was often not pleasant (as many period movies would show) and was often discriminatory, but its existence changed narrative paradigms and the visions of possible futures for women.[12] Female celebrities foregrounded the new diversity of women's lives—varying from the beautiful lawyer and suffragist Inez Milholland Boissevain, who seemingly had it all before dying at thirty-one, to the self-promoting sexually libertine writer Mary MacLane, to reformers and social workers like Jane Addams and Louise de Koven Bowen, to a host of screen and stage stars, conveying a wide range of (public) feminine ideals and identities. With more freedom in their social lives and recreation, women recognized that feminine roles were unfixed, granting them more agency and control over their goals.[13] If fame increasingly appeared to be a more reasonable choice, it was partly because these transitions undermined the certainties that traditionally limited women. Certainly, the Progressive Era was not a utopian period, but its transformations likely encouraged dreams that previously appeared unattainable—including the transition from private individual to star, based on little other than appearance and the desire to move into another, more enticing, realm of life.

Star-search contests, the fame they promised, and the Progressive Era's culture of celebrity more generally would not have been possible without photography. A technology that allowed many working- and middle-class citizens to preserve and circulate their image even after death, photography opened up forms of self-staging formerly associated only with the famous and most renowned.[14] It was domesticated, democratized, and turned into a mass consumer technology during the Progressive Era when Kodak introduced the Brownie, the first affordable camera, in 1900. Photography would participate in Progressivism's erosion of public and private, allowing the masses to see the details of tenement life (as in Jacob Riis's photos), the luxury inside film stars' homes, and the conditions inside factories, office buildings, or upper-level government institutions. Like film, it focused public attention on individuals' appearance, demeanor, and lifestyles while making people more aware of their own image and encouraging them to find ways to best represent themselves. Photography was therefore as much a venue for self-staging and self-presentation—practices central to both the Progressive Era and celebrity—as it was for memory and preservation.[15] It helped to establish and distribute visions of the spectacular feminine self more widely than before and with greater detail and "authenticity," facilitating the presentation of a more publicly circulating femininity associated with public life while creating a new and more complex relationship between agency, self, and appearance. All the period's star-search competitions depended on widespread access to cheap and reliable photography and were furthermore embedded in these associations and their promise of feminine mobility, self-improvement, and self-actualization. Photographs were the cost of admission; contestants were judged on them, whether by their peers or a panel of experts and were (briefly) known through the circulation of their images. This was not how the film industry operated; still photographs were overwhelmingly *not* considered a measure of screen presence—even if truthful, they measured something the motion picture camera might not register, pointing to the specific and mystical qualities of cinema and film fame.

Celebrity in Progressive Era America

Fame thrilled the Progressive Era public, both as a spectacle and as something to which many aspired, especially those women who saw it as a route into a more public, self-actualizing and attractive life. Mo-

Celebrity, Self-Awareness, and the Consciousness of Self

tion pictures escalated interest in celebrity, exceeding the kinds of fame already seen in theater and other amusements.[16] During the 1910s, the number of film stars would be higher than at almost any period in the medium's history, partly in response to the increase in production companies, all needing signature stars, and partly to accommodate viewers' fascination with fame.[17] Although famous figures had captivated America since the nineteenth century, whether on stage, the lecture circuit, or in the pages of popular newspapers and magazines, the Progressive Era's celebrity fascination was different, in scale as well as in terms of what it represented. There were institutional reasons for the increased number of celebrities: mass media (first print, then film) increasingly required subjects that grabbed public interest, both to fill pages on schedule (the celebrity profile is important here) and boost sales.[18] Heightened competition for newspaper circulation further bolstered celebrity mania while presenting additional opportunities for fame seekers.[19] Even local theater bulletins depended on stardom, constructing theaters as places where patrons could come closer to its aura and the possibilities for self-advancement it offered.

Although film stardom is important, as a product of the culture as well as an important industry commodity, it is not my primary focus. Instead, I explore manifestations of what today would be called celebrity. Celebrity and stardom overlap and gain meaning from each other, but they nonetheless refer to somewhat different phenomena. I use the term *celebrity* in this chapter as it more accurately and concisely describes something that period writers struggled to express. This exact word was in circulation but not widely used; instead, terms like *personality* and *star* were employed, even if the person in question was not a star in any accepted sense. At this time, *star* alternately designated production companies' leading players (many of them more accurately described as actors) or those who had great popularity and could be considered true stars, although it had other applications, including referring to figures whom studios were priming as future stars. Many so-called stars were effectively celebrities, in today's sense of the word—figures who were known more for their press coverage than screen roles, even though studios orchestrated most of this reportage.

I use the term *celebrity* to evoke a broader and more diffuse cultural formation that was widespread during the Progressive Era, sometimes distinct from stardom, sometimes enveloping it. There were many types of celebrity, including the celebrity of people who were famous for multiple reasons and in multiple media—like Lillian Russell who was known as a beauty, actress, singer, and newspaper columnist. In an era where the variety stage still held sway, multiple accomplishments might attest to some celebrities' greater talents, even if they erased the original source of their fame. Other luminaries like Thomas Edison achieved fame outside their profession because their accomplishments affected many areas of life and because they promoted themselves as modern heroes. According to Charles Ponce de Leon, these figures were attractive to print media because "they could be counted on to produce interesting remarks on topics both serious and mundane."[20] Celebrity was thereby associated with specific individual's capacities to transcend cultural boundaries, whether those separating different fields or those delineating private and public life. As such, it opened up the multifaceted nature of modern individuality for mass attention, steering public curiosity toward the private lives of notable figures. As an exploration of the modern self and its relationship to contemporary society, celebrity participated in Progressivism's broader process of self-examination.[21]

Fame was particularly attractive to Progressive Era women, particularly younger women who wanted to experience a more public life and take advantage of new opportunities.[22] Whether real or simply imagined through vehicles like stage, screen, and the printed page, modern life appeared to offer more than domesticity or drudgery. Contests capitalized on these desires, offering a shot at fame, even as fan magazines warned young women that movie stardom was hard work and harder to achieve. These accounts traced fundamental associations between femininity and screen ambitions. As Susan A. Glenn has pointed out with regard to the stage, Progressive Era women were often interested in self-display, in "assertive self-spectacle," even as they risked their own images being contained and used against them.[23] She argues that this very "self-spectacle . . . obliterated the ideological dividing line between the private sphere (associated with femininity) and the wider public sphere (associated with masculinity) [and] had more than commercial value . . . [it was] a symbol of woman's longing for personhood."[24] Along these lines, film fame represented more than social mobility and participation in a much-beloved industry. It articulated a new modern subjectivity that played with the new variety of roles opening up for women without limiting them to just one—all while demonstrating the power of visibility for women seeking full personhood in an intensely visual modern culture. As Liz Conor has observed: "modernity has intensified the visual scene and specularized women within it. Consequently, feminine subjectivity has come to be increasingly performed within the visual register. The conditions of modernity constituted certain visually typed subject positions . . . marked by a dramatic historical shift: women were invited to articulate themselves as modern subjects by constituting themselves as spectacles."[25] This desire to be visible—and to control one's own representation—contributed to women's interest in fame and enhanced cinema's allure, particularly by the mid-1910s when it became clear that most popular stars were young women. This phenomenon encouraged many star aspirants to imagine the industry as saturated with feminine power and agency. In turn, this ethos of visibility repositioned cinema as a site that permitted women to demonstrate their mastery of detail, appearance, and visual literacy. They could study film, fashion, and beauty (topics that were increasingly linked in the new fan magazines like *Photoplay*, *Motion Picture Classic*, and *Shadowland*) and present this expertise via their self-presentation and through their evaluation of other like-minded women. Here they might construct their own roles and their own off-screen personas, fostering a new self-aware femininity while using those same skills the stars of stage and screen used. Glenn's observations about the stage can therefore be applied to the screen: "By opening up a space for female performers to become *both* spectacles and personalities, the popular theater promoted the development of the first self-consciously 'modern' expression of new womanhood."[26]

Not all Progressive Era celebrities were remarkable figures like Edison or Lillian Russell. Some had few accomplishments and were famous because of their lifestyles, their high birth, involvement in scandal, or from their own self-promotion, making celebrity and fame seem a more democratic route to self-advancement. Such personalities were more like celebrities in the contemporary sense, staging themselves in public, regardless of work or talent, suggesting a form of fame opposed to stardom. Whereas stardom asserts the importance of work, talent, and the auratic individual, celebrity seeks the rewards of upward mobility. This kind of coverage defined star-search contests, which required entrants to create a persona and market themselves to a public, even though they could only sell themselves and their photo: until they won, there was no screen work to promote. Few contestants or winners acquired any substantial stardom before Clara Bow, although her accomplishments had more to do with her determination than the prize she won.

Leo Braudy, Daniel Boorstin, and Joshua Gamson have suggested that this form of celebrity is *the* modern incarnation of fame, predicated on specific forms of visibility created through mass culture that divorce accomplishment from renown.[27] During the Progressive Era, celebrity did not necessarily preclude talent or accomplishment, but it did not require it either. The sheer variation in the period's celebrities and their accomplishments revealed broader confusion about how social mobility could be attained, and in what measure individual talent, hard work, and integrity mattered, questions that permeated discourses on film stardom. Celebrity thus constituted a discourse on the very social mobility that was key to American national identity but was often absent from many people's experience of grueling, dull, or dead-end work, especially working-class and immigrant women. Stressing leisure over work and the sudden rise to fame, celebrity offered a site where these issues could be explored, permitting evaluation of different forms of individuality and different paths to success. It also allowed ordinary women to indulge in the pleasure of imaging themselves as public figures, their visibility attesting to their personhood and the pleasures of self-creation afforded by a consumer culture that severed some of the links between biology and destiny. Star-search contests were an important part of this process, helping reveal the limits and promises inherent in Progressive Era discourses on fame.

Increased interest in celebrities fed fascination with the private lives of the famous, encouraging the public to link some celebrities' fame to their personality, recreation, and intimate affairs, not their work.[28] Celebrities were increasingly perceived as exceptional because of their innate individuality, *not* because of their accomplishments. Such beliefs could suggest work was unnecessary as greatness/distinction was found in the individual, even if this personality was essentially the

Celebrity, Self-Awareness, and the Consciousness of Self

creation of personal fantasies, consumer goods, and sheer willpower. This perspective influenced coverage of film actors, which moved away from discussions of their professional life, presenting problems for the industry as it attempted to shift attention back to their work.[29] Celebrity's emphasis on the exceptional individual clearly responded to the Progressive Era's concern with the different new collective social formations that modernity had produced. In emphasizing distinctive individuals, celebrity did not necessarily present solutions to the problem of self but offered examples that could be held up to public scrutiny and analyzed in detail as an example to all. As Richard Abel points out, it was widely agreed that stars had personality, a term "Susman found in his research [that] was widely used in self-improvement manuals between 1900 and 1920 as a means of resolving the problem of how the individual could be distinguished from the *crowd* in modern society" (italics in original).[30] The pleasures of analyzing stars and celebrities therefore often circulated around discussions of how they constructed their individual identities.

Susman's influential work on personality and the construction of self in Progressive Era culture provides important insights into celebrity and the role of the modern self. Nineteenth-century urbanization and mass culture eroded earlier ideas of a "natural" self and validated concepts of the self-made individual. Media increasingly made citizens aware of the ways they drafted their existence, inviting people to see themselves at the center of some narrative or representation. Furthermore, twentieth-century self-help manuals (many ostensibly penned by stars like Douglas Fairbanks or columns ghostwritten for the likes of Mary Pickford), popular journalism, star profiles, and consumerist forms of self-improvement helped present the inner and outer self as malleable commodities, a movement in which cinema also participated.[31] Whereas earlier ideals, like character, a concept that arose in the seventeenth century, were based on self-mastery and restraint and focused on learned moral imperatives, qualities necessary for work as well as religious life, the later model of personality responded to the rise of consumerism and mass society. It depended on self-realization, creating an attractive and visible self at the center of society that could be distinguished from the crowd.[32] Personality was necessarily affiliated with leisure, consumer society, and performance, especially as it involved "the unique qualities of an individual and the performing self that attracts others."[33] Unlike character, which involves the sublimation of self, personality relied on its "externalization," again linking visibility to full personhood.[34]

To different degrees, celebrity and film stardom both embodied personality and participated in the Progressive Era's broader efforts to stabilize modernity, particularly at the level of managing the self. As Jennifer Bean has shown, stars resituated a modernist humanism at the center of cinema, arguably transforming the medium into an important supplement to broader cults of personality.[35] While stardom gained momentum from performers in stunt-filled serial films, it eclipsed these modernist spectacles, asserting the importance of these personalities above all else. These magnetic, fascinating individuals would underscore Progressivism's shift away from a modernity of shock, sensation, and attractions to another, later, modernity fascinated with viewing others, assessing oneself, and seeing other people's private lives propelled into the public sphere.[36] Unsurprisingly, viewers wanted to participate in these forms of fame, especially as movies combined heightened identification with stars (and the models of individuality they represented), making both appear deceptively close to many spectators. This desire to participate was even greater among women who saw in celebrity and screen fame the chance for a public existence that combined self-actualization with the pleasures of the visible body, newly accorded them by modern consumer culture, mass media, and cheaper photography.

Cinema, Celebrity, and Self-Awareness

The early star system was not the only way in which the film industry catered to increased public interest in fame. By the early 1910s, producers started featuring well-known personalities on screen, including nonactors/performers.[37] Examples included artists' model Audrey Munson; ballet dancer Anna Pavlova; opera diva Geraldine Farrar; Ben Lindsey, a social reformer, judge, and Progressive Party politician; suffragette, labor lawyer, and society beauty Inez Milholland Boissevain; Andrew Carnegie; and Mexican rebel Pancho Villa.[38] Most notable, perhaps, was Evelyn Nesbit, the showgirl/model at the center of the scan-

Celebrity, Self-Awareness, and the Consciousness of Self

dalous 1906 Thaw-White murder who Lee Grieveson considers "the first person to capitalize on a scandal to become a film star."[39] Many of these figures did not have extensive screen ambitions, allowing the industry to engage the public's fascination with fame without negative consequences, such as the higher salaries associated with increased interest in a star. Even if they were ostensibly playing someone else, the line separating the celebrity's real life was usually thin, as in *Redemption* (Joseph A. Golden/Julius Steger, Triumph Films, 1917). Here Nesbit played Alice Loring, a character suspiciously like herself, who was involved with a philandering architect. Her son, Russell, even played Loring's son, Harry.[40]

One particularly telling instance of the intersection of celebrity, cinema, and Progressivism can be seen in the single film appearance of scandalous young female memoirist Mary MacLane, whose image again emphasized young women's interrelated desires for visibility, personhood, self-realization, and public life. A sensation at twenty-one when she published her erotic biography, 1902's *The Story of Mary MacLane*, which sold almost one hundred thousand copies in its first month, McLane was particularly popular among young women.[41] She subsequently cultivated her reputation as an outspoken and daring bisexual feminist who broke taboos, using her private life and erotic fantasies as material for books and newspaper columns. Her only film, *Men Who Have Made Love to Me* (Arthur Bertelet, Perfection-Essanay, 1918), capitalized on this image, focusing on six of her affairs, including one with a married man. The *Motion Picture News* observed that, "It is to be expected that with all the advertising Mary MacLane has had in the past—with all that Essanay is giving her in the present, that there will be a public eagerly awaiting the picture."[42] According to the *News* the now-lost film started with shots of MacLane looking into the camera lens and smoking alternated with titles, the first of which read: "So that you may know me, I, Mary MacLane, will tell you of six piquant love episodes in my life—all of them damnably real."[43] Reviews indicate that these relationships were intercut with images of MacLane "discussing" them directly on camera, presenting "her view of each lover 'as a specimen to be stuck on pins and examined under a microscope.'"[44] The film thus offered the novelty of seeing a famous and popular author playing herself—both as the character in her books and as the person analyzing her own actions—presenting itself as an authentic celebrity text. James S. McQuade even commented that "it is the first time in my remembrance that I have seen on the screen author and actress concentrated in the same person, and that person acting over again love scenes in her own life with a matter-of-fact realism."[45] Surviving reviews indicate that this film foregrounded the kind of self-analysis at the root of much of the period's celebrity phenomenon, something print media first made possible, and that cinema (with its intimacy, glamour, and ability to document movement) took to a new level. It is a perfect example of celebrity enabling the self-examination inherent in Progressivism—both for the famous persons themselves and the public who were involved by proxy. MacLane exemplified one kind of celebrity found in Progressivism—she was a self-absorbed self-promoter, an ordinary girl who created and monitored her own extraordinary image—but her antics and writings grabbed public attention and were linked to the broader feminist cause for self-actualization.[46]

I term this inward look *self-awareness*, but not in the sense that it displayed complete self-knowledge, including the subject's recognition of their place in the world. Rather, this self-awareness involved a heightened consciousness of oneself, an inward turn that recognized how each action might be seen by others and thus had to be self-monitored. While it derived from Progressive culture's investment in reform, oversight, and its general efforts to study, and thereby improve, society, this self-awareness testified to the importance of self-creation, the desire to present a public persona that articulated fantasies of a socially mobile self. Stardom and the rise of visual culture further complicated structures of looking and being looked at, making the latter a highly desirable position rather than something largely associated with control, scrutiny, and reform. Celebrity and personality thus combined to create (or reveal) a culture in thrall with itself, yet vexed about the correct ways to self-police, a feminine position that also epitomized women's ventures into visibility and their investment in a more public life. Such anxiety and self-fascination broadly shaped this culture, as seen in Progressivism's numerous surveys, reports, and studies of everyday life, as well as its concerns with constructing a suitable national identity. Self-awareness was also manifested among a population who became more mindful of both their own gaze and how they presented themselves,

Celebrity, Self-Awareness, and the Consciousness of Self

partly to avoid policing, partly to attract favorable attention, again a position closely linked to the modern feminine condition. Whether looking at others or recognizing the possibility that one was being looked at, the public became more aware of the importance of self-presentation in an increasingly public world. All this made self-awareness one of the most important facets of Progressivism, as well as an increasingly cinematic tendency that capitalized on the medium's strengths in staging personalities and presenting them for public examination.

Indeed, celebrity co-opted impulses to see and be seen, allowing the viewing public to play the role of those in power regardless of whether they were the ones being surveyed or the ones granting stars power through giving them attention. Women particularly enjoyed this new power of looking at and monitoring others accorded them by cinema, fan magazines, and the new feminine consumer culture, especially as it encouraged them to self-monitor and self-evaluate in terms linked to stardom and other forms of public representation. A dynamic of female power, associated with the female look, marked star polls in fan magazines as well as contests where the public "elected" new stars, most of whom faded away before their films were released—as seen in the *Chicago Herald* contests discussed in this chapter. The fascination with looking at stars seemed inexhaustible, leading to the production of movies like the independently produced feature from 1915, *How Molly Made Good* (Lawrence B. McGill, Kulee), that was exclusively structured around the fascination of watching famous people. In the process, this film reveals how stardom eclipsed other attractions while linking celebrity's power to female professionalism.

How Molly Made Good: *Modernity and the Attraction of Fame*

Besides demonstrating the allure of celebrity, *How Molly Made Good* illustrates how ideals of personality might facilitate women's professional advancement. The film's premise is simple—stars fascinate, particularly when they are at leisure, and somehow, they might offer a route to self-advancement, particularly for women. Aspiring writer Molly Malone arrives in New York from Ireland expecting to meet her brother only to find he has left for war some weeks earlier. Heading to his office at the *New York Tribune*, she overhears an editor reprimand a young female correspondent, Alma Hinton, for failing to interview temperamental opera singer Madame Fjorde, who Molly had befriended on the boat. Seizing the opportunity, Molly asks for a job, presenting a portfolio of clips. The editor gives her a task—if she completes it, he will hire her. She is to meet with a series of stage luminaries, but he will only give her one name and address. She has to use her personality, her winning ability to get along with others, to get contacts from each actor and complete the task on deadline. Like the serial format, to which the film alludes, *Molly* presents a discourse on female professionalism that tests its heroine's resolve, abilities, and, significantly, her personality. Although she is a trained journalist and has the ability to get a story and fend off assailants, she completes the job because she gets on well with others.

The bulk of the film features Molly racing up, down, and across suburban New York in a variety of vehicles (including an airplane), followed by the evil Hinton and a series of other villains who try to destroy her. Instead of each challenge building to a resolution, as in a serial, Molly overcomes increasingly spectacular obstacles to meet with theater stars, visit their homes, and see them at rest. The attraction of meeting famous people overwhelms any narrative progression, something the *World* noted in its very positive review: "more important than the story, more important than anything else in the picture, in fact, are the intimate glimpses of stage stars which it affords. . . . We see all of these people at close range [and] enjoy views of their attractive estates."[47] Indeed, the spectacle of celebrities even eclipsed the film's more visceral interests, including the car crashes and airplane rides, attractions typical of slightly earlier modernity. Molly's adventures are all based on finding a star, and her adventures, perils, and stunts are clearly secondary to the pleasure of seeing celebrities at home. If cinema's prior shocks, sensations, and attractions represent an earlier incarnation of modernity, the dialectic between celebrity, stardom, and cinema characterized Progressivism's later incarnation, where famous figures deliver the most significant thrills. This point underscores the diminution of attractions that occurred around 1911, coinciding with the establishment of a star system, pointing to the transfer of energies from attraction to star.[48] Besides capturing audiences' attention, attractions and stars both gestured outside the text, whether through the

Celebrity, Self-Awareness, and the Consciousness of Self

former's use of display or the latter's evocation of other performances, off-screen lives, and the overarching celebrity culture. While it is a novelty, and thus not typical, *Molly* nevertheless reveals how stardom superseded the attractions of an earlier cinema, pointing to a changed configuration of modernity on- and off-screen.

Molly's advertising prominently featured the thrill of seeing famous stage stars in their summer homes. The *New York Times* notes that, "The plan was to find a scenario that would show [its stars] in their respective homes amid their families, livestock, flowers, automobiles, and other signs of prosperity."[49] The film's writer-producer, Burns Mantle, had access to his stars, as he was the drama critic for the *New York Evening Mail* and would later review films for *Photoplay*. He may also have had some insight to these actors' future screen ambitions: virtually all *Molly*'s stage luminaries—Julian Eltinge, May Robson, Robert Edeson, Julia Dean, Cyril Scott, Henry Kolker, Charles J. Ross, Leo Ditrichstein, and Henrietta Crosman—later moved into cinema, generally with limited success. In some cases, this was not their first film appearance—only Lulu Scott and Julia Dean did not try for film careers.[50] As each vignette purportedly placed each actor in their "natural" environment, these scenes likely crafted appropriate images for future screen careers, effectively acting as auditions for roles in a medium that demanded intimacy and still presented many stars as regular folks. Yet because all these figures are stage stars, they are presented as celebrities, an important distinction the film's exclusive focus on their leisure, domesticity, and off-stage lives reinforces—none of them plays a role, they all appear as themselves, but these selves are of interest because of their fame.

Each star is shown in everyday routines. May Robson drinks tea with her daughter and grandson in their gardens, Mrs. Henry Kolker picks fruit, Charles J. Ross plays with a litter of new puppies, famed female impersonator Julian Eltinge works on his car. Most are very friendly, greeting Molly warmly and inviting her into their homes.[51] Some help her out of tough spots: Leo Ditrichstein rebuffs Irwin, the villainous moneylender who stalks Molly, getting his gardener and driver to remove him from the premises. Charles J. Ross invites her to stay and interview the Queen of the Carnival and drives her to the station. Notably, these stars are not hidden away, but are well known to their neighbors; although each actor gives Molly just a name and a

CHAPTER 3

town, she is able to find them by asking the locals who know where they live.[52] Graeme Turner has suggested that celebrity, at least in its more contemporary manifestations, is symptomatic of the loss of community.[53] *Molly* goes to great ends to suggest that this was not the case—these celebrities are good citizens because they participate in local life, a very Progressive ideal (or fantasy).

While it is difficult to say how closely each star's image matched their public profiles, it is worth looking briefly at one particularly interesting case: Julian Eltinge. The era's dominant female impersonator, Eltinge had a short but notable film career in the late 1910s, largely after *Molly*'s release. Perhaps not surprisingly, his off-stage image was highly masculine—"a regular fellow" in *Photoplay*'s words.[54] As well as offsetting homosexual connotations (he was engaged but never married), his masculinity foregrounded the work and talent involved in turning this "husky, two-fisted" man into a woman.[55] According to publicity, Eltinge went by his real name off stage—Bill Dalton—and liked to drink beer, work out with rowing machines and medicine balls, smoke cigars, and race cars.[56] Dressing like a woman and mastering female gestures reportedly did not come naturally. According to *Photoplay*, "When he started in, Bill didn't know the difference between chiffon and a bias tuck . . . He had to get up on all that dope which is a life work in itself."[57] In keeping with this, *Molly*'s Eltinge is rugged, stands with his legs apart, and downs a beer in a single gulp. He even looks at Molly lasciviously as she leaves.

More an example of the era's prevalent celebrity discourse than a study in star images, *Molly* presents its stage stars solely in terms of their private lives, which are presumably more fascinating than their work. Although period audiences would likely have some familiarity with these actors (without it, the film is pretty dull and has little point), there is no effort to integrate their work on screen or to explain who they are. Like much celebrity discourse, the film relies on extratextual information that is already sufficiently well known, revealing another important way in which early features—and films of the mid-1910s more broadly—are not completely hermetic, closed, or self-sufficient. *Molly* also highlighted cinema's capacity to trump other celebrity media, something that newsreels would also capitalize on, particularly titles devoted to Hollywood and screen stardom like *Photoplay*'s "Screen

Celebrity, Self-Awareness, and the Consciousness of Self

Supplement" and *Screenland*'s own eponymous series that documented the professional and private lives of the stars in vivid moving images.

"How To Get In": Aspiring to Fame

While *Molly* capitalized on public fascination with fame, it presented it primarily as a spectator sport, offering an alternate, more work-oriented and pragmatic model of feminine social mobility through its plucky immigrant-turned-journalist. Other films explored the desire to be famous and break into movies, although it must be noted that these were few and far between. In attempting to correct public fantasies about screen life, films like *A Girl's Folly* (Maurice Tourneur, World, 1917) presented film stardom in terms of its relationship to work and talent rather than seeing it as an easy alternative to a more mundane career, even as they acknowledged some stars' vanity and laziness. Patrons would be familiar with these accounts of stardom as hard work, given their widespread circulation in fan magazines. But such repetition indicated that the message was likely not getting across to a public—particularly a feminine public—who believed that stardom really involved leisure, consumerism, self-realization, and an escape from routine. During the 1910s, fan magazines continually reminded their largely female readers that the only players of merit were those who avoided the spotlight and put work first—and these were the stars whom the readers adored, like Marguerite Clark, May Allison, Pearl White, Mae Marsh, and Norma Talmadge. These actors recognized that they were employees, were disciplined and self-controlled. In January 1918, for example, *Photoplay* noted that "the popular belief that a film player's life is one round of pleasure was a fallacy . . . you don't see [stars] about . . . because they have to work so hard. They all tell harrowing tales about getting home at 6 or 7 o'clock, 'just so tired,' and being obliged to be on their way again in the morning between 8 and 9 o'clock."[58] Accordingly, stars' public images—like their on-screen presence—were approached as the product of labor so consuming that it eclipsed private lives. Industry discourses were clearly designed to focus attention on the screen, contain stars' power, and deter hopefuls from flocking to studios. They advance a self-sacrificial model much like Susman's character, not a more contemporary ideal of personality

111

CHAPTER 3

and infinite self-realization and reinvention. The industry clearly drew on these earlier—and dated—models of self for tactical reasons, deglamorizing stardom to retain power over the business, its texts, and their reception. This process was not successful.

Character-centered publicity established stars as talented and self-effacing individuals who deserved acclaim. Some reports even mention the dangers of their work, as Bean points out, suggesting that stardom—for all its fame and visibility—might ultimately end with the obliteration of self.[59] These perils varied from the physical risks some actors took, to the general rigors of the work, its long days, travel, and personal demands. As Bean observes: "The strenuous demands made of the film player's body explained, to many, why dramatic luminaries like Sarah Bernhardt never quite 'got over' with the filmgoing public, whereas those who succeeded in the crossover . . . were praised specifically for their physical stamina and courage."[60] This sacrificial, work-first ethos structured much publicity on stars' off-screen lives—particularly female stars—with their private life reportedly taking second place to professional duties as the industry tried to contain their allure. Audiences did not accept this account, however, and it was not entirely true. As stardom increasingly transcended texts and the industry's preferred reading contexts, it became associated with celebrity, something that was more social and thus more difficult to contain and resisted incorporation in the discourses of professionalism the industry employed.

While fan magazines insisted that work, talent, and experience made stars, their readers increasingly suspected that this may not be the case. Instead, movie fame increasingly appeared to depend on chance, a break, access, and self-assertion, instilling doubts about the degree of work or talent needed to be a screen success while foregrounding the appeal of stardom's rewards for those fortunate enough to succeed. Movie stardom thus became mired in the logic of celebrity—of appearance, leisure, and consumption—even as the industry maintained otherwise.

Even fan magazines occasionally admitted that screen success could be mystifying. In January 1918, *Photoplay* mentioned a query from "a sick, tired little girl" who asked why "lucky chances make stars of some women while others with perhaps as much talent, working just as hard,

Celebrity, Self-Awareness, and the Consciousness of Self

passing, as she says, 'through fire and brimstone' . . . get nowhere." The magazine admitted that this was "the eternal, unanswerable question," agreeing that stars often owed success "to a bit of luck." Still, they rationalized this, adding: "if that luck had not come their way, it is not probable that the genius for success would still have won its place?" In this account work and talent ultimately produced success if the individual persevered.[61] Although the magazine came close to suggesting that stardom came from luck, it backed away from this conclusion. Admitting it would have undermined the institution: affiliating stardom (and the film industry) with chance and thus devaluing its merit while encouraging even more girls to head to studio gates. If stardom did not solely derive from work or talent, then perhaps it came from personality, something that was conveniently difficult to describe but could justify film fame.

Shelley Stamp has discussed the problems the desire for screen fame created for the industry by the early 1910s as would-be stars flocked to Hollywood.[62] As producers dispensed with stock companies around 1913, they relied more on extras, opening up some work at the same time celebrity culture fast compounded movie stars' new fame. While fan magazines initially fed this desire with columns about how to make it in film, there were signs of change by the mid-1910s. Articles emphasized the difficulties in achieving screen success, responding to the spate of girls who arrived in Los Angeles seeking a break and those whose hopes had started to fade.[63] Columns on how to get into the movies became a fan magazine staple, particularly as it became increasingly difficult, often providing little hope. The *Classic* and its sister publication, *Motion Picture Magazine*, ran a series of articles in 1916 based on the personal experiences of a number of (largely female) stars. The *Classic* stated, "Every publication, producer, director and player is constantly flooded with inquiries asking How to Get In, and these articles are to cover the field exhaustively and conclusively by the greatest experts in the business."[64] They noted that advice varied and acknowledged that they were not inviting people into "this already overcrowded business." Parents were advised to read these largely cautionary articles. Even though the *Classic* promised surprises, much of the information followed the standard line: work hard, gain experience, and you can work your way in, particularly if you are intelligent and beautiful.[65]

CHAPTER 3

Some features offered professional advice from the sources that mattered most—female stars, emphasizing links between feminine expertise and screen success. Some stars, like Florence LaBadie, observed that directors would hire newcomers if they fit a role, noting that many stars had no prior experience. Lillian Walker was more realistic, stating: "It's hard to advise beginners how to get into the pictures. Some can get in without much difficulty, and some might never get in."[66] She suggested extra work, but did not mention that it, too, was hard to find. Like LaBadie, she recommended experience, hard work, and starting at the bottom, adding: "so many look on Moving Picture work as play and join the business to have a good time. These people will not succeed and had better seek some other form of employment."[67] As Walker's comment suggests, the allure of the screen, its association with audiences' own leisure, and the discourses of consumption that increasingly surrounded stars (endorsing goods as well as posing in fashionable gowns and within beautiful homes) coalesced in fantasies of a star's perfect life.[68] Still, the sheer numbers of women seeking stardom suggests that there was something specific about the screen that encouraged these ambitions. Cinema's unprecedented visibility, the importance Progressive Era culture accorded recreation, and the movies' associations with fans' own leisure were all factors building the fascination with, and desire for, screen stardom—as was the possibility of unlimited protean identities and the process of self-actualization in a more visual modern world.

The term most commonly used to describe the ineffable quality that made a star—*personality*—conveniently resisted description and invalidated any easy formulas for success. As a manager of a western motion picture company cited in *Motion Picture Classic* (then called *Motion Picture Supplement*) reportedly stated: "'Film Personality! Why it's—it's when a woman or a man can 'get over' on the screen! What makes 'em get over? Hard to tell in words but, say, just look over there at Miss Pickford—she's getting over!"[69] Similar quotations litter trades and fan magazines, suggesting that personality was not always defined in the way that Susman points out. This kind of personality definitely could *not* be acquired or learned, regardless of what it was (and the consensus was generally that it could be recognized but not defined); it was specific to screen presence and owed little to, say, the quality of

Celebrity, Self-Awareness, and the Consciousness of Self

a photograph, looks, talent, or the charisma of a stage star. As with so much else, motion pictures were transformative, and thus it was often impossible to know with any certainty what would work on screen.

Personality suggested two things: screen success was inherently linked to highly *individual* traits and only a few experts (like D. W. Griffith) could recognize it in its raw forms and know in advance who could be a movie star.[70] Consequently, film stardom could not be learned or, ironically, worked for—although screen acting was still work—and it was not self-evident, rendering individual self-evaluations useless. Many fan magazines featured articles that told stories of beautiful girls turned away by a director because their beauty—or personality—was unsuited to movies.[71] Some of this was couched in scientific terms—blue eyes did not register as well on camera as brown—while journalists admitted that some looks did not translate to film, often for unknown reasons.[72] In turn, of course, this meant that a "positively homely" person could "go before the cinematograph and, by reason of their personality, be transformed on the screen into extremely good-looking types."[73] Given the consistency with which such advice appeared in fan magazines and newspaper columns, some readers might think that they had what it took—no matter how improbable—but their star presence could only be confirmed—or denied—by appearing on screen. Consequently, the screen test became the Holy Grail. Screen tests were difficult to get, of course. But they were available at industry conventions (like the 1916 and 1917 Chicago Movie Expositions), constituting powerful public attractions. These tests went against the industry's largely cautionary rhetoric, even as they lured the public to buy tickets. Still, screen tests were no minor hurdle, as *Photoplay* noted:

> Some of the most celebratedly beautiful women, on and not on, the footlighted stage, have been conspicuous studio failures when they faced the photoplay camera! Their faces simply wouldn't do for the screen. The skin that was lovely to look at was a texture that would not photograph; or the smile would not "register"; or grace of movement would not reproduce except in lying awkwardness; or—but there are so *many* "ors" in front of the crucifying eye of the movie camera! No one can know until the test is over! (Emphasis in original)[74]

As if to prove this point, the *Chicago Herald* pointed out that the "least attractive girl" in *Photoplay*'s "Beauty and Brains" contest looked the best on camera, while another "pretty as a wax doll in reality, simply could not register in the eye of the camera."[75] Unsurprisingly, newspapers like the *Herald* would soon use the promise of a screen test or the greater lure of a film role to stimulate their own circulation.

Seeking a Lucky Break: Star-Search Contests and Local Celebrity

The star contests that mushroomed during the mid-1910s offered a different discourse on stardom from those the motion picture industry offered, whether in fan magazines, interviews, promotions, or in films themselves. These competitions focused on the lucky break, the most irrational yet essential element in becoming a star that escaped individual control. Luck clearly undermined assumptions about talent, work ethic, professionalism, and success that fan magazines and the industry used to ground stardom.[76] In offering "lucky breaks" as prizes, these contests foregrounded the difficulty of getting into movies, rationalizing themselves as efforts to correct systematic failures by offering solutions like a prize role, exposure in the press, a screen test, and opportunities to meet with movie executives. As such, they appeared to side with frustrated readers who believed the system was broken, blocking access to deserving aspirants, leaving matters to fate and personal connections.

But this altruism hid a larger economic rationale. Contests capitalized on star mania to promote products and build circulation. The two extensive movie star competitions the *Chicago Herald* conducted in 1915 and 1916 were designed to sell subscriptions on the back of broader public interest in film fame, particularly among women. The *Herald* even advertised these contests in the *Moving Picture World*, in the process emphasizing the paper's developed movie coverage and favorable theater advertising. Besides playing with associations between film stardom and social mobility and self-awareness, these local contests balanced ideals of individuality and community, rooting stars in their neighborhoods while simultaneously promising to transport them to Hollywood and the mystical world of the screen itself.

Celebrity, Self-Awareness, and the Consciousness of Self

"Sue"

In November 1914, the *Herald* announced they were helping Essanay find "the prettiest and most popular girl in Chicago" to star in a film called *Sue*.[77] (The *Herald*'s used of the term "popular" recalls personality's emphasis on attracting others as well as the community loyalties this contest evoked.) The first competition of its kind in Chicago, "Sue" stirred up neighborhood pride and star mania, extending the magnetism associated with personality and stardom to the community-oriented spaces of neighborhood theaters. For Chicagoans, this localizing of fame had additional resonance, as uptown producers Essanay partnered with the *Herald* in both its star-search contests. Essanay also made other films of local interest, like *The Lady of the Snows* (1915), written by Mrs. Carter Harrison, the novelist wife of Chicago's mayor (1911–15).[78] They were only distributed within the city, revealing the studio's efforts to distinguish itself as a national giant with local pride. The "Sue" contest was distinctly local: while the *World*'s James S. McQuade discussed the frenzy it incited in his "Chicago News Letter," the finished film was not reviewed or mentioned in the trades or in any paper other than the *Herald*.

"Sue" encouraged readers to submit pictures of the prettiest local girls for publication in each day's paper, each representing her neighborhood. Throughout the contest's duration, the paper emphasized neighborhood loyalties: "All you have to do is vote for the prettiest girl entered from the locality in which you live. You are not actually forced to vote for just the candidate from your district, although you will probably want to."[79] After the finalists had been selected, slides of the top forty were shown in local theaters.[80] Once all the girls' photos had been published, the public could vote.[81] Each vote's value depended on the number of coupons submitted with it—a coupon worth five votes was printed in the *Herald* each day. To increase theater attendance (another of the contest's aims), votes had to be validated at a local Essanay theater.[82] This press/film synergy was designed to boost the *Herald*'s circulation while steering viewers toward theaters showing the General Film (GFC) program.

"Sue" promised its winner recognition and celebrity, offering a more straightforward, seductive, and potentially misleading star discourse that suggested—unlike fan magazines—that beauty and a photograph

CHAPTER 3

were proof of star potential. Even though its prize was the starring role in a one-reel film, the leading contestants ultimately received more exposure from the highly touted months-long citywide contest than from the finished movie. The contest was so popular that its deadlines were extended several times, with vote tallies published daily to create suspense.[83] This change in rules—the contest was originally going to last only long enough for all the girls' pictures to be published—testified to the structuring impulses of celebrity. Rather than just cataloguing the contestants, the competition's attraction depended on the allure of seeing favorites repeatedly, reading about them and building them into local figures—even though none of them had "earned" their fame. But they had been transformed into widely seen images—and this, perhaps, was the point. On Monday, December 14, 1914, the twelve leading contestants made their first appearance on film in that day's installment of the *Herald Movies*—films that like all local productions were another important site for self-staging.[84] As excitement spread, songs were composed then performed at local theaters and dance halls, leading contestants appeared together at local expositions in front of large audiences, and Chicago sculptor Maximillian A. Hoffman promised to create a statue of the winning contestant. Meanwhile, the Loew-Victor Company vowed that they would tie her name to the prow of their finest hydroplane and draw it over Lake Michigan.[85] Yet nobody knew much about the girls, other than their names, how old they were, where they lived, and what they looked like. Their images and their ability to attract others were literally all that mattered.

The actual prizes paled besides this fervor—a diamond ring worth $200 for the winner, and $300 worth of prizes divided among three runners-up.[86] Even the film—and with it, the possibility for the winners to show their talent—seemed incidental as the contest became a celebration of local celebrity. The readers of the *Herald* had taken local girls and made them famous, displaying their neighborhood loyalties and their readers' ability to participate in the process of star creation. Communities were formed around each aspiring star as readers established clubs to support favorite contestants, meeting in neighborhood theaters to drum up support.[87] "Sue" thus mobilized the community loyalties so central to Progressivism, as neighborhood theaters became sites where readers could meet their favorites, vote for them, and even

Celebrity, Self-Awareness, and the Consciousness of Self

forge relationships with these local icons. These activities imbued the theater with the aura of celebrity, moving screen fame into local auditoriums and lobbies.[88]

"Sue" ended on Sunday, March 7, 1915, as the *Herald* announced the winner of a supposedly tense battle: Dorothy Warshauer from the North Side.[89] But the competition was not so tight: as the *World* had pointed out a week earlier, Warshauer "has got so far ahead that it now seems impossible for her closest competitors to reach her."[90] Essanay claimed to have offered her a contract to star in other productions, but nothing materialized.[91] The other leading competitors won bit parts in the film (directed by Wallace Beery), which was a dramatization of the contest with a love story tagged on, shot at the *Herald* offices and Essanay's Chicago studios.[92] As the film only had a local release and was not reviewed anywhere other than the *Herald*, it was not going to break a girl. *Sue's* release on Wednesday, May 5, 1915, was an anticlimax, a postscript to the contest, not its culmination. The film quickly vanished (it is likely lost). Even the *Herald*'s own Louella Parsons had a subdued reaction to the city's new star:

> All the "fans" and voters will have a natural curiosity to see whether she justifies their choice. I think she does. . . . Dorothy makes such a winsome and attractive Sue. Her little uncertainty of manner can be called a natural shyness. Of course, she isn't an actress by profession, but she apparently needed little coaching. . . . There isn't much to review about this single reel, written to order tale, because all our interest centers around "Dorothy of Our Choice." She is worth reviewing and she deserves our congratulations for becoming so charming a motion picture actress over night.[93]

On its own, as its reception suggests, the film had little value. Fascination lay in the contest, which transformed ordinary people into widely circulated images, if only within this one city. As with most other contests, its winners disappeared, partly because the prize-winning roles were typically in cheap productions that had limited screen interest, partly because the contest, with all its attendant publicity, was really the starring event.[94] It was therefore ironic that such competitions proved the industry's maxim that stars couldn't emerge from publicity or from the sheer desire for fame as these girls' renown immediately evaporated.

Rather than finding stars, these contests attested to the public's insatiable appetite for film-related celebrity. They further testified to cinema's seemingly mythical powers to transform the individual into something new and auratic, a process that only worked inconsistently. The *Herald* immediately followed "Sue" with a nationwide beauty contest sponsored by Universal in conjunction with forty-six newspapers across the United States. This time, candidates would sell *Herald* subscriptions to get bonus votes. Like "Sue," it stretched out over several months, its first stage running from April 1 to May 15, 1915. Two winners would represent the state at a beauty contest at the San Francisco and San Diego fairs, one from Chicago and one from Illinois. Prizes included an expenses-paid trip, the choice of a wedding trousseau or "a home furnished for a bride" up to the cost of $500, and, of course, the chance to become a movie star. The winner would star in a Universal picture, written by serial queen Grace Cunard. All the local finalists visited Los Angeles in July, and other events ran into September before the winners were announced. Newspapers were not the only ones to benefit, as Universal sold sponsorship to a number of other companies, including Colgate, which gave each finalist toiletries for her trip to Los Angeles. Doubleday and Sons donated an autographed copy of a special edition of their 1914 bestseller, *Bambi*, to each girl; the *Ladies' World* gave each girl a three-month subscription; the International Handkerchief Company presented them with a set of hankies, and the E. T. Welch Grape Juice Company provided all drinks. The *World* commented on strong public interest, with many papers devoting nearly a page a day to its coverage. Again, the victor—and their short film—made no impact on Hollywood, although the sponsors benefited from the exposure.[95]

The People's Movie Star Contest

The next year, the *Herald* organized another movie star contest that ran from September to December 1916, hoping to replicate "Sue's" success.[96] Although the "People's Movie Star Contest" offered many more prizes, it was a lesser draw. It aimed to find eighty-nine players to fill the

Celebrity, Self-Awareness, and the Consciousness of Self

cast of another Essanay film (later called *The Sunshine Line*): "Four persons—woman, man, little girl and boy—for stellar roles. Five women and five men substars for leading parts. Seventy-five young women and young men for minor roles."[97] Unlike *Sue*, it was originally supposed to be a multiple-reel film, and there were rumors that it might be distributed outside Chicago, although this was not to be.[98] The initial announcement emphasized that its prime purpose was exposing undiscovered talent, giving them the publicity they needed to succeed:

> During the contest . . . the stars will have gained wide publicity because of the great and rapidly growing circulation of the HERALD, and additional fame will come to them when they are declared winners and have posed for the film, which will be viewed by hundreds of thousands over the course of its run, first at a leading loop theater and later at scores of Chicago's outlying picture houses. And that's when the big movie concerns will begin to hold out allurements to the members of the company to join this or that company of players.[99]

In other words, Essanay would not offer contracts to the winners.

The rules were effectively the same as before: all entrants must be amateurs, and readers were asked to nominate and vote on contestants (they could self-nominate) using coupons published in each day's paper. Once again, the competition was extended due to public interest, prolonging the excitement, while giving contestants more exposure. Nomination coupons were good for five hundred votes, weekday and Saturday editions featured a regular one-vote coupon, while Sunday papers had a ten-vote coupon. Six-month subscription forms (available from the *Herald*'s office) were worth an impressive one thousand votes, effectively forcing contestants to sell subscriptions.[100] Each coupon was good for a week, and readers could vote as often as they liked, increasing circulation as voters and contestants purchased multiple copies of the paper for its coupons. Again, the *Herald* stressed that it was the most qualified paper in the world to offer such a contest because:

> The HERALD's movie program is by far the most extensive of any appearing in any daily newspaper, not alone in the United States, but in the world. . . . It prints more about movies every day in the week than

all the other Chicago papers combined, and its movie readers are in like proportions. . . . It has three-fourths of the cream of Chicago picture theaters advertising in its movie directory daily. . . . Film magnates and exhibitors the country over recognize the HERALD as the greatest of all newspaper boosters for the movie game."[101]

The number of prizes likely limited the contest's appeal, diffusing attention away from a single winner: eighty-nine roles were a lot, and many would be very small. Unlike *Sue*, this movie would feature no professional players, further downgrading its value. The possibility that a local newspaper could find and break a star—even one in a city as big as Chicago—was further diminished given the failure of the major "Sue" aspirants. Only one candidate, Alice McChesney who came in eighth, had been kept on at Essanay, appearing in a handful of films between 1916 and 1917 and finally receiving the lead in a one-reel film, *Books Made to Balance* (Richard Foster Baker, Essanay, 1916), whose release was curiously timed to coincide with this contest. Louella O. Parsons reported on McChesney's success in September 1916 as the new competition got underway, and she was featured in an ad for it later that month. Here, she was billed as "a winner in a previous *Herald* contest," and readers were reminded: "had Miss McChesney neglected her opportunity to enter this contest, about two years ago, she would doubtless now be unknown in screendom."[102]

The *Herald* ran a number of similar ads, most featuring major stars, like Anita Stewart or Mae Marsh, reminding readers that despite their talent, they too needed a break.[103] Tellingly none of them had found fame in a contest. Marsh's ad was headed "From Schoolgirl to Movie Star Overnight." Her chance discovery by D. W. Griffith was used to remind readers, "YOU may have that inherent talent, those unrealized attributes for which every director in screenland is ever searching."[104] These ads ran during the nomination phase that lasted until October 9, 1916. Such was the lure of the lucky break that entrants came from rural Illinois, Wisconsin, Indiana, Iowa, Minnesota, and Michigan. One hopeful made news when she moved to Chicago from Minneapolis to improve her odds of winning.[105] The paper's contest editor, BAB, further fanned interest, urging contestants to work harder (and sell more subscriptions).[106] By the end of the nomination period, about one

Celebrity, Self-Awareness, and the Consciousness of Self

thousand people had entered.[107] Free theater tickets were distributed several times to the leading candidates (often those who sold the most subscriptions), who usually received the best seats in the house.[108] Voting was strong—with one day's tally promoted as rivaling that of the presidential election held a few days earlier (of course, there were no one thousand vote coupons in that election).[109]

Louella Parsons praised the contest, noting that "three-fourths of [the five hundred weekly letters she received] are from men, women and children who want to be motion picture stars and want a word of advice on how to get into pictures."[110] Many contestants the paper interviewed co-opted aspects of fan magazine discourse on stardom, stressing that they were born to do this and would work very hard to win—a work ethos encouraged in the *Herald*'s own commentary.[111] What exactly this work might involve remained unclear—other than selling *Herald* subscriptions to get one thousand vote coupons and, possibly, lobbying coworkers and employers to vote for them. Still, their words demonstrated widespread faith that work could overcome the odds and deliver that lucky break.[112] But there was no screen work for these young men and women to show their worth. Instead, they were effectively toiling at an unpaid second job—selling newspaper subscriptions—hoping for the social mobility and satisfaction missing from their real jobs and lives. Tellingly, letters printed in the *Herald* reveal that many aspirants hoped to escape the burden of work, much of it thankless labor, something all the more frustrating in an era of increased expectations and more opportunities for women. One read, "I am a working girl of almost 17, and I would like to enter your movie contest, as I am working in a laundry and find it very unpleasant." Another wrote, "Is there room in the contest for a brown curly haired girl? I am a housemaid and take care of twelve rooms."[113]

As with "Sue," the contest migrated into neighborhood theaters. Nobody could win without the community support necessary to sell subscriptions and to attract votes, which were doubled when coupons were stamped at neighborhood houses (courtesy of a stamp the *Herald* provided). Theaters capitalized on this publicity, staging popularity contests and running slides, while contestants were encouraged to work with exhibitors and make personal appearances to get more exposure, build loyalty, disseminate their image, and lobby patrons for

CHAPTER 3

votes.[114] Incidentally, these activities created structural parallels with real movie stardom as they tested contestants' popularity with theater audiences, albeit before they appeared on screen.

As the contest drew to a close, Louella O. Parsons (who wrote the prize picture) announced that Essanay president George K. Spoor would personally coach its winners.[115] Then the *Herald* noted that there might be room for more contestants in the prize film, finally choosing 102 players when the results were announced on December 10, 1916. Contest editor BAB reminded those with small parts that a film company might still notice them.[116] More information was given the next week: the film was to be a two- or possibly three-reeler, likely a film of college life, although details were still being finalized. The big scene would be "a masquerade ball in which the entire company will take part, including 'Charlie Chaplin' and 'Mary Pickford' [impersonated by two cast members]. This will give a fine opportunity for unique, grotesque and beautiful costumes."[117] Significantly, BAB said nothing about the film offering ways to showcase the winners' talents. Before penning the play, Parsons met with the cast at the *Herald* offices, hoping to give everybody a chance to show what they could do. On February 11, 1917, the *Herald* reported that all the big scenes of the film, *The Sunshine Line* (Charles Haydon, Essanay-KESE), had been completed, with the players reportedly working night and day without breaks, even coming in on Sundays. Evidently, they required extra training because they were not professionals—descriptions that did little to advance them as future stars.[118] Notably, all subsequent ads, including those from Essanay, emphasized the film's amateur cast rather than framing the film within star discourse.

Entrants saw *The Sunshine Line* differently, including those who had not received a role. The *Herald* printed some of their letters, accompanied by a drawing from a losing contestant, Elsa Lenn, titled "To Movieland," that depicted the winners (including Pete Fagin, the lucky dog winner) flying off to Hollywood on a magic carpet while other contestants waved and wished them luck.[119] This sketch revealed how Hollywood figured in the public imagination as a mystical and fantastic other place, one far away from Chicago's neighborhoods, while also revealing the "losers'" good-natured community spirit. A similar community ideal was evidenced in one of the minor winner's suggestions that all contestants form a *Herald* Movie Club for social purposes.[120]

Celebrity, Self-Awareness, and the Consciousness of Self

The Sunshine Line opened in two of the smaller downtown houses on March 26, 1917—not the promised large Loop theater.[121] It was not even a headline attraction: the Pastime (66 West Madison) billed it as an extra and teamed it with Max Linder's *Max Wants a Divorce* (Max Linder, Essanay-KESE, 1917). The Alcazar (69 West Madison) promoted it with a photo of its little boy "star," Harry Moir Jr.—the owner's son.[122] Advertising revealed its cast had now grown to 125, including Pete Fagin, the dog—over 10 percent of the contestants, potentially leading more friends, family, and supporters to buy tickets. Again, the trades and national fan magazines ignored *The Sunshine Line*. Judging from advertising in the *Herald*, it did not run for long in local theaters either. Even its sponsor quickly lost interest, although there are considerable difficulties in assessing its reception. The *Herald* appears not to have reviewed *The Sunshine Line*, but it is possible that it was featured in what appears to have been the paper's last film section, unfortunately missing from the extant microfilm. America's entry into World War I, and the preceding increase in hostilities, might also have overshadowed its release. Nonetheless, *The Sunshine Line* marked a turning point in the *Herald*'s movie coverage. Shortly after its completion, the paper sharply decreased its film coverage, and its film advertising dropped off, possibly because the financial problems then facing exhibitors caused them to limit advertising. The paper was struggling and its vaunted film coverage had clearly not saved it. In March 1917, the *Herald* dropped its separate Sunday movie section, replacing it with "City Life," folding its now considerably reduced film coverage back in with the theater section. Film reporting only briefly perked up during the 1917 Movie Exposition, likely because the paper's participation in this event had been arranged months earlier, declining rapidly thereafter.

Searching for Stars at the 1917 Chicago Movie Exposition

The *Herald* participated in a final, less ambitious star contest during the seventh annual convention of the Motion Picture Exhibitors' League of America (held at Chicago's Coliseum just like the previous year). Although intended for serious business—like discussions of censorship, Sunday openings, star salaries, summer closings, war taxes, film depos-

CHAPTER 3

its, and open bookings—this event was open to the public, its prime attraction being the chance to meet stars at company booths. Large crowds arrived, hoping to see popular stars like Mae Marsh, Lillian Walker, Francis X. Bushman, Beverly Bayne, Alice Brady, Edith Storey, Viola Dana, Bryant Washburn, and Carlyle Blackwell. Schedules announced when each player would be available to meet the public, with megaphones announcing their entrance into the Coliseum.[123] As fans came in record numbers, previously unannounced names, like Pearl White, Doris Kenyon, Fannie Ward, and Jack Dean, arrived at the show, further increasing ticket sales.[124]

Attendees were not just interested in seeing stars. One of the Expo's attractions was a mini film studio run by Rothacker that allowed the public to act in front of the camera, with the promise that major producers would view their screen tests. This machine had been featured at the 1916 meeting and the turnout had been overwhelming.[125] Capitalizing on this attraction, the *Herald* orchestrated a more modest star search contest in conjunction with Universal, this time seeking a male lead—but in a way that upheld feminine expertise and cinematic knowledge. The studio's publicity department claimed that its young star, Violet Mersereau, was looking for a man "with the ideal movie face," and "enlisted" the *Herald*'s help in finding him: "'I just had a fleeting glimpse of him,' said Miss Mersereau, 'but he is exactly the type I want and never could find in New York. I am not familiar with Chicago, so I cannot say just where I saw him, nor can I recall the color of his eyes, and a hat covered the hair.'"[126]

Even though Mersereau could not provide any details, she was prepared to pay for his salary and his transportation to New York. This was unnecessary, however, as Carl Laemmle and the *Herald* were determined to find him. To accomplish this, Mersereau would be at the *Herald*'s exposition booth each day from 3 to 5 p.m. and 9 to 10:30 p.m. Young men matching her (purposefully) vague description could come by, register, leave a photo, and meet her in person. On the last night of the convention, she would choose the best fit, a set-up that played to a specifically feminine ability to recognize screen charisma, and he would receive a part in her next Universal picture. Mersereau had been a child actress and later appeared in Biograph films. As Laemmle was trying to build her into a star at this time, she was frequently featured in fan magazines.[127] This stunt was clearly designed to expose her further, not find a new leading man; indeed, the paper did not identify any winning entrant or mention the matter again after the convention closed.

Celebrity, Self-Awareness, and the Modern Self

Progressive Era fascination with celebrity attested to the culture's deep self-analysis and fascination with its own machinations. Like reform, celebrity focused attention to the self more generally, increasing awareness of the ways that other people might evaluate one's identity, appearance, and conduct—as was incidentally the practice in a screen test or a star contest—producing greater self-consciousness. Once again, feminine expertise was important, positioning these skills as valuable in negotiating modern life. Consequently, widespread interest in celebrity suggested something akin to a cultural narcissism, whereby the public studied the famous to explore how they lived and flourished, to learn more about their lifestyles, and, by extension, to understand the culture and the correct constitution of the modern self. Looking at famous people was pleasurable in part because it evoked fantasies of being in their place, something the industry capitalized on with star contests and stories about ordinary men and particularly women's transformation into screen stars.

Even though it represents a discourse on, and inquiry into, self, celebrity has a complicated relationship to Progressivism's efforts to stabilize modernity, especially when seen in the context of its relationship to motion pictures. Although stardom can be annexed to character and narrative, it still represents potentially destabilizing excess, as has often been noted.[128] The energy of celebrity—and part of its appeal—involved this transfer of excitement toward the self—particularly the female self, divorced from the need to attend to others and a commitment to duty, even if this phase was elusive or at best short-lived for many women. Star search contests and movies about stardom like the ones I have discussed fascinated because they promised to reveal how this kind of visibility worked, how it could be produced, how people could be represented in public, how they could gain fame, if briefly and for trivial reasons, and how women might escape the strictures of everyday life and enjoy the rights to personhood and self-assertion associated with full citizenship. Contests tantalized participants with the possibility of fulfilling their dreams while endorsing the pleasures of self-presentation. Even the poses contestants adopted in their photos were often modeled on those of the stars, revealing that private citizens, particularly women, were thinking about their image in ways formerly reserved for the famous. As most nonfamous people didn't get their pictures in the paper or their slides shown in movie theaters alongside those of stars—let alone in *Photoplay*—even getting this far transformed these women, affording them the chance to experience being part of representation itself.[129] As such, star search contests evoked discourses on celebrity that played with the public's recognition that they were both part of representation—as an audience, its existence was predicated on their patronage—and distanced from it—they could not participate in it directly, other than through fantasy or in limited ways linked to polls and contests. As such, these contests reinscribed the gap that defined celebrity representation so that the fortunate few could stage themselves as their own individual self-creations. In the process, they held out the possibility that this success might be open for others, highlighting the social mobility that was so central to the American dream.

The star contests of the mid-1910s reveal that this distance between the famous and the unknown, between screen representations and real life, frustrated many audiences, who believed their own ambitions and social mobility were blocked. Given Progressive society's stress on forging a strong American identity, one that incorporated and stabilized the changes wrought by modernity and new waves of immigrants under a renewed national strength, this inability to enter the film industry represented nothing less than a foreclosure of the American Dream. Some members of the public believed they were prevented from establishing the kind of identity they wanted, one that corresponded with the ethos of celebrity culture. Audiences might attend movies religiously, read about the industry and their favorite players, yet they could not apply this knowledge into a form of work that would fulfill them and allow them to fully actualize themselves.

This frustration was only compounded as the film industry continually marketed itself as specifically American (ignoring the French hegemony of just a few years earlier). Discussing his emphasis on solely

Celebrity, Self-Awareness, and the Consciousness of Self

American films, *Photoplay*'s Julian Johnson argued that cinema was an American medium, in contrast to the stage, which borrowed material from England and its form from France. While he acknowledged that the films he reviewed were shorter and less prestigious than many plays, he noted: "the big American thought is here. The transcript of our life is here, and when it comes to truth expressed, a brochure is as potent as a two-volume novel—more so, because the big book scares folks away."[130] This emphasis on cinema's essential American-ness also marks star discourse. As Richard Abel has shown, stars can be linked to the process of Americanization as "this discourse on movie stars introduces an intriguing spin on the contentious process of imagining a national identity." He adds that by late 1912, picture players were admired and possibly emulated, even by "the foreigner" seeking insight into "the customs and habits of the country of his adoption," so players "had to be no less American than anything else on the screen."[131] Similar associations among stardom, movies, and national identity appeared in descriptions of entrants in star-search contests, who are consistently described as "real American beauties"; "perfect types of the American girl"; "this all-American Eleven" representing "the pluck of American womanhood"; "the native player . . . whose first and only study is the shadow stage, and who brings to it no prejudices of the theater."[132]

Besides exploring individuality, then, celebrity evoked community ideals—both nationally and locally. This combination was powerful and attractive, as seen in the success of star contests like "Sue" with their more inclusive ideals of stardom that emphasized audience participation and rooted celebrity in a specific physical place—one very much like home. In opening up the many identifications stardom made possible, these contests extended personality's appeal beyond the screen and steered it toward local communities. In the process, they demonstrated how celebrity could articulate desires for belonging, facilitating interactions with other patrons and highlighting shared interests and local loyalties. As such, these contests capitalized on the very qualities at the heart of neighborhood theaters' success during the 1910s, testifying to the characteristics that made them the most important form of exhibition during the decade. In the next chapter, I explore these institutions and their dominance, focusing on their community appeal—a quality that would become central to cinema during the Progressive Era.

FOUR

Private Pleasures and Public Space
Community Culture and the Dominance of Neighborhood Theaters

> The neighborhood or family theatre has reached a stage in its growth where it may be said to be an important factor in the lives of millions of people daily—that is, so far as their theatrical amusement is concerned. As a pioneer in the neighborhood theatre I have had the opportunity of watching its progress from a lowly improvised storeroom theatre to the present palaces dedicated to it. The neighborhood motion picture theatre, in which the splendid screen productions of the present day are now so satisfactorily presented, is one of the most powerful agencies for good, despite the continuous hue and cry that so-called reformers are putting up.
> —Alfred Hamburger, Chicago theater magnate, 1917

Often overlooked in favor of the nickelodeon and picture palaces, the community-centered neighborhood theaters constituted the most important form of exhibition between 1908 and 1917. Movies found their greatest success in these areas, repositioning cinema as a fundamentally local pleasure deeply linked to family and community. "Neighborhood" referred to more than a space, evoking the wholesome values threatened by urbanization and modernity that were miraculously preserved in these more residential areas, making them privileged and protected sites in much Progressive Era rhetoric. Part of broader efforts to improve the medium's reputation, these theaters were established around the same time that formal and narrative changes helped establish cinema's moral discourse, with both displaying a similar investment in uplift.[1] Positioned as communities in their own right, exhibitors encouraged their patrons to connect with one another while waiting in the lobby, to linger after a show, and they fostered audience interaction via program staples like illustrated songs and prize contests. The trade press and exhibitors' manuals emphasized the importance of running these theaters as preeminently social spaces, defining exhibitors' expertise by the way they treated patrons as well as their choice of films, although the two were not unrelated.[2] Exhibitors were advised to emphasize their deep knowledge of, and care for, their audiences and to root themselves in their communities, presenting their theaters as valued civic institutions. Locating cinema in these largely residential districts was not without risk—citizens might fight for their removal to protect the more wholesome neighborhood ideals. Yet the process was surprisingly easy, attesting to audiences' desire for recreation close to home, the medium's improved reputation, and exhibitors' skills in working with their communities. By 1914, many neighborhood theaters were sizeable structures, seating more patrons in greater luxury and comfort than first-run downtown houses, yet they still promised intimacy and emphasized community, rewarding loyal patrons with prizes and coupons and arranging shows for local charities. By offering personalized amenities like children's playrooms, lobbies, and waiting rooms to enhance spectators' comfort, exhibitors emphasized their care for their patrons.

By 1909, neighborhood theaters had almost completely replaced storefront nickelodeons, becoming Chicago's dominant form of exhibition. Many were purpose built, feeding a mid-1910s construction boom that responded to demand for motion pictures close to home. Between approximately 1909 and 1917, the city's largest, most modern, and most elaborate theaters would be situated in Chicago's neighborhoods, with seating capacities of over one thousand quite common—years before the Balaban and Katz Theater Corporation invested in large theaters in these very areas.[3] Neighborhood theater chains quickly formed, using profits from these increasingly lucrative houses to support their parent companies' first-run establishments. By 1916, they had become the primary venue for feature films, helping the form become dominant by eliminating the need to travel downtown to see such titles. Speaking in 1915, Edison's production manager, Horace Plimpton, remarked: "I suppose that the theaters in residential sections are more likely to do better with long films because families are able, or more apt, to make an evening's entertainment out of their visit, whereas those catering to more transient trade are better off with more and shorter subjects."[4] Neighborhood theaters are also important, then, in challenging accepted wisdom about the transition to features and related assumptions about a two-tier system—luxury downtown theaters showing features and smaller local nickel theaters that stayed with short programs.

The community address of these "intimate and friendly" neighborhood theaters was perhaps their most important feature, distinguishing these often-overlooked venues from other forms of exhibition like first-run establishments downtown and the cheaper houses customarily found in entertainment districts.[5] Unlike their neighborhood counterparts, theaters in entertainment districts were part of a broader and more maligned public amusement culture. Downtown first-run theaters similarly catered to an itinerant and anonymous public, albeit a more respectable one with their more public, auratic address. Unlike some reformers and moralists who grouped all theaters together, the public, film industry, and city council understood exhibition's structured variety, recognizing that theater location determined audiences, profitability, programming, and address more than any other factor. This distinction was built into the city's licensing structure as well as the widespread understanding that downtown Chicago's two-hundred-seat Fine Arts was a major first-run theater, whereas the North Side's nine-hundred-seat Royal (Belmont and Lincoln) was not.

Given their incorporation of neighborhood values and their self-presentation as protected, semiprivate public spaces, these theaters should be considered in terms of Progressivism's reconfigured social spheres. In this era's more public culture, many activities formerly associated with the Victorian private sphere—like relaxation and moral rejuvenation—migrated into public space. Movie theaters were an important part of Progressivism's more public way of life, responding to the occlusion of private space in increasingly crowded cities. By accommodating demands for privacy, even at a more illusory level linked to film consumption, neighborhood theaters associated themselves with an idealized and readily available private sphere, emphasizing their intimacy and domesticity. This combination of private pleasures in public space was not only good for business but it also helped counter concerns about commercial recreation corrupting the public's need for leisure.

Leisure was so important for Progressive Era society that it was upheld as an essential sphere of human activity that warranted professional study, monitoring, and regulation. It was also a relatively new development. As late as 1860, the term *recreation* was practically unknown, and there were few commercial amusements, even in New York City.[6] As leisure was disassociated from religious and secular holidays during the nineteenth century, consumerism, industrialization, and urbanization helped create a mass audience with spare money and free time. During the Progressive Era, recreation increasingly took on the functions of moral and physical rejuvenation formerly associated with the Victorian home and was soon seen as an essential and necessary sphere of human activity. Studies showed that rest and recreation bolstered worker productivity, leading to reductions in the working week from an average of sixty-six hours in 1850 to fifty-five in 1914.[7] As the new commercial entertainments opened access to all social classes, leisure expanded public life.[8] Concerns soon emerged about its available forms: many of the new leisure researchers and professionals warned about the dangers of perverting the healthy desire for clean, uplifting, and athletic recreation. Reformers worried that cheap amusements like cheap vaudeville, arcades, saloons, dance halls, amusement parks, and, later, cinema fostered a distracted, pleasure-seeking population and tried to steer workers toward more uplifting entertainment with stronger moral, cultural, and social values.[9]

Neighborhood theaters responded to these presumptions about commercial amusements, countering charges that their offerings corrupted the broader social need for leisure. They instead emphasized their nonexploitative, socially situated, and textually inscribed model of spectatorship—the patron. From their inception around 1907–8, neighborhood theaters rarely referred to customers, only *patrons*, a term evoking respect and service. Evoking a community "where everybody knew everybody else," patronage countered charges that modern mass culture alienated consumers from family and society, contrasting cinema from rival commercial entertainments.[10] As both individuals and part of a community, patrons visited their local theater for more than even the most edifying and enjoyable films. Ironically, the term *patron* had its roots in the very neighborhood vaudeville, stock, and musical theaters that movie theaters displaced, taking over their premises and customers during the late 1900s and 1910s. Implicitly personal and modeled on a more old-fashioned idea of courtesy and respect, patronage offset the commercialization that had tainted so much modern recreations. Writing in 1915, sociologist Richard Henry Edwards noted that movies were unusual in resisting these tendencies: "Commercial management has been well characterized as tending to sever the individual from the community, to prefer miscellaneous crowds to neighborly groups, to neglect the interests of the child, and to make no provision aside from moving pictures for the mother of the wage earning family."[11] As with the neighborhood theater, patronage helped cinema distinguish itself as a unique form of modern mass culture, devoted to "personalised care" and treating customers as "guests in every sense of the word."[12] Family patronage was particularly desirable as it associated movies with domestic values, helped by neighborhood theaters' cheap ticket prices.[13] As Walter Prichard Eaton noted in 1915, with "fifty per cent of the wage earners of [Chicago and New York] receiv[ing] but $500 per year," movies were one of the few recreations adults and children could attend together, further cementing the neighborhood theater's quasi-domestic appeal.[14] Drawing on all these characteristics, the neighborhood theater positioned itself as a suitably public Progressive equivalent of the middle-class Victorian home—an uplifting and restorative space, offering intimacy, respect, and showcasing the highest community ideals.

The War on Nickelodeons: Neighborhood Theaters, City Zoning, and Licensing Laws

In Chicago at least, neighborhood theaters were not solely a film industry initiative, emerging after municipal clean-up campaigns led to the implementation of new building regulations and zoning laws.

Nickelodeons were particularly badly affected and failed to maintain their foothold in Chicago's downtown districts after strict regulations were imposed on them between 1907 and 1911. Exhibitors had little choice other than to move to the city's neighborhoods after building regulations and zoning forced cheap entertainments out of most of downtown Chicago by the end of 1907. At the same time, prohibitive regulations were applied to smaller storefront theaters (including nickelodeons) to preserve land values in central districts.[15] Before the implementation of the city's 1907 amusement code, cheap vaudeville, nickelodeons, and amusement arcades had flourished in the Loop, and movies could be found in small storefronts as well as in vaudeville, stock, and burlesque houses like the Haymarket, Criterion, Bijou, Academy of Music, Alhambra, Marlowe, Sid Euson's, and the Columbia.[16] New laws closed most of these establishments and made it difficult for motion pictures to be shown in others.[17]

Smaller film theaters suffered the most due to increased licensing fees and new requirements mandating expensive alterations that exhibitors could not afford and landlords refused to finance. Commercial amusements subsequently migrated into largely unregulated amusement districts and residential neighborhoods.[18] New entertainment districts emerged in areas abutting downtown in areas where regulations were lax, like West Madison and South State Street. Here cheap movie theaters flourished amid the high-density cheap duplexes and shanties that housed mainly African Americans and immigrants from southern Europe.[19] Small theaters also sprung up around South Halsted Street in the shadows of slums, factories, and warehouses, troubling Progressive reformers who tried to establish alternative entertainments in settlement houses, albeit with limited success. Moving cinema into the city's neighborhoods was initially far from the failsafe option: if movies were seen as attracting (unwanted) outsiders and were perceived as potentially transitory institutions, they risked protests and bans, particularly in "better" neighborhoods. In February 1908, for instance, the civic committee of the Illinois Federation of Women's Clubs advised their affiliated groups to "Prevent the establishment of 5-cent theaters in your community, abolish those already in operation and urge the licensing of hotels."[20] Exhibitors hoped some of these objections would be irrelevant if they could prove that they knew their clientele and suc-

CHAPTER 4

cessfully rebranded cinema as an institution that bound the community together, not one that attracted unwanted outsiders.

The city continued its aggressive attacks on nickelodeons: in 1907, the council responded to complaints about cheap theaters by closing all nickelodeons in some neighborhoods, although they ignored theaters in low-rent districts. In November 1907—the very month the city established its censorship board—tighter building ordinances signaled the nickelodeon's demise. This new code was part of a comprehensive rezoning program designed to make Chicago safer, eradicate slums, and improve transit. Charles B. Ball was hired to head (and strengthen) the office in 1907, and his regulations shuttered many theaters while the rest of the nation experienced an unprecedented nickelodeon boom.[21] Under the new law, the city licensed theaters into twenty-one ranked categories, strictly regulating the lower classes and making it very difficult for them to stay in business. One of its targets, nickelodeons were rated fourth class, below legitimate theater, vaudeville variety, opera, drama, lectures, panopticons, museums, concerts, recitals, and live music but above amateur dramatics (often seen as a cover for illicit activities, especially with children), amusement parks, and wrestling matches.

In December 1907, building commissioner Downey warned 150 five-cent theater managers to comply with the code before January 1, 1908, or close down.[22] The *Motion Picture World* estimated that these new standards threatened half of Chicago's five-cent theaters and severely limited any new business prospects.[23] Over one hundred new theater licenses were rejected in the code's first two months, representing about 25 percent of the city's four hundred licensed five-cent houses. The building inspector was subsequently accused of waging "active warfare against the five-cent theatre houses," after he found only sixty of 140 licensed premises up to code in 1908. Despite legal appeals, many theaters closed while others were forced to upgrade.[24] Even the city's larger exhibitors were not immune: in March 1908, five nickel theaters were shuttered, all run by Hubert Daniels, who then operated more movie houses than anyone citywide, effectively destroying his business.[25] The *Record-Herald* complained that the laws were unjustified and pointed to an underlying prejudice against cheap film shows: "There is no necessary connection between the safety of a structure and the moral quality of the entertainment given in it. But . . . strict enforcement of the building ordinances is one of the most effective ways of reaching and regulating the moving picture 'shows.'"[26] Much of the new code specifically attacked nickelodeons. As movies were considered a "fire-prone industry," they could be banned downtown; safety ordinances 1612–1624 focused on flammable nitrate stock to limit theater construction and drive existing establishments out of the Loop.[27] These regulations could have closed all Chicago's exchanges—the nation's most important—but for reasons that are unclear, they survived, possibly because they were seen as businesses not amusements. Small downtown exhibitors were not so lucky, and many closed forever.

These assaults continued throughout 1908 with theaters closed for minor and easily corrected misdemeanors, including "chairs scattered about the auditorium, no red lights, rear exists obstructed, overcrowding and having dressing-rooms."[28] Faced with exhibitor protests, the city announced they would arrest "all operators and managers who attempt to run without licenses," and fine them $10 to $200 a day, quelling further protests.[29] The only solution was to escape the restrictive Class IV zoning strictures altogether, something that was only possible if exhibitors moved into larger premises—potentially increasing profits for those who could afford it.[30] Those who could not either left the business or relocated to the less reputable amusement districts where rents were lower and regulation lax.

License fee increases during 1909–10 further accelerated tendencies to show movies in large theaters. Class IV storefronts had to pay substantially higher prices, effectively subsidizing their larger and more expensive counterparts.[31] Exhibitors protested and their trade organizations sued.[32] This time exhibitors won as the court ruled that the city could not base license fees on ticket prices. This did not save the nickelodeon, but instead meant that the relationship between theater size and ticket price collapsed, keeping ticket prices low in neighborhood theaters and hastening the storefronts' demise as patrons could go to a more lavish theater for the same five cents.[33] Finally, in July 1910, the council stopped issuing permits to open Class IV theaters, unless they seated *fewer* than three hundred persons, a move that was essentially irrelevant as most new theaters were decidedly larger.

CHAPTER 4

Although the nickelodeon was short-lived, excessive competition meant that nickel pricing dominated Chicago far longer than most cities. Ticket prices remained at five cents until around 1915–16, when increased costs, including feature film rentals, forced admissions up to an average of ten to fifteen cents. Some independent exhibitors struggled, but theater chains flourished as they could offset low prices through economies of scale and their involvement in states rights film distribution. Patrons' reluctance to pay more than a nickel meant that some of the first large neighborhood theaters quickly closed. In March 1909 the city's leading exchange man, William H. Swanson, opened the six-hundred-seat Cottage Grove Theater, charging ten cents during the evenings (five cents during the day), but patrons balked and it soon folded. Still, descriptions of the Cottage Grove give a sense of the facilities early neighborhood theaters offered and their difference from storefront nickelodeons (Class IV theaters). A highly decorative building, with its ticket booth framed by an arch and stained glass, it was decorated inside in gold leaf and green, had state-of-the-art ventilation, and at night its exterior was lit by "several thousand incandescent lights and an electric sign, over twenty feet high, with a vast revolving star."[34] With its three projectors, double stereopticon, and sound-effects machines, it offered three reels of film and song slides seven times a day from 1 p.m. to 11 p.m.[35] Within three years, far more elaborate facilities would be standard.

Although the trade press and the film industry initially protested the city's attacks, they soon changed tactics. Recognizing that neighborhood theaters bolstered cinema's claims to respectability, the uplift-minded industry started calling for improved accommodations. In July 1912, for instance, the trade press and exhibitors' organizations supported new laws that led building commissioner Ericsson to close all movie theaters located above the ground floor. He refused licenses to eighty such establishments, calling them "menaces to life":

> 75 of the 80 . . . refused to obey his orders for important changes to conform with the law. Eight of these houses, he stated, are on second floors and one on a third floor above street level [and he] asked the city council to pass an ordinance prohibiting theaters above the ground floor. The latter houses are at present within the law, but the Commissioner presented an ordinance condemning them as nuisances.[36]

Private Pleasures and Public Space

With no organized industry opposition, this law passed in February 1913.[37] Even though the *Motion Picture World* had consistently praised two of the closed theaters—the Iola (1238 Milwaukee) and Sittner's Criterion (235 West North)—for the quality of their shows, they now agreed with the city, admitting that "it must be conceded, in all fairness, that they were a menace to the exhibiting of pictures in Chicago while they stayed open."[38] Theater safety was important for an industry in search of uplift and respectability.[39]

By 1913, an estimated two-thirds of Chicago's remaining small theaters could not afford to comply with the city's latest round of safety, zoning, and licensing regulations and had to close.[40] On Friday, October 24, 1913, Alderman Shafer, representing these exhibitors, met with the city Health Department, with Shafer claiming that the 1913 ordinance, if applied consistently, would also shutter most churches and lodge halls.[41] Henry Horner, attorney for the Chicago Motion Picture Exhibitors' Association, called it "unenforceable," predicting it would result in 90 percent of the city's theaters closing. He suggested it had been designed to "favor certain theaters" and to force less prestigious houses out of business.[42] This was likely the case. By this time, small theaters were no longer popular, replaced by the larger neighborhood theaters that successfully appealed to both audiences and community ideals.

Neighborhood Theaters

In March 1907, *Billboard* somewhat inelegantly dubbed Chicago "one of the foremost cities in the world in the matter of neighborhood theaters," adding "the hold which these outlying houses have upon their patrons was never better expressed."[43] They referred to vaudeville, but movies would soon take their place, often literally, as larger vaudeville houses were converted into the first neighborhood movie theaters. Movies first appeared in Chicago's bigger neighborhood vaudeville houses (like the Haymarket on the West Side) during the 1908 summer off-season, and some of these establishments soon converted to movies year round.[44] The "spacious, family-oriented" 1,200-seat Hamlin (3826 West Madison) was first, becoming one of the Chicago's most important local movie theaters after its October 1910 renovations.[45] Most residential neighborhoods soon had several houses in limited competition. By 1914, the city's largest theaters were in neighborhoods, attracting audiences year round and resisting the summer slump that customarily hit movies by offering facilities that compensated for—or tried to mitigate—the off-putting heat. Indeed, these theaters were so convenient that audiences returned many times each week, setting up the conditions for community formation and intimacy, as well as economic success.[46]

Neighborhood theaters consciously adopted Progressive doctrines to frame cinema as a community-oriented and healthy recreation, fit for the whole family.[47] If movie theaters were community institutions, surveillance would be unnecessary—communities protect their institutions and their patrons. To these ends, neighborhood exhibitors made themselves known to their public, offering audiences activities, services, and gifts, displaying a duty of care while masking the commercial impulse at the heart of their business under a broader philanthropic appeal.[48] Free gifts and prize contests rewarded viewers for their loyalty and encouraged them to return. For example, during Christmas 1912, Chicago's Bonaventure Theater gave souvenir calendars to patrons, each "adorned with a postcard of some photoplayer . . . most of the patrons being advertised that they could have their choice, expressed their preference without hesitation."[49] As exhibitors invited feedback and placed comment boxes in lobbies—all activities recommended by the trades—audiences were reminded that they played an active role in *their* neighborhood theater. Their appeal did not lie in their film programs alone, but in the context surrounding them, in the theater's facilities, its possibilities for social contact, and the entire atmosphere of the show.

The importance of community—and its strangeness—is evident when one considers that in 1917, over 10 percent of Chicago's 450 licensed movie theaters seated over one thousand—almost all of them neighborhood establishments.[50] While some audience members might know one another, most likely did not—and it would have required amazing diligence for managers to know their patrons personally, let alone chat to them about what films they might like. Clearly, the concept of the neighborhood theater as a community was often more dis-

Private Pleasures and Public Space

cursive than real, but the idea's very ubiquity reveals much about the importance of loyalty and intimacy while demonstrating the embrace of Progressive values in programming and promotions.

Descriptions of the new decorative neighborhood theaters started appearing in the trades as early as 1907. Their intricate ornamentation, fixed seating, large capacity, enclosed projection booths, purpose-built screens, lobbies, freestanding box offices, murals, decorative plasterwork, carpets, fountains, lounges, and other physical features distinguished them from bare-walled nickelodeons.[51] Notable neighborhood theaters included the eight-hundred-seat Jefferson, at the corner of 55th and Lake, which opened in 1912; the nine-hundred-seat Kedzie Annex (3204 West Madison), which opened in May 1912; and the 1,200-seat Clark Theater (4533 North Clark), "the second largest and finest outlying vaudeville theater in Chicago," which converted to licensed movies that March.[52] By 1915, Louella Parsons observed that "many of the outlying theaters contained architecture, inside structures and pipe organs that place them in the category of Chicago's finest."[53] The table below represents the most important establishments operating in October 1914, almost all of them far bigger than the biggest Loop movie theaters—the nine-hundred-seat Studebaker and LaSalle.[54] They were scattered around the city, making them convenient for patrons

Table 4.1

Theater	Address	Capacity	Neighborhood
Crawford	Crawford near W. Madison	1,210 seats	West Side
Hamlin	3826–36 W. Madison	1,200 seats	West Side
Lyda	315 N. Cicero	905 seats	West Side
Kedzie Annex	3204 W. Madison	900 seats	West Side
Kedzie	3202 W. Madison	1, 396 seats	West Side
Monogram	3510 S. Halsted	1,100 seats	South West Side
Halfield	55th and Halsted	952 seats	South West Side

141

CHAPTER 4

Theater	Address	Capacity	Neighborhood
Harper	53rd and Harper	1,500 seats	South Side
Twentieth Century	4708 S. Prairie	1,000 seats	South Side
E.A.R.	69th and Wentworth	890 seats	South Side
Jefferson	55th and Lake	800 Seats	South Side
Linden Photodrome	743 W. 63rd	780 seats	South Side
Biograph	2433 N. Lincoln	942 seats	Near North Side/ Lincoln Park
Parkway	2736 N. Clark	750 seats	Near North Side
Clark	4533 N. Clark	1,2000	North Side
Bryn Mawr	1125 Bryn Mawr	768 seats	Far North Side/ Rogers Park

citywide. To show this, I have organized them by neighborhood (table 4.1).

This boom in large outlying houses continued throughout the 1910s, reinforcing audience preferences to see movies close to home. By 1914–15, most neighborhood theaters were purpose-built as part of some larger complex that often covered an entire city block, with their coherent architecture integrating the building's many different functions.[55]

Exterior, decoration, lighting effects, and interior embellishments attracted customers, as can be seen in a 1915 program for the Savoy (4346 West Madison) that proclaimed: "The entire theater has been painted throughout and redecorated, thus giving it a pleasing appearance to the eye. *You will be proud to be seen in this place among your neighbors*" (my emphasis).[56] This comment addressed the self-staging, self-awareness, desire for social mobility—and even narcissism—characteristic of Progressivism, something theaters increasingly capitalized upon with their elaborate amenities and decor. Architects rethought theater design to accommodate patrons' comfort. J. Bowles's Morse Theater in Rogers Park (1328 West Morse Avenue, 650 seats, opened

1913) did not feature the then traditional round ticket box outside the theater but moved it inside, to the side of the theater's long marble-finished lobby. Bowles observed:

> It is not very courteous to ask a woman to stand on the sidewalk, especially when it is cold and nasty weather, and have her to remove her gloves, to fish for the desired coin, or to have a lady stand in front of such boxes on rainy days in a pool of water, an umbrella in one hand. It is not very polite to tell a woman and children that they cannot enter the doors of the lobby before they have purchased their tickets, or to force them to stand in line, in front of the little round ticket box, exposed to winds, rain or snow.
> There is still another reason. A woman does not like to open her purse in front of an idle crowd looking at the posters.[57]

Bowles's account of his remodeling emphasizes courtesy and concern for his patrons, using language typical of the community-minded exhibitor as well as the importance of female audiences and the need to protect them, their clothes, and their safety.[58]

The importance of customer care led exhibitors to offer services not usually associated with entertainment. Many theaters, like the Hamlin, catered to basic requirements, like child care, in surprisingly lavish ways. Its management boasted that it was "the originator of an idea that appeals to the mothers of their patrons. They have a room especially equipped with merry-go-rounds, swings and all sorts of toys. . . . A nurse in charge of the children keeps them amused while their parents enjoy the pictures."[59] Besides addressing needs—including child care—that might prevent patrons from attending movies, these theaters presented themselves as ideal homes, creating fantasies of social mobility for their patrons with grand staircases, velvet seats, decorative tile, and even fountains. Idealized domestic settings reinforced these theaters' intimacy, encouraging audiences to think of these premises as their space, places where they can feel at home and recuperate. As quasi-private sites for relaxation, neighborhood theaters took on the restorative functions formerly associated with the Victorian home and, in characteristic Progressive fashion, moved these into public spaces. It is thus not surprising that popular theater names included the Home,

CHAPTER 4

Cozy, Palace, and People's. Screen fantasies of improved domestic life could thereby be extended to the patron's experience of relaxing inside their premises. Lounges gave tired patrons a place to rest; child care facilities allowed mothers a chance to indulge themselves, while balconies, mezzanines, luxurious bathrooms, and even male-only smoking rooms reminiscent of wealthy homes allowed audiences to experience (and wander freely through) spaces they could otherwise only dream about—or watch on screen. One South Side house, Louis Weinberg's Avenue Theater (3110 South Indiana Avenue, seating capacity 636), claimed to have a "comfortable, home-like atmosphere," but descriptions suggest this was no ordinary home, with its elaborate paintings and corps of uniformed female "maid ushers." Its tiled lobby had a mosaic floor, was decorated with large murals, palm trees, and freshly cut flowers, and featured an eight-foot wainscot of English-veined marble with in-built brass poster display frames. The lobby led into the foyer, which featured drinking fountains, mirrors, two dressing rooms, and toilets, while its walls were "decorated in old rose and ivory, in art nouveau style, [with patterns] worked out in soft delicate greens, browns and crimsons." A mezzanine reached by two large marble staircases, one at each side of the lobby, led to a lounge painted in ivory and rose, carpeted in red velvet, and furnished with Louis XVI–style furniture. The auditorium featured an allegorical mural titled "The Goddess of Flowers," and was subdivided with ornamented beams while its walls were decorated with ivory, gold, and rose reliefs. Eight boxes were similarly embellished.[60] While undeniably lavish, these features were essentially domestic: couches, lounges, restrooms, child care, flowers, murals, and upholstery (albeit velvets and brocades), presenting the neighborhood theater as recuperative space of patrons' dreams. With their multiple rooms and high ceilings, these theaters provided a welcome sense of space for cramped urban residents while their furnishing encouraged audiences to linger, suggesting that exhibitors did not simply want to get patrons in and out as quickly as possible.[61]

The neighborhood theater's best-known (and most frequently touted) property was its association with community. As the *Moving Picture World*'s "Chicago News Letter" noted in 1916: "In the neighborhood theater, the exhibitor has become an important member of the community. He knows most of his patrons personally and frequently holds conversations with them regarding his show. They tell him their likes and dislikes, and while he may be unable to please all of them, he aims at pleasing as many of them as possible."[62] While clearly idealized, and somewhat prescriptive, this description was consistently echoed throughout the trade press. In his well-known exhibitor's manual from 1915, Epes Winthrop Sargent advised exhibitors to exploit the "personality of the Exhibitor and the personality of his house." The "clever exhibitor" would develop a regular clientele while linking his business with community, not the atomization and anonymity that bred crowds.[63] He urged exhibitors to know their customers and invite feedback, rewarding viewers for their loyalty to their theater.[64] Exhibitors could turn their audiences into a community (whatever that might have meant) or integrate theaters into the local community; most successful neighborhood theaters did both.

Many exhibitors raised money for local charities or lent their facilities to churches and community groups.[65] In December 1911, John Bell of the Bell Theater (Western Avenue and Madison Street) worked with the Red Cross and Chicago Tuberculosis Association, using his theater to educate the public while offering free admissions to these charities' employees.[66] In April 1913, the Vaudette (92nd Street and Houston Avenue) ran a benefit for victims of the Indiana and Ohio floods; in October 1914, the Royal (1369 Milwaukee Avenue) and Triangle Theater (7219 Wentworth Avenue) raised money for toys for European war orphans, while in July 1915, neighborhood theaters across the city ran benefits for the victims of the Eastland pleasure-boat disaster.[67] Such responses prompted the *Herald* to comment: "The hearts and pocketbooks of the motion picture people are always open to cases of disaster."[68]

More often, the community appeal of local theaters was somewhat intangible, based on the relationships between exhibitor-patron and exhibitor-neighborhood rather than specific activities, architectural features, gifts, or programming. Specific examples of community-based activities are not easy to find, partly because most were promoted in forms—like theater bulletins—that no longer exist, or manifested themselves in everyday interactions that went unrecorded. Theater bulletins document these theaters' community appeal, providing more than program information: they published local news, stories of neighborhood interest, and film-related features, often culled from items in

CHAPTER 4

distributor publications. One of these, the *Triangle News*, a four-page weekly bulletin issued by Chicago's Triangle Theater (seating capacity six hundred), covered neighborhood issues such as the status of street lighting in the area. *Motography* praised it, noting: "While it fully explains all matters that the patron is interested in about the theater and is therefore certain of popularity it is most interesting to those living in the neighborhood because of the community news it carries."[69] Many bulletins also included small prize contests, polls where patrons could vote for their favorite stars, letters pages, and numbers for the theater's own lottery. Patrons were invited to submit copy on items of local or cinematic interests and comment on exhibition conditions and program choices. Advertising space helped exhibitors strengthen ties with local business while presumably covering the publication's costs.[70]

Most exhibitors distributed free gifts and keepsakes, tokens that masked commercial considerations, instead evoking friendship and goodwill. Many were household goods or fashionable trifles, further reinforcing theaters' domestic address and emphasizing how exhibitors catered to feminine needs and fantasies. In December 1912, Milwaukee Avenue's Star Theater ran daily souvenir days when they gave away silverware, predating the popular Depression-era dish nights by nearly two decades but appealing to the same feminine desire to have an attractive place setting at home.[71] Between October 19 and 26, 1914, John H. Hodgson, manager of the Oak Park Theater on Wisconsin Avenue, gave roses to all women patrons to thank them for their attendance over the past year.[72] This personal touch was likely cheaper, more touching, more memorable, and more effective than newspaper advertising, ensuring each woman felt recognized and encouraging them to continue patronizing his theater. Even owners of neighborhood theater chains distributed gifts: in December 1916, Alfred Hamburger played Santa Claus at all his neighborhood theaters on the two Saturdays preceding Christmas, dressing up in furs and giving "toys and keepsakes" to patrons. Here he positioned himself as a kindly patriarch who cared about his patrons' happiness, not the owner of the city's largest theater chain.[73] One of the largest and most widespread promotions was the kinematographic grocery, a variant on the lottery that was popular during the mid-1910s. Audiences filled in a card as they entered the theater and winning numbers were drawn at the end of the program, with boxes of groceries disbursed to winners from the stage. As it often rivaled the final film, variants soon emerged, including comic forms where the most inappropriate prizes were handed out—a comb for a bald man or baby food for a teenage boy.[74]

Distributors offered similar promotions, demonstrating industry-wide investments in positioning and maintaining the neighborhood theater as a community space. Mutual gave exhibitors free trademark "wing-ed clock" lamps for their theaters and provided copies of their trademark serial, *Our Mutual Girl*, and of *Our Mutual Girl's Magazine* for free during 1914. Universal responded with free Alkali Ike dolls, based on the lead character from their popular comic western series, *Snakesville*.[75] Distributors also offered promotions that stimulated activities inside theaters, like Universal's 1915 movie game, based on guessing film titles represented by a strip of illustrations printed in local newspapers. Its theatrical component used short films, available for a small fee from their exchanges—Universal recommended showing these about a week after the print version ran in newspapers to allow players time to think about the puzzles.[76]

Neighborhood Theaters and Theater Chains: The Case of Alfred Hamburger

One of the clearest signs of the neighborhood theater's success was the growth of theater chains based on their appeal, a development that theater historian Robert Grau considered one of Chicago's most significant contributions to the industry (along with the consolidation of national film distribution).[77] Two chains dominated exhibition in Chicago until at least 1917: Jones, Linick and Schaefer (JLS) (Aaron J. Jones, president; Adolph Linick, financial executive; and Peter J. Schaefer, real estate magnate) and Alfred Hamburger, although both approached the business in very different ways. JLS retained strong ties to the legitimate world and vaudeville; as late as 1914 they saw movies as a training ground for future theatergoers, believing that fall 1914's boom in legitimate and vaudeville attendance resulted from films stimulating audiences' desire for "the real thing."[78] Perhaps unsurprisingly, JLS focused their efforts on the Loop, hoping to transform it into Chicago's own Broadway, while Hamburger sought the greater profits found in

CHAPTER 4

subsequent-run exhibition.[79] His downtown theaters promoted first-run films largely to boost takings in his circuit of subsequent-run neighborhood houses.[80] His business strategies best fit the market and served as a model for other chains (like Lubliner and Trinz, Ascher Brothers, Henry Schoendstadt, and, most famously, Balaban and Katz) whose success was based on bigger and better neighborhood houses, not downtown theaters.

Hamburger shared Progressive Era sentiments about neighborhoods, seeing them as a force for good, emphasizing family-friendly entertainment and positioning his theaters as community-centered institutions. As Louella Parsons observed in 1914: "Mr. Hamburger stands for clean films, is in accord with the censor, and is doing everything in his power to uplift the film business to a status that will be recognized as a dignified business proposition."[81] With this policy, he dominated exhibition until 1916–17, even though he was also the second largest owner of first-run downtown movie theaters behind Jones, Linick and Schaefer. He valued the song and dance contests, vaudeville, and other popular attractions found in neighborhood theaters, instructing his company's promotional director, "P. A." Jacoby to emphasize their community aspects. One of the more extreme examples was a wedding conducted on the stage of his Albany Park Theater in April 1917.[82]

Born in Bavaria in 1877, Hamburger came to Chicago at three years of age, starting his career as an office boy in a wholesale woolen house. He studied commerce and bookkeeping in night school, entering the printing industry where he rose to own his own company.[83] He turned to exhibition in 1909 (although he did not sell his printing business until 1914)—three years after Aaron Jones (of Jones, Linick and Schaefer) opened his first theater.[84] While most of his holdings were located on the South Side, he owned over twenty "high class" movie theaters in central and outlying neighborhoods by 1915.[85] He also claimed to be the first to raise neighborhood admissions from five cents to ten cents and to charge twenty-five cents for feature exhibition downtown. In 1916, his chain included the following nineteen houses, although like all theater circuits, these holdings were subject to change, as he traded theaters to maintain profits and quality (table 4.2).[86] All Hamburger houses were promoted as comfortable establishments, each "perfectly

Table 4.2

Theater	Address	Seating Capacity	Program (where known)
Ziegfeld	624 Michigan Blvd.	677	First-run features
Fine Arts	410 Michigan Blvd.	200	First-run features
Langley Hippodrome	63rd and Langley	1,200	Shorts, subsequent-run features, vaudeville
Albany Park	4816 N. Kedzie	1,000	
Beverley Bayne, purpose built opened June 1915	Sheridan Rd., just north of Wilson Ave	1,000	Subsequent run features and short program
Willard	51st and Calumet	1,000	Subsequent-run features direct from the Ziegfeld and Fine Arts
Shakespeare	43rd Street and Ellis	954	Mixed program with 2-reelers, some subsequent run features.
Drexel	858 E. 63rd Street	834	Subsequent-run features, including Famous Players releases
20th Century	47th and Prairie	750	2-reelers and Hearst-Selig newsreel; subsequent-run features alternate days
Argmore	Argyle and Kenmore	676	Subsequent run features and short program

CHAPTER 4

Theater	Address	Seating Capacity	Program (where known)
Panorama	5110 Prairie	671 (closed 1917)	
Pine Grove	717 Sheridan Road	633	
Apollo	526 E. 47th Street	550	Features; shorts; weekends "high-class" vaudeville
Ellis	63rd and Ellis		4 vaudeville acts, subsequent-run features, tango contests on Weds.
Oakgrand, opened 1916—adjacent hotel under separate management	Grand Blvd. at Oakwood		
Pickford (formerly the Lux)	35th and Michigan		Daily change of subsequent-run features
Prairie Avenue	58th St.		
Ravenswood	Kedzie and Lawrence		
20th Century	47th and Prairie		

ventilated, [with] excellent music, courteous service, and the highest type of photoplays."[87]

Hamburger started in partnership with Nathan Ascher, who later formed the Ascher Brothers circuit. Together with a third partner, Ludwig Siegell, they formed the Louise Amusement Company, incorporated in July 1909 with capital stock of $2,500.[88] In September 1911, his company, now named Hamburger & Co., purchased the President Theater on 55th Street, a movie-only establishment, converting it to a combination of small-time vaudeville and "a cheap picture service."[89] In 1912, he acquired two large South Side vaudeville houses, the Langley Hippodrome and the Drexel, and changed both into high-class, predominantly first-run picture houses, charging ten cents admission for licensed films. According to the *Moving Picture World*, other local theaters "use films aged 10 to 30 days . . . and charge 5 cents admission," but Hamburger insisted on newer, higher-quality prints, maintaining quality in all areas of his business throughout the 1910s.[90] His neighborhood-theater-centered policies paid off as outlying houses reported unprecedented business starting in summer 1914.[91] By March 1917, his chain was the largest in the city, comprising eighteen theaters.[92] He built the Easterly Theater, Lincoln Avenue and Diversey Boulevard, in April 1917; the Speedway Theater, Indiana Avenue and Forty-Seventh Street; and took over the leases on two Ascher Brothers houses, the Panorama and the President, in November 1917.[93] The last parts of this expansion occurred after his firm was reincorporated as the Continental Theater Corporation.[94]

Although Hamburger focused on large neighborhood houses, he leased two downtown theaters by 1914—neither of them as centrally located or as large as Jones, Linick and Schaefer's holdings. These were used to promote features before they played in his neighborhood theaters where most of the revenue could be made (hardly surprising given their greater size). Hamburger pioneered this strategy in Chicago, and it made perfect economic sense as the big profits were in neighborhood exhibition, as the *Chicago Sunday Herald* noted in 1914:

> After a feature picture has had a long run in a downtown theater its value is greatly increased for the outlying theaters. . . . That this idea is correct is proved in Chicago by *The Spoilers*, *The Christian*, *The Traffic in Souls*, *The Battle of the Sexes*, *The Sea Wolf*, *The Squaw Man* and other features, which bring big money to exhibitors all the time and any time, while such resurrected films as those of Mary Pickford [the Imp shorts rereleased during the summer and fall of 1914] excel most "first-run" arguments.[95]

Hamburger's downtown holdings were the Ziegfeld next door to the Blackstone Hotel (described by the *Herald* as "a little far down the boulevard for the convenience of the public [but] naturally suggestive of class"). He also ran the relatively tiny two-hundred-seat Fine Arts, which he first rented in May 1914 for *Neptune's Daughter* (Herbert Bre-

CHAPTER 4

non, Universal, 1914). This theater was pretty far south on Michigan Avenue, although it was opposite the La Salle Street station. It was housed in the same complex as the Studebaker Theater as well as "several of the city's most influential clubs and social organizations such as the Chicago Women's Club, the Fortnightly Club and the Daughters of the American Revolution."[96] After *Neptune's Daughter*'s eleven-week run broke records (admittedly easier in such a small house), he signed a long-term lease to make this "very probably . . . the only high class theater downtown in Chicago devoted exclusively to feature 'pictures.'"[97] *Neptune's Daughter* was not typical of most of the features playing in the city's high-priced downtown theaters at this time, which were predominantly imported epics or theatrical adaptations. Instead, it was a celebrity-driven fantasy starring the "Diving Venus," famed swimmer, vaudevillian, and beauty Annette Kellerman. It was therefore possible that audiences for this picture were not the same as those for earlier epics like *Quo Vadis?*, revealing Hamburger's emphasis on middlebrow entertainment.

Hamburger soon applied the neighborhood theater's community-oriented strategies to downtown exhibition. He reinvented the Ziegfeld as a place where mothers could take their children in the afternoon, printing coupons in the *Herald* during August 1914 for free admission "Good for One Lady to the Ziegfeld."[98] In mid-March 1915 he announced Children's Week at the Ziegfeld in the wake of the successful children's matinees at Orchestra Hall, where "children accompanied by their parents will be admitted to any performance except Saturday at a reduced admission charge."[99] He also tried to import some of his neighborhood theaters' camaraderie and programming strategies into other Loop theaters. When the Fine Arts opened for spring and summer 1916 with *The Ne'er Do Well* (Colin Campbell, Selig Polyscope–VLSE, 1916), Hamburger presented pink carnations to all his "guests," combining intimacy with the aura of a special downtown event.[100] In March 1917, he offered regular patrons admission discounts, selling a "handy book of admission coupons. By purchasing one of these books the fan effects a twenty percent reduction in admission price, and the coupons are good in any Hamburger theater."[101] As with neighborhood theaters, these "gifts" transformed the relationship between theater and patron

Private Pleasures and Public Space

into something more intimate, rather than the anonymity that typified downtown entertainments.

Hamburger's success foregrounds the significance of neighborhood theaters as economic and cultural entities during the mid-1910s. He drew on local pride to promote his chain, even naming one of his neighborhood theaters after Essanay's popular star, Beverley Bayne.[102] She responded, stating: "I appreciate the great honor Mr. Hamburger has conferred on me, and I am especially pleased to have the theater located in my own neighborhood."[103] He displayed concern for his audience's tastes, soliciting patrons' opinions before screening controversial films, promoting his cinemas as respectable and family friendly. In June 1915, for example, he offered a prize of $25 to the person writing the best letter about whether *The New Governor* (Edgar Lewis, Fox Film Corporation, 1915), a film based on Edward Sheldon's racist play, *The Nigger*, should be allowed to play in his neighborhood theaters.[104] At this very time, the film was playing at the Ziegfeld, indicating the different standards for downtown exhibition with their largely itinerant audiences.

Downtown Exhibition: More Public Pleasures

Although Chicago's four downtown first-run movie theaters received a lot of attention, they were generally small- to mid-sized establishments, all owned by chains and primarily used for promotion rather than being successful attractions in their own right. The few attempts at offering regular lavish exhibition downtown generally failed, even as features were filling up newly built neighborhood theaters seating more than a thousand. Loop theaters had a difficult and narrowly circumscribed role in Chicago's market. With the rise of features, road showing, and the trend for "De Luxe" screenings, producers needed prestigious theaters, yet without financial support from film companies, they struggled in a market where large neighborhood houses were the central draw. These theaters had to differentiate themselves to justify higher ticket prices and the trip downtown, something that became harder as neighborhood theaters grew larger and more ornate. While even the largest neighborhood theaters were positioned as elaborate domestic spaces, Loop houses stressed their more public status,

CHAPTER 4

whether through such innovations as all-night screenings, decor that emphasized exotic or outdoor spaces, or by offering more anonymous pleasures. Their more public orientation reinforced movie theaters' own public/private continuum.

The Loop's surviving entertainment districts (like those on West Madison and South State Street) offered both high-class exhibition and the remnants of low-end exhibition to largely itinerant audiences—the Loop had few residents of its own. Although there was no theater district comparable to New York's, Chicago's larger downtown theaters were generally found on South Michigan, West Randolph, and Clark, while the bulk of the smaller houses were on West Madison and South State, known for their cheap amusements. Some of Chicago's first movie theaters had been established on the central blocks of South State Street, most notably the Lyric and the Bijou Dream, a house dubbed "the most magnificent five cent theatre in the west" when it opened in June 1907 in the heart of the downtown's shopping district.[105] The "new and elaborate" Lyric opened later that month near the junction of State Street and Jackson Boulevard.[106] It was a purpose-built movie theater whose elaborate decor (costing an estimated $15,000) marked it as something "new and different."[107] These theaters cornered the market for higher-end exhibition early on, along with the nearby Orpheum, a 677-seat theater at 110 South State Street. At first, the Orpheum premiered major early features, but after 1914 it offered less prestigious fare. Jones, Linick and Schaefer owned all three, and their decision to cluster their theaters suggests that they knew more people would come downtown if they had a variety of options. This reveals a different way of thinking about cinema—rather than placing movies close to people's homes, they could be part of a larger entertainment scene that might be part of a day—or a night—out. This approach defined the city's entertainment districts where patrons were encouraged to wander in and out of various establishments, indicating their more public status and proximity to street life and culture.

Despite strict zoning, a few small movie theaters flourished in the Loop well into the 1910s, mainly offering subsequent-run features and film programs from the major exchanges. Unlike neighborhood theaters, these establishments did not shy away from adult content and were often directly associated with the area's nightlife. Some, like the Lyric, a house located on "one of the liveliest corners in the city," opened all night, a practice it pioneered in March 1911 and one that reportedly covered all its costs.[108] Like other such theaters, it mainly catered to men returning from bars, shows, and business dinners, but there were always some women in attendance, reportedly gossiping through the films. Other regulars included insomniacs, night workers, socialites, people who had missed trains, and the homeless and itinerant, ironically leading local authorities to praise the management for cleaning up the city streets.[109] Not surprisingly, adult material was a popular attraction. The Bandbox (125 West Madison at LaSalle, opened October 1915) established a "women only" policy starting in 1916 so audiences could watch films like *The Unborn* (Otis B. Fair, Kulee Features/States Rights, 1916), an antiabortion melodrama capitalizing on the success of *Where Are My Children?* that censors had found too sensitive for mixed sex audiences.[110] Here, manager Jack Haag's strategy anticipated the mixture of paternalism and the promise of salacious content that later characterized exploitation cinema and was rarely, if ever, found in neighborhood houses.[111]

At the other extreme, the Loop was noted for high-end screenings of first-run features. The first such films shown in Chicago during summer 1913, like *Quo Vadis?* and *Les Misérables* (Albert Capellani, Pathé, France, 1913), were exhibited in legitimate theaters during the off-season, helping movies gain a foothold on Broadway and the Loop while attracting more middle-class audiences.[112] These screenings proved that cinema could be part of legitimate culture if the right films were shown and handled properly.[113] These were not routine releases though: they sought different audiences and tried to offer an experience akin to opera or the legitimate stage, not the regular film program. Although these first feature screenings played to relatively small audiences, they received the first film reviews and serious movie commentary in Chicago's newspapers. In bringing these artistic movies to public attention, they helped improve the medium's reputation, making it visible and offsetting its links to shadowy establishments in bad areas. Initially a big draw even in the worst heat, these prestigious films seemed to be a more viable year-round entertainment than live theater, but their popularity was short lived.

CHAPTER 4

Nevertheless, at their peak in July 1914, these features resisted the "summer slump," attracting larger audiences than the previous summer when screenings were still uncommon, leading to some overoptimistic predictions about their continued success.[114] In August, "reports from the managers of the Loop film houses [revealed] unprecedented box office returns for this season of the year prov[ing] that the photoplay is heat resistant and cold proof and is here to stay."[115] That month the Illinois Theater announced that *Cabiria* would extend its run until September 1, making this "the first time in the history of the theater that a photo-spectacle, maintaining the regular dramatic scale of prices, has continued throughout the summer at a Chicago playhouse, or, in fact, at any theater in America."[116] Although the Illinois ultimately returned to legitimate drama, *Cabiria* continued at the Ziegfeld.[117] Four downtown theaters stuck with movies into the early fall—the Ziegfeld, Orchestra Hall, the Fine Arts, and the Princess, but the trend was fading fast—these theaters were merely rented out to fill gaps between legitimate engagements.[118] The Princess quickly returned to legitimate drama in the second week of September, while Orchestra Hall went back to music on October 1, 1914 (it was rented out for first-run features during the 1910s). By October, the Comedy had returned to drama, followed, in November, by the Fine Arts, which briefly interrupted its legitimate season to screen the six-reel *Damon and Pythias* (Otis Turner, Universal, 1914) that December.[119] The Fine Arts returned to movies full time in April 1915 after being acquired by Alfred Hamburger.[120] Films remained on vaudeville bills, with the Majestic featuring weekly changes of the General Film Company's *War Series* (1914), but these were usually minor attractions.[121] Continuous first-run movie exhibition did not come to the Loop until the 1914–15 season, when the Studebaker and Ziegfeld were booked exclusively for film exhibition.[122]

While impressive, these developments responded more to the rise in high-end states rights features during 1913–15, which required the rentals of major theaters, and therefore did not necessarily reflect a greater interest in cinema among either the public or legitimate theater managers.[123] Despite widespread theater construction elsewhere in the city, only two larger movie theaters opened downtown during the mid-1910s: the World (61 West Randolph Street, opposite the Garrick

Theater), and the Bandbox, advertised as a "New $150,000 Photoplay Palace."[124] Neither was used for first-run features. Tellingly, some of the medium's most stalwart supporters expressed doubts about the viability of big features downtown. In November 1914, the *Herald* declared: "motion pictures were being overdone when four or five big houses in the loop [*sic*] attempted to live upon them at the same time, and some of the managers frankly confessed that the big theaters were being kept open for the 'movies' chiefly for the benefit of the advertising that would accrue to plays [films] so exhibited."[125] Local geography may have played a part in this decline: the Loop's larger movie theaters were not particularly close to its shops or the West Madison and South State Street entertainments. Theaters like the Fine Arts, Studebaker, Orchestra Hall, and Ziegfeld were considered out of the way, even though they were near train stations, likely making them less valuable to the legitimate trade as well, explaining why they were rented out for film exhibition.

Other factors made downtown less amenable to feature films. As people were primarily there to work, shop, or for some other specific reason, time was a factor, making features an impossible indulgence. Louella O. Parsons noted in October 1914: "Many persons might drop into an attractive downtown theater to see a short film who would not care to go in to see a long one—for lack of time if no other reason."[126] As patrons spent leisure hours in their neighborhoods, they had the time to watch features: in October 1914, the very month it expressed uncertainty about the prospects of longer films downtown, the *Herald* reported on the popularity of features in neighborhood houses.[127] (As this paper did not have a vested interest in a specific kind of production or exhibition, like the short film program, it is likely a more reliable source than the trades.) Another report in the *Chicago Sunday Herald* indicates that the kinds of theaters downtown patrons wanted may not have been economically viable, again indicating that shorter films were more compatible with viewers' schedules:

> Attractive theaters on the well-traveled streets, a compromise in size between the big Michigan avenue houses and the smaller theaters already in the loop district, are regarded by some persons as being the thing needed—*places where the thousands can drop in for a few minutes while wait-*

CHAPTER 4

> *ing to keep an appointment, or sometimes largely merely in order to rest.* Such theaters, it is estimated, would have to have attractive entrances and provide first-class attractions, although not necessarily big features. On the other hand, it is pointed out that theaters not now getting this type of patronage would have to be in locations which would make the rent an impossibility for a 10 or 15 cent show. (My emphasis)[128]

With few people living downtown, theaters had to cater to workers, shoppers, nighttime revelers, and tourists who generally wanted shorter shows in luxurious yet cheap theaters, seeing movies as a quick diversion rather than a full evening's entertainment. The conflict between what the public desired and what was economically possible was irresolvable, but this was not a problem in the city's neighborhoods where rents were cheaper and patrons had more time.[129]

By the mid-1910s, first-run Loop movie theaters had split into two categories: medium-sized houses (seating well under one thousand) that were the flagships for major local chains like Alfred Hamburger or Jones, Linick and Schaefer and De Luxe theaters hired specifically for road-show engagements on short-term leases. The chains' four flagship theaters were Hamburger's Ziegfeld and Fine Arts and JLS's nine-hundred-seat Studebaker (203 South Michigan Avenue near Van Buren) and the nine-hundred-seat La Salle (110 West Madison). All occasionally returned to legitimate or musical attractions during movie slumps, and none had a particularly large seating capacity by period standards. They were far smaller than the theaters leased for roadshow engagements that usually sat over one thousand, the most important of which I have tabulated below (table 4.3).[130] These larger theaters were generally associated with De Luxe staging, a trend that received a lot of publicity and was particularly successful in New York City. Still, it struggled in Chicago, likely because cinema was entrenched in the city's neighborhoods in theaters that rivaled—if not exceeded—those downtown in terms of the quality of their amenities and presentation.

Theaters De Luxe: The New Strand and the Colonial

The Theater De Luxe was the most dramatic and extravagant trend of its time and was reserved solely for first runs of important feature

Table 4.3

Theater	Address	Capacity	Notable Films Shown
Orchestra Hall	Michigan Ave. between Jackson and Randolph	2,500	Rented by Strand Theater Company, summer 1915 (road-showed prestige pictures in Chicago).
Colonial	24 W. Randolph	1,724	*The Birth of a Nation* (transferred from the Illinois). Often used for big roadshow screenings.
Palace Music Hall	127 N. Clark near Randolph	1,500	Documentary and travelogues during summer 1914 (e.g., Paul J. Rainey's *Series of 1914: African Hunt Pictures*). Otherwise rarely used for films.
Illinois	65 E. Jackson	1,304	Opened *The Birth of a Nation*. Occasionally used for big road-showed attractions.
Princess	319 S. Clark	900	*Traffic in Souls* Only screened features in 1913 when they were novelties.
Comedy	Van Buren near Michigan Ave.		Continued run of *Traffic in Souls*.
Olympic	51 Clark near Randolph		Rented out for occasional features in summer theatrical off season.

films. These presentations could only be found in the most important downtown theaters. Films were screened among elaborate (often purpose-built) settings to form a larger *gestamkunstwerk* combining (and sometimes overwhelming) all the senses. Acted prologues, oratory, and

CHAPTER 4

orchestral overtures preceded films, while choirs, actors' voices, music, colored lights, and themed perfumes often accompanied screenings. Flowers, fountains, decorative frames around the screen, lavish decor, and specially costumed ushers rounded out the experience, ostensibly to foreground the film's pictorial and artistic properties. The Theater De Luxe was most closely associated with Samuel "Roxy" Rothapfel, whose grandiose Belasco-style theatrical presentations at Minneapolis's Lyric and the Knickerbocker in New York soon became legendary. Eileen Bowser describes one of these early Minneapolis shows, *The Passion Play* (1911):

> There was a prelude of two silent films with no music and no sound effects: *Wild Birds in Their Haunts* and *The Holy Land*, both from Pathé. When the audience was settled in, the doors closed, the house darkened, the stage curtain lowered. There was a distant pealing of chimes. "The Holy City" was played by the pipe organ. The curtain was raised and perfumes of lilies wafted over the house. Twenty choirboys in white vestments were onstage. The baritone sang "Holy City," the choirboys joined in, a pale blue light was gradually diffused, fountains played with pale blue lights beneath, and several dozen roses were carefully strewn on the steps and stage. Then, with the showing of the feature, there was a performance of "Holy Night," "Adeste Fideles," "Christmas Carol," "Praise Ye the Father," "The Palms," and "Calvary."[131]

As this account suggests, De Luxe staging created something very different from the neighborhood theater's "intimate and friendly" address. It was designed to inspire awe and wonder while simultaneously creating the distance associated with receiving works of art. These presentations purposefully divorced films from the routine of everyday life and placed them as a more public spectacle.

Chicago's most prominent exponent of De Luxe exhibition, the Strand Theater Company, programmed movies at the 2,500-seat Orchestra Hall (home of the Chicago Symphony Orchestra) during the 1915 summer off-season. Local dignitaries, society folk, film critics, and W. Hodkins, president of Paramount, were invited to witness the April 30, 1915, unveiling of their renovations, which were designed to inspire awe, even in the most illustrious onlookers:

That $5,000 was spent in beautifying. . . . Orchestra Hall does not sound extravagant when one sees the Venetian garden effect with the masses of green background and flowers grouped against the back of the stage. Fountains with water playing over colored lights and an inclosure [sic] of pink buds for the orchestra added to the artistic appearance of the stage. The lights in the body of the house were covered with flowers.[132]

This description of the newly renovated interior points to key differences from even the most grand neighborhood houses. Rather than offering domestic luxuries to build a more intimate relationship with the audience, these theaters wanted to dazzle spectators. Auditoriums were compared to public spaces like museums, art galleries, palaces, and even cathedrals. Promotional discourse stressed exoticism and evoked the thrills of seeing a famous and often foreign tourist destination. The Venetian garden and its fountains mentioned above clearly denoted an experience that transported viewers out of the city and away from familiar spaces in contrast to the neighborhood theater's luxurious domesticity.

After a temporary residency at Orchestra Hall, owners of the Strand opened their own downtown theater, the New Strand, on Friday, October 15, 1915, but this enterprise was short-lived. This conversion of the 1,500-seat former Globe Theater (opposite the Blackstone Hotel at 700 Wabash at Seventh Street) was the only theater of its kind in Chicago.[133] On opening, it received rave reviews, as did its first screening, the local premiere of Cecil B. DeMille's *Carmen* (Paramount–Famous Players–Lasky, 1915) teamed with William Selig's personal rare, hand-tinted copy of *The Coming of Columbus* (Colin Campbell, Selig Polyscope–GFC, 1912).[134] Louella O. Parsons praised the theater's transformation, describing how "Japanese blue rugs cover the floor and upholster the Circassian walnut chairs. Scarlet hangings fall softly from the stage, with artistic lights shedding a subdued radiance here and there."[135] The New Strand lasted for less than a year as a De Luxe movie theater, pointing to the difficulties in running such an establishment year round without industry support, even in the nation's second largest city. Even Samuel Rothapfel failed at running a De Luxe theater, lasting less than a month as manager of the Colonial (formerly the

CHAPTER 4

Iroquois) in early 1916.[136] This 1,724-seat theater at 24 West Randolph was the site of the notorious December 1903 fire that had killed nearly six hundred people, including 212 children.[137] Rothapfel had previously worked in Chicago for a month during June 1912 as general manager of the Schuberts' chain of first-class houses and had previously presented De Luxe pictures at the Lyric.[138] The Colonial had had previous success with *The Birth of a Nation* (D. W. Griffith, Epoch Pictures, 1915), which had transferred from the Illinois, and had briefly been used for the biggest Chicago roadshows and premieres.[139] After it reopened in February 1916 under Rothapfel's management, Louella Parsons noted it was "something very like the Strand," sharing its "subdued lights, soft music and artistic surroundings"—trends Rothapfel pioneered. His other signature touches included a turbaned "Hindu" doorman and the transformation of the stage into a highly decorative pictorial background for the pictures—very popular in high-end urban houses at this time.[140] Even before he departed, the Colonial was not a success, and he quickly changed its approach, screening multiple features (mainly routine programmers). The Strand's E. C. Divine briefly took over before Jones, Linick and Schaefer purchased its lease for legitimate attractions just one month later.[141]

After these failures, De Luxe staging was reserved for limited-term openings of roadshowed prestige pictures. Its failure revealed that movies were more successful when integrated into everyday life, as they were in neighborhood theaters, rather than being presented as special events, as something artistic, foreign or exotic, possibly revealing patrons' desires to get closer to the screen and have an intimate relationship with its stars. Under intense competition, the Loop fast fell behind the city's neighborhoods as an important movie district with all its major theaters closing for redecoration in 1916 to compete with the new outlying theaters.[142] Only Hamburger's female-friendly Ziegfeld operated as usual.[143]

Entertainment Districts

Movie theaters in the city's entertainment districts, including those inside the Loop, constituted the other major form of exhibition. Although they initially appear more like neighborhood theaters, these

Private Pleasures and Public Space

establishments shared the public address associated with downtown exhibition. Entertainment districts were often located in some of the city's poorest districts where rents were low and regulation lax. Cheap theaters were clustered together, with patrons visiting at least one show and combining it with other recreations amid a vibrant street culture. Audiences usually wandered in and out of nearby theaters, dissolving boundaries between theaters and street, often visiting different types of entertainment on a single night out.[144] Chicago's business directories reveal that entertainment districts were relatively stable even though the businesses they housed were often short-lived. A comparison of listings in *Lakeside Classified Directory* from 1910 to 1914 reveals, for example, that most of theaters in the South Halsted entertainment district either changed hands or moved to other buildings, but the same clusters of theaters remained.[145] Advertisements reveal that these theaters offered a program of mixed shorts and vaudeville far later than elsewhere in the city.[146]

Entertainment districts were lively places that usually attracted working-class, ethnic, and immigrant audiences.[147] Some were found in business areas like the poorer reaches of the Loop, where the highest concentration of small movie theaters could be found on West Madison Street, whose easternmost blocks were nicknamed "Celluloid Row." These largely catered to workers taking a break after work.[148] Five of the area's most successful small movie theaters were clustered here on a single block: the Casino (58 West Madison, 288 seats), Boston (60 West Madison, 750 seats), Rose (63 West Madison, 299 seats), Alcazar (67 West Madison, 298 seats), and Pastime (66 West Madison, 390 seats). In April 1910 the *Moving Picture World* noted that these small theaters had a quick audience turnover and their short programs were "generally put on badly," reserving their sole praise for the Pastime.[149] A few months later, their correspondent noted that conditions on the central part of the street had somewhat improved: the Boston was "beautifully decorated," but still had poor projection, was dirty inside and had no ushers, although there was plenty of room between seats, good song slides, and music.[150]

Three West Madison theaters—the Alcazar, Boston, and Rose—were owned by Harry Moir, owner of the Morrison Hotel, and managed by H. C. Miller.[151] His theaters were probably the most respectable

CHAPTER 4

establishments of their kind, but they still provide some insight into how such theaters operated. The Alcazar and Boston opened during the nickelodeon boom, but their decorative facades (courtesy of Chicago's Decorator's Supply Company), prosceniums, theatrical seating, and sidewalk box offices distinguished them from rival storefronts. The Boston was an early convert to the movie craze, previously housing one of the city's best-known small-time vaudeville shows.[152] In 1908 the Alcazar acquired "one of the earliest, if not the very earliest pipe organ specifically installed in a moving picture house in that city."[153] Unlike his rivals, Moir advertised his theaters in the local press, ensuring name recognition and regular mentions in local movie columns. His theaters were always advertised as a group, with audiences encouraged to drop into one and then visit another. Films generally moved from the Boston to the Rose, while by 1917 the Alcazar was open until 5 a.m. to catch the last late-night moviegoers. It had plain but "tasteful" decorations, uniformed ushers, "excellent music and projection," and its own unique feature—a rear section of the auditorium fully lit so patrons could read newspapers.[154] The idea was profitable, and the practice spread to the Rose as well as nearby competitors like the Casino and Rialto.[155]

Small houses also did well on the downtown blocks of South State Street, an area specializing in cheap amusements and shorter shows, catering to shoppers and workers on lunch and afternoon breaks (table 4.4). These theaters rarely advertised or caught the eyes of the trades or local newspaper columnists so little is known about them, but this lack of promotion suggests they were well known to their target clientele. As several older establishments specializing in cheap musical theater and burlesque were located nearby, like the Gaeity Hippodrome, 220 South State, it would appear that the area specialized in relatively lowbrow cheap entertainment, so many of these theaters likely did the same.

Reformers paid close attention to these theaters, visiting them and using their findings to justify increased regulation, censorship, and calls for the medium's abolition.[156] This attention is unsurprising as entertainment districts, save the one in the Loop, were usually located in low rent residential neighborhoods that were home to the poor, immigrants, and ethnic minorities, like the South Halsted Street entertain-

Table 4.4

Theater	Address	Capacity, if known
Royal	408 S. State	900
Orpheum (larger theater, at times used for first run features)	110 S. State	800
Gem	450 S. State	434
Motion Picture Theater	700 S. State	325
Castle, established 1912	6. N. State	300
Lyric	348. S. State	290
State-Harrison	546 S. State	288—storefront
Chicago	614 S. State	270
New Paris, constructed 1914	618 S. State	274
Five Cent Theater	714 S. State	
Fisher Paramount	36 S. State	300
Old Paris	557 S. State	275
Premier	336 S. State	

ment district.[157] Hull House (800 South Halsted), the Juvenile Protective Association (816 South Halsted), and Halsted Street Institutional Church Settlement (1935 South Halsted) were all nearby—Hull House even offered educational films in an unsuccessful attempt to lure away audiences.[158] At twenty-two miles, Halsted Street was then the longest commercial street in the world.[159] A narrow, crowded thoroughfare that crossed some of the poorest districts in the city, it formed a "vision of the urban inferno in all its horror."[160] The architect of the Chicago Plan, Daniel Burnham, described it as follows:

> There the smoke from railroad shops and yards and from standing locomotives combines with the soot sent up by nearly four hundred trains that come and go each day . . . the nearby tanneries contribute their odors . . . and the streets are covered with the sawdust, coal, and dirt spilled from thousands of wagons. . . . Close [by] is a cosmopolitan dis-

CHAPTER 4

trict inhabited by a mixture of races living in surroundings which are a menace to the moral and physical health of the community."[161]

Greeks, Italians, Jews, Russians, Bohemians, and Arabs were among the immigrant groups living and working along South Halsted Street.[162] The Italian neighborhood, or nineteenth ward, roughly encompassed the area below West Van Buren between the 100 and 1300 blocks of Halsted, stretching from Racine Avenue East to the riverfront, was one of the city's worst neighborhoods.[163] In 1910, reformer and social worker Edith Wyatt described the areas as "very closely packed in housing almost unbelievably bad . . . most of the tenements are low and old, built with frame siding and jammed in behind each other."[164]

The entertainment district located here housed many five- and ten-cent movie theaters, attracting passers-by, visitors from outside the district as well as locals. Many of these moviegoers were reportedly of poor repute. In 1910, Wyatt observed:

> The penny arcades and the five-cent theaters of moving pictures are close together here. In this evening, phonographs clank and scream before them on the pavements and barkers call their attractions. Some of these kinetoscopes represent the familiar subjects of moving trains with comic characters . . . or other expressions of that sort of completely harmless and senseless, light-hearted fooling of which every normally constituted nature probably likes at least a little. Others of these moving pictures make an appeal so debased that they can only fill you with a sense of shame that there should be in existence human beings whose experience and opportunities can have given them so degraded a sense of life.[165]

She was more sympathetic to movies than many other Chicago reformers, and her description captures some of the typical characteristics of movies in entertainment districts—the fluid movement between streets and theaters, the loud barkers, the proximity to other entertainments, bars and cafes, as well as the tendency to show comic, sensational, or salacious films.

Ethnic theaters could also be found here and usually offered somewhat more respectable entertainment to a more loyal and regular clientele. In June 1910, C. Young visited a theater in the Italian neighborhood off South Halsted Street on the near west side "patronized exclusively by Italians" and found a well-received song and comic sketch in Italian offered alongside Independent films ("all the Italian films are Independent," as he noted). A cluster of six such theaters existed in the heart of the Italian district (between the 900 and 1300 blocks of South Halsted), all catering to the immigrant trade.[166] In the nearby Jewish ghetto, along Halsted between 12th and 14th streets, movie theaters offered Yiddish vaudeville.[167] This kind of ethnic exhibition went largely undocumented other than in the foreign language press, but it appears to have been more popular before 1912.

Distinctions between neighborhood theaters and exhibition in entertainment districts extended to significant differences in reception. Besides being much larger and more lavishly decorated, neighborhood theaters took a community-minded approach while entertainment districts catered to those seeking thrills rather than uplift, usually attracting itinerant audiences who sought excitement, not known patrons. Rather than the family-friendly films found in neighborhood houses, viewers might encounter "adult only" pictures, films that the city censors only considered suitable for those over twenty-one years old, and that many neighborhoods exhibitors prohibited.[168] Although 1914's adult-only rating was intended for important films, it rapidly became synonymous with exploitation.[169] Short film programs were also popular as many audiences did not want to spend an evening in one place but rather enjoy the ambience and excitement these districts offered, sampling multiple entertainments.

Despite some diversity, the neighborhood theater dominated exhibition, with other forms, like De Luxe staging and exhibition in entertainment districts, essentially modeling themselves as alternatives to this norm. The neighborhood theater's "intimate and friendly" address established a period standard, demonstrating patrons' desire to integrate movies into their lives and the film industry's efforts to affiliate their product with neighborhood values rather than glamour, excitement, or sensation. Seen in the context of the period's celebrity culture, these theaters' intimate address likely facilitated patrons' desire to be close to the screen and its stars. Their comfortable amenities and service may have even encouraged viewers to see the social mobility of

CHAPTER 4

stars as attainable, given that patrons experienced something similarly elevating when they entered these lavish premises. While the distanced and auratic protocols of first-run and De Luxe exhibition had its own appeals, proximity was far more suited to movies in the age of celebrity culture, and this was available in neighborhood houses. The neighborhood theater's dominance is thus profoundly important, as it speaks to the importance of the social dimensions of exhibition as well as its fundamentally communal nature, begging reassessment of the thesis that a largely text-based spectatorship emerged in the mid-1910s. The neighborhood theater attests that reception remained fundamentally social, while different forms of theater catered to different spectatorship practices. Indeed, all three principal forms of exhibition handled Progressivism's more public life and culture differently, variously celebrating the chaos of the city, the pleasures of anonymity, and luring viewers with a more domestic, more communal, semiprivate experience that mediated the old and the new.

With its emphasis on community and its efforts to balance the public with the private, the neighborhood theater revealed how the film industry affiliated itself with mainstream Progressive values. Still, movies continued to trouble some social reformers and others in power—like many politicians and press barons—who argued that films needed to be tempered and regulated for the greater social good. Ironically, these reformers and their politician allies were more concerned about cinema's influence *after* the neighborhood theater dominated exhibition. As the industry became more respectable, it also acquired greater power over spectators and the culture. Many newspaper barons, reformers, and local politicians attacked cinema because it threatened their authority as it became more respectable and reached more middle-class patrons. Ironically, the medium's improved social standing motivated more strident calls for stricter censorship between 1907 and 1914—even as the film industry gently advanced a more benign form of censorship to demonstrate its concerns with uplift and social order, issues I discuss at length in the following chapter, which examines Chicago's film censorship and its relation to local politics.

FIVE

Oversight and Regulation
Film Censorship, Local Government,
and Social Reform

As cinema became more respectable, it made the remarkable jump from a cheap amusement, based on thrills and sensations, to a potentially powerful source of cultural influence and authority. This more reputable guise ironically posed a greater threat to traditional sources of authority, including some reformers, politicians, and press barons. While conventional wisdom suggests that the movies' efforts at uplift and moral authority would offset calls for censorship, this would not be the case in Chicago. Although the city implemented its first forms of censorship in 1907—before neighborhood theaters and the adoption of more morally charged narrative discourses—its most punitive and oppressive regime came as the medium attained greater cultural and artistic acclaim in the early to mid-1910s. While far cheaper and more "vice-laden" amusements escaped such clampdowns because they knew their place, the movies' overt middle-class aspirations allowed them to cross class lines and reach deep into community life, factors that enraged Chicago's strict film censors. Cinema's artistic aspirations—as seen the 1913–16 trend toward epics and literary adaptations—and its efforts to speak on matters of political and international significance, like World War I, aggravated Chicago's most rigorous censorship advocates more than the earliest cheap films. Indeed, the censors' biggest battles were

CHAPTER 5

not over tawdry sensational films but major and high-minded titles that aspired to both art and speech, like *Traffic in Souls*, *The Birth of a Nation*, and *The Little American* (Cecil B. DeMille, Mary Pickford Company–Paramount, 1917).

While similar battles occurred nationwide, Chicago's censors were unusual in fighting these battles for so long and with such acrimony. As Lee Grieveson has shown, the question of cinema's authority and its right to speak on matters of public interest played out over this period until the medium was redefined as "harmless entertainment," a process that culminated with the verdict of *Mutual v. Ohio* (1915):

> Legal decisions, combined with those internal to the mainstream film industry in this period, gradually established a consensus that mainstream cinema should principally offer harmless and culturally affirmative entertainment and not pretend to the loftier purposes of the press or to the purpose of cultural negation that post-romantic cultural theory accorded the category of "art."[1]

The question of cinema's authority to speak on such matters was central to the period's censorship debates, along with more obvious issues like the medium's quality and its effects on audiences and society. While some reformers and cultural custodians wanted cinema not to speak on such matters, others hoped the movies would take a more interventionist role, addressing topics like temperance and morality, educating audiences, and improving society.[2] These more progressive reformers advocated cinema as an alternative to the saloon, providing the films were of sufficient cultural and artistic merit.[3] Other leading reformers such as the Reverend Allan Hoben, theology professor at the University of Chicago and field secretary of the Juvenile Protective Association (JPA) (1910–13), wanted a more punitive censorship regime, even calling for total abolition of the movies, seeing them as beyond redemption.[4]

Censorship battles were not black and white. The film industry was not uniformly and unilaterally opposed to it, as shown in its own informal efforts at self-regulation through the National Board, as well as its initial acceptance of Chicago's first censorship regime. As censorship could be linked to respectability, accountability, and uplift—as well as pointing to an out-of-control industry—it could help the industry police itself and improve its reputation. Similarly, the press, local politicians, and reformers were not entirely unified in their opposition to cinema. Chicago's *Herald*, a popular, middlebrow newspaper, courted cinema, although it was the city's sole such title until 1914–15. Politicians like Mayor Fred Busse and William Hale Thompson were not unsympathetic to cinema, and some reformers, like Jane Addams, believed the medium could be used for the greater good, revealing clearly marked political and ideological differences within all these groups. Still, the vocal antimovie sentiment voiced in papers like the *Chicago Tribune*, the city's paper of record with strong links to social reformers, and the lowbrow *Evening American* influenced local politicians' actions, and both were linked to the formation of Chicago's censorship board, the nation's first.[5] This board was initially quite benign and tried to offset the pressure from conservative reformers and the press, who were not so easily placated.

Censorship was a particularly Progressive response to the perceived social problem cinema presented. In addition to displaying the powers this culture gave government to manage social problems, it relied upon one of the era's favored strategies to diagnose problems and restore order—oversight or monitoring. The practice of examining all aspects of culture then using these findings to calm modernity's disruptive influences more generally marked the period's investigations into urban life. Oversight also played a role in the period's broader realignment of public and private, making the private public, both through its exposure and by turning it into a matter of public significance, transforming it, in turn, into municipal policy. As these designated observers were those of "good" character and upright values—usually members of the social elite who feared that new modern culture threatened their cultural power—oversight often became a conservative strategy. This ideology characterized Chicago's censorship board during its most visible and notorious years (1913–17) when it was largely run by conservative social reformers. Still, censorship was not necessarily an assault on cinema; indeed, its orientation depended on the censors' approach to society and cultural politics. Although some of Chicago's censors had an old-fashioned approach, others (particularly members of the earlier police board) were more pragmatic, even forward looking, believing censorship should advance movies' social standing.

The various incarnations of the Chicago censorship board thus need to be considered in relation to local politics and the way this determined their approaches to cinema. Ironically, while censorship was initially implemented to placate those who believed movies were damaging society, Chicago's first censors essentially supported American film and had the approval of the uplift-minded film industry. This board infuriated those who campaigned for its implementation, with antimovie papers like the *Tribune* and *Examiner* subsequently stepping up reports that linked movies to immorality and crime and lobbying for tougher censorship. In finding mainstream American productions acceptable while clamping down on foreign films and those from fly-by-night companies, Chicago's first censors effectively confirmed the film industry's moral compass and protected their market share. The industry's endorsement of these early censors further revealed the industry's investment in Progressive uplift. The industry staunchly opposed the subsequent tighter censorship regime that emerged around 1911–14 in response to a new political administration that feared cinema's increased influence and systematically targeted longer, more narratively integrated films. While these battles over the medium's aesthetics, content, and social force revealed politicians' concerns about cinema's more central role in urban life, it should be noted that these figures were not necessarily representative of public sentiment, hence the backlash over the city's censorship regime under Major M. L. C. Funkhouser and Mayor Carter Harrison II.

Censorship arrived in 1907 during the fiction-film led nickelodeon boom. It was strengthened in 1910 when the one-reel drama became the new standard and again in 1913, after the emergence of serials and early features. The punitive 1913–17 censorship regime coincided with the film industry's most concerted attempts at uplift, seen in feature-length adaptations of stage and literary classics as well as the debut of newsreels. These films' increased power and influence likely explain why so many upper-class reformers and press barons, like the *Tribune*'s McCormicks, began lobbying the city to curb the medium's power in 1907, 1909, and, again, in 1913–15. Other more conservative social institutions similarly responded to cinema's increasingly powerful hold on audiences.[6] It is far from coincidental that the most vigorous fights over censorship occurred between 1914 and 1918, a time when movies were largely accepted, with some of the most contentious battles centering on respectable and well-reviewed films.

The history of Chicago's censorship board falls into three periods, each defined by a different mayoral regime. Although Republican mayors Fred A. Busse (1907–11) and William Hale Thompson (1915–23) did not consider cinema a major problem, Democrat mayor Carter Harrison II (1911–15) entered office pledging to clean up the city and deliver the strict censorship his allies in the reform community wanted, even though he had little personal animus toward cinema. He made significant changes, most notably appointing the notorious Major Funkhouser as head censor, setting the stage for arguably the nation's most pronounced conflict over cinema and morality. This censorship regime fruitlessly battled movies against a background of increasingly positive newspapers and magazine coverage. The board subsequently lost much of its power under Mayor Thompson, who ordered a commission to investigate its operations. Besides marking changes in political regimes, these censorship battles indicated residual uncertainty about how leisure might be annexed to social uplift. Censorship could be used punitively to keep cinema in its place, one that some reformers and politicians hoped would be marginal at best, a belief that defined the Funkhouser era.[7] Alternatively, it could be used for uplift, maintaining movies as a sanitized and healthy pastime, as was predominantly the case under both Busse and Thompson.

History of Chicago's Film Censorship

Like the neighborhood theater, Chicago's film censorship arose out of clean-up campaigns designed to distance the city from its earlier reputation for "vulgarity, crudeness and commercialism."[8] The most important were 1907's citywide cleanup and the 1910 Vice Commission, a landmark examination of urban vice and recreation. While the former led to censorship, the latter significantly changed its administration. Crackdowns on popular culture were important issues in the 1907 and 1911 mayoral elections, making them a central part of the public agenda while further testifying to the importance of leisure dur-

CHAPTER 5

ing the Progressive Era. As Lauren Rabinovitz points out, these battles over motion picture censorship constituted struggles over the direction of American culture: "In the process of determining what form regulation would take, the movies themselves became publicly defined as an important cultural institution. For movie audiences, for civic leaders, and for film industry entrepreneurs, basic notions about cinema became instituted through arguments about the moral regulation of the nickel theaters"[9] Still, there was little consensus about the movies' social role, even among those calling for film censorship. Some of Chicago's leading citizens, like Frederic Siedenburg, SJ, dean of the School of Sociology at Chicago's Loyola University, believed censorship was necessary because cinema was a *central* part of contemporary life: "The movie is an indispensible [*sic*] means of supplying a need of that sort and therefore it needs to be supervised just as we supervise our water supply and our milk supply. We ought to supervise the movie[s] . . . and have them comply with sane and legitimate standards . . . whatever is bad for moral health should be eliminated on the same principle that we eliminate what is bad for our physical health."[10]

Investigations into public amusements were a standard feature of the Progressive Era.[11] Even before the invention of cinema, Chicago's reformers had focused on the small Loop theaters that housed a variety of cheap and sometimes disreputable entertainments (like penny arcades). Located near the Levée (the segregated vice district), these attracted the poor, workers, and children, leading reformers to see them as dangerous places where the vulnerable could be lured into greater evils, like prostitution, alcohol, or drugs.[12] Reformers soon turned their attention to movies, which were subsequently blamed for Chicago's crime wave of late 1906–early 1907.[13] As Grieveson observes, "the audiences singled out by early reports about nickelodeons and the *Tribune* were part of a population that seemed to many middle-class Americans at the time visibly out of control."[14] During spring 1907, the *Tribune* published daily reports about motion pictures' potentially horrific influence, calling for tighter regulation and censorship.[15] The JPA, the City Club, and charity worker Sherman C. Kingsley mounted a series of investigations at the same time and drew the same conclusions—or rather searched for evidence to support their campaigns against cinema. All these reports were likely timed to influence that April's mayoral elections, as reformers and the press hoped to make film censorship a priority for the new administration. These campaigners were particularly vocal, as, for the first time, a mayor would now be elected for four years, not two. Groups consequently worked harder to get their concerns on the new mayor's agenda.

Many reformers were particularly concerned about cinema's influence on children, with the *Tribune*'s 1907 campaign against nickelodeons and the debates on film censorship it ignited both, linking movies to juvenile crime.[16] The Chicago City Club, a reform organization of middle-class men, ran their own investigations into the city's theaters, seeking to ban children under thirteen from attending films. They asked the courts to study the links between movies and juvenile crime, believing the medium's suggestive influence to be so strong that juveniles copied what they saw on screen—convictions underpinned by crowd theory. Their report (published April 1907) was one of the most important documents presented in support of film censorship in Chicago in 1907.[17] As it would be difficult to keep young people out of theaters, reformers insisted on a formal censorship process to make movies suitable for children.

Unofficial censorship emerged out of one of the city's larger cleanup campaigns conducted during February and March 1907, primarily to clean garbage from the streets, eliminate smoke, and improve air quality. Associations between this detritus and motion pictures were unmistakable. These preliminary measures allowed appointed police officers to view unreleased films in film exchanges' private viewing rooms, a process that, as George Kleine later recalled, "gradually crystallized into a formula which forbade certain kinds of action such as robbery, murder, and other crimes."[18] Although police supervision implicitly linked movies to crime, these officers were more broadminded than later censors and were not concerned with the cultural debates and questions about urban governance that preoccupied the later reform-filled board.

Mayor Busse

Censorship advocates were likely disappointed in the outcome of the mayoral election. Its victor, Mayor Fred A. Busse (Republican, 1907–

CHAPTER 5

11), was probusiness and had little interest in intervening in others' affairs, including cinema. Still, with the *Tribune*'s movie investigations in full force, he had to do something and hoped quick action would make the matter go away. Although Busse implemented the city's first official and mandatory film censorship, his board was moderate and his censors generally well regarded by the film industry. His opponents were more tenacious, however, and were not pleased with the way his censors effectively endorsed most mainstream American films from Trust companies.

On taking office, Busse assigned his new police chief, Shippy, to investigate downtown's beleaguered five-cent theaters and penny arcades, something intended as a temporary measure designed to silence cinema's critics. On May 1, 1907, the first day of Busse's administration, Shippy announced a new motion picture era:

> There will be no more moving pictures of "The Thaw Case" or of disrobing scenes. The police force has the power to take the license from any place giving an objectionable performance and henceforth no such places will be permitted. They cannot be stamped out in a day, but all of the places will be kept under surveillance, and any objectionable features will be stamped out as soon as they are found.[19]

Shippy put theaters under continual surveillance, a technique previously used for the city's dance halls.[20] Lieutenant Alexander McDonald was appointed to head a newly formed "nickel theater squad" and each day received Shippy's police reports on Loop movie houses. These ceremonies were largely orchestrated for the benefit of the local press, publicly demonstrating the new administration's actions as the mayor tried to please strict censorship advocates without alienating exhibitors.

On his first day in office, McDonald met with the City Club's commission on charitable reform and penal institutions and with its chair, Sherman C. Kingsley, launched a combined effort "to suppress what the new [police] chief considers one of the greatest evils in the city"—cheap theaters attracting children with suggestive films. The investigating officers, sergeants Miller and Muchowski, voiced then standard complaints about cinema's influence on child audiences, but, significantly, they indicated that the problem was already under control:

> A penny arcade at 129 South Clark street, conducted by Samuel Schwartz . . . contained moving pictures of a dance unfit for any young person to see. The sergeant's report intimated that many of the immoral pictures recently had been removed from the places visited, but he said that there were still some suggestive features to be found. These . . . were to be seen at 276, 288, 388, 310 and 329 State street. Sergeant Miller reported objectionable pictures in the arcades at 252, 278 340 State Street . . . "Some good may have been accomplished already," said Mr. Kingsley . . . "The reports . . . show conditions that should not be tolerated in any civilized community. In all sections of the city these places have been in operation and have worked for evil among the children who have been lured inside their doors. We are glad to co-operate with the police department, and I am certain that much good will be accomplished."[21]

The city simultaneously cracked down on live theater's Friday "amateur nights," particularly those featuring children singing and dancing between reels that violated child labor laws and the attendant social prohibitions on looking at child performers.[22] A little over a week later, Busse and Shippy announced plans to censor five-cent theaters, ordering the destruction of "any pictures . . . of a morbid or criminal nature." They assigned "Ten detectives, commanded by a lieutenant . . . to maintain the censorship," forming the first de facto censorship board six months before censorship was officially implemented.[23]

Just one month later, in June 1907, McDonald pronounced the experiment a success. The 158 five-cent theaters and vaudeville houses his men had under "constant watch" and "whose patrons are, for the most part children," had evidently improved their shows: "Where formerly pictures of the 'train robber' type were exhibited, more instructive and still equally amusing are now used."[24] This sudden transformation in film content seems unlikely, instead suggesting that Busse had no interest in further action and believed he had taken sufficient steps to manage the procensorship lobby.

The local press and their allies in the reform community were not placated, however, and stepped up their protests. In May 1907, at the height of Busse and Shippy's investigations, the *Chicago Daily Tribune* published its famous anticinema editorial, demanding stringent mu-

CHAPTER 5

nicipal regulation and censorship and calling the mayor's recent actions inadequate.[25] At this time, Chicago's newspapers were among the most hostile to cinema in the nation.[26] They had a vested interest in containing cinema's popularity partly because they were in the midst of a circulation war that would lead to the collapse of several titles and the June 1914 merger of three dailies (the *Record-Herald*, *Inter-Ocean*, and *Times*) into the new *Chicago Herald*. Perceiving movies as a rival and a threat, they linked cinema to crime, vice, mental decline, and urban decay. The situation only changed in 1913–14, as publishers increasingly realized that film stars, story serialization, and film reviews drew readers and advertisers.[27] Nonetheless, the *Tribune* and *American* continued to demand strict censorship well into 1914, seeing movies as a threat to their authority, especially after film companies started producing newsreels.

Despite pressure from the press and reformers, it took several months before official censorship was established.[28] In June 1907, Alderman John Z. Uhlir first proposed that a police board censor all films to be shown in the city, something that appeared possibly unconstitutional and in excess of the city's powers. The bill moved to the report stage before being passed in November.[29] In the interim, leading reform groups like the JPA, the Relief and Aid Society, and Hull House voluntarily helped police patrol local nickelodeons. They worked with Shippy's theater and dance hall inspectors, removing disreputable films from downtown five-cent houses and releasing reports to sympathetic papers, like the *Tribune*.[30] Once again, they claimed the number of sensational films shown in Chicago's theaters had recently surged and demanded the city censor motion pictures.

On November 4, 1907, film censorship was finally made official as part of a three-pronged municipal program designed to improve the city and maintain physical, social, and moral order.[31] As such, it was not solely established as a repressive enterprise but as part of a general plan of uplift. Grieveson points out that the Chicago board moved their "focus from building regulations to the regulation of morality," adding, "Shifting focus to a policing of representation, the censorship ordinance marks an important moment, and innovation, in the development of a structure of governance for cinema."[32] Now distributors would have to get a permit for a film and send a copy to the police censor board. To administer this new regime, the city created a ten-man board headed by the general superintendent of police to issue permits for commercial motion picture exhibition. Its head censor was initially appointed annually, although this changed under subsequent administrations. Prior censorship was now mandatory for all films shown citywide, except those shown by religious organizations, educational establishments, libraries, museums, or private societies—exemptions that later allowed the notorious Major Funkhouser to show reformers material cut from films to rally support for his cause.[33] Distributors would have to cut any footage the city found offensive and physically present it to the censor to get a permit. For this they were charged fifty cents per film (raised to $1 under Major Funkhouser). As there was initially no written record describing the approved print, enforcement was problematic.[34] More controversially, there were no specific guidelines regarding acceptable content, leading to widespread critique.

Local exhibitors fought back, charging the city with illegal behavior and un-American conduct. In May 1908, exhibitor Jacob Block filed a suit in the superior court (the *Block* case) claiming "the city ordinance prohibiting the exhibition of moving pictures without a permit from the chief of police is held to be class legislation."[35] He claimed the ordinance was unconstitutional because it discriminated against moving pictures and did not apply to all entertainments.[36] Some debates were quelled when this case came to court and the Illinois Supreme Court authorized the city's censorship in April 1909.[37] It stated:

1. The City has power to regulate the motion picture business;
2. That an ordinance passed under express powers can not [*sic*] be held void or unreasonable;
3. That the ordinance is not invalid because the Chief of Police is to determine whether or not the pictures are obscene or immoral;
4. That the ordinance prohibiting the exhibition of immoral or obscene pictures is not invalid because it fixes no definite or certain standard;
5. That a picture may be immoral, although it illustrates scenes connected with history; and
6. That a person is not deprived of his constitutional rights without due process of law when not permitted to show a picture that violates the provisions of the ordinance.[38]

CHAPTER 5

The Illinois Supreme Court decided not to affix a standard of morality or define the meaning of "obscenity," however. This decision allowed censors to ban films on seemingly subjective grounds, making appeals difficult. This lack of specificity remained a central issue for several years, leading to lawsuits and charges of caprice, corruption, and abuse.[39] Legal challenges targeting both the board's operations and its constitutionality continued throughout its years of operation, culminating in the 1917–18 public hearings that radically curtailed the censors' powers.

Although they welcomed the new board, reformers and the local press (especially the *Tribune*) immediately complained that it was too lax. The film industry initially endorsed it, recognizing censorship could support their efforts at uplift.[40] They were also pleased because the censors focused on their rivals, including market-leading Pathé, and emergent independent producers. As Richard Abel has shown, attacks on foreign films reveal how cinema was linked to the period's investment in constructing a "'morally superior' national identity."[41] During the board's early days, Chicago's censors found particular fault with films that were based on foreign materials (including Shakespeare) or were too "exotic."[42] Abel notes that French cinema (and European films more generally) subsequently acquired a contradictory reputation as potentially both high quality art or as morally lax, sensational, and distasteful. Making matters worse, Chicago's ethnic audiences often preferred Pathé films because they had few intertitles, troubling reformers because cinema was the most influential entertainment in immigrant communities.[43] Yet the paradoxical position of European films was also underscored in the popularity of Pathé titles among reformers (like Jane Addams), again revealing minimal consensus about film content.[44]

Even after the head censor changed, attacks on foreign film continued. In 1908, Joel Smith replaced censor McDonald. Smith particularly disliked foreign culture and handled American melodramas more leniently than their foreign counterparts, although he was toughest on American-made films adapted from European material.[45] In one widely reported decision, he cut two feet of *Macbeth* because he considered "Shakespeare's exuberant imagination . . . too strong for babies and sucklings." Footage of Macbeth stabbing the sleeping king and wiping his blade on his pantaloons was removed because it was too realistic and violent for children, with Smith explaining, "you never see that on the stage, but the film-makers stuck it in to improve the piece." He protested French films' fondness for detailed love affairs and complained that Italian films cared "more for knifing and blood."[46] In June 1908 the *Record-Herald* argued that Smith was blinded by his patriotism, referring to his fondness for the Second Amendment. Although guns were banned from the city's screens, "the lieutenant's loyalty to the history of his country will not permit him to place the ban on the cowboy's six-shooter," on the grounds that "a cow-puncher don't look real without his arsenal."[47] This kind of inconsistency made the censor's decisions appear random and subjective with Smith's lowbrow tastes, lack of familiarity with European literature, and fondness for popular American drama, giving Chicago's censors an early reputation for mindless "butchery." In one of the earliest defenses of cinema from a Chicago newspaper, the *Record-Herald* attacked Smith for blocking cinema's attempts to become a mature art: "He has been greatly shocked at the innate depravity of the modern French school, and even Shakespeare he views askance. He dotes on plays like *East Lynne* and *Damon and Pythias* because they satisfy his ethical sense. He believes that art should be made the handmaiden of morality, but he doubts whether it is."[48] The other local titles disagreed, however, claiming that Smith gave too much latitude to sensational American films, prompting yet another series of reform investigations and calls for tougher censorship.

The *Tribune* and its reform allies responded to the formation of the censorship board by stepping up attacks on cinema. Finding the censors too lax, they lobbied for stricter standards. In tandem with local churches, they investigated local theaters and published scandalous stories about the movies to keep pressure on the city. Many clergy were upset that censorship did not include provisions about preserving the sanctity of each faith. Movies threatened their social and spiritual leadership, particularly in immigrant neighborhoods where the neighborhood theater had usurped the church or synagogue's position.[49] Between 1907 and 1914, many clergy sermonized against motion pictures, with the *Tribune* dutifully reporting their words. On May 16, 1908, the Reverend John W. Powers called on Chicago's Catholic laity to oppose cinema, dubbing the five-cent theater a "sink-hole of vice" and "one of

CHAPTER 5

the greatest forces for immorality among children."⁵⁰ A week later, the Reverend J. F. Callaghan of Saint Malachy's Roman Catholic Church (Western Avenue and Walnut Street) denounced the movie theater "as a demoralizer of the young," adding that "parents who permit their boys and girls to frequent these places without investigating the environment . . . were as traitorous to their country as is the man 'who would tear the flag from the staff and trample upon it.'"⁵¹ He urged parents and the city to take a greater role, noting that "priests are not policemen, but it is your duty—a duty you owe to God, to your home and to your country—to bring your children up to be good citizens. And that you cannot do if you permit them to roam the streets at night."⁵² Many of these sermons revealed widespread fear that cinema derailed immigrants' "correct" assimilation, threatening national identity in the process.⁵³

Despite continued press hostility, Mayor Busse appointed another moderate figure in November 1908 as the next year's censor. Sergeant Charles E. O'Donnell quickly became known in the trades as a man who elevated the medium without unnecessary interference, being "broad minded and . . . familiar with the motion picture industry." He only banned pictures that tended "towards obscenity or morbid sensationalism" and considered cinema a vast improvement over rivals like the saloon.⁵⁴ Significantly (and with a definite nod to neighborhood theaters), he called the movies a "boon to any community," noting that the medium "affords entertainment for young and old and my observation has been that it has a tendency to bring together parents and children who spend the evening in the neighborhood picture house."⁵⁵ His faith in cinema's ability to strengthen community and family infuriated the by-now familiar antimovie coalition of press, reformers, and the church, leading to more press outrage while increasing reformers' efforts to show that the medium was fundamentally immoral.

O'Donnell made the censorship process more systematic. For the first time, the board kept a complete record of each film, including the date of its inspection, and details of excised footage were recorded on the permit. Each print was stamped several times with the city's seal of approval and each reel given its own certificate. If permits were lost, officials could now ensure that only properly censored prints were shown.⁵⁶ Any violation would lead to the film's confiscation, a fine, and possible imprisonment for the distributor or exhibitor. Through this process, O'Donnell tackled an important problem that his predecessors had overlooked. Because Chicago was a national film distribution center, exchanges usually replaced the excised footage in prints intended for out-of-town exhibition. As a result, uncut films circulated within the city. O'Donnell forced exchanges to destroy objectionable footage. Still, this new system could not be fully implemented until the Illinois Supreme Court found for the city in the *Block* case in March 1909, as this suit threatened the board's existence.[57] While the board's new processes were undoubtedly more rigorous, the censors were still interested in uplifting the medium, eliminating films that brought the industry into disrepute and holding wayward distributors in line.[58]

Later in 1909, the Chicago board faced another challenge from the new Motion Picture Patents Company (MPPC)–supported National Board of Censorship of Motion Pictures (later the National Board of Review). Yet reformers preferred local censorship, as it was more open to their influence, seeing the national board as an industry-sponsored attack on the city's regulation.[59] Supported by a levy from each reel of film reviewed (the MPPC and, later, Mutual, Universal, and a number of other exchanges submitted all films prior to release), the board produced cinema's educational pamphlets describing improvements in movies to offset local and national censorship.[60] Even though many renowned northeastern reformers supported the national board, they had already promoted movies as a force for communal good—like John Collier, secretary of the People's Institute of New York and Orrin G. Cocks of the Laity League of the Federation of Churches. The board also had links to the People's Institute, an uplift-minded reform group, which organized cut-price screenings of "quality" films as reputable entertainment.[61] Indeed, the national board was not interested in prohibition but in establishing an overall moral content, as Grieveson observes: "Regulation by the board was not simply repressive . . . but was *productive* of a certain configuration of filmic discourse and of particular narrative patterns, fundamentally encouraging filmmaking based on a moral discourse."[62] As many of Chicago's reformers believed cinema had no positive value, they now threw themselves behind the Chicago board, which had no industry affiliation and could potentially implement strict censorship.[63] Still, they did not necessarily approve of its current operations, which essentially followed the same uplifting ideals as the national board.

Many Chicago reformers launched new high-profile investigations into cinema, like the Juvenile Protective Association's 1909 survey, to force the city to implement stricter censorship.[64] Under Louise de Koven Bowen's supervision, JPA workers made 1,156 visits to 298 of Chicago's 405 "cheap theaters," where they found an unspecified "demoralized condition of affairs and 216 violations of the law," which they reported to local authorities.[65] Particular concerns included the "lurid advertisements and sensational posters" that attracted crowds of children outside theaters; the late hours of shows; the cheap ticket prices; poor ventilation, darkness, and inadequate exits; and the popularity of films containing "scenes of brutality and revenge calculated to arouse coarse and brutal emotions" that had slipped past lax censors:[66]

> The Juvenile Protective Association would report a film of this kind to the Chief of Police and it would be removed at once, but it would turn up shortly in another part of town, and would again be reported. The Association, feeling that it was necessary to take some decisive step in the matter, found that an ordinance had been passed previously which provided that a censorship committee should be appointed by the Chief of Police and that every film should be passed upon by this committee and signed by the Chief before it could be shown in a licensed theater; also that a license to show the film should be posted in the theater.[67]

Considering the scope of the JPA investigation (and their 1911 follow-up), it is disappointing to find few details in their report. Still, the city's censors responded with temporarily tighter standards, infuriating the film industry. The trade press pointed to such absurd decisions as December 1909's ban on Centaur's children's film *Santa Claus and the Miner's Child*, even though there was "nothing gruesome, repulsive or immoral about it," with the *Moving Picture World* demanding, "The action of the Chicago police . . . calls for some explanation."[68] Although this clampdown was temporary, the Chicago board would later earn a reputation for capricious and heavy-handed actions as well as for its willful inability to evaluate film as art after the election of Mayor Harrison in 1915. A new mayoral administration and a major investigation into urban leisure produced these changes as the city established a new Morals Court that took over film censorship, giving reformers, not police, jurisdiction over its operation.

Carter Harrison II, Major M. L. C. Funkhouser, the Vice Commission, and the Morals Court

By 1910, Chicago's censors were under attack from all sides: reformers, churches, the press, and the film industry. The 1910 Vice Commission offered one way out of this impasse, even though its main focus lay elsewhere. Conducted by a group of "men and women who command the respect of the public at large," the Vice Commission was a major investigation into the city's saloons, amusement parks, dance halls, and brothels.[69] It was dissolved on June 1, 1911, and a book-length study of its findings (published later that year as *The Social Evil in Chicago*) recommended tighter surveillance and regulation of working-class/ immigrant leisure to eliminate urban vice.[70] In response, the city united reformers, local politicians, city officials, leaders of organized religion, the police, university-trained social workers, and sociologists in a comprehensive program to manage all forms of public amusement. Besides implementing more regulation (censorship, building ordinances) and supervision (organized community playgrounds, settlement houses, church-sponsored recreation), the city funded more "healthy" and uplifting collective amusements (like those offered in settlement houses, university extension classes, or church-sponsored outings).

The report's most visible outcome was the closing of the segregated vice district on November 1912 that was replaced by the Morals Court in April 1913 after a series of public hearings.[71] The first court of its kind nationwide, it was established to prosecute crimes against public morality *and* to oversee cheap public amusements, including cinema, testifying to the reform community's belief that these issues were closely linked.[72] Movies were now bracketed together with vice as film censorship was placed under the Morals Court's jurisdiction and the police board replaced with reformers. After the court failed to reduce vice and affiliated crimes—which were clearly not easily resolved—it focused on film censorship, which it tackled with aggressive zeal.[73]

CHAPTER 5

Significantly, the Vice Commission's report barely mentioned cinema, yet its findings formed the blueprint for the city's new leisure ordinances—including film censorship. Movies were only mentioned once in the over-four-hundred-page report in an unnamed social worker's testimony that the city repeated many times to justify its actions:[74]

> I think the nickel theaters have an immoral tendency. While I believe some are instructive, the general tendency is towards immorality. I know a good many of my young girls have told me their first wrong came when they attended nickel theaters. . . . I think the nickel theater is a recruiting station for vice. In the first place, from the pictures often shown there; in the second place from the association. Often young people are without supervision, and it is an easy matter for a wrong character to get acquainted with a girl. Evil minded men can very easily make an acquaintance there, when it wouldn't be possible under other circumstances.[75]

Even here, cinema is treated with ambivalence—at worst, movies were seen as a gateway to other "evils." This testimonial was just one person's opinion and was not supported by any evidence, indicating that cinema was not the threat to public morals that the censors believed.

The city's interpretation of the Vice Commission's report was tactical and owed much to change in the city's administration. Although Mayor Busse had established the Vice Commission, its findings were implemented under his successor, Democrat Carter Harrison II (1911–15). Film censorship was an important part of his social agenda and was at the forefront of the city's subsequent crackdown on vice. The gap between what was acceptable in Chicago and the rest of the nation increased under his administration, prompting an onslaught of lawsuits and widespread criticism of the city's censors. Instead of establishing community standards, Harrison's board displayed its distance from public tastes through its hostility toward cinema.

The election of a new mayor in 1911 transformed the city's censorship regime. During the 1910 elections, Carter Harrison II campaigned as the man who would clean up the city, a task he claimed Busse had neglected. Part of a local political dynasty, Harrison and his father would share the period's record for the longest terms as the city's mayor

(Harrison Sr., 1879–86; Harrison II, 1897–1904, 1911–15).[76] Harrison II was an avowed vice crusader: in his first term, he had tackled saloons and fruitlessly attempted to close the Levée's brothels, making him the reformers' choice—the man whose record qualified him to act on the Vice Commission's pending recommendations.[77] Throughout his campaign, he reminded voters that thousands-strong groups like the Women's Christian Temperance Union and the Church Federation had to force the reluctant Busse to tackle vice.[78] He promised to do things differently. On election, he immediately closed bookmakers, removed prostitutes from Michigan Avenue, closed "call houses and cheap hotels on the avenue from 12th to 35th streets," and, most symbolically, shut down the city's finest and most visible brothel, the Everleigh Club.[79] Movies were his next target, leading to his wholesale revision of city censorship.

In January 1912, Harrison started tightening Chicago's censorship codes, amending the law to allow the city to confiscate "immoral" films and punish "any person putting objectionable films into circulation." Any person circulating or exhibiting a prohibited film could be fined $50 to $200 per offense, and the film would be confiscated. Appeals could only be made to the mayor, and his decision was final, giving Harrison more authority over cinema than his predecessor.[80] The code was now deliberately punitive, although its severity was initially tempered by chief censor Jeremiah O'Connor (a Busse appointee), who had won the industry's respect for "his admiration for good picture subjects" and for recommending his son's boarding school install a movie theater.[81] But he was soon forced to act differently in the face of rumors that he was to be replaced, although he managed to keep his job for another year.[82] Under pressure, O'Connor announced a review of all films over six months old in February 1912, highlighting the stricter standards now in place. Distributors and exhibitors would now have to pay for new permits at fifty cents per print (and in the event exhibitors lost them, another fifty cents for a replacement).[83] The new system outraged the film industry, as the *Moving Picture World* observed:

> Motion picture companies selling in Chicago . . . are complaining bitterly over the treatment received at the hands of the city police censorship board.

CHAPTER 5

>Of late, the police department has tightened the reins almost to breaking point. Not only are all murders, suicides, burglaries, confidence games, etc., which always have received the official ban, barred, but many little incidents essential to the story, are seized upon by police inspectors and ordered out.[84]

Despite the board's new severity, the *Tribune*, *Evening American*, and *Chicago Examiner* stepped up attacks on motion pictures, aware that the mayor was on their side, with the *Examiner* chastising O'Connor (dubbed "a careless, indifferent, unthinking official") for his leniency toward "exhibitions of a crime-provoking nature."[85]

More wholesale changes were afoot. In December 1912 the city created the new office of second deputy of police to head the censor board and announced that eleven specially appointed fellow censors would replace the police as part of the board's migration to the Morals Court.[86] As the 1907 ordinance was not repealed, there was some confusion about who was in charge: the general superintendent of police, the mayor, or the new second deputy?[87] As head of the board since 1911, O'Connor was the first person appointed second deputy of police, but he was at the end of his term and under increased attack from reformers, their newspaper allies, and the mayor.[88] He was not representative of the new regime, but in a vain attempt to placate his critics, he made two decisions that alienated his allies.[89] In 1912 he ordered a store not to display the painting *September Morn* because it showed a naked human figure, leading many newspapers to mock him as a philistine. His new disregard for artistic license was further demonstrated in his March 1913 banning of *The Miracle* (1912), directed by the acclaimed theater director Max Reinhardt from a play by the 1911 Nobel Prize–winning Belgian symbolist dramatist Maurice Maeterlink. Even the *Tribune* condemned this decision as "excessive and unenlightened."[90] The writing was on the wall. As James McQuade noted, "What with women's societies pestering him about laxity in the discharge of his duties and soreheads kicking because of the cut-outs insisted upon in various films . . . it would seem as if his cup were already full. . . . *He is a victim of conditions*" (my emphasis).[91]

O'Connor tried to defend himself. He claimed that any apparent inconsistencies in his judgments derived from the conditions under which films were viewed. He told *Motography*'s Mabel Condon that he was too short-staffed to cope with the vastly increased number of releases, a complaint that was likely true: "there is always better censorship . . . when I can assign my men in pairs to view films. But with only ten men and an almost hourly demand for them every day, I can only send one."[92] If an inspector had any doubts about a film, it was screened again in front of O'Connor and one or two of his men, adding to their workload. Still, he tried to be objective, appointing men who were "broad minded . . . and unprejudiced."[93] But this was not what Harrison wanted. On March 22, 1913, he appointed a new second deputy, Major M. L. C. Funkhouser, and there was speculation he would name a new board, alarming the city's exhibitors and distributors.[94] Despite insisting "there would be no changes," Funkhouser quickly overhauled the entire process.[95]

Funkhouser

Funkhouser's appointment came about partly as a result of institutional change. In March 1913, Harrison had placed the city's censorship board under the jurisdiction of the Morals Court, which his friend and ally Funkhouser already headed. Under this leadership, the Morals Court had turned away from policing organized vice and toward regulating popular amusements, particularly "moving picture theaters of both the loop and outlying districts. The Levée—south, west, and north sides. Café and restaurant cabarets [and] dance halls."[96] Funkhouser disliked popular culture and cracked down on it. He banned the tango from downtown cafés and prohibited dancing in restaurants as of midnight on August 29, 1913.[97] He regulated fashion, banning the translucent chiffon and figure-hugging dresses, slit skirts, and skirtless swimming costumes that accommodated women's increased physical activity and arrested offenders, despite Jane Addams's protests that "the less clothes we can wear with modesty the better."[98] As head of the film censorship board, he attacked cinema with the same zeal, his tenure representing the board's most visible, harsh, powerful, and controversial period. An ex-military man who valued traditional morality, Funkhouser believed in rigorous policing, prosecution, and the careful surveillance of all places where crime and wrongdoing potentially lingered.[99] He was

CHAPTER 5

particularly proud of his German American heritage and aggressively opposed to America entering the Great War on the Allied side, later using his position to advance his own ideas on the war, patriotism, and national identity, as discussed in chapter 7.

Funkhouser had previously worked with the Chicago Women's Club on their fight against commercialized vice and was well liked by the most conservative reformers.[100] After his appointment, he immediately called a meeting on censorship, inviting representatives from local churches, schools, and newspapers, and legal and medical experts and reformers. In an unusual show of grace, he even called on film industry personnel to form an advisory delegation.[101] But this meeting was staged to present him as fair and neutral, a man who responded to the community's needs and standards. He soon made it clear that in its current state, cinema was compatible with neither. In July 1913, he called Chicago "a moral city," and proclaimed that the only reason moviegoers had tolerated "low caliber" films was "because they had to take what the managers offered."[102] He claimed his tougher censorship had already greatly increased patronage at neighborhood theaters because he censored films based "on the theory that four fifths of the patrons of moving picture houses are children, and films that would be all right for older persons are cut out on that account."[103] He neglected to mention other reasons for this increase—including nationwide surges in audiences, more lavish theaters, and the rise of the star system.

Under his jurisdiction, film censorship followed a strict and punitive path that was increasingly out of touch with public perceptions—in Chicago and across the nation—of movies as respectable entertainment that met community standards. Funkhouser announced censorship would be guided by "four fundamental rules," banning films that "depict crime, show degradation of women, ridicule constituted authority or make heroes of criminals," but extended his reach far beyond this.[104] The severity of his regime was manifested through changes in the board's constitution and operations. He immediately banned censors from socializing with film company employees, claiming that such activities had previously resulted in "certain manufacturers getting permits for pictures."[105] In October 1913 he called the police censors inept, largely because they allowed many film companies' appeals, and asked Mayor Harrison to replace the police board with a new group of

Oversight and Regulation

censors hired as civil servants, allowing Funkhouser to appoint friends and like-minded associates.[106] Even some advocates of strict censorship critiqued his actions. In December 1913, the Women's National Council dubbed Chicago "a prudish old maid" after witnessing the censors' work.[107]

The film industry quickly responded. On November 8, 1913, Chicago's distributors and exhibitors held a conference to organize its members and hired prominent local attorneys Henry J. Toner and David K. Toner.[108] One member noted:

> During the week ending November 3, it is stated [Funkhouser] killed seventeen subjects, some of which were features, also cut about fifteen others to such an extent the story of the film was injured. In the past a film has been passed by one censor and killed by another . . . *In organizing it is not the intention of the motion picture interests to do away with censorship, but merely to get clean intelligent and just censorship.* (My emphasis)[109]

Matters only got worse. In February 1914, Funkhouser appointed "clergymen, representatives of various civic welfare, social uplift, and other reform organizations" to his censorship board.[110] For three months, these temporary hires, Funkhouser's friends and allies, replaced O'Connor's police officers while he searched for ten new appointees and waited for them to pass their civil service exams. The interim censors included some of the city's (and the world's) most renowned reformers (table 5.1).

They were joined by less well-known reformers Mrs. George M. Shirk, Mrs. Charles G. Snow, and Kate Addams.[111] Funkhouser subsequently added theater magnate William A. Brady to the board. At the time, Brady repeatedly shared his dislike of cinema with the press. In January 1914, for instance, he told the *Chicago Examiner*, "The people are tired of moving pictures with their butcher-actors."[112] Aghast at his appointment, the *Moving Picture World* lamented: "William A. Brady [who] has shown his bias against moving pictures, has been selected as one of the members of the censor board in Chicago . . . What next?"[113] Ironically, a career in the film industry: Brady then formed World Pictures, one of the leading production companies of the mid-late 1910s that featured his daughter, Alice, among its most popular stars.

CHAPTER 5

Table 5.1

Name	Occupation	Biography
Gertrude Howe Britton	Director and superintendent of the Bureau of Social Service of Cook County, Marriage and Divorce Division	Health expert and author, active member of the JPA, senior worker at Hull House.*
Louise de Koven Bowen	President of the JPA, vice president of the United States Charities, treasurer and trustee of Hull House	Author of several books; member of the Chicago Women's Club, the Friday Club, the Fortnightly, and the Women's City Club.**
Mrs. Herman Landauer	Chair of the Ordinance Committee of the Reform Department of the Chicago Woman's Club	Author of *Ordinances You Ought To Know*.***
Minnie Low	Superintendent of the Bureau of Personal Service	Charter member and founder of the Chicago Council of Social Agencies; "a recognized leader in the welfare field" specializing in the care of "defective" and dependent children.****
Frederic Siedenburg, SJ	Dean of the School of Sociology at Loyola University	
Dr. Graham Taylor	Professor of social economics, University of Chicago Theological Seminary	One of the nation's most respected reformers. Cofounder of the Chicago Settlement.*****
Harriet Vittum	Head resident, Northwestern University Settlement	Ardent campaigner for suffrage and children's rights. Independent candidate for Alderman of the 17th Ward, 1914.******

192

Name	Occupation	Biography
Mrs. Virginia Brooks Washburn	Founder and first president of the Hammond Settlement	Renowned local lecturer, Member of the Women's City Club.*******

Notes

* Valeria D. McDermott and Annie Elizabeth Trotter, *Chicago Social Services Directory* (Chicago: Burmeister Printing Corporation, 1915).
** Agness G. Gilman and Gertrude M. Gilman, *Who's Who in Illinois: Women-Makers of History* (Chicago: Eclectic Publishers, 1927), 48–49.
*** Frank and Hofer Jerome, *The Annals of the Chicago Women's Club for the First Forty Years of Its Organization, 1876–1916*, 297.
**** Kathleen McCarthy, *Noblesse Oblige: Charity and Cultural Philanthropy in Chicago, 1849–1929* (Chicago: University of Chicago Press, 1982), 137.
***** *Who's Who in America*, vol. 8 (Chicago: Albert Nelson Marquis, 1914–15), 2308.
****** *Report of the Chicago Motion Picture Commission*, 74; McDermott and Trotter, *Chicago Social Services Directory*; Gilman and Gilman, *Who's Who in Illinois: Women-Makers of History*, 243.
******* *Who's Who in America*, vol. 8, 286.

In March 1914, Funkhouser selected six of his ten new censors from names submitted by allies in the city's women's clubs, social settlement workers, and leading reform groups. Despite his earlier insistence that all censors should be civil servants, this group (Miss Eva Loeb, Mrs. Christine Field, Mrs. G. F. Karr, Miss Katherine A. Birmingham, Mrs. Florence B. Kirk, and Samuel Block) was hired before passing their exams.[114] On March 13, 1914, three more censors were appointed for a year: Reverend Archibald J. Carey, Wallace Rice, and John S. Dankowski. Rice, a newspaperman and member of the Press Club of Chicago, left almost immediately, claiming defective eyesight. The two other appointments were made to heighten the board's racial and ethnic sensitivities. German and Polish organizations recommended Dankowski, while Carey, a leading African American reformer and minister of the Institutional Church (West Thirty-Eighth and South Dearborn Streets) had an impressive record fighting racial inequality.[115] Funkhouser would not comment on Carey's appointment, but noted

CHAPTER 5

that it "followed the receipt of several requests."[116] Each received an annual salary of $1,320, for which they were expected to work eight-hour days with Funkhouser retaining the right to veto their decisions.[117] Some temporary appointees, including Louise de Koven Bowen, Gertrude Howe Britton, and members of the City Club were retained as part of a new censorship advisory board.[118] The board was reorganized again in September 1914. For the first time, positions were open to the public; 235 people applied with twenty-five passing the civil service exams, including three standing members (Block, Kirk, and Loeb).[119] The old censors advised them, preserving the board's conservative tastes.[120]

The board's activities were widely publicized during this time. Although standards were tightened during Funkhouser's initial months in office, the censorship process remained the same, guided by the 1911 rulings of the Illinois Supreme Court.[121] All pictures now had to be censored from the perspective of a child, and any references to white slavery and gunplay were banned.[122] Films were watched by at least three censors with Funkhouser recording eliminations and confiscating the offending footage rather than keeping detailed records of approved prints.[123] Most films were scrutinized in a new municipal screening room on the tenth floor of City Hall, although censors still visited local theaters to ensure only authorized prints were shown.[124]

As censorship became more extreme during spring 1914, the *Tribune* and *Herald* published daily lists of "cut-outs" so the public could read about the scenes they were not allowed to watch. Much of it makes little sense as no plot information was given, but the point was clear—most cuts were irrational. Eliminated footage featured scenes of murder, violence, bribery, child kidnapping, vice, gambling, women smoking cigarettes, excessive drinking or drunkenness, indecent or excessive exposure of male or female bodies, "table dances," tangoing, people being overpowered by wild animals, and shots of money or stamps.[125] Other cuts included reductions in the length of kisses, embraces, and battles while even elliptical suggestions of crime, sexuality, or any other sensitive topic were eliminated. Titles were removed if they featured religious, ethnic, or racial slurs, or substituted for, referred to, or clarified any acts of violence, crime, or immorality. Films were completely rejected if the police or "constituted authority" were shown in a negative light, if the main protagonists were immoral, criminals, or prostitutes, if they glorified crime or insulted any established religion or ethnicity.[126]

While the *Tribune* initially used these cut-outs to vindicate the censors' actions, their details soon reflected badly on the city. There were so many cuts for petty or inane reasons that readers likely laughed, if the tone of press coverage is any guide. By mid-1914, even the *Tribune* followed the *Herald*'s lead in ridiculing the process, indicating that the censors—not the film industry—were out of touch with the community. Tighter censorship led to another series of lawsuits.[127] On December 20, 1913, the World's Special Film Corporation, Mutual Film Corporation, H. & H. Film Service, and August Zilligen filed a forty-one-page complaint in the federal court. They wanted censorship abolished on the grounds that it was unconstitutional (they listed eight grounds) and called for the abolition of the fifty-cent permit.[128] They lost their case on June 1, 1914.[129] Three days later, another exchange, the Trans-Oceanic Film Company, sued the city's censors for banning five of their films in six days (the low-budget three-reelers *Slaves of Morphine, Mendel Beilis, Lieutenant Saring, Gorky, the Dragon*, and the four-reel *The Magic Veil*).[130] In February 1914, Mutual (the industry leader in fighting censorship ordinances through the courts) filed a second injunction with the United States District Court restraining the city of Chicago, chief of police Gleason, and Major Funkhouser from unconstitutionally "interfering with their films." In language echoing the landmark *Mutual v. Ohio* case, they claimed that

> Gleason has delegated censorship powers bestowed on him to a deputy [Funkhouser]; That such censorship deprives the Mutual [film company] of liberty without due process of the law, and prevents a jury trial of disputed films; That the ordinance gives judicial powers to the police; That the exaction of a fee is not properly an inspection tax and is an unnecessary one on interstate commerce; That the Mutual purchases or produces no films that are obscene, riotous, immoral or indecent.[131]

By November 1914, local film organizations had moved their challenge to the state level, even writing a bill for a state board "which will have complete authority and will do away with the local . . . censors."[132] This bill also failed, leaving the city's board unchallenged.

CHAPTER 5

Significantly, many of these challenges accepted censorship in theory but not its current form. In February 1914, the Amusement Protective League, a trade organization representing all aspects of the film industry, composed a censorship ordinance that it placed "before the Board of Aldermen empowering Mayor Harrison to appoint a board of three censors, instead of having the censoring done by one man, as at present."[133] Headed by Funkhouser's old antagonist, Joseph Hopp, the league was backed by industry heavyweights like Mutual, Laemmle Film Service, Warner's Features, Famous Players Film Company, and the General Film Company. They proposed strategies to fight the current regime, including raising audience awareness with slides stating: "Should any picture be exhibited on this screen that is in any way disconnected, ask your alderman. He knows why."[134] Other picture men opted to stand for local office: in February 1914, the Motion Picture Operators' Union's Mr. Baker and Joseph Hopp, head of the Union Film Company, both ran for alderman.[135]

Funkhouser stepped up his assault. To prevent theaters showing uncensored prints, he went undercover, accompanied by a coterie of reformers. These infamous visits became known as "raids" and were widely condemned.[136] He was twice prohibited from policing theaters in this way (in April 1914 and May 1915), only to have the privilege quickly reinstated.[137] Still, the city's status as a distribution center and its proximity to two other state lines justified his paranoia, as some theaters obtained prints meant for distribution outside Chicago, most often the "Wisconsin Copies" that were uncensored and could easily travel over state lines. If caught, exchanges usually claimed an office boy or messenger had sent the wrong version.[138]

This combination of aggressive censorship and unwavering press coverage made Funkhouser's board the nation's most visible, making it *the* battleground for censorship debates. In February 1914 it became more controversial when it decided to allow appeals from reformers, but *not* producers and exhibitors.[139] As *Motography* noted:

> The film may pass the National Censorship Board and the City Police Board and be on its way two or three days before some neighborhood reformer gets a slant at it. This alleged reformer writes a letter to Chicago's notorious Major Funkhouser lodging complaint against the film,

and without further investigation all the prints are withdrawn. . . . Censorship in Chicago has developed into one of the farces of the continent. It will soon have reached an international reputation.[140]

Funkhouser quickly backed down, letting the film industry appeal verdicts from March 1914, a decision that led to many lawsuits over the next few years, including the case involving the Mary Pickford vehicle, *The Little American*, discussed in chapter 7.[141] These lawsuits further eroded the board's authority, especially as the censors usually lost.

As there were few specific censorship guidelines, the board was often accused of making "arbitrary and unreasonable" decisions.[142] Critics singled out its more outrageous decisions, including banning *Traffic In Souls* despite its wide acclaim as an important and moral film; prohibiting exhibition of *The Merchant of Venice* (Phillips Smalley and Lois Weber, Universal, 1914) on the grounds of anti-Semitism; and banning *The Scarlet Letter* (David Miles, Kinemacolor, 1913) because it featured an adulterous heroine. By censoring the classics, it justified claims that Funkhouser was unable to identify "art," and was therefore unqualified for the job.[143] An order to cut shots of nude female statues from Victor's *The Panama Exposition* was considered the ultimate "puerility of the censors' work."[144] As respected cultural journals like *The Independent* and *Harpers* started publishing motion picture columns around this time (1914) and film appreciation and educational film movements became more widespread, Funkhouser's inability to distinguish between "serious" films and run-of-the-mill exploitation became more pronounced. Even the *Tribune* spoke out in an April 1914 editorial that condemned the censors' inability to recognize art.[145] But once again, this crackdown was tactical: the more motion pictures aspired to art, the more the conservative forces within the city wanted to limit their power. Like all Progressives, they wanted to manage modernity, but they took a repressive and old-fashioned approach, trying to contain it and eliminate its threat rather than integrate it into a forward-looking culture. As such, the industry's move to more respectable and artistic subjects threatened the censors as it undermined their understanding of a modernity sullied by harmful mass culture and potentially eliminated the justification for censorship, further challenging their authority.

CHAPTER 5

Funkhouser's Demise: Challenges to Chicago's Censorship Regime

Given the close links between local politics and film censorship, it was not surprising that Funkhouser lost much of his power and municipal support after Harrison's defeat in April 1915.[146] The new Republican mayor, William Hale Thompson, did not share his predecessor's beliefs about cinema. His preelection clean-up campaign on the city's South Side targeted crime, brothels, and saloons and left movies alone.[147] Before and after his election, Thompson vowed to build more playgrounds and clean up the city but refused to attack cinema.[148] Just one day after taking office, he introduced an investigation into Funkhouser's conduct as head censor, and, in the interim, reduced his powers, limited his duties, and reassigned his police officers.[149] As the *Herald* noted: "Funkhouser's men can no longer make raids . . . they can gather no evidence . . . they cannot testify in court . . . they must simply investigate complaints of citizens as to vice conditions . . . they must submit evidence of vice to the chief of police instead of acting without his knowledge."[150] Funkhouser simultaneously faced another threat, this time from the state. In May 1915, the Illinois legislature approved an African American–supported bill for a state censorship board that effectively eliminated the city's censors. This prospect terrified conservative reform groups and Christian organizations that claimed it was the work of the film industry.[151] The bill failed to make it into law, however, and Chicago's censorship board remained intact.

Funkhouser was renowned for his tenacity and would not relinquish his position, as a February 1916 suit illustrates. He delayed giving a verdict on *The Right to Live* (C. H. Ferrell, United Photo Plays, 1916), a feature based on Mayor Thompson's notorious Sunday closing order for Chicago's saloons (Thompson attacked alcohol in the same way his predecessor treated cinema). Its distributor, United Photoplays, subsequently sued the city.[152] Police chief Healey went over Funkhouser's head, issuing a permit after showing the film to the corporation's counsel.[153] This raised the question of who had the ultimate authority to censor films—Healey or Funkhouser? This dilemma was partially resolved that April, when the city counsel, Ettleson, approved Essanay's *The Little Girl Next Door* (Richard Foster Baker/M. Blair Coan, 1916), an eight-reel picture based on the findings of the senate's O'Hara Vice

Commission.¹⁵⁴ Ettleson "made forty modifications and cut-outs. Permission to exhibit the film was given following an opinion by Mr. Ettleson that Chief of Police Healey and not Second Deputy Funkhouser [who rejected the film] is the highest officer authorized to censor cinema productions."¹⁵⁵ A six-reel version of the film, cut by Healey, made it into theaters.

Soon afterward, Thompson set up a major investigation into the city's censorship.¹⁵⁶ Louella Parsons argued that Funkhouser was particularly vulnerable: "because Corporation Counsel Ettelson's ruling that Chief Healey has authority practically to nullify the motion picture findings of Second Deputy Funkhouser . . . Mr. Ettelson is going to compile a statement of all the ordinances covering motion picture censorship. Incidentally, he says that Mr. Funkhouser was wrong . . . [Ettelson said] 'The chief may overrule the second deputy in every case he sees fit. Under the law he could in effect destroy the second deputy's power.'"¹⁵⁷ Comptroller Pike subsequently cut the censor board's annual budget from $36,000 to $21,600, forcing Funkhouser to cut three of his ten vice investigators and reduce their daily allowance to $1.50—a sum that the *Herald* considered "obviously inadequate for obtaining necessary evidence in certain well-known classes of cases."¹⁵⁸ Funkhouser's allies, aldermen Merriam and Nance, immediately called for an inquiry.¹⁵⁹

In March 1916, police chief Healey suspended Funkhouser for disobeying orders (showing cut-out reels to aldermen, reform groups, churches, and women's clubs in the censor board's offices) and appointed Wilbur F. Willis as head censor. Healey's coup failed and Funkhouser was restored to office because of corruption surrounding his replacement. The mayor's brother-in-law, William Burkhardt, deputy commissioner of public works and owner of the Kenmore Theater, had allegedly conspired with Harry Igle, a Mutual, Universal, and Triangle representative, to ensure Willis became head censor.¹⁶⁰ Even Funkhouser's enemies like the promovie *Chicago Herald* withheld support.¹⁶¹ City club women, reformers, civic workers, and ministers protested, declaring "the move to oust the major is another attempt to make possible the reopening of the old 'red light' districts and curb the censorship of motion pictures."¹⁶² On Saturday, March 18—the day after Willis's interim appointment—three thousand Funkhouser sup-

CHAPTER 5

porters, including such noted reformers as Sophonisba Breckenridge, Louise de Koven Bowen, and Harriet Vittum, staged a protest at the Auditorium Theater, an event the *Sunday Herald* dubbed "one of the most dramatic political gatherings in the city's history."[163] A few days later, Healey restored Funkhouser's office, although he insisted the censor's performance was "far from satisfactory," and his conduct would be investigated.[164] As Funkhouser's power was solely restored due to political corruption, his standing was, at best, tenuous.

These incidents further strengthened reformers' dislike of Mayor Thompson, however, and they stepped up efforts to prove an ever stronger need for film censorship. Women's groups launched another clean-up campaign under the direction of Mrs. Guy Blanchard to preserve the city's censorship regime while Funkhouser's supporters issued statements decrying the new state of affairs: Frederic Seidenburg insisted that "from the time Chief Healy [sic] took charge censorship has been going down," while Louise de Koven Bowen claimed her JPA investigators found a dramatic decline in standards:[165] "unrestrained indecency prevails in and about many amusement parks, *that the cheap theaters are rapidly returning to the demoralized condition of 1909*; that restrictions on public dance halls are more honored in the breach than the observance; that police connivance with the filthy cabarets, now the most flagrant class of vice markets, is commonly assumed by their employers and their frequenters" (my emphasis).[166] Reformers maintained cinema's moral standards were in sharp decline, although once again they gave no details. The Chicago Political Equity League claimed: "Despite the activity of Chicago's municipal censors, less that 62 per cent of the movies shown in the city's theaters are morally good."[167] Yet the films playing in the city at this very time refute their claims: in addition to theatrical/literary adaptations (like Mutual's *Silas Marner* [Ernest Warde, Thanhouser, 1916]) found in larger Loop theaters, there were a large number of high-budget family-oriented features, like Mary Pickford's *Poor Little Peppina* (Sidney Olcott, Famous Players–Mary Pickford Corporation–Paramount, 1916), and Mary Miles Minter's *Dimples* (Edgar Jones, Columbia/Metro, 1916), and war documentaries, serials, melodramas, comedies, and westerns were also popular.[168] The picture was much the same in neighborhood theaters. Indeed, throughout 1916 the film industry concentrated resources on stage adaptations featuring well-known theatrical stars as part of an aggressive move to uplift its product. Nowhere else in the country did reformers make such claims, and given Chicago's strict censorship, it was unlikely that salacious films would only be available in that city.

Once again, these investigations fought a very public battle for control of commercial entertainment, but now they just appeared hysterical and out of touch. As movies expanded their reach, there was a smaller audience for the reformers' work. At the same time, Healey and Thompson entered into their own crackdown on public entertainment. But they did not touch movies, instead focusing on cabaret and burlesque, closing seven such theaters in 1916, including three small Loop houses, the Gem, Omar, and National.[169] These actions reveal that the city's leading officials were not blind to vice but did not see motion pictures as a public threat, tacitly acknowledging the medium's new respectability.

Even with reformers' faithful support, Funkhouser was in trouble. Despite occasional victories (like his July 1917 legal vindication over the banning of *Birth* [Eugenic Film Company, 1917]), an "obscene" early exploitation film, the courts increasingly sided with the film industry.[170] In March 1917, Eli Guggenheim successfully appealed the ban on his film of Clifford Roe's vice exposés, *The Sins of the Sons*, which Funkhouser found "immoral, obscene, disorderly, riotous, and not conducive to public peace." Witnesses at the trial merely found it boring: "Ladies of the half-world were shown attired in conventional evening dress. The 'riotous' cabaret scenes consisted of a few men and women throwing confetti on New Year's Eve." After seeing the film and hearing all evidence, the judge leaped to his feet, exclaiming that Funkhouser's definition of immorality was completely unfounded: "If there is an ordinance in effect which permits the city censors to pass on pictures from that point of view . . . I hold that such an ordinance is not law—absolutely not. If that is immorality, then all the great works that have ever been produced—all the books, plays, pictures, stories, are immoral. . . . This is too much! I instruct the jury to turn in an immediate verdict for the film company."[171] As this statement threatened the very basis of censorship in the city, women's organizations insisted Funkhouser appeal to the Supreme Court. But his support was collapsing, even among reformers and the church. In March 1917, the Reverend

CHAPTER 5

M. P. Boynton of Woodlawn Baptist Church gave a passionate sermon against censorship, reserving his fiercest criticisms for Funkhouser, noting that "a number of clergymen, clubwomen and other prominent citizens had asked the Major to pass the film, but were coldly turned down. 'We retired from the presence of this "high authority" in morals,' said Dr. Boynton, 'amazed at the stupidity, discouraged by the arbitrariness, and disgusted at the bombast.'"[172]

As his authority wanted, Funkhouser's judgments were increasingly overthrown. In July 1917, he lost a yearlong fight with Pathé over their backstage drama, *New York* (George Fitzmorris, 1916), which finally opened at the Star theater.[173] In September 1917, Vitagraph successfully appealed his ban on *Within the Law* (William P. S. Earle, VLSE, 1917). After this film had been refused a permit, Vitagraph organized a private screening at the Studebaker, invited 1,200 of the city's most prominent residents, and polled them after the show. All found it an important picture that required no cuts and, armed with these findings, their attorney, Louis F. Jacobson, marched to Funkhouser and Schuettler, demanded a permit, and after one was denied, immediately filed suit.[174] Vitagraph's actions were carefully orchestrated, based on a clause in the Chicago city charter "which provides that the city is authorized . . . through the general superintendent of police to refuse or grant permits for motion pictures as the general superintendent may determine. An enactment of the City Council, later passed stipulated that the second deputy, who shall not be a member of the police department shall censor motion pictures, but does not provide in what manner the censoring shall be done."[175] Although Vitagraph's appeal was successful, the city's censorship was not overthrown (possibly their intent). Meanwhile, the censor placed himself and the city in contempt of court by refusing Vitagraph a permit.[176] Once again, the *Tribune* distanced itself from his actions, commenting that "it is hard to find justification for Chicago's censorship of films," just as a city council judiciary subcommittee considered amending the current ordinance to curb Funkhouser's power.[177] He fought back yet again, claiming his decisions were not arbitrary and calling clubwomen to "fight against licentious films." Declaring his actions were designed to protect local audiences from the movies' powerful and immoral East Coast influence, he maintained: "It is not the Chicago firms, but those from outside whose pictures I am called upon to censor. I must wash New York's dirty linen."[178] The Vitagraph case marshaled his opposition, however, leading to rumors that Chicago exchanges and the nation's leading producers were planning to oust Funkhouser for "his alleged antagonistic, arbitrary and *unpatriotic* interference with the showing of feature films in this city" (my emphasis).[179]

With local censorship in disarray, the city council's judiciary subcommittee embarked on a series of public hearings during November and December 1917. At stake was a new ordinance, introduced by Alderman Walter P. Steffen, aimed at eviscerating Funkhouser's powers: "where a picture is judged immoral or obscene, a permit cannot be refused until the picture has been submitted to a board of ten censors, none of whom shall be connected with the police department, and a majority of the board condemns it. The first deputy of police would still issue the permits."[180] With censorship itself in question, major film companies like Vitagraph and Fox began opening their major films in the city's largest theaters without permits. In the battle over public opinion, these premieres forced censors to defend their attacks on cinema, calling on the public—not city officials—to judge their work. One such event was William Fox's Chicago premiere of the Theda Bara *Cleopatra* (J. Gordon Edwards, 1917), attended by no less than Mayor Thompson and his wife, confirming this assault on Funkhouser's authority and endorsing the film industry's tactics.[181]

In May 1918 a judiciary subcommittee concluded that the second deputy (Funkhouser) did not have the right to control film censorship.[182] As Funkhouser's position now officially had no legal authority or responsibilities, it was eliminated.[183] With the fate of the board in question, further public hearings were held in September 1918, centering on the relationship between motion pictures and public morals.[184] Besides investigating Funkhouser's conduct, the commission reconsidered whether movie censorship was a criminal or civil matter to be supervised by police or civil servants. Reversing established procedure, they removed censorship from the Morals Court *and* lifted it from police jurisdiction. In a judgment that simultaneously highlighted the postwar decline of Progressive politics, the decreased significance of the city's reformers, the movie's own changed status in American cultural and social life, and the strength of the film industry, film censorship

CHAPTER 5

was separated from police control in December 1918.[185] A downsized board of three to five salaried civil servants would now be appointed to three-year terms by the mayor, with film companies granted the direct right of appeal to the board, obviating expensive and time-consuming lawsuits.[186] The commission considered repealing the pink permits for adults only films, but tabled the matter.[187] Despite consensus that all films should be suitable for children, they found a need for motivated license in motion picture art.[188]

Funkhouser's censorship regime did not collapse just because he lost support after the election of a new mayor, but because the board was wildly out of touch with community standards. If censors are not seen to be acting on behalf of their community, preventing the circulation of material that threatens its standards and the fabric of society, their authority is void, as was the case here. It was admittedly difficult to establish community standards at a time of change; in fact, there was much debate on this very issue during the Progressive Era. But the censors' aggressive actions effectively ceded the establishment and maintenance of community standards to the film industry and its neighborhood theaters. This became obvious as pictures like *The Birth of a Nation*; *The Battle Cry of Peace* (J. Stuart Blackton, Wilfrid North, Vitagraph-VLSE, 1915); *Intolerance* (D. W. Griffith, Wark-Triangle, 1916); and *Civilization* (Reginald Barker, Thomas H. Ince, Thomas H. Ince Corporation–Triangle, 1916) demonstrated the industry's move toward art and its ability to make statements (some contentious) on significant contemporary issues. In addition, the turn toward family pictures, like those starring children (Mary Miles Minter, Baby Marie Osbourne, and others) or adults impersonating children (most notably Mary Pickford and Marguerite Clark), revealed cinema's investment in "wholesome" values, making it increasingly difficult to argue for its moral danger.

Perhaps more than concerns about morality, censorship expressed anxieties about the social and cultural changes represented by a more powerful and influential cinema, including fears about challenges to traditional sources of power and influence, like local government, elite social classes, and reformers. Cinema's increasing respectability made it more threatening—it was not a known quantity like vice, and it became increasingly difficult to support claims that it led citizens astray and placed them in moral danger. More paranoid concerns about cinema's links to crime and its suggestibility can be seen as part of a discourse on its changes in style and address between approximately 1907 and 1915, expressing concerns about its increased cultural influence and capacity to engage audiences so deeply. While most of society welcomed this more reputable cinema—as seen in the Busse and Thompson administrations—others had major reservations about this medium and what it might become, perhaps using traditional fears to articulate something that resisted expression.

Chicago's film censorship was deeply saturated in politics, testifying to the medium's growing cultural significance. This relationship would become increasingly important after 1914 as the federal government grappled with decisions about how the nation should respond to the outbreak of war in Europe. In response, the film industry used its already proven community appeal in the service of shoring up national identity in the wake of global conflicts that threatened to tear it asunder. In seeking to establish itself as a national medium, the film industry tried to speak for America, forge national consciousness, and produce a national community, all while trying to solve still very real Progressive Era anxieties about national identity. In the next two chapters, I look at these efforts in the context of two particular forces that undermined national unity: racial conflicts and the outbreak of World War I. Andrew Higson has shown that it is the task of a national cinema to hold together the shifting range of antagonisms and conflicts that often define healthy, democratic nations, rather than asserting a monolithic vision (possibly more the sign of a nation in crisis).[189] In the following chapter, I focus on the dilemma facing Chicago's black film audiences: accept cinema's predominantly white vision of nation and become part of its national address or establish a black cinema and take up a marginal identity. In the final chapter, I explore how World War I further fragmented national identity in Chicago, foregrounding local differences from national consensus. Besides looking the challenges of articulating national identity during wartime, I examine how this war marked the end of the Progressive Era, its cultural politics, and its distinct way of seeing.

SIX

Citizenship and Black Cinema

One of the Progressive Era's top priorities was to stabilize and secure national identity, something that mass immigration and modernity made more fraught as both challenged foundational American ideals. Progressive Era anxieties over definitions of national identity also testified to the lingering significance of historical events. As Rivka Shpak Lissak observes, "the trauma of national disunity caused by the Civil War, along with the huge immigration from eastern and southern Europe that had begun after the 1880s, led native-born Americans to a reassessment of what was called the American Idea in relation to nationalism, nationality (later called ethnicity), and culture during the Progressive period."[1] Since the middle of the nineteenth century the culture had been broadly invested in "the American Idea," a concept closely related to manifest destiny and American exceptionalism that linked citizens together through their hopes for the future, their faith in a new, democratic way of living rather than their shared ethnic traditions.[2] While American identity was implicitly based more on the future than the past, modernity begged questions about the very nature of this future by introducing an unprecedented degree of unpredictability and change.[3] Besides evoking key Progressive concepts like community and self-awareness, dilemmas around national identity returned to the period's signature issue of managing and stabilizing modernity.

Cinema participated in broader efforts to reestablish a cohesive and modern American national ideal that could manage the nation's diversity and synthesize past, present, and future into a new shared culture, one marked by the medium's shared pleasures. The industry's attempts to establish film as *the* national medium were also somewhat strategic, designed to offset outside intervention, assert cinema's respectability, and show leadership while capitalizing on its ability to reach large audiences. Movies had already proven that they could fuse tradition and modernity, commemorate history, disseminate information, communicate through a "universal language," create communities, and instill powerful loyalties and identification. These qualities could all be used to cement a broader national consensus and produce a firmer, more strongly defined sense of nation. In doing this work for the nation and putting the medium in America's service, the film industry would also reap the benefits, using its power for the public good and placing itself as an unimpeachable force of authority and national good.

Despite sharing Progressivism's emphasis on community formation and its keen interest in national identity, American cinema's visions of nation were often far from inclusive. No issue illustrates this better than race, particularly in terms of the production and reception of African American screen images. *The Birth of a Nation* offers perhaps the most obvious and notorious example: Linda Williams quotes William Walker, an audience member who saw the film in 1916 in a black theater and declared: "You had the worse feeling in the world. You felt like you were not counted. You were out of existence." Williams links these words to *Birth*'s "visceral logic of black disappearance" rather than its "specific instances of white-on-black violence or even of more explicit depictions of black men attacking white women."[4] While it is an extreme example and not the focus of this chapter, *The Birth of a Nation* offers a useful starting point as it testifies to American film's interest in establishing itself as a national cinema and reveals some of the terms it might take.[5] Williams follows Clyde R. Taylor in acknowledging how *Birth* established "an allegory of national identity founded on the exclusion of blacks as a co-defining anti-type," which then permitted a post–Civil War reunion of North and South.⁶

The consequences of these practices were strongly felt in the black community, which had developed a strong interest in movies well before the release of *The Birth of a Nation*.⁷ The black community's response to *Birth*—as well as the reactions of white citizens opposed to the film—foregrounded issues central to national cinema, and national identity as a whole, including belonging. Rejecting *Birth* posed problems for any African American spectators who found themselves unable to accept its national address, one more easily taken up by large numbers of white Americans. While arguably a limit case, *Birth* emphasized the dilemmas circulating around black cinema, spectatorship, citizenship, and the concept of national cinema, bringing them into the national spotlight. Citizenship was a primary concern for the black public, structuring much discourse in the black press during the Progressive Era. With mainstream movies' turn toward national cinema, it appeared that moving pictures would be yet another venue that refused African Americans full citizenship. Black moviegoers and filmmakers found ways to extend cinema's national address to include themselves, as I show throughout this chapter, even at the cost of conflicting allegiances and subject positions. It is notable that the black public's major concerns—citizenship, community, uplift, and managing modernity—mirrored those of the Progressive Era, although this should not be surprising, as all cultures were shaped by, and helped shape, this prevailing zeitgeist.

Throughout this period, the *Chicago Defender* repeatedly raised the topic of citizenship in relation to cinema, first through its coverage of segregation, then in its treatment of black cinema (or "race films"). Racial loyalties often transcended national allegiances due to widespread discrimination and the awareness that black citizens were often not included in national address, cinematic or otherwise. Many African Americans instead turned to their own communities to advance their social, economic, and political standing, foregrounding white culture's refusal to recognize their status as full and equal citizens. But many recognized that these strategies risked further marginalizing blackness rather than asserting it as a central part of American identity. In the face of cinema's increased popularity, black audiences explored the question of how they should engage with white mainstream cinema and the undeniable pleasures it gave them.

Black moviegoing and film production in Chicago were different tactics used to assert black citizenship. Both need to be contextualized within American cinema's increasing success in positioning itself as a national medium, making mainstream movies both more problematic and more important for the black community. One of Progressivism's greatest concerns, national identity was linked to issues of community, uplift, and the "correct" integration of new immigrants. This process was not limited to whites: Chicago's African American community also confronted the different cultural practices and expectations of new migrants from the south, expanding cultural diversity in ways that could be similarly problematic. Furthermore, with so much focus on the possible assimilation of white (and even Asian) immigrants and the ongoing efforts to redefine and reassert American identity, African Americans wanted to ensure that they were included as full citizens, their civil rights upheld, and their contributions to history acknowledged. In a climate where movies were rapidly becoming a national medium, black cinema offered a potential solution, particularly as it simultaneously made black institutions and black history more visible. Early black filmmaking and black exhibition strived to include the African American community in the national consciousness, something that was not simple and was recognized as a struggle at the time. Citizenship and community both became central to Black cinema's exhibition, reception, and production practices.

Several important works attest to the significance of Chicago's black movie theaters, black filmmakers, and black film criticism during the silent era, most notably those by Jacqueline Najuma Stewart, Anna Everett, and Mary Carbine.[8] All demonstrate how black cinema primarily involved exhibition and reception strategies centered on mainstream white films—black filmmaking was marginal and rare. Carbine and Stewart have both shown how music, black theater staff and ownership, theater location, and black patronage helped transform mainstream white films into black cinema. But the question of black patrons' film preferences has been largely overlooked, along with consideration of the textual strategies that made these films resonate. Despite the attention paid to the ways black audiences reworked white films into

CHAPTER 6

forms of African American culture, less consideration has been given to another structuring impulse: the desire to be addressed by films, to be part of the national cinema they helped constitute. As already marginalized African American communities sought inclusion (through consumption of mainstream film and access to predominantly white theaters) and simultaneously looked for their own cultural and social space through black theaters and black films, cinema evoked issues of local and national community, albeit in ways that were not always compatible or straightforward. Black cinema—in all of its forms—effectively complicated discourses of belonging associated with national cinema.[9]

Chicago was the center of the nation's nascent black film industry, a largely artisan enterprise hampered by limited funding and distribution. Black movies lacked the infrastructure that characterized black vaudeville and musical comedy circuits, with filmmakers struggling to cover production costs despite strong audience demand.[10] Still, concerns like the Foster Photoplay Company and the Peter P. Jones Photoplay Company made popular films that featured positive representations of contemporary urban black middle-class life, black history, and black military service. In the process, they sought to advance black citizenship, counter stereotypes, increase visibility, and arouse audiences' social conscience. Other filmmakers capitalized on the novelty of black performers for black and white audiences alike, with some predominantly white producers making stereotype-laden works that were primarily intended for white audiences. These were roundly disparaged if screened in Chicago's black theaters.[11]

It is important to look at the kinds of films—both mainstream and black productions—that were popular in the black community and try to understand their appeal. Certain genres and stars were strongly favored, indicating black audiences had marked preferences.[12] Some mainstream movies could be recuperated more than others, engaging patrons who might even prefer them over black productions, possibly because of their higher budgets, their narrative and aesthetic strategies, and their ability to accommodate tastes for glamour, escapism, and celebrity—characteristics that revealed desires for social mobility and inclusion in mainstream culture. Black patrons wanted to attend theaters throughout the city, raising broader issues about segregation and discrimination that emphasize the links between mobility, agency, and citizenship. A number of highly publicized cases of illegal segregation in film theaters exacerbated cinema's racially ambivalent reputation during the 1910s, constituting a direct assault on black citizenship.[13] Any black preference for white films thus involved more than simple assimilation, as Stewart makes clear in her discussion of reconstructive spectatorship.[14]

Black reception of white films asserted black citizenship differently from race films, revealing a not unproblematic participation in national cinema. Still, even the most recuperative readings of white films could not easily accommodate black desires to be fully recognized. Ironically, black citizenship could not be completely asserted through black-produced films either, largely because these were part of a marginal cinema, whose consumption evoked a similarly marginal citizenry. Consequently, tensions between inclusion and segregation shaped all levels of black film practice—from production and exhibition to reception and film criticism—with both forms, and their conflicts and intersections, defining the intricacies of asserting black citizenship. After all, black reception involved negotiating white screen images as well as social phenomena like theater employment and ownership, segregation, and the ways audiences were treated inside theaters.

Life and Leisure in African American Chicago

During the 1910s, Chicago had a small but active and well-established African American population (around 1 percent). It reputedly offered more opportunities for African Americans than any other northern city, although the relatively hermetic nature of its black neighborhoods (and later racial conflicts over neighborhoods like Hyde Park) reveal a far from ideal situation. By 1914, with the Great Migration underway, the city's African American population topped sixty thousand (out of a total population around 2.4 million), primarily concentrated in a number of self-contained communities to the south and west of the Loop.[15] That year, the *Defender* noted: "Forty-five thousand . . . Afro-Americans in Chicago reside on the South Side, and most of these are in the district bordered on the north by Twenty-sixth street, on the west by Federal street, on the east by the lake and on the south by Sixty-third

CHAPTER 6

street. Along State street can be found nearly every line of business conducted and conducted successfully by race people."[16] Not all members of the black community liked the city's newfound fame, believing (in the words of one *Defender* editorial) "that reputation works more harm than good to the older residents. For each year from the South come hundreds who have heard of this haven, who instead of going slow and learning the Northern ways, sail right in where angels fear to tread, and undo all the good that has been done."[17] Black cultural differences were foregrounded as hundreds of thousands of African Americans left the south between 1890 and 1930—a movement Stewart parallels to the impact of European immigration on white working-class communities. Besides creating new definitions of blackness (including the modern idea of the "New Negro," an essentially northern, upwardly mobile, urbane, and middle-class figure who countered antebellum stereotypes), these migrants revealed different social expectations within the black community.[18] Many new arrivals experienced a greater sense of freedom than in the segregated south, moving into spaces that the established black community had often avoided, leading to more de facto segregation. Meanwhile, established communities were concerned about newcomers' behavior, often seeing southern migrants as damaging their hard-earned respectability and still precarious social status.

As Stewart suggests, issues of belonging and definitions of community were not simple: the black community was diverse, not fixed or singular.[19] It "grew during the late nineteenth and early twentieth centuries [becoming] increasingly conspicuous and diverse," encompassing professionals, elites, businessmen, and working-class families, with stratifications of class, culture, and social origins adding to debates about suitable racial identities.[20] Black elites, including those writing for the black press, favored middle-class visions of uplift and propriety that resembled those associated with white social reformers, foregrounding the value of African American culture and enterprise. Not all black citizens lived up to such ideals, however, prompting the black press to critique cultural practices it found distasteful, especially those that might confirm white prejudices and stereotypes.

This discourse of uplift was emblematically Progressive, shaping reports in the black press that remains one of the few sources on the

Citizenship and Black Cinema

period's black life and leisure. It informed the *Defender*'s coverage of cinema, a medium that the paper largely ignored until around 1911, and only rarely featured until 1913. Despite its strong support for black filmmakers, the *Defender* was concerned about the respectability of commercial amusements long before cinema, dismissing many of them (including movies) as lowbrow.[21] Black elites shared these concerns, participating in social reform like their white counterparts, seeing commercial amusements as unsafe, demoralizing, debasing, and discriminatory.[22] Stewart suggests that many of these risks were exaggerated "to justify [reformers'] uplift activities and to maintain their roles as guardians of Black public life and the Black public image."[23] Meanwhile, new residents forged new communities around leisure to offset their homesickness and isolation, making amusements like cinema central sites for the redefinition and reassertion of black identity and citizenship—albeit ones that, again, challenged black reformers' ideals.[24] As Stewart suggests, these recreations offered new urban migrants something akin to "the community life they left behind," constituting "public spheres that were more commercialized but also more 'free' than the traditional structures of social life in the South."[25] Once again, as was generally the case in Progressive America, cinema became a central site for the negotiation of community and identity. Still, this was not easy—cultural differences within and outside the black community complicated and sometimes undermined this process.

Black Theaters

Black movie theaters were located in or near African American districts, like Chicago's Black Belt, and served primarily black patrons, although they also catered to whites seeking something different. Chicago's Black Metropolis had its own entertainment district, located around South State Street, south of the Loop and just north of the Levée. Carbine notes that many theaters were found in the area "encompassing the Douglas, Grand and Washington Park districts . . . stretch[ing] thirty blocks southward along State Street, parallel to the stockyards."[26] Stewart counts at least eighteen theaters showing films here, eleven of them concentrating on motion pictures. Most opened after 1913 (one of the most important, the Vendome, opened in 1918) or turned to cinema during the early 1910s, revealing the surge in black exhibition around 1913.[27] I provide a table of these theaters below (table 6.1).[28] Like most neighborhood houses, black theaters emphasized their duty of care toward patrons, promoting their amenities toward these ends. Although there is no evidence that black theaters existed elsewhere in the city, the possibility cannot be ruled out.

Table 6.1

Theater Name	Address	Offerings/Specialties/ Seating Capacity
Atlas	4711 S. State Street	650 seats, 1 story, exterior terracotta decorations.
Elba	31st Street and Indiana Ave. (3115 S. Indiana Ave.)	300 seats. Owned by O. C. Hammond, proprietors of the Fountain, Pickford, Phoenix, and Vendome.
Fountain	35th Street and Grand Boulevard	Featured children's matinees.
Franklin		
Grand	3100 S. State Street	500 seats. Initially music and vaudeville theater but by 1917 focused on high-class motion pictures and vaudeville.
Lincoln	3132 S. State Street	350 seats. Opened 1912. Owned by Nathan Joseph then operator of States and Owl theaters. Renowned for its music.
Merit	35th Street and S. State Street	
Owl	4653 S. State Street	1,200 extra large seats.
Phoenix	3104 S. State Street	321 seats. First successful movie theater in the area, occupying the site of the old Grand. Renowned for its respectable entertainment and considered suitable for children. One of the most popular houses on the Stroll.

Theater Name	Address	Offerings/Specialties/ Seating Capacity
Pickford (formerly Lux)	35th Street and S. Michigan Ave	800 seats. Lavish theater with 4-piece orchestra. High-end theater, appealing to black elites. Also catered to white audiences. Subsequent-run features a specialty.
Star	3833–35 S. State Street	First black-owned and run theater. Tony Langston was manager from 1915 to 1917, followed by William Foster. Renowned for its feature films.
States	3507 S. State Street	708 seats. Renowned for its film dramas and music (hired Pekin orchestra in 1913). Specialized in features from 1915 onward.
Washington	3440 S. State Street	
Vendome	3145 S. State Street	Opened 1918. 1,265 seats. Elaborately decorated, luxurious French Renaissance style theater with a very large stage.

Limited records, and the *Defender*'s editorial slant, make it difficult to ascertain exactly when black interest in movies started. As Stewart and Anna Everett note, these factors have led some historians to assume black audiences were not interested in cinema, interpreting black protests against *The Birth of a Nation* in this light.[29] But the situation was more complicated, possibly reflecting black critics' bias against movies as a not entirely respectable and overwhelmingly white form.[30] In 1910, for example, the *Defender*'s Sylvester Russell inveigled against white entertainment, likely referring obliquely to cinema: "there is one thing certain, the people of an African neighborhood do not care for white attractions and especially when they come by the subordination of mediocrity like stale oysters on the half shell ignored and relegated from the booking of a big time vaudeville theatre. . . . What they will want on State street is good clean intelligent, well dressed artistic colored performers."[31]

CHAPTER 6

An April 1911 *Defender* story set in a movie theater offers further insight into cinema's low social standing in the eyes of those "respectable" black citizens who disliked movies even more than their white middle-class counterparts, at least in this paper's eyes. As Stewart notes, such fictional references to black spectatorship are useful as they "open up facets of the moviegoing experience that tend to be overlooked by academic film criticism . . . [suggesting] ways to bridge the gaps between 'spectator' as textual point of address and 'viewer' as empirical unit."³² Besides providing historical insights into black audiences' understandings of spectatorship and cinema's cultural status, they also offer details of the experience that, as Stewart notes, are not found elsewhere.³³ In this short story, country cousin, Beth, comes to Chicago to visit the sophisticated Laura, and they attend a vaudeville show in the Black Metropolis that features motion pictures:

> "You don't want to stay for the pictures, do you?" asked Laura in the tone of one who expects the answer to be, "No."
>
> Beth blushed. She took a childish delight in motion pictures, but from the chatter about her, she gathered that it was considered childish to sit through the whole performance. . . . [During the screening] the property man and his fellows on the stage supplied the clinging of the bells and the screech of the whistles and to Beth it was all very real. . . . The audience shrieked at the pantomimic humor. . . . She left her seat and with trembling limbs started up the aisle. Laura followed her country cousin curiously. An usher directed her to the balcony where the machine was operated, and she waited until the operator had finished.³⁴

Beth conforms to a fictional archetype where "Black spectators are frequently characterized as members of the working-class 'masses,' prominently including southern migrants living in the urban North."³⁵ In contrast, Laura represents the New Negro, who finds movies childish and keeps her distance from the screen, pointing to the *Defender*'s approved model of spectatorship. Beth is entranced but recognizes this is an improper response, even as the films affect her physically. She forces herself to leave, yet she is incapable of autonomous movement, a response that signals suggestion and hypnosis. A third reaction is documented—that of the audience. They make noise, talk, shriek with laughter, indicating their lack of manners and culture—comments that reveal the *Defender*'s thoughts on movies at this time.[36] Rather than forging community, then, the movies fracture it in this story, revealing stratifications of class and taste.

Prior to 1913 the *Defender*'s entertainment columnists were reticent to discuss cinema, despite evidence of strong audience interest in motion pictures. Sylvester Russell, the paper's music and drama correspondent until 1911, ignored movies even as he reviewed live acts or music from the very same program.[37] As Everett observes, his efforts "to accommodate 'the motion picture craze' were minimal . . . little more than footnotes wherein he simply catalogs the weekly film offerings at neighborhood nickelodeons."[38] Although he later praised the area's reputable movie theaters, he was primarily interested in music. Still, two rare (and telling) mentions of film reveal the medium's growing popularity with black audiences. In April 1910, Russell observed that "the moving picture craze has developed a wonderful stampede among the Negro and Yiddish theater goers."[39] In summer 1911, he noted, "The moving picture business is going up now. The people seem to like them and this house [Phoenix, 3104 State Street] is doing good business."[40] His successor, Minnie Addams, ignored movies throughout her 1911–12 tenure.[41] Any expansion in black film theaters occurring between October 1911 and March 1913 therefore went undocumented during what was evidently a pivotal time for film exhibition in the area known as the Stroll, judging from advertisements in the black press. With the 1913 appointment of Tony Langston, a local black exhibitor who took over management of the Star in July 1915, the *Defender* expanded its movie coverage.[42] Still, it remained limited: few films were reviewed and the most developed items were short exhibitor reports about upcoming films, listing successful releases from the previous week.

Advertisements offer more insight into cinema's popularity, revealing the presence of first- and second-run movie houses on the Stroll as early as 1911, although earlier establishments likely existed. The Phoenix was possibly the area's first successful movie theater, a 321-seat house on the former site of the old Grand offering "comedies, westerns, serials and many features to Black Belt moviegoers."[43] Further evidence of the medium's popularity can be found in a June 1911

CHAPTER 6

advertisement for the Phoenix, billing motion pictures first (capitalized and in a larger font) above "high class vocal and instrumental music, first class colored orchestra."[44] By March 1913, four local movie-only theaters advertised regularly in the *Defender*, the Washington, Merit, Lux, and Phoenix.[45] Films also spread into other theaters: the States and Pekin did not specialize in movies but screened films during the vaudeville off-season that summer, while the area's new film theaters like the Lincoln, Lux, Washington, and Phoenix attracted full houses.[46]

New movie theaters like the Phoenix participated in the Stroll's southern expansion, hurting the older live theaters on northern blocks and marking a shift in more than the area's geography. In May 1912, J. Hockley Smith stated that the blocks between 27th and 31st streets "have been the popular promenade and always will," but this was no longer true just two years later:[47] "Now the gay part of the street is from 31st to 35th streets. Thirty-fifth street is the center of attraction. Several popular theaters and a number of moving picture houses are off from the corner and the crowd likes the sport."[48] By 1917 as a cluster of popular movie theaters opened even farther south—The Owl and Atlas were near 47th Street—northernmost houses, like the Pekin (State and 27th) struggled. Significantly, all these failing houses concentrated on music and live attractions and were outdrawn by the picture theaters to the south, with their movies and increasingly elaborate decor.[49] The eight-hundred-seat Lux had a four-piece orchestra and a "celebrated ventilation system"; the 1,200-seat Owl had extra-large seats and a "beautiful lobby"; while the States featured a canopy loaded with electric lights, "architecture and decorations pleasing to the eye, and to add to the enjoyment of patrons, a mammoth $10,000 organ and orchestra."[50] On September 26, 1914, the 650-seat Atlas opened, featuring "an improved ventilating system [that] constantly suppl[ies] the patrons with pure air. Among the attractive features will be a $5,000 organ in a special loft, the latest idea in a sanitary bubbling drinking fountain, the wash rooms with hot and cold water . . . 'Gee, that place looks like heaven, it's so pretty,' said [one patron] who told everyone he met not to miss it."[51] As Stewart points out, "By boasting quality films and fine musical performances and amenities in beautiful surroundings, Black Belt theaters promoted themselves as refuges from squalor, exclusion and discrimination."[52] Their promised high-class films and luxury amenities addressed black audiences as discriminating, upwardly mobile citizens who deserved this care, combining discourses of Progressive uplift and black citizenship.

Like other neighborhood theaters, each black theater had its own identity. Small houses like the 350-seat Lincoln thrived alongside theaters like the Owl with capacities of more than one thousand; the Fountain regularly scheduled children's matinees where they distributed free candy to ladies and children, while as early as November 1913, the Lux offered big features (like *Quo Vadis?*) fresh from the Loop.[53] Meanwhile, the Phoenix featured entertainments of a "high moral character" to a "good class of young people," prompting Russell to comment: "The Phoenix theatre is the place for the children and we are glad to see them go. The picture plays are moral and humorous."[54] Members of black society—"the silk-stocking element"—patronized the Pickford, which specialized in exclusive first-run features and whose audience was otherwise "about 60 percent Caucasian."[55] In his 1917 annual review of movie houses in the Black Metropolis, Tony Langston noted that the States "houses the finest . . . and most famous productions," while the Phoenix, evidently the most popular house on the Stroll, specialized in romantic dramas, although "it is a common sight to see the sidewalks jammed in front of this theater with the sign board announcing a Wm. S. Hart or Douglas Fairbanks special."[56] As Carbine has pointed out, music played a significant role in differentiating black exhibition.[57] When the States Theater signed Joe Jordan and his famous Pekin Orchestra in August 1913, its audiences doubled.[58] The Lincoln's patronage likewise surged after its new orchestra was dubbed "the best on the Stroll."[59] In May 1916, the Pickford introduced song and dance contests, the most popular of which were its "Walkin' the Dog" nights.[60] In March 1917, the Phoenix followed suit and in January 1917, the Star began an all-professional song review on Friday nights, which was evidently a "real attraction."[61] Other promotions in black houses resembled those popular in other neighborhood theaters. In August 1915, the Lincoln gave out coupons for free or reduced admissions imprinted with lottery numbers with watches for the lucky winners while the Star gave away coupons for free admission.[62]

The New Star's identity hinged on something more substantial: it was the city's first and only black-owned and operated movie theater. Run by W. J. Riley, it opened in November 1913.[63] Its facade was festooned with electric lights that reportedly "made the prettiest theater on State Street. . . . Pictures that are the best on the market are shown and changed nightly."[64] The *Defender* urged readers to patronize this "race enterprise" noting: "It has everything to recommend it—cozy and homelike, comfortable seats, tastefully decorated and has one of the most perfect heating and ventilating systems . . . three and four reels of first-run pictures are shown with appropriate music, all of this for five cents. Is it to be wondered at that they are playing to overflow houses at each performance?"[65] From its opening, the New Star was a black institution, employing some of the major figures in early black cinema. In 1915, Tony Langston became manager, and under his guidance, a three-reel feature was shown every day, responding to black audiences' interest in longer films.[66] Within months, he had bought the theater and instituted an ambitious policy of booking features, like the six-reeler, *Arizona*.[67] From 1917, it was managed by Will Foster, the city's pioneer black filmmaker, and owned by Henry "Teenan" Jones, gambling boss, community leader, entrepreneur, and the only important African American entrepreneur in Chicago to invest in exhibition.[68]

Given the paucity of black films, greater importance was attached to black ownership, management, all-black orchestras (another source of employment)—even black ushers and ticket sellers. Besides offering employment, a predominantly African American staff revealed that a theater belonged to the community, partly offsetting the films' whiteness. As Stewart notes, "Black audiences did not have to fear the unpleasant treatment by white ushers and managers that they often experienced in downtown theaters."[69] Although white-owned, the Phoenix, the Stroll's first popular movie theater, employed African Americans in senior positions: in 1915 the *Defender* noted that is was "the *only theater on the Stroll* that has a member of the race [Al Gaines] as manager" (my emphasis).[70] In 1917, the *Defender* praised the newly opened Owl Theater for its employment policies, noting:

> Mr. Soloman, the genial gentleman who has the management of the theater . . . promised that he will employ as many members of the Race as it is possible for him to use and it looks to us as if the success of the New Owl is already assured.[71]

Shortly afterward, they offered further praise:

> In attending this theater, you will notice that all employees are members of the Race, with one exception, and that the operator is a member of local 110, which means that one of our boys is responsible for the proper showings of the of the offerings on the screen. This all will mean the continued success of this theater, and the environments call for a first-class attendance.[72]

This report ascribes black projectionists a degree of authorship as trained professionals who controlled the picture on the screen. Unsurprisingly, theaters promoted employment policies: in one of its ads, the States proclaimed: "A member of the Race fills every position from the box office to the operating room—fifteen people in all—and the advertising is handled exclusively through the Langston Advertising Bureau [owned by Tony Langston]."[73]

These appointments must be read in the context of the small number of African Americans employed in higher ranks of the entertainment industry. The *Defender* acknowledged, "the colored race has not as yet produced any managers in musical comedy who were not actors, and only two who take rank in that capacity," while Allan H. Spear has observed that even the Stroll's lauded vaudeville and stock counterparts were generally white owned and operated.[74] Indeed, Sylvester Russell argued that much improvement was needed within the black entertainment community:

> We observe that white men have already built colored theaters and we must understand that the word "colored" means that such theaters are built principally for colored people in such localities where they number the thickest and in which houses they are assured of all their public rights and privileges. . . . White proprietors of these houses in many cases have offered jobs to men said to be colored managers. . . . So, if white men who build do this, we can only expect colored managers to hire any man who qualifies to keep the house running successfully. But the duty of colored managers will be to develop managers from supes and stage managers whom they employ."[75]

CHAPTER 6

While black staff might have masked white theater ownership, audience awareness of the substantial differences between (white mainstream) film production and local exhibition could not be as easily erased, although this was not necessarily a problem for audiences wanting to engage in the national culture cinema increasingly represented.[76]

Segregation, Civil Rights, and Spectatorship

Black audiences did not stay in the Stroll, often attending movies elsewhere in the city, revealing a variety of entertainment needs and the desire to participate fully in urban life. When they left the area, however, they risked persecution, racism, and segregation.[77] Participating in all types of entertainment was central to modern life, and the black press recognized its importance for full citizenship.[78] Furthermore, the state's civil rights ordinance—the only one in the land—promised all Illinois residents the right to travel throughout the state and attend public events without color lines. Still, it was not universally obeyed, with segregation still structuring life for many black citizens who "always had to be prepared to face discrimination . . . but . . . the different contours of race relations . . . were not as consistent and inflexible as those in the South."[79]

Throughout the 1910s, the *Defender* attacked theater segregation, reminding readers they were "responsible for all that is heaped on them by keeping their mouths closed."[80] They listed key signs that a theater was breaking the law and told readers how to act:

> A great amount of timidity is shown among our people in assisting their rights against the whites. After obtaining your tickets for the theatre, be sure that the seat check or stub is not thrown in the ticket box, make sure that you have the short end of the ticket, not the deal. It is customary in theaters of cheap caliber and cheap amusement houses to huddle all of our people together. Where this occurs, you have good grounds for suit and don't fail to take advantage such a golden opportunity. . . . But be it known that with the intellect we have in Illinois (the only State with a law for us) we do not cater to the drain and outcasts of other States (without this law), but encourage the influx of the Negroes who

wish to establish a precedent and help us keep the cob-webs [*sic*] off the Civil Right Law.⁸¹

Here, the *Defender* drew its own line, welcoming only black citizens prepared to fight segregation, not those passive "outcasts of other states." As part of this mission, the *Defender* closely followed court hearings and established a fund to cover plaintiffs' costs. In repeatedly couching these as battles over full citizenship, it implicitly underscored how entertainment had become central to national identity. As important sites on the threshold between public and private spheres, free access to movie theaters became part of the right to participate fully in modern public life.

Reports on segregation consistently linked attendance at entertainment venues to full citizenship. For example, in June 1910, the *Defender* celebrated attorney E. H. Morris's victory against the Colonial Theater, a vaudeville house that refused to sell Frank D. Donaldson advance tickets for the front of the balcony, then denied him access to his seats on the main floor on the grounds that they were for another date. Donaldson had overheard an usher say, "These are niggers: how did they get these tickets?" Although he hired the best civil rights attorney in the state, the trial was a farce. The Colonial's sole witness could not remember anything, and their lawyer attacked prosecuting attorney Morris's credentials, unaware that he had cowritten the state's civil rights law. In his summary Morris instructed the jury "not to consider the case from a prejudiced standpoint but as a case of a citizen of the State being refused his rights as a citizen." He won despite the presence of a juror who "stated that Negroes should go to the Pekin and not to the downtown theaters." Donaldson received $100 damages, but the real victory lay in seeing the law upheld.⁸²

Another color-line case made headlines in February 1911 when an all-white jury found the American Music Hall guilty of violating the civil rights of Albert W. Merriweather, who received $75 in damages. Two years later, the *Defender* reported that the Majestic refused renowned black soprano and vaudevillian Abbie Mitchell a first-class seat, revealing that fame was no insurance against discrimination.⁸³ Soon after, a vicious attack at the Merit revealed that black patrons might not be safe in their own theaters. Projectionist James W. Slonaker (originally from

CHAPTER 6

Mississippi) grabbed Mrs. Barr's breast. She fought back, aided by black and white patrons alike, and Slonaker fled. When caught, he became abusive, claiming "'down home' he could do as he pleased with any 'woman of color,' but he evidently learned that Chicago was not Mississippi when he was fined $25 and costs in the Thirty-fifth and Halsted streets court the next day."[84] Slonaker kept his job and the theater maintained its black patronage, indicating that charges of discrimination could have minimal impact even within the black community. Even the *Defender* spoke positively about some theaters that had practiced segregation in the past, as Stewart points out, and continued featuring ads and reports from the Merit.[85]

This (apparent) resurgence in racial discrimination continued. In September 1913, Luther Hall sued the Avenue Theater, 31st and Indiana Avenue—mere blocks away from the Black Belt—for allowing only whites and Jews into the main floor and restricting blacks to the balcony.[86] The *Defender* orchestrated a letter-writing campaign to Mayor Harrison and police chief McWeeny: "The Grand Theater, three blocks away, [a black theater] sells seats to all American citizens—the Avenue Theater must be made to respect Illinois, or the management should be deported to his home country—the American citizens of color who fought in all America's wars will not stand the insult."[87] After a series of protests organized by middle-class "colored college men" supported by white sympathizers who occupied the main floor, the Avenue changed its policy.[88] This was unusual because there was generally a lack of interracial collaboration on racial issues.

One month later, the issue exploded when Judge Edward T. Wade endorsed theater segregation during the case of Robert Anderson versus the Monarch Theater, 461 East 31st Street. Following the Monarch's policy of letting patrons seat themselves, the Andersons headed to the main floor, but were told to go upstairs. When they refused, manager Louis Zimmerman threatened them, shouting "upstairs or get out," leading to a near-show-stopping dispute. When the case reached court, Judge Wade called for dismissal, claiming that Zimmerman's actions were not discriminatory. After a heated argument, he agreed to hear the trial then summarily dismissed it: his prejudices were so well known that other judges and municipal attorneys had wagered he would throw the case out of court.[89] Urging readers to write to the mayor and police chief, the *Defender* again reminded them, "you are just as much a citizen as the Italian emigrant that arrived here yesterday—remember your brother or uncle . . . wounded or killed at Fort Pillar, or made that desperate charge at Gettysburg."⁹⁰

After this flurry of cases, reports of segregation died down. It is not clear why. Exhibitors may have stopped discriminating, or (more likely) audiences may have failed to file suit, stopped attending certain theaters or trying to get better seats. Word of mouth likely played a role, with black audiences sharing information about welcoming theaters. Still, even with these reports, it is difficult to gauge the extent of segregation. Most cases were likely overlooked and patrons presumably avoided places that did not welcome them. Most likely, the release of films like *The New Governor* (Edgar Lewis, Fox, 1915) and, most famously, *The Birth of a Nation* shifted battles from the auditorium to the screen. *The New Governor* was a major release, based on Edward Sheldon's white-supremacist drama *The Nigger*. Although reasonably well reviewed in the white press, it had a difficult time with Chicago's censors but passed with cuts and revisions.⁹¹ The *Defender* condemned the film, but chose not to fight it: "It is one of those pictures you couldn't get excited about if you tried. It was made from a table of ingredients aimed at an emotional hot tamale effect, but we are so used to them that they provide no novelty of sensation. . . . The best thing for us to do is to let it die a natural death—agitation only keeps it alive."⁹² Two other racist films had caught the *Defender*'s eye a year earlier, but neither were significant releases. One was *Levinsky's Holiday*, which featured "a group of men throwing balls at the head of a colored boy protruding from a hole in a canvas on which was painted in large letters 'Hit the Nigger.'"⁹³ During a Monday night screening at the Grand, the *Defender*'s correspondent was horrified that this house "crowded with Afro-Americans" was "evidently insult proof for they laughed and applauded."⁹⁴ This laughter raises a number of issues, including black audiences' pleasure and the censors' acceptance of overtly racist films, despite their sensitivity to other forms of discrimination; indeed, black reformers were not represented on the city's board until the Reverend Archibald J. Carey, a powerful black reformer and Methodist minister, was appointed as a censor in March 1914.⁹⁵

CHAPTER 6

As Stewart has shown, segregation affected more than mobility. It shaped black spectatorship as the practices that produced all-black seating areas created social contexts that mediated the overwhelmingly white images on screen, undermining straightforward identification.[96] Viewers could offset racism on screen by turning away to the predominantly black social space of the theater, recognizing themselves as "embodied subjects" as they interacted with their peers: "mediat[ing] engagements with the text and/or exert[ing] pressures on individual viewers to perform in particular ways." Audiences' racial constitution therefore allowed spectators to "reconstitute themselves as viewing subjects in the face of a racially exclusionary cinematic institution and social order."[97] Stewart suggests that these social horizons could explain some black patrons' almost inexplicable enjoyment of racist films—like *Levinsky's Holiday*—as the presence of other African Americans and the resultant awareness of discrepancies between on- and off-screen images provoked different forms of laughter, directed at the follies of such representations.[98]

These arguments are important, especially because black spectatorship overwhelmingly involved white films, raising questions about pleasure, reception, and belonging. Although not necessarily as white as movies from later years—partly because of the black (or blackface) presence in Civil War anniversary films—cinema was not exactly racially progressive during the 1910s. This did not make black cinephilia impossible, as Stewart and Everett point out, although Stewart argues it may have kept it a "primitive" level—arguing that the predominance of all black seating may have limited absorption into the screen by foregrounding racial difference. Here absorption and identification might be resistant strategies, refusing the marginal space accorded black spectators.[99] Nevertheless, Stewart's explanation does not really address why African American audiences were drawn to the screen and to its white stars, something that likely cannot be answered fully. Still, the forms of mainstream white cinema singled out in advertisements and reports in the black press as black favorites offer some clues. In general, it appears that these films allowed readings that challenged dominant white culture while simultaneously accommodating black spectators' desires for full citizenship without these patrons having to renounce their pleasure in the screen.

Mainstream Hollywood and Black Taste

As Everett points out, black film criticism reveals black interest in movies as texts: even films like *The Birth of a Nation* were critically evaluated on aesthetic grounds despite their reprehensible content.[100] Other discourses in the black press—including reports on audience's star and genre preferences—highlight filmgoers' interest in the details of films while revealing firm favorites. Black film production further indicates an investment in the medium that cannot be explained away. Although it is important not to make generalizations about tastes given the diversity of the black community, certain mainstream genres—vamp pictures, serials, and westerns—stood out as particularly popular, with audiences having somewhat different tastes from their white counterparts.

Black audiences were interested in feature films almost from the start, with these films appearing in Black Belt theaters quite early, booked fresh from their first-runs in the Loop. White neighborhood theaters would follow suit several months later. Advertisements in the *Defender* reveal that features were shown in Black Belt theaters by 1913. The five-reel *Satan* was screened at the States Theater in September 1913, reportedly "by special request." This film—likely Ambrosio's *Satana* (Luigi Maggi, 1912)—was partly based on Milton's *Paradise Lost*, allowing audiences to indulge in sensation under the guise of religious and cultural improvement.[101] *Quo Vadis?* played the Lux for one weekend in November 1913, billed as "a rare treat," with audiences advised to arrive early to ensure admission. The *Defender* noted that this would be the full two-and-a-half-hour film, adding that the Lux "has gained an enviable reputation for presenting high-class pictures and it justly deserves it, for there is nothing too good in the market, so the genial manager says, for [its] patrons."[102] By 1914, several theaters were screening features on Sundays, including the Lincoln, Washington, and States, usually charging ten cents—twice their normal admission.[103] By October 1915, the States had moved over to all feature bills.[104] Not surprisingly, *The Birth of a Nation* did not play the Black Metropolis, but the other epics that opened in its wake, like *The Battle Cry of Peace*, were strong draws. *Battle Cry* played the States for two days in January 1916, just three months after its opening, inaugurating the theater's new pol-

CHAPTER 6

icy of screening major features for two or three days a week shortly after their Loop run.[105] After Teenan Jones took over the Star, he took Metro productions directly from Jones, Linick and Schaefer's Loop theaters.[106] *Intolerance* even played in the Stroll, heralded as a spectacle, complete with "125,000 People! 7,000 Horses! 1,500 Chariots!" not as a work of Griffith's genius.[107] By August 1917, black theaters were placing large ads illustrated with publicity stills for their biggest weekend bookings, by then mostly all features.[108]

Westerns

Between 1913 and 1917, several mainstream genres established themselves as clear favorites with black audiences. Significantly, African American filmmakers did not work in many of these forms (like the vamp, sex picture, and serials), indicating difference in black film reception as well as budgetary constraints. Ads and exhibitor reports give some sense of black tastes, although the information is still limited. Still, it appears that westerns and war films were particularly popular around 1911–13: in 1911, Sylvester Russell remarked that *The Railroad Managers*, *The Flag Didn't Rise*, *Cattle Thieves of 62*, and *Range Pals* were particular favorites.[109] During the last week of February 1913, Tony Langston reported that westerns were the featured attractions in three theaters: the Washington offered the two-reel *The Cowboy Millionaire* on Sunday and an unnamed two-reel western war drama on Thursday, while the Merit was "taxed to capacity almost nightly [after] several exciting western dramas were shown," and planned more of the same for the following week.[110] In March 1913 Langston commented on the strong following for Broncho Billy pictures at the Phoenix and reported that "several exciting western dramas" filled the Merit.[111]

Clearly, the western drew on discourses like nation and citizenship that greatly concerned the black community. Conceptually too, the Great West and the frontier played important roles in mythologizing American exceptionalism, manifest destiny, and framing the nation's image of itself, making westerns arguably *the* national genre. But as Richard Abel notes, it is worth asking: "What 'imagined community of nationality' did they tend to produce? Moreover, who were the audiences invited to share this knowing. . . . Americans of various kinds may have been attracted to the 'authentic' geographic landscapes of the West . . . but what those meant for specific audiences was not always the same."[112] It is too easy to link black tastes for westerns to fantasies of full American citizenship, but, as Stewart points out, this was clearly *part* of their appeal, especially in the westerns made by Noble Johnson and Oscar Micheaux.[113] But the kind of citizenship 1910s mainstream westerns evoked for black audiences, and the stakes involved in accepting their address, were far from straightforward. As Abel has shown, many westerns (like the Broncho Billy series) assumed white middle-class ideals of self and social order, despite the occasional presence of part Native American actors like Kalem's Mona Darkfeather, while minorities, particularly Mexican Americans, generally played the roles of villains, although exceptions existed.[114] This begs the question of black identification. Was it a disruptive force, identifying with resistance against whites, empathizing with Native Americans, Latinos, or other minorities? Stewart suggests such identifications were unlikely, pointing to the reception of the black film *The Trooper of Troop K* (Lincoln Motion Picture Company, 1916) that documented the Carrizal Incident and pitted African American soldiers against Mexicans.[115] During its Chicago release, black spectators screamed in support, "align[ing] themselves against Mexicans," presumably "not considering "how alliances with Asians or Latinos might advance their struggles against white racism."[116]

Clearly this film's reception, and its racial identifications, did not necessarily mirror those in white westerns. But the relative absence of African Americans in these films suggests an entirely more complex and flexible set of identifications. Stewart's point about the general absence of racial alliances between nonwhites is important, especially given the prominence of period civil rights discourse that set black citizens against immigrants, suggesting that in some instances, black subjects might identify against ethnic others, especially given these films' textual address. While evidence is scant, and therefore comments have to be somewhat speculative, calls for full black citizenship consistently evoked African Americans' history as *non*immigrant subjects, demanding equality on grounds of national origin. Although white immigrants were its primary focus, this discourse could also apply to Latinos, suggesting that black spectators might have allied themselves with white

CHAPTER 6

western heroes as Americans and as national pioneers. The maverick quality of some western heroes and their distance from the (southern) cultures associated with traditions of segregation and inequality may have enhanced this identification.

Westerns (and Indian films like those from Bison-101) that included a Native American presence raised another set of possibilities. Like African Americans, Native Americans shared the experience of being nonimmigrants discriminated against by whites. Abel points to the ambivalent position of Native Americans in many films, caught between their realization that their culture and tradition is lost and their need to accept, if not assimilate into, a white future.[117] Identifying with Native Americans would appear to pose a series of problems in a culture in which the Indian was increasingly seen as a romanticized but "defeated other."[118] If the Indian was the past, whose conquest set the terms for the birth of an American nation, then black identification could not represent the incorporation of black subjects into the nation, but the opposite: a perpetual position on the margins. Even brief moments of victory had to be framed in terms of this knowledge: they could only be temporary upswings in an otherwise lost cause. If anything, then, Indians' fights—and their ultimate acquiescence—suggested a path *not* to take toward full black citizenship.

Abel argues that for immigrants, identification with the Indian—an "in-between" figure—could be read "as a worthy figure of their own assimilation," while noting that for white assimilated audiences "that same figure [could be] reason for finding one or even both of the others unfit for assimilation."[119] He omits any possible black response, but it is not implausible that Indians might simultaneously evoke pity, sympathy, and even abjection. Black viewers may have even reconfigured the Indian as a figure with whom they could not identify because it embodied loss—of land, power, and the rights to their own culture. For a black community seeking full citizenship after a history of marginalization, the Indian inverted everything they stood for. Yet, as Abel suggests, this ambivalent response was shared throughout the population, facilitating the kind of belonging a national cinema necessarily evokes. "Indian pictures may well have worked to forge," in Hansen's words, "an *American* 'mass public out of an ethnically and culturally heterogeneous society,' yet one in which some degree of separation still marked their 'constellated communities' or audiences" (emphasis in original).[120]

Obviously, identification involves more than characters and exists across race, but these factors need to be considered, especially given the western's popularity with black audiences *and* its significance as a black film genre. Stewart and Pearl Bowser offer another perspective on these films' appeal, suggesting that black patrons' fondness for the genre likely came from the west's mythical position as a fresh start, a new empty space representing utopian possibilities and evoking a new improved order, one that would afford African Americans possibilities for self-realization.[121] Yet mainstream westerns represented this space as already in the process of being fully assimilated into white mainstream culture, something at odds with the above sentiments. This process nevertheless opened up a space for black filmmakers to correct the images of nation the western offered, injecting hopes for other possibilities.

Serials and Sensation

Although westerns remained popular, black preferences extended to more "feminine" genres between 1914 and 1917, as serials and sensational forms like white slavery, vamp, and fallen woman films became big draws.[122] Despite their overtly feminine address, serials had roots in the western, particularly in "cowboy girl westerns" like *Ranch Girls on the Rampage* (Kalem, 1912) that featured active female protagonists.[123] By June 1914, serials' popularity among Chicago's black audiences was evident: the Washington screened three different episodes of *Lucille Love: The Girl of Mystery* (Francis Ford, Universal, 1914) during one week, drawing capacity crowds, while all the area's other movie theaters listed serials as top draws.[124] They maintained their popularity even after their appeal faded in the city's white neighborhood theaters.[125] As Singer points out, serials—"the bad sheep of the picture family"—predominantly appealed to groups without social capital, making them perhaps predictable favorites.[126] They continued to be popular in small houses, rural neighborhoods, and in black theaters throughout the 1910s, even as they were held in low esteem by the industry as a whole.[127]

CHAPTER 6

Serials were extremely popular on the Stroll throughout 1917, despite doing badly elsewhere in the city: in July 1917, the *Motion Picture News'* Chicago correspondent reported: "Serials were emphatically out of it here for many months past. Seldom are they seen except in the smallest theatres of the five-cent variety in neighborhood sections."[128] Yet their popularity in the Black Belt was unabated: January, the Star noted that they were "using two serials in our regular booking and the great *Girl From Frisco* [a western serial] episodes are a real drawing card."[129] The same month, the Lincoln screened five serials—*Liberty* (another western serial); *The Shielding Shadow* (a supernatural serial queen mystery); *The Lass of the Lumberlands* (Helen Holmes out west); *The Crimson Stain* (another supernatural thriller); and *The Vampires*—"and they all have a great following." At the same time, the Washington ran three serials, *The Penalty of Treason* (the sequel to *The Diamond from the Sky*), *Liberty*, and *The Vampires*. The Star featured two: *The Shielding Shadow* and the ninth episode of *The Girl From Frisco*, "The Web of Guilt," which "drew well." The Atlas offered *The Shielding Shadow* and reran 1915's *The Diamond From the Sky*.[130] In May, the Lincoln announced, "We are using many serials now, and they all have a following. These are *The Great Secret*, *The Voice on the Wire*, *Patria* [a preparedness serial that represented Mexicans and Japanese as enemies intent on invading the United States], and *The Double Cross*."[131]

It is possible that serials' play with women's attempts to seize full agency in public space appealed to African Americans who read these gendered struggles in racial terms. Some serials explicitly linked their heroines' activity to their desires for expanded citizenship, inviting black identification, as with *Patria*, whose heroine, Patria Channing, organized her own army/militia, associating women's activity with more than just (temporary) liberation. But this freedom—like women's ability to participate in the public sphere—did not come easily. Like other serial heroines, Patria had to struggle against the forces seeking to contain her, here the villainous Morales and Baron Huroki, who repeatedly captured her to stop her investigating their plans to invade America.[132] Tellingly, Patria's actions were paralleled with those of her African American servant, at least in the serial's first episode, likely encouraging black spectators to associate her actions with more than gendered freedoms. After entering a secret passage that she discovered behind her fireplace, Patria, her fiancé Donald, and her servant find a dead body, which they carry upstairs. Shortly afterward, Huroki holds the servant hostage and then captures Patria, setting fire to her house. While there are clear differences in class and power, Patria and her manservant work together and for the same cause—American freedom—even though it paradoxically leads to their entrapment while Donald remains free. Given the fragmentary state of this film, it is unclear what role this character had in future episodes—even if he escapes—but in the Museum of Modern Art's surviving footage, he is presented as a team member, not just a loyal servant. In defending his country against a Mexican-Japanese alliance, his role reinforces Stewart's point about the lack of interracial collaboration against white hegemony (he works with whites; Asians and Latinos are the enemy) while establishing a race-gender alliance that might have informed the reception of serials more generally.

As Stamp has shown, serials' dialectic of entrapment and freedom articulated female audience's frustrations with social limitations, something that likely resonated with African American audiences.[133] Their representation of workplace discrimination also addressed women's struggles in public space, as seen in *The Hazards of Helen* (J. P. McGowan and others, Kalem, 1914–17) and *What Happened to Mary?* (Charles Brabin, Edison, 1912). These heroines had to work—the search for work was one of *Mary*'s major plot points—and performed well despite confronting prejudices.[134] This recognition of discrimination combined with narratives of female ability and success highlighted the struggles inherent in forging a more heterogeneous and inclusive public sphere, something with significant racial implications.[135] Identification with these heroines could support calls for greater citizenship while providing thrilling escapes into worlds of crime and/or luxury. Although serials may have spoken more to the needs, interests, and pleasures of black women, the black press offered no discussion of gendered preferences, perhaps because this risked fragmenting the community, directing attention toward gender, not race.

CHAPTER 6

Sensational Dramas and Adult-only Films

Almost all genres popular with black patrons shared a tendency toward sensation, a byword of the mid-1910s in the *Defender*'s exhibitor reports. Its appeal was not limited to the black community, working-class audiences also flocked to serials that had their roots in 10-20-30 melodrama.[136] As these texts addressed social change while expressing "the inherent anxiety and disarray of the postfeudal, postsacred world of nascent capitalism," they were clearly appropriate vehicles for mediating issues about status and community.[137] Sensational pictures generally focused on the plight of the innocent and the unrecognized, positions with which many black audiences could identify, even if the characters' specific situations were otherwise alien (as they would have been for most white viewers). In responding to a culture that "had not fully adjusted to the sensory upheavals of urban modernity," sensation may have appealed more strongly to recent black migrants from the rural south.[138] Nevertheless, its combination of thrilling action and empathy for those not in conventional positions of power made these melodramatic forms resonant vehicles for the concerns of a black population seeking social mobility, visibility, and recognition as well as diversion and distraction.

Another sensational form popular with audiences in Chicago's Black Metropolis was the adult-only feature film. Singer reminds us that: "Sensational melodrama remained a prominent genre as the feature film emerged in the early Teens (a fact that should be borne in mind in light of the tendency to oversimplify the feature film as an emblem of the film industry's gentrification)."[139] Many adult-only films were sexual melodramas, although crime films and politically sensitive material like *The Birth of a Nation* and *The Little American* also received pink permits. By 1917, all the movie theaters featured in the *Defender*'s weekly entertainment page routinely screened adult-only films—at a time when these were shunned in the city's white neighborhood houses. Under manager Will Foster, at least one of the States' weekly features was reportedly pink.[140] By 1917, the States, Phoenix, Lincoln, Washington, Star, Atlas, Pickford, and Fountain all screened pinks at weekends, whether more pedigreed theatrical adaptations (like *Damaged Goods* [Richard Bennett and Tom Ricketts, American-Mutual, 1914]), lurid films with big stars (particularly Theda Bara and Clara Kimball Young), or less reputable films like *The Unborn* (Otis B. Fair, Kulee, 1916), which played to "record-breaking crowds," as did the white slavery pictures shunned elsewhere in the city.[141] A preference for sensational features, especially those centering on female sexuality, marks the States Theater's program for November 29–December 21, 1917. Nine bills are listed, some with a single feature, others with an added two-reel attraction. Five were sensational melodramas dealing with female sexuality and criminality: *Her Hour* (George Cowl, World, 1917); *Camille* (J. Gordon Edwards, Fox, 1917); *The Woman God Forgot* (Cecil B. DeMille, Artcraft-Paramount, 1917); the white-slavery melodrama, *Who Is Your Neighbor?* (S. Rankin Drew, Master Drama Features Inc., 1917); and *Within the Law* (William P. S. Earle, Vitagraph-VLSE, 1917).[142] Three were adult-only films (*Her Hour, Camille, Who Is Your Neighbor?*), while a fourth, *Within the Law*, was shown only by "Special Court Permit."

Strikingly, several of these films emphasized struggles against injustice and prejudice, foregrounding how discrimination made it difficult to find suitable employment. *Within the Law*, based on the 1912 Bayard Veiller stage melodrama, focused on Mary, a woman jailed for a crime she did not commit who becomes a swindler, as she cannot get legitimate work. She marries a man she does not love to get vengeance on his father, the employer who originally sent her to jail, and is then is accused of a murder committed by her true love, Joe, who finally confesses to the killing. *Her Hour* focuses on Rita, who is fired from her department store job after refusing her supervisor's advances. She later works for a lawyer and succumbs to him to save her job. She then marries a young widower and they have a daughter, but when the widower discovers her past, he discards her. She becomes a lobbyist to bring down the lawyer who ruined her reputation but is told that this will ruin the life of her now adult daughter. After the lawyer's campaign manager breaks into her home and attacks her daughter, Rita kills him and is put on trial, with her old foe prosecuting her. She then dies of a heart attack, hiding the fact that the lawyer is really her daughter's father. Both films dealt with women's struggles after their professional reputations were ruined, focusing on the consequences for their working and romantic lives. Their narratives suggest that people who experience discrimination *will* seek alternate paths to social mobility whether that involves crime or acceding to male lust, blaming the system for

CHAPTER 6

these injustices. While part of their appeal came from identifying with the unfairly maligned, resonating with African American spectators' own experiences of discrimination, these films also offered the thrill of watching beautiful white women suffer, commit crimes, and indulge in sexual escapades.

Stardom

In addition to their genre preferences, black audiences were particularly interested in movie stars, although many white favorites like Mary Pickford had limited appeal. As was the case elsewhere in the city, black theaters were decorated with star ephemera, with the lavish Owl Theater featuring a "rotunda decorated with oil paintings of movie stars."[143] Not surprisingly, actors who routinely appeared in sensational films were particularly popular with black audiences, particularly Theda Bara and Clara Kimball Young, with Bara outranking her nearest rivals.[144] Other favorites included William S. Hart, Dorothy Gish, and Charles Chaplin, but none were mentioned in the black press as often as Bara and Kimball Young.[145] According to some of her early publicity, Kimball Young was supposedly semiaristocratic, "a descendant of Lord and Lady Becour," although the public knew her as the wife (then ex-wife) of her director, James Young.[146] She specialized in playing suffering women, some virtuous, some led astray by their sexuality. While capable of vampiric sexual behavior, her characters usually felt remorse, often because her conduct stemmed from malign male influence, as in *Lola* (James Young, Schubert-World, 1914) and *Trilby* (Maurice Tourneur, Equitable-World, 1915). Consequently, many of her films ended tragically.[147] Bara's characters, while far more varied than her iconic vamp, were usually excessive, fashionably dressed sexual women who were far less repentant than Kimball Young's (if reviews, commentary, and plot descriptions are any guide). Often triumphant in her power over men, her use of her sexuality and her ability to make her way through society, Bara presented a very different and highly performative take on sexual transgression and feminine resolve. Black patrons seem to have appreciated her abnegation of white middle-class morality and her pleasure in defying the norms even more than Kimball Young's suffering.

Bara's stardom evokes issues of race, at least for white audiences. As some critics have pointed out, her exoticism implied that she was nonwhite or positioned her as a racially liminal figure.[148] Publicity often presented her in Orientalist terms, posing with Egyptian mummies or kneeling in front of Buddhas, wearing elaborate headdresses with her eyes darkly outlined. But any sense of Bara as less than wholly white was scant even among white patrons, as audiences were in on the joke. Fan magazine profiles recognized her as Theodosia Goodman from Cincinnati, especially after she became an established star and started playing more varied roles like Juliet and one of *The Two Orphans* (Herbert Brenon, Fox Film Corporation, 1915). It is highly unlikely that black spectators read her as a nonwhite presence—nothing about Bara's persona linked her to the African American community save the popularity of her films.

Still, these beloved white players did not quell demand for black stars, figures who could counter mainstream images and signify African American success.[149] Audiences so craved black stars (if they were in white films, so much the better in terms of visibility and success) that the very presence of a black actor in a mainstream film could forcefully change reception strategies—even if they played a villain or marginal role.[150] Properly handled, black stardom might open up possibilities for blackness and black citizenry that were yet unfulfilled—especially given period fascination with celebrity. Ideally, these stars would not elicit white attention to an exotic, stereotypical blackness, but would evoke important aspects of black culture through their roles and star images, something the black press linked to uplift and the middle-class black ideal.[151] While a few respected black vaudevillians, most notably Bert Williams, appeared in white productions, their acts were often transcribed in ways that echoed racial ambiguities: Williams was an intelligent and socially conscious man forced into blackface because of the expectations of vaudeville circuits and their white audiences.[152] His brief entrée into film with Biograph during 1916 (the very end of the studio's active years) involved the same compromises. While he wrote, directed, and produced both Biograph releases, *Fish* and *A Natural Born Gambler*, he wore blackface and engaged in what would be seen as stereotypical behaviors like gambling and drinking. The intertitles in *A Natural Born Gambler* were written in a crude approximation of work-

CHAPTER 6

ing-class black pidgin while its cast combined African Americans and white actors blacked up (although without the exaggerated minstrel make-up Williams wore here and on stage). These films were primarily aimed at white audiences and were heavily advertised in the trade press but curiously not in the *Defender*. This lack of coverage makes it difficult to know whether they played the Stroll and perhaps reveals black leaders' hesitation in addressing such texts. They were the creative work of a leading black vaudevillian, starring vehicles produced by a company that was formerly an industry leader, yet they posed the same problems as his vaudeville act that was aimed at white audiences yet was also his own creation. Rather than criticize successful African Americans or endorse the kinds of low black comedy the paper otherwise opposed, it was perhaps best to leave the matter alone.

While no black actor reached the heights of stardom, there were players who received moderate success in mainstream films. In 1917, Pathé Balboa featured the young African American boy actor, Peggy Williams, alongside their juvenile lead Baby Marie Osborne in the five-reel Gold Rooster brand film, *Told at Twilight* (Henry King, Pathé Balboa). It played at the States as an Easter Sunday special, and was warmly received. Even though it appears that Williams's role was marginal, he was acclaimed as one of the film's stars.[153] Universal employed the actor who came closest to black stardom, Noble M. Johnson, who simultaneously starred in race films from the Lincoln Motion Picture Company, until he had to resign from his own company in 1918.[154] He appeared with Claire McDowell in *The Lady from the Sea*; supported Ruth Stonehouse in *Kincaid—Gambler*, a Bluebird feature; and acted in the five-reel Red Feather releases, *Love Aflame* and *The Caravan*.[155] A light-skinned actor, dubbed the "'Ebony Francis Bushman' . . . by his many lady admirers," Johnson was cast in many "ethnic" roles.[156] He worked in Hollywood until the 1950s, appearing in blockbusters like *King Kong*, and continued his career on television, making him the most significant African American film actor of his day. But Johnson was only a star to black audiences; for whites, he was at best a supporting actor. Although he made blackness visible, his race was often disguised, limiting the circulation of this African American image among white audiences: "Johnson played diverse racial roles (including Native Americans, Mexicans, Arabs, and even whites); in fact, Johnson almost never played Black characters in his Hollywood film appearances. Black audiences celebrated and patronized Johnson's films, regardless of the race of his characters and despite the fact that he played villains in many Hollywood productions. For Black audiences, Johnson's star text undercut the classical diegetic world of mainstream films."[157] Johnson's unique parallel trajectory as a star and producer of black films and as a contract player in mainstream films helped transformed these representations for black audiences in the 1910s. In his work with Lincoln, he usually played the kind of upright, intelligent, middle-class hero the black press endorsed as a racial ideal. His mainstream releases and race films may have been read alongside one another to elicit another understanding of Johnson as a black man who could only fully express himself and his identity in the context of black films. But these more mainstream texts were important, as they really allowed audiences to claim Johnson as a star. Still, black stardom in the fullest sense could really only be constituted in black films at this time, another reason why they were so significant and longed for despite their limited circulation and restricted power.

Black Filmmaking: Genre and Address

Although Chicago pioneered black filmmaking and was home to perhaps its first director, William Foster, these films were far from routine attractions in area theaters.[158] Financing was difficult, and few such movies were made. All these films are lost, there are limited reports on them in the black press, and they were not mentioned in the trades, leading most scholars to mine the same materials from the *Defender* to trace their reception and content.[159] Like local film productions (with which they share many characteristics), black films were low-budget forms that allowed audiences to see themselves and their neighborhoods on screen, constituting important community practices in their own right. For economic, cultural, and political reasons, these filmmakers often worked in a relatively narrow range of genres—comedy, newsreels, war pictures, and westerns—revealing telling discrepancies between the mainstream white material black patrons favored and the subjects that lent themselves to black authorship. With limited budgets, filmmakers had to be strategic and make the films they considered

CHAPTER 6

most necessary, so black films necessarily functioned differently from their white counterparts, but this did not mean that they neglected entertainment. Still, critical reception was less playful: black films were perceived as important social statements and had to manage greater expectations of "authenticity," correcting misapprehensions about black life, often in tandem with their middle-class emphasis.

The earliest black films were comedies, a genre that was already popular with black audiences and worked well with filmmakers' low budgets, particularly given comedy's association with the short film. Still, Pearl Bowser, Louise Spence, and Stewart recognize that this strategy was not without risks as these films frustrated race leaders both by foregrounding the heterogeneity in the black community (in the face of efforts to present a united front) and by causing blacks to laugh at one another.[160] Stewart argues that many early comedies "juxtapose different 'types' of Black characters based on their geographic background and/or location," as well as presumably class and other forms of stratification, evoking the humor that could arise in black interactions.[161] Furthermore, comedy fits uneasily with the black press's rhetoric of uplift: writing about Oscar Micheaux's work of the 1920s, Bowser and Spence note that drama was the black press's preferred genre because:

> the social urgency of the times had led some . . . members of the black bourgeoisie to the deluded belief that positive representations of cultural vitality and achievement would demonstrate the Negro's basic humanity to the world and win the rights of full citizenship. This acceptance, however precarious, depended on setting themselves apart from, or denying, the socially abject. However, in attempting to prove that they were modern and not so different from the American mainstream, these blacks were sacrificing their autonomy.[162]

Still, comedy was not without its redeeming qualities. William Foster's early work spoke directly to his community, picking up on shared references and insider knowledge while focusing on African American middle-class life to counter racial stereotypes.[163] Offering more than just stereotypes, comedy presented insider parodies, critiques of black life, situations and customs to stimulate the laughter of recognition, binding audiences together and cementing belonging, something very much like the practice of signifying Henry Louis Gates elaborated.[164] As these films focused on black knowledge, audiences appreciated this privileged address and realized other groups would not get the jokes.

By the mid-1910s, a number of low budget producers started offering more crude and stereotypical black comedies, making the genre's reception more contentious. Despite their support for early (and worthy) efforts by the likes of Foster, the black press turned against comedy, even when used by black filmmakers. After a reader wrote to the *Defender* in 1916 expressing her disgust with the Ebony Company's comedies, Tony Langston agreed, telling audiences to stay away from "all-colored comedies," mentioning that he had advised black exhibitors to do the same.[165] A few months later, J. Dooley (manager of the Atlas Theater) criticized black filmmakers who specialized in that "cheap and low stuff called 'comedy.'"[166] While Foster managed to balance uplift and comedy—partly because of his use of middle-class settings—the genre became increasingly controversial. As Stewart notes, "the comic, often parodic, treatment of black characters in Ebony films, along with Black representations in other white-controlled companies, impelled other African American producers to settle on drama as the appropriate genre for presenting the 'positive' and unifying implications of migration and patriotism for African-Americans."[167] The *Defender* was particularly troubled by black patrons liking for comedies filled with negative stereotypes, causing its journalists to bemoan audiences' apparent self-deprecation.[168]

The other foundational black film genre was the newsreel/actuality/documentary, emphasizing local black social institutions and community leadership. The black press fully endorsed these films, just as they would the slightly later black dramas that typically took up issues of citizenship. Many of these later films were war films and westerns, genres already associated with the national experience that were reworked to foreground black history, agency, and national ideals. Some filmmakers like Peter P. Jones and Noble and George Johnson effectively created a black national cinema, focusing on African American history and contributions to American society. All these films explored belonging, positioning blackness within the parameters of nation and showing the community values at its heart.

CHAPTER 6

Black spectatorship of race films cannot be seen as akin to white spectatorship of mainstream films. Audiences were aware that these texts were exceptional and recognized their differences (further touted in promotions and reviews), and they clearly stood out on bills of otherwise white films. Even though black films may have been closer to their culture and experience, they would be measured against white mainstream cinema that constituted the norm. These films not only told different stories and featured different actors/characters but also looked different, as their lower budgets affected film style and photographic quality. Unlike most headline attractions, they were often just one- or two-reels long (especially at first), again foregrounding their difference.

Two of the most important early black film companies were Chicago's Foster Films and the Peter P. Jones Photoplay Company. Both were undercapitalized, making production sporadic and therefore short-lived, despite critical acclaim and public demand for their work. While each had their own approach to filmmaking, they worked with similar genres and subjects. Besides emphasizing middle-class African American experiences, both companies made comedies, films about black military service, and actualities commemorating important local events. Other black filmmakers may have existed: in 1915, Foster estimated that there were currently about "ten or twelve" active African American producers who together could not begin to satisfy demand for their films. While likely exaggerated, his comment suggests figures may have vanished from this sketchy historical record.

The *Defender* occasionally referred to another kind of black film production: degrading and stereotype-laden comedies like those from the Chicago-based white-owned and managed Trykay Film Company. Established by former Keystone man Ogden K. Hunsaker and newspaperman E. F. Hurley, they released several all-black titles that were screened in black theaters, but not discussed in the Black press, although their primary audience seems to have been rural whites.[169] In September 1917, they announced they would specialize in "colored comedies . . . plain black comedies, with the casts made up of negroes. They are to be of two-reel lengths. The first is to be known as *The Darktown Fire Brigade*."[170] This was the title of a popular lantern slide and lithographic series from 1885 featuring incompetent African

Citizenship and Black Cinema

American firefighters, presumably the film's inspiration. Adapted into a minstrel show in 1908, the subject was infamous among black audiences, suggesting that the resultant film—if released—would not be well received.[171] Such examples reveal that black films involved more than African American actors: they needed to express a black point of view, come from black creators, and address themselves to the needs of black communities.

The Foster Photoplay Company

Probably the nation's first black filmmaker, William Foster was a pioneer showman with close ties to the black theater.[172] Under the alias "Juli Jones" he was formerly entertainment columnist for the black newspaper the *Indianapolis Freeman*. He wrote for the *Defender*, worked as press agent for African American comedians Bert Williams and George Walker, and later managed the States Theater.[173] As Jane Gaines points out, "In his ties with the *Chicago Defender*, Foster illustrates as well what was distinctive about the early African American film industry—it diverged from the white mainstream in the strengths of its connections with widely circulating black newspapers."[174] Foster claimed to have founded the Foster Photoplay Company in 1910 (Lynn Kirby also lists this date) but would not release films for over a year.[175] Even though his company was headquartered in the Black Metropolis at 3110 South State Street, his films took time reaching Chicago's black theaters. *The Railroad Porter*, his first major success, was completed in 1912 but did not premiere in Chicago until July or August 1913, appearing in New York in September 1913 at the Lafayette Theater.[176] Histories of his work are scant and riddled with inconsistencies, partly because all his films are lost and partly because he favored promotional bluster over more objective accounts.[177] His tendency to promote films years before he started production, and sometimes under variants of their release titles, presents further difficulties in discerning what films he made—and when they were produced and released.[178]

Despite claims that *The Railroad Porter* was his first film—and maybe the first ever black-produced motion picture—reports in the *Defender* reveal that Foster's first two films were actualities, pictures of the dedication of the black YMCA in 1913 and the parade that followed, both

CHAPTER 6

missing from filmographies.[179] This was a strategic way to launch a career: the YMCA opened in 1911 and was an important black cultural institution, even though some found it elitist because of its high membership fees and its affiliations with black social reform.[180] By filming its commemoration, Foster marked the founding of one major black institution (the YMCA) by forming another: black filmmaking. These actualities presented him as a serious community representative, recording important events for what appeared to be posterity, placing his work in the service of black history and culture from the start. His other early actuality was *The Colored Championship Base Ball Game* (1913), featuring highlights from the Negro League Championship. According to the *Defender*, four thousand people flocked to these actualities in their opening week (July 19, 1913) and both ran successfully for a number of weeks in houses along the Stroll.[181] Foster's early work captured the black community's desire to see itself and its institutions on screen, be they a Negro League game, a parade, or the YMCA. His fiction films were all shot in Chicago's Black Metropolis, so audiences could see their culture *and* their neighborhood on film for the first time. This recognition had to be significant and pleasurable, establishing an unprecedented proximity to the image for local audiences used to mainstream white films that had some distance from their lives.

Foster further displayed his pride in his culture when he announced his forthcoming fiction films and promised they would present "the better side of the race on canvas [rather] than . . . some Negro making an ass of himself."[182] His early actualities established his name, built an audience, and likely helped raise money for more expensive fiction films.[183] They also gave him a platform to promote his upcoming comedies—*The Railroad Porter* and a then unnamed movie (*The Grafter and the Maid*) focusing on a black butler who worked for a white family.[184] *The Railroad Porter* featured Kid Brown in the title role, Lottie Grady as his wife, Cassie Burch Slaughter as her friend, Edgar Ellison as a waiter, and Bell Coles as a policeman.[185] Brown had a lengthy career as a comedian-actor-singer in black vaudeville, but Lottie Grady was a star.[186] Before playing in *The Railroad Porter*, she was a leading actress in the Pekin stock company and worked on the New York stage. In 1910, she appeared in a solo show at the Monogram earning the highest salary then paid to a single black performer in Chicago—$100 a week.

She also toured on the Western vaudeville circuit and would appear on Broadway a couple of years after filming Foster's first comedy.[187] Casting her was a big coup, and her salary was presumably high, suggesting that these comedies may not have been so low budget. Indeed, her performance would have been one of the film's major attractions, suggesting that the railroad porter's flirtatious wife may have been a more significant figure than extant plot descriptions suggest. In casting Grady, Foster created something like a black film star whose presence asserted the centrality of contemporary African American life and culture.

The Railroad Porter debuted to crowded houses at the States Theater in early August 1913. In an unprecedented departure from the theater's customary daily change, it played all week, with matinees on Mondays, Thursdays, and Saturdays, attracting so many patrons that the States contracted for the first run of all Foster's subsequent pictures.[188] Two weeks later, it moved to the Grand as the featured attraction—quite remarkable for a short—where it "kept the audience in convulsions of laughter."[189] It then played sold-out shows at the Pekin before moving to the Majestic for one night in November and then, reportedly, onto black theaters nationwide.[190] It was also featured on vaudeville bills. *The Railroad Porter* returned to the Stroll several times through this period, being bought back to the Star in July 1917 by local demand.[191] Not surprisingly, the film is lost: there were likely few prints, probably played until they wore out.

Stewart notes that *The Railroad Porter* "features a range of New Negro types." Both its male characters—the husband and the fashionably dressed waiter with whom his wife has a flirtation—were employed in positions that "reflect exciting new opportunities available to African American men—uniformed, well-traveled Pullman porters were often treated as cultural heroes within the Black community."[192] Foster's fictional world was an urban, modern, black middle-class milieu, and its comedy potentially derived "from the disruptions posed by these attractive features of modern life—travel, consumer culture, and the glamour of the Stroll café scene."[193] Other commentators focused on its extramarital flirtation and the slapstick chase that follows the husband's discovery of his wife's dalliance.[194] As the film is lost, it is difficult to ascertain its address and how it positioned the black community,

CHAPTER 6

but it likely accommodated a diverse black audience, the members of which hoped to see black culture finally represented "authentically" on screen. For some, this might involve seeing the Stroll, for others, a representation of middle-class life or even Lottie Grady's performance, while others enjoyed the jokes.

Foster immediately announced that he was constructing a movie studio to produce four- and five-reel pictures that would rival any on the market. This did not come to pass and may have been promotional bluster. Nonetheless, the *Defender* predicted success, adding: "It is always gratifying to see a member of our race embark into a new field of endeavor. Long live the Foster Film Company."[195] In September 1913, his next film, the short Jerry Mills drama *The Grafter and the Maid*, opened at the States. Mills was an actor and musical comedy writer who had been a member of Bob Cole's All Star Stock Company in New York (the first professional African American stock company and theater school) before joining the Pekin stock company.[196] He appeared in several Foster films and later worked with Oscar Micheaux on *The Homesteader* (1920). The *Defender* admired *Grafter*'s greatly improved photography, possibly indicating one of *The Railroad* limitations.[197] The next month, the States premiered Foster's third short comedy, *The Fall Guy*, which the *Defender* acclaimed as "a marked improvement over some of the preceding ones and simply goes to prove that practice makes perfect."[198]

That November, the *Defender* heralded Foster as a pioneer, ironically, exactly as his productivity sharply declined: "Foster saw into the future. He knew that moving pictures were here to stay and that the moment he could get *real Negro life* in one of his pictures he would have solved the problem, a picture of his ideas seen at big houses. *The Railroad Porter* was enacted. He conceived it and had it played and took it with his own machine and put all the trimmings in to make it go . . . Foster's 'movies' are a success" (my emphasis).[199] This article may have been designed to help him raise funds or find more reliable distribution: with the exception of *The Grafter and the Maid*, which the Soundies Distributing Company distributed, he distributed his own work.[200] In an interview with the *Defender* seven months later, Foster announced he had signed a distribution contract with the Warner Feature Film Company, then a relatively minor player specializing in states rights features. This would have been a coup for a small independent, but it may have been another piece of showmanship: Warners never released any Foster films.[201] His subsequent releases—*Mother* (1917), *Brother* (1918), *Fool and Fire* (1918), and *A Woman's Worst Enemy* (1918)—were all self-distributed.[202]

These subsequent releases were far more sporadic. The nearly three-year gap between *The Grafter and the Maid* and *The Barber* suggests possible financial problems, although his mode of distribution might account for some of this delay. Foster traveled with his films, like later black filmmakers, touring the south with *The Railroad Porter*, *The Fall Guy*, *The Butler*, and *The Grafter and the Maid* in 1914, presumably affecting his production and release patterns.[203] After releasing several films locally, he hit the road, presumably waiting until he had a full program. This was more efficient than touring with each short but reveals the strain on a filmmaker with no official distribution and limited funds for multiple prints. Foster claimed southern blacks "were wild about [his] films," and maintained that his films pictures were a "big hit throughout Europe."[204] While possibly wishful thinking, references to the popularity of black films in international markets were not uncommon, as Everett points out.[205] This internationalism positioned African Americans as part of a global public—even if these citizens weren't fully recognized at home.

Returning to Chicago, Foster continued writing for the black press under the alias Juli Jones. He did not resume film production until July 1916 after receiving backing from gambler-entrepreneur Henry "Teenan" Jones, who hired Foster to manage his Star Theater in 1917.[206] His next release was a self-penned comedy, *The Barber*, starring Anna Holt, vaudevillian Howard Kelly, and Edgar Lillison. The *Defender* welcomed him back, noting: "It has always been a source of wonder why the Foster company did not continue to produce after the success it had with *The Fall Guy*, *The Grafter and The Girl*, *The Butler* and others. There never was as great a demand for pictures of this kind as at present."[207] The scenario for *The Barber* was printed in full in the *Defender*, which was unprecedented in a publication that only featured limited film criticism. Like its predecessors, *The Barber* was a slapstick comedy of manners centered on a wife's seduction. This time Foster featured black society protagonists and a wily barber who disguises himself as

CHAPTER 6

a Mexican music teacher to seduce a wealthy and beautiful wife.[208] Another success, it played in several theaters on the Stroll, booked for return engagements alongside his earlier work.

By now, other black filmmakers like Peter P. Jones and the Lincoln Motion Picture Company had entered into production, possibly influencing Foster to make more ambitious films.[209] While managing the Star, he started working on multireel films on more weighty topics.[210] *Mother* (1917) was his first serious drama, a six-reel World War I film, boasting "fifty scenes [and] 4,000 people."[211] It focused on one of the most important issues in the black community: black military service and its relationship to full civil rights. War films foregrounded African Americans' role in creating and protecting this country—military service was central to the period's black civil rights, an issue that was all the more pressing as the nation moved to war.[212] These dramas also exposed the institutional racism black soldiers experienced, reinforcing what Stewart calls "the optimistic notion that the cinema—as both a representational medium and a public space—could potentially improve the social and political position of Black American citizens."[213] Foster's *Brother* (1918)—one of three features he released that year—was another six-reel drama, showing the last thirty years of African American history from a black perspective. (His other 1918 releases were the vamp/western hybrid *A Woman's Worst Enemy* and the five-reel vamp film *Fool and Fire*.) While he claimed *Brother* was a direct response to *The Birth of a Nation*, it seems not to have been a radical film, instead featuring "the bad colored man, the bad white man, the good colored man, and the good white man." He presented his work in terms that curiously echoed those Griffith used to defend *The Birth of a Nation*, as Foster argued: "No race of man is better than its women. Not every white man in the South is a race hater."[214]

This statement lies uneasily with some of Foster's other comments. In his 1915 *Defender* essay, "Moving Pictures Offer the Greatest Opportunity to the Race," he discussed how film could become an important African American institution, providing employment, opportunities to showcase black creative talents, and accomplishments while offsetting "so many insults to the race."[215] He urged others to make films to honor African American history and culture and "tell their side of the birth of this great nation . . . show what a great man Frederic Douglas [*sic*] was, the work of Tousant LaOverture [*sic*], Don Pedro and the battles of San Juan Hill, the things that will never be told only by the Negroes themselves. The world is very anxious to know more of the set-aside race, that has kept America in a political and social argument for the next two hundred and fifty years [*sic*]."[216] In contrast to the retrograde individualism used in his promotional copy for *Brother*, Foster furthers cinema's role in fighting discrimination, advancing black citizenship and improving his community. He believed filmmaking was inherently political and maintained that all-black motion pictures could be his race's most important cultural form—and its most lucrative.[217] He was an advocate for black filmmaking—in October 1915, he urged African Americans to enter the business now that movie equipment was available on the open market. Still he cautioned (presumably on the basis of his own experience) that "the past failure of colored men handling such things [motion picture production/distribution] teaches us that no one can handle a big corporation by himself."[218] His words reveal the scope of his ambitions: for black filmmaking to rival white mainstream films. "The public alike all over the world wants novelty. The colored plays would enter the field as a novelty. If they made good—of which there is not the slightest doubt—the plays would be a factor to stay."[219]

Peter P. Jones Photoplay Company

Chicago's other notable black film company, the Peter P. Jones Photoplay Company, specialized in serious nonfiction films emphasizing black history, culture, citizenship, and military accomplishments. Jones produced, directed, and self-distributed his films and was active between 1914 and 1917. He was a renowned black photographer, lauded for his retouching skills, who had taken pictures of such luminaries as Booker T. Washington, W. E. B. Du Bois, and Henry O. Tanner as well as members of the city's African American community.[220] In 1914, he announced plans to establish a studio on the Stroll with his partners Marshall and J. T. Bell to produce films that revealed "the progress of the Afro-American in the United States," some with "well-laid love plots," others revealing black business acumen, all featuring some degree of humor: "There will be no chicken-stealing scenes or crap games.... The pictures will be placed upon a high order and... will

CHAPTER 6

tend to awaken the consciences of men and women to do the right thing in life and will discourage drunkenness, dishonesty and licentiousness. There will be love scenes of the purest type, ones that children, maids and patrons will relish with pleasure."[221] Everett points out that the *Defender* heralded Jones's entry into filmmaking with a first-page story discussing his plans to form an international company in Brazil to make actualities. As there were no follow-up reports on this enterprise, she assumes it was a success.[222] It seems more likely that these plans failed even though Jones would later successfully release actualities in Chicago: had any earlier films existed, the *Defender* would certainly have commented on them.

While known for his serious work, Jones started in comedy, a genre he immediately abandoned. His first film, *The Troubles of Sambo and Dinah*, was released in June 1914, starring comedian Matt Marshall, a former member of the Pekin stock company.[223] As Everett observes, it is odd that a black film entrepreneur, especially one from Jones's background, would produce a film with such an offensive title and even stranger that the *Defender* failed to comment on a "wholesome and refined [film] . . . where one of the principal characters is derisively named 'Sambo.'"[224] His next release was *For the Honor of the 8th Illinois Regiment*, an actuality featuring the famous all-black company meeting Governor Dunne, fighting in Cuba during the Spanish-American War, and celebrating victory.[225] The following year, he covered Chicago's Lincoln Jubilee celebrations, held from August 21 to September 16, 1915, marking "the progress of the Negro after 50 years of freedom from slavery."[226] These films commemorated landmark events in African American culture and their relationship to black history, emphasizing the values of the culture and the contributions of black citizenship, in keeping with Jones's intent.

Jones's most productive year was 1916. He released five films, all representing African American progress, military prowess, citizenship, and culture. One of these, *Re-Birth of a Nation* (1916), was a direct response to Griffith's defamations. His subsequent two-reel military actualities, *Colored Soldiers Fighting in Mexico* and *Negro Soldiers Fighting for Uncle Sam*, focused on two wars. The first followed the 8th Illinois under their white commander, Colonel Franklin, fighting Villa's troops in Mexico, the second showed black soldiers training for active duty in

World War I.[227] *Progress of a Negro* was a newsreel stressing black cultural developments, African American pride, and the continued need to fight for civil rights. It featured Booker T. Washington, the Tuskegee Institute, and Mound Bayon, Mississippi, a city "built by ex-slaves."[228] His final 1916 release, *The Dawn of Truth*, edited together scenes from his other films with footage from the War Department, combined with comedy and drama to form a "movie spectacle," in the words of its publicity."[229]

Jones's two 1917 releases were fictions dealing with historical inequities and the progress African Americans made, urging them to rise beyond the limitations of both facets of their identities—the African and the American. *The Slaver* was set in Africa, where a black chieftain "reverses the slavery pattern," and "purchases a white girl from a White Sea captain. A Black cabin boy sacrifices himself to free her."[230] Through role reversal, the narrative exposes the ludicrousness of slavery while recasting the African American male as the white maiden's protector, countering images of lecherous blacks chasing after white purity. In the process, it encouraged black audiences to rise above prejudice while foregrounding the bizarre logic of white supremacy. His second 1917 release, *The Slacker*, was "an inspirational World War I film" not unlike *Joan the Woman*. A Dickensian melodrama, it featured the "ghost of wars past" inspiring a man to enlist, leading him to become a hero in France.[231] In placing a black man as a national icon in a white man's war, Jones reminded viewers that his community had maintained their side of the citizen-state contract, despite frequent betrayals. He ceased production in 1917, likely because of high production costs and limited distribution, although the exact reason is unclear. His work arguably represents the earliest serious and sustained attempt to explore the period's black life in the context of both American and African American history, foregrounding the relationship between black and white America to advance the cause of full black citizenship.

Clearly, mainstream films dominated black screens, offering a different form of address to black audiences, one that sometimes evoked the potential for belonging and full citizenship, albeit not without struggle. There may have been some comfort in seeing that this struggle was not restricted to African Americans, but was more broadly shared by women and many in the working classes. Black films' investment

CHAPTER 6

in African American citizenship was more clearly marked, but while these texts offered a welcome visibility and black perspective, it came with the awareness that this address evoked a parallel community that was not commensurate with the full citizenship patrons demanded. As American cinema became an explicitly national cinema during the 1910s, the black community faced the difficulties of being attracted to a medium that did not fully include them as citizens, as evidenced in the paucity of black roles and the absence of black stars, let alone texts presented from a nonwhite perspective. Yet refusing mainstream cinema's address meant isolating themselves from the sense of belonging that all national cinemas evoke, as well as sacrificing its pleasures—something few black citizens wanted.

Although black consumption of white films necessarily involved recuperation, in terms of both exhibition and spectatorship, mainstream films would be a necessary part of black cinema, especially for an audience who wanted to be considered full citizens. Still, the relationship between mainstream and race films reveals the need to present difference and maintain visibility on one's own terms. Black spectators consequently occupied an ambivalent position, caught between issues of belonging and the race-based forms of self-definition seen in black film production, black exhibition practices, and black film criticism. Even as national cinema became increasingly significant during the 1910s, the question of American identity remained unsettled. Race was only one area of dissent. Local, class, and ethnic allegiances all complicated and fragmented definitions of national identity. These debates were heightened in Chicago after the outbreak of war in Europe in 1914. As I point out in the next chapter, cinema's capacity to produce communities and stir audiences' emotions would take on a new resonance, showcasing its ability to consolidate or fragment definitions of national identity during a time of crisis.

SEVEN

Patriotism and Patronage
Regional and National Identity in
Chicago's Theaters during World War I

Films touching on national identity and American history and culture constituted an important and prestigious production trend during the 1910s. By 1914, feature-length films dealing with the national experience had supplanted the European epics like *Cabiria, Les Misérables,* and *Quo Vadis?* that had dominated Chicago's downtown theaters the previous summer. Vitagraph and Selig invested heavily in this trend with often epic-length national spectacles like *The Coming of Columbus* (Selig, 1912); *The Crisis* (Selig, 1916); and *The Battle Cry of Peace* (Vitagraph, 1915) and *Womanhood: The Glory of the Nation* (Vitagraph, 1917), texts that were usually surrounded by exhibition strategies designed to heighten audience identification and foster patriotism. Also popular were films based on (or set amid) events of national significance (like the Civil War, then celebrating its fiftieth anniversary), pictures adapted from American classics, and those exploring the modern American experience—like immigration, the move west, and contemporary consumer culture. Together, these forms positioned motion pictures as a powerful, accessible, and uplifting national form. Many were prestige productions, presenting national identity as one of the industry's primary and most vaunted concerns, a tactic clearly designed to enhance

CHAPTER 7

motion pictures' social standing and cultural renown while responding to and trying to alleviate contemporary uncertainties.

As seen in the publicity surrounding *The Birth of a Nation*, this emergent national cinema attempted to position the medium—and its "universal language"—as specifically American. Many of these films, including *The Battle Cry of Peace*, *Intolerance*, and *Civilization* (Reginald Barker, Thomas Ince, Triangle, 1916), combined national history or current events with allegory to link American destiny to eternal truth. Yet all maintained very different visions of nation, attesting to Progressive Era concerns about defining and shoring up national identity while illustrating the problems inherent in any effort to establish a "national" medium. Critically acclaimed and often controversial, these films highlighted difficulties in establishing consensus around national identity. Even as Progressive Era policies tried to foster immigrant assimilation and develop civic awareness through culture and education, it was clear modernity, the changed role of government, urbanization, and the closing of the frontier all placed American identity under stress. Shifting international relations further challenged any coherent national image as events like 1898's Spanish-American War, Pancho Villa's skirmishes on the US-Mexico border, and, most importantly, the outbreak of World War I challenged national security and made patriotism more pressing. With social anxieties circulating around the loss of a shared culture, the film industry used this opportunity to capitalize on its popularity and simultaneously improve its reputation. Ideally, cinema's "universal language" and its shared culture might help transcend audiences' former loyalties, reinventing motion pictures as a more civic medium, particularly during the Civil War anniversary and the run-up to World War I.[1]

The emergence of national cinema in the United States during the Progressive Era testified to the period's widespread tensions over definitions of nation and culture. Although diversity was a hallmark of American identity, it was not considered a stable ideal but more an interim position:

> Persistent diversity was not an ideal Americans aspired to but a temporary, inevitable situation to be dealt with in a democratic and humane manner. . . . The ideal was brotherhood, amalgamation, harmony.

Americans believed that common blood was not necessary to create unity, but they did not consider permanent group diversity to be desirable for American nationalism or culture. On the other hand, there was a view that racial and cultural amalgamation would create a better nationality type and national culture. In this way Americans dealt with the tension between unity and diversity.[2]

This idea of a "temporary" state of diversity was something that Progressive Era culture addressed, sometimes in prohibitionist terms, with campaigns that were designed to limit immigration or stop it entirely, such as the Immigration Restriction League (formed 1894). Laws were passed to restrict immigration and more broadly limit mobility, varying from the Chinese Exclusion Act (1882) to the 1910 Mann Act (which was used not just to prohibit women being taken over state lines for immoral purposes but to prevent interracial marriage where necessary, as with the case of Jack Johnson)—all designed to stabilize geographic and cultural change.[3] Less extreme, and more widespread, were efforts to balance new national loyalties and cultures with those of the old. There was, however, no consensus about how this balancing act could be achieved or what exactly this new American identity might look like. Reformers, sociologists, politicians—even the film industry—all tried to play a role here, as seen in the ideals cinema touted, like community, universal language, and patriotism. Diversity offered a temporary solution—one the film industry adopted—allowing numerous competing sentiments and beliefs to be fudged together as simultaneously "American" and patriotic. This practice reached its limits during wartime, however, when certain positions and identifications became controversial or untenable.

National cinema is a complex matter involving more than just texts, as Andrew Higson, Richard Abel, Paul Willemen, Philip Rosen, Sabine Hake, Stephen Crofts, and many others have shown.[4] National cinemas variously strive to bolster a nation's self-image as they present specific identities to the world, engage with state mandates, or seek to produce or reinvent a national culture where one may be absent or in turmoil.[5] They work to naturalize the concept of nation, masking its ideological and historical creation to render it timeless or alternatively evoking history to bolster tradition, loyalties, and a sense of continuity. As both

Philip Schlesinger and Andrew Higson have observed, they draw on the idea of the nation as a communicative space, establishing boundaries of inclusion and exclusion, even though these may be questionable, fragile, or contentious. As Higson notes, this practice involves constant work, as "the public sphere of the nation and the discourses of patriotism are . . . bound up in a constant struggle to transform the facts of dispersal, variegation and homelessness into the experience of rooted community."[6] National cinemas often play on emotions, try to evoke recognition in audiences, construct national communities, and market a nation while positioning cinema as both a leading source and a product of a discernable national culture. While they play with textuality, reception practices, and history/historiography, they rely upon—or attempt to secure—concepts of nation as "a minimally coherent entity," a task that often appears elusive and one that was certainly a leading Progressive Era concern.[7]

American national cinema of the 1910s demonstrates how address, reception, promotion, and exhibition could potentially transform a variety of texts into national cinema, albeit with varying degrees of coherence. In positioning itself as a national cinema, American film tried to negotiate Progressive Era tensions surrounding American identity without fragmenting already fragile national consensus, further threatened by World War I. Aided by careful promotions, exhibitors extended cinema's established community appeal to the national level to inculcate belonging and patriotism in audiences. Particularly effective at first, this tactic oscillated between the local and the national, often masking very real differences around patriotism and national identity as both could be expressed as communal sentiments. But as the war progressed, such strategies could not mask important differences that divided the American public and fundamentally challenged Progressivism's community ethos. As a conflict seemingly imposed upon the American people, World War I increased distrust in federal government, positioning it as a potentially untrammeled power rather than a force for the greater good. Meanwhile, the nation's entry into the war undermined Progressivism's overwhelming faith in progress, questioning the very concept that American life could only improve if carefully monitored.

World War I was both a symptom and a cause of national and international instability, embodying the period's clash between modernity and tradition.[8] After the outbreak of war in Europe in 1914, American definitions of national identity became more fraught and more dependent on international relationships, something with significant consequences in immigrant-heavy cities like Chicago.[9] Consequently, neutrality, preparedness, isolationism, and questions of partisanship played an increasingly important role in shaping America's sense of self, as did some citizens' lingering allegiances to different European nations. The Great War's influence on—and challenges to—American ideals further frustrated those who were not of European descent or believed in American exceptionalism and necessary distance from the Old World—after all, why should a European war intervene in American society and its self-definition? In Chicago, these beliefs were often at odds with dominant visions of national identity the federal government perpetuated, something that became increasingly visible in local movie theaters thwarting efforts to bolster national ideals within the city.

To understand the impact of World War I on American national identity, it is necessary to consider earlier efforts to specify national ideals. Before the war, German heritage was often privileged in accounts of American identity, as David A. Gerstner has shown, particularly those linked with efficiency, progress, and eugenics, all matters of importance during the Progressive era.[10] The war led to a shift away from these beliefs, marking a profound change in national self-conception. Unsurprisingly, many Chicago residents adhered to these national ideals given that many were of German ancestry—the city supported several German-language publications catering both to new residents and longtime citizens. Some of its most prominent leaders, including Mayor Thompson and head censor Major M. L. C. Funkhouser, opposed the United States' pro-British partisanship and were concerned about the ways these allegiances might shape national ideals. Social class and ethnic background further influenced understandings of national identity in sometimes surprising ways, sentiments further crystallized by war. In general, the city's social elite supported the British cause, as did East Coast high society. Its most recent immigrants (mainly from southern and eastern Europe) followed a national consensus that was alternately neutral then pro-British, unlike the majority of German-leaning assimilated residents who declared themselves fully American. Meanwhile, Chicago's African American population expressed a different kind of frustration, angry that their military contributions were erased in an all-white history while they were not given full civil rights.[11] Movie theaters attended to all these different ideals even after the outbreak of war while still extolling cinema as a national medium par excellence.

War brought neighborhood theaters' affiliation with community to another level as exhibitors imbued films with patriotism to mask often contentious differences over national identity. But many Chicago residents' objections could not be easily papered over, with patriotic appeals alienating many audiences after the United States entered the war on the Allies' side. Major film producers were aware of this dissent and largely avoided explicit and partisan war themes, especially in features, revealing how disagreements about the war mirrored debates about American ideals.[12] History films were a better option for bolstering national identity, using nostalgia to bring viewers together, as seen in the presentation of Civil War films like *The Littlest Rebel* (Edgar Lewis, Photoplay Productions, 1914). Taking advantage of historical distance, these films capitalized on the current anniversary celebrations to evoke patriotism without dealing with the turmoil over contemporary national identity.

Chicago's pro-German leanings were nonetheless evidenced in the war films shown in the city's theaters and in their modes of presentation. Downtown theaters were the first to express alternate, pro-German versions of national identity: the city's major newspapers—the *Tribune*, *Herald*, and *Evening American*—all made, financed, and imported pro-German war films that were linked to American patriotism both in theaters and in the press. Dissent from national consensus was particularly strong during 1917, manifested in local exhibition strategies, battles over film censorship, and protests over war taxes. Still, the film industry was not unified in its approach to the war: while many exhibitors did little to hide German partisanship, the city's producers, particularly Essanay's George Spoor, worked closely with the government, supporting official national war policies. The city's big theater chains' initial support for the war diminished once this strategy affected business.

Asserting Nation, Commemorating the Civil War, Declaring Neutrality

By 1914, feature films on matters of national interest had become a significant production trend. Unlike the European epics of the previous summer, these films appealed to a wide audience and transferred well to neighborhood theaters.[13] Specifically American subjects, like the filmed stage play *America* (Lawrence B. McGill, All Star Feature Film Corp.–World, 1914), dominated the Loop's first-run schedules well into the fall, while westerns and Americana remained popular throughout the city's theaters.[14] As Richard Abel has shown, the overwhelming popularity of westerns and Civil War films between 1909 and 1914 pointed to this national fascination with exploring American history and cultural identity.[15] Like westerns, Civil War films allowed the film industry to negotiate action, history, and nation, making the Civil War, in Tony Horowitz's words, "a badge of citizenship."[16] In balancing tensions that were never completely reconciled, these films addressed American national identity in all its complexity and dissent.

Of all the films shown in first-run Loop theaters during summer 1914, the Civil War melodrama *The Littlest Rebel* stands out, partly because of its excessive presentation. The first explicitly nationalistic American feature to hit Chicago's downtown screens, *Rebel* drew attention to itself through its patriotic trappings. Adapted from the Edward Peple play, *Rebel* covered familiar and conventional ground (the film is lost).[17] It centered on six-year-old Virgie, the daughter of a Confederate officer who is captured by Union troops after returning home to his plantation. Virgie charms her father's estranged brother, a Union officer, who then tries to save her father, leading to the siblings' arrest and near execution. The film featured the Civil War tropes that, for Abel, typified reunion culture: nostalgia for the South, Confederate-friendly point of view, innocent North-South romance (Virgie emblematized Southern innocence, with her name echoing the first colony and youthful purity), female action (albeit through a child), feminization of the South, and emphasis on "domestic or family-oriented stories."[18] Many World War I films (like *The Battle Cry of Peace* and *The Little American*) would later use these same tropes to exhort action, preparedness, or even neutrality, revealing how Civil War narratives influenced filmic

CHAPTER 7

discourses around the Great War and took on a structural role in articulating national mythology.

Rebel was one of many Civil War films produced during its golden anniversary (1911–15). Locally at least, it owed some of its significance to chance: its Chicago opening coincided with the outbreak of war in Europe. Tensions escalated over a week as first Austria-Hungary declared war on Russia on July 28, then Germany declared war on France. On August 4, Germany invaded neutral Belgium, prompting England to go to war against Germany. *Rebel*'s exhibitor immediately capitalized on the conflict, transforming the film into a statement about American national identity in the face of the current global situation, benefiting its box office. As the *Herald* noted: "No photoplay shown in Chicago this season has caught the public fancy more quickly than *The Littlest Rebel*. . . . Attendance has increased by leaps and bounds daily, probably because of the war spirit permeating Chicago, resulting from the interest in the war clouds which are engulfing the European nations."[19] Initial publicity linked nationalism and the American child, presenting *Rebel* as both civics lesson and national allegory. The Monday after it opened, the First Cavalry of the Illinois National Guard attended the evening show, something that was advertised in advance as part of the attraction.[20] A week later, on August 2, 1914 (promoted as "Patriotic Sunday"), every child under twelve carrying an American flag was admitted free to afternoon screenings, cementing the film's associations between youthful innocence and a future-oriented American identity.[21] The next week's promotions explicitly referenced the new European war, indicating a key shift in address. "International Color Week" emphasized Chicago's—and America's—heterogeneous origins with all children under twelve who carried American flags or wore the colors of European nations admitted free to any daytime show.[22] This promotion fused three separate discourses. The first played with characteristics of Civil War commemoration, as these patriotic children echoed the strength of the film's heroine, symbolizing a new beginning and national reunification. The second highlighted the American melting pot, while the third evoked Europe at war—although acknowledging all sides equally, showing American distance from the conflict and the nation's impartiality. *Rebel*'s somewhat inchoate exhibition thus represents an early example of how World War I initially provided an opportunity to bolster and reshape definitions of national identity, presenting the United States as separate from Europe, while unifying its diverse people as those who were wise enough to recognize war's costs.

Rebel's promotions constitute an early example of Civil War films being used to comment on World War I, here managed exclusively through its presentation. One war was used to reflect upon another, making a political statement about peace and American identity: any sense that the Civil War evoked still-contested national ideals paled in comparison to Europe's current conflicts over national sovereignty. *Rebel*'s child protagonist—and the veil of nostalgia more generally surrounding these fiftieth anniversary commemorations—further linked the Civil War to an innocence missing from accounts of the brutal European conflict. As images of a more modern and barbaric European war began appearing on screen and in print, Americans were reminded that their war was history, just like hoop skirts and stovepipe hats. America appeared different from Europe; it had moved away from battles and its formerly contested national ideals were in its past, reassuring audiences while temporarily masking very real debates and anxieties about national identity.

Neutrality

Initially, the European war helped stabilized definitions of American identity, particularly after President Woodrow Wilson addressed the nation on August 19, 1914, making neutrality a key, if short-lived, component of (official) national identity. Neutrality was *not* the absence of sentiment, but a policy in which America avoided taking sides, transcending the quarrels of the beleaguered Old World while evoking American exceptionalism and ability to rise above such conflicts. Once again, Wilson's declaration explicitly linked the European war and the Civil War: his childhood memories of the latter had turned him into a pacifist, shaping his response to the current conflict.[23] Conveniently for the film industry, its stock of Civil War films could now be used to support neutrality (with the right promotions), reminding audiences of war's high costs and limited benefits. Still, it was soon apparent that neutrality would not be universally accepted, and, as such, it was not a panacea for anxieties over national ideals.

CHAPTER 7

Hoping to display cinema's capacity to shore up national identity, major film producers quickly endorsed Wilson. Universal even produced a two-reel film, *Be Neutral* (Francis Ford, Powers-Universal, 1914), just forty-eight hours after his 1914 declaration.[24] It dealt with two men who argued about the war, then rioted, its cautionary tale suggesting cinema's ability to reach diverse patrons and assuage conflicts. In September, the film industry released a statement supporting Wilson, suggesting that the movies would help maintain the "local peace and national dignity" he requested:

> The importance of the sentiment expressed in the proclamation of President Wilson to the effect that the people of this country should refrain from taking sides in the European war, for the purpose of avoiding any unnecessary expression of feeling likely to be engendered by the sympathies of our diversified population was recognized by the film industry.
>
> The National Board of Censorship saw in the appeal an opportunity for exhibitors throughout the country to perform a service in the interest of local peace and national dignity. The organization has issued a request to exhibitors to run a caption before war films asking audiences to refrain from uttering any partisan expressions.[25]

While linking America's unique identity to its diverse population, this statement acknowledged its problems, as not all audiences would support neutrality. Consequently, exhibitors had to assert their authority to preserve the stable communities associated with their theaters. Few films focused on neutrality—possibly because it was not narratively compelling—with most released in 1915 and 1916 as this stance became heavily contested.

A few pacifist films were immediately available, however. Although different from neutrality, these were used to support Wilson. The most notable was *Lay Down Your Arms* (Holger-Madsen, Nordisk, Denmark, 1914), which played at the La Salle in September 1914 (otherwise not showing films at this time) before transferring to the Orpheum. *Arms* was widely acclaimed for its epic scope, four-part narrative, and vivid portrayal of "the horror of war."[26] It had originally been booked for Vienna's 21st International Peace Congress, an event that was postponed

Patriotism and Patronage

because of the war.[27] Based on leading pacifist Bertha von Suttner's novel, it was used in the United States "to support President Wilson's neutrality proclamation."[28]

Despite the National Board's statement, exhibitors often circumvented neutrality, responding to their audiences' loyalties. Some theaters tried to maintain the appearance of impartiality, alternating between war films from either side while capitalizing on fascination with the war. For instance, in November 1915, Chicago's Olympic Theater screened the anti-German preparedness tract, *The Battle Cry of Peace*, then presented German war propaganda, *The Warring Millions* (The American Correspondent Film Company, 1915). Produced by a company linked directly to the Austrian government, *Millions* featured battles shot at the German front from the German perspective, focusing on the capture of Ivangorod.[29] This strategy continued after America entered the war: in July 1917, for instance, Orchestra Hall followed the anti-British Revolutionary War drama *The Spirit of '76* (Frank Montgomery, Continental Producing Company, 1917) with the Official British Government War Pictures' *The British Tanks at the Battle of Ancre*, where all proceeds were split between the United States and British Red Cross.[30] Throughout this conflict, short war films and newsreels became very important as they offered an easy way for exhibitors to capitalize on war, express partisan leanings, and change the political stance of their show. Newsreels also demonstrated that cinema could perform an important social function, informing the public, quelling tensions, and thereby maintain order at a time of crisis.

The War on Film: Newsreels and Documentaries

As war escalated during August 1914, Chicago's worried immigrants flocked to newsreels, which, along with documentaries, constituted almost all early World War I movies. These films were often more popular than top-billed features, even though most were faked.[31] Cinema's visual immediacy attracted audiences, boosting the medium's claims to be a "visual newspaper" while promoting these emergent film services. The *Herald Movies'* war service started on Wednesday, August 5, 1914, with pictures projected on the front of the Herald Building at 163 West Washington Street. The previous night, equipment was tested, and

CHAPTER 7

"several hundred persons . . . [saw] a stirring war 'movie' and read the bulletin just received from London saying that Germany and England had declared war against each other and that the English fleet had left before dawn for the North Sea."[32] Using language later associated with the liveness of broadcast technologies, the *Herald* promised intertitles that would transcribe "to the minute" reports sent using "Marconi wireless" and "copied in Arlington, Va., at Panama, by the American fleet off Vera Cruz and on the Atlantic seaboard." The films were reportedly shot and projected on new, lightweight equipment that supposedly allowed "for the transmission of news instantaneously." Besides being technically impossible, these pictures were likely fakes. According to Craig W. Campbell, there was no authentic war footage before late October 1914, as authorities prevented photographers and war correspondents from going to the front: "Charles G. Rosher, a correspondent . . . wrote to *Moving Picture World* in September, 'Impossible to get from England to the Continent with a motion picture camera . . .' A September 5 letter to Carl Laemmle from his London representative said, 'Anything you see in America of any consequence is fake. I do not care what it is, if it is relative to the trouble on the Continent.'"[33] The *Herald*'s stunt is noteworthy in demonstrating how the war changed discourses about cinema's social function. The newspaper promised films that would alleviate public fears, letting movie, vaudeville, and musical comedy patrons enjoy their entertainment knowing that if anything happened, managers would inform them instantly by having "the *Herald* war bulletins read or thrown on a screen."[34] This description reveals the ways in which modernity's leisure technologies might inform and comfort rather than foster shock, sensation, or distraction, annexing cinema to social order at a time of crisis. Cinema's capacity to present information (almost) as it happens was linked here to concentration and relaxation, making a visit to the movies a productive activity. War coverage thus signified another crucial turning point where cinema took on social and cultural leadership while binding the nation together. This kind of modernity certainly did not need to be managed, tamed, or ordered.

From the very start of the European war, short war documentaries and newsreels were popular in larger Loop theaters (yet evidently not so much in neighborhood houses), although their attraction was relatively short-lived. Starting Monday, February 1, 1915, the Ziegfeld added the *Herald War Movies*, billing them second to its Paramount features.³⁵ Reports suggest that these films were not patronized by the "usual" moviegoers but instead brought new audiences into central theaters, including worried immigrants, those who had previously shunned movies, as well as those interested in combat.³⁶ The first war "documentary" (as opposed to a newsreel) shown in Chicago was Edwin F. Weigle's staunchly pro-German *Belgian War Pictures* (Chicago Tribune Company, 1914), which played for four weeks at the Studebaker (from Friday, November 13, to Friday, December 11, 1914) and likely featured authentic footage.³⁷ Originally booked for a short run, it was so popular that it displaced the scheduled headliner, the society drama *Aristocracy* (Thomas N. Heffron, Famous Players–Paramount, 1914) and the next three Paramount features.³⁸ The Studebaker's manager observed: "Many of those who came to the theater yesterday remained through more than one running of the reel. The theater was crowded the whole day."³⁹ Loop exhibitors were not sure that war films could draw audiences, hence the initial short-term booking, but their concerns were quickly resolved. As war pictures were in short supply, there was often some time between releases: after the success of the *Belgian War Pictures*, no war actualities played the Loop until February 19, 1915, when the *Herald's German War Pictures* ran for one week at the Ziegfeld on a double bill with the romantic comedy *David Harum* (Allan Dwan, Famous Players–Paramount, 1915). Like most early war films, the *Belgian War Pictures* and the *German War Pictures* were independently produced and/or imported and markedly pro-German.⁴⁰ A documentary billed as *War Pictures* (most likely the *Staats-Zeitung War Pictures*, a pro-German six-reel film of German, Austrian, and Turkish battles) opened at the Studebaker on August 19, 1915, and was possibly the same film shown at the Ziegfeld in August. The next such film screened in the Loop was the German propaganda picture *The Warring Millions*, which played the Olympic for three weeks, starting November 25.⁴¹ By late 1915, an onslaught of pro-German war films in major Loop theaters provided insight into many residents' sympathies. This partisanship was even more pronounced in the German-language press. In February 1915, the *Illinois Staats Zeitung*, the state's major German newspaper, wrote to Chicago's daily papers to complain about the pro-Allied Forces bias in the *New York Sun*.⁴² Further signs of Chicago's emergent sympathies came in the Ziegfeld's advertising for the *Herald's German War Movies*, screened that very month. This copy read: "GERMANS! ATTENTION! Just Arrived From Germany, NEW SERIES OF GERMAN WAR PICTURES Kaiser Wilhelm in front with great army showing armies in actual battle."⁴³

While major producers carefully stressed the neutrality of their war documentaries (if they made them), the smaller companies who made most war films were overtly partisan, often formed solely to distribute material that was little more than propaganda.⁴⁴ Major producers initially hid their feelings, waiting to gauge audience sympathies: Vitagraph's J. Stuart Blackton was a strong Allies supporter, but it was a year before he made *The Battle Cry of Peace*. Other companies took even longer and instead dealt with such issues indirectly, often through historical dramas, Ruritanian romances set against fictional intra-European conflicts, and Civil War films. Still, official national policy would soon veer in a completely different direction, encouraging some major producers to express their own views on war and American national identity more openly.⁴⁵

Preparedness

An emergent preparedness movement, advocating the buildup of military defenses in case of war, soon challenged neutrality, adding yet another national discourse to an increasingly uncertain mix. The earliest preparedness movements were largely associated with the East Coast and the National Security League, which started in 1914. Preparedness sentiments were generally not so welcome in Chicago, as they positioned Germany as an antagonist and potential threat. While preparedness shorts were produced during 1914–15, the evidence suggests that these did not play in Chicago, or that they were not advertised or otherwise mentioned in the German-leaning press.⁴⁶ Nationwide, these sentiments increased after the sinking of the British passenger liner *Lusitania* on May 7, 1915, when 128 US citizens died, including a number of Chicago residents. This was a turning point as "influential politicians, such as Theodore Roosevelt began to campaign for involvement, arms manufacturers pressed for preparedness and Wilson sent notes of protest to Berlin."⁴⁷ Things were different in Chicago, where pro-German sentiments remained strong. The *Herald* even published an editorial on the *Lusitania* in May 1915 reminding readers to think of Germany's losses.⁴⁸ Preparedness gained further momentum in 1916, after former American ally, Pancho Villa, attacked the United States on the Mexican border. As Wilson moved in this direction, Chicago's opposition to official national sentiments became more pronounced, acknowledging threats from Mexico but not Germany.

Although relatively few war features were shown in Chicago's first-run theaters during 1915, this changed after the anti-German preparedness feature *The Battle Cry of Peace* opened its six-week run at the Olympic around October 14, 1915 (it also played one week at the LaSalle in January 1916). The year's other controversial epic, *The Birth of a Nation*, was playing at the Colonial at this time. Film critics set up a rivalry, presenting each as an American manifesto, although *Birth* was generally better received.⁴⁹ Both films were fiercely patriotic, tracing the contours of key debates on national identity like federalism, states rights, and preparedness, but taking a radically different stance. *Birth*'s southern emphasis on states rights clearly opposed the kind of federal armies the futuristic *Battle Cry* endorsed in the name of national security.⁵⁰ Touting itself as "The greatest of all Photo Spectacles. An Inspired and Inspiring Appeal to National Patriotism!," *Battle Cry*'s advertisements reproduced a handwritten letter from Theodore Roosevelt, dated July 12, 1914, endorsing the film and exhorting all free men to fight for liberty.⁵¹ It was printed under the following header: "One Great American: On the momentous subject that inspired J. Stuart Blackton to write the thrilling patriotic Photo-Spectacle." According to Gerstner, *Battle Cry* was formally influenced by an American doctrine of realism that paradoxically owed much to Teddy Roosevelt's pro-German interpretation of American identity, linking patriotism to a masculinity that was not afraid to fight. Blackton enlisted many leading military figures, including Franklin Delano Roosevelt, then assistant secretary of the navy, and Admiral Dewey, to support his film, reinforcing this masculine military dictum.⁵²

Battle Cry was specifically aimed at changing current US policy, making it one of the first films to combine epic feature entertainment with explicit propaganda—Blackton made it as "a call to arms," as he admitted years later.⁵³ It presented what the *New York Times* called "an animated, arresting, and sometimes lurid argument for the immediate and radical improvement of our national defenses":⁵⁴

> *The Battle Cry of Peace* is the picture version of Mr. Maxim's [book] *Defenseless America*. It was Mr. Blackton's argument that, with the screens of the country at his disposal, he could reach the people with the Maxim data at a much more rapid pace than the book itself could possibly achieve. . . . There is nothing in the least subtle about [it] . . . the accent of authority is given to the picture by the presence on screen of Admiral Dewey, General Wood, and Secretary Garrison. Furthermore, the Commodore [Blackton] claims for his film the indorsement [sic] and co-operation of many a notable, from Theodore Roosevelt to Secretary Lansing. . . . You . . . see a good many ugly things . . . bombs drop on the swaying crowd in Times Square . . . Long Island houses go up in flames, and the Capitol at Washington crumbling. . . . *The Battle Cry for Peace* [sic] is done on a large scale but it represents no advance in the motion picture art, *nor indeed, does it pretend to do so. That is not what it is for.* (My emphasis)⁵⁵

Battle Cry took on the near future (1921), dealing with the destruction of an unprepared New York by an unnamed enemy in a narrative that reportedly ran for four reels, followed by some two reels of allegorical material (the film is now lost, only fragments and a condensed one-reel version survive). It played with the well-known conventions of Civil War films, albeit from more of an urban northern perspective, its cautionary message inverting their romance of reunion, moving away from earlier tracts about the futility of war. It focused on two families: one, the Vandergriffs, welcome a fellow pacifist into their home who turns out to be a foreign spy, bent on their destruction. The other, the Harrisons (whose son is in love with the elder Vandergriff daughter) are more aware, trying to convince Mr. Vandergriff that preparedness was necessary. They fail in these efforts, and New York is attacked as Vandergriff presides over a peace meeting. The resultant deaths, destruction, and near rape (Mrs. Vandergriff kills her daughters to save their honor) underlined the importance of preparedness.⁵⁶ As Campbell notes, the film's allegorical tableau "further enforced this message,

Patriotism and Patronage

contrasting Columbia trampled by a triumphant foe with Columbia living in honorable peace because of adequate defenses. Then there were views of American defenses and military forces."[57] Columbia, a poetic feminized personification of the United States, displayed the need for national protection, again reinforcing preparedness as a correct masculine stance. Blackton toured with his film, introducing it to audiences in major cities and accompanying it to state capitals and military encampments.[58]

For its Chicago opening, *Battle Cry* was surrounded with military trappings, the first film presented this way since *Rebel* a year earlier. As was the case in other major US cities, the UK-born Blackton, who had recently assumed American citizenship, spoke at the premiere, proclaiming, "Any foreign-born American who is offended by this picture has no right in this country at any time . . . the only way to spell peace . . . is the new phonetic way, P-O-W-E-R." Even Chicago's pro-German Mayor Thompson, nicknamed "Kaiser Bill," met with representatives of the National Security League at the screening and addressed the audience on the topic of preparedness.[59] Thompson was anti-Allies and staunchly anti-English, publicly sympathizing with both the Germans and the Irish Republican cause, so his attendance was odd, indicative of his desire to reorient preparedness away from Germany, as was reportedly evidenced in his speech.[60] It is difficult to imagine this tactic was successful, particularly as *Battle Cry*'s enemy soldiers wore German uniforms, revealing limits to the strategy whereby exhibition context changed a film's address.[61] Furthermore, reviewers like the *Herald*'s Louella Parsons, who were strongly opposed to America's entry into the war, dismissed the film as misguided, indicating that its intended message came across very clearly.[62]

Battle Cry's release coincided with the screening of several pro-German war films in Chicago, which reoriented, if not undermined, conventional preparedness efforts. The anti-British documentary *The Warring Millions* followed *Battle Cry* at the Olympic, running for three weeks. One week later, the feature-length film *On the Fighting Lines with the Germans* (Industrial Moving Picture Company, 1915) played for three weeks at the Fine Arts before moving to the La Salle on December 24, 1915, for another three weeks. According to Anthony Slide, this "anti-British film . . . was made for the *Chicago Tribune*, a very anti-

CHAPTER 7

British publication."[63] Between December 3 and December 17, two of the six first-run Loop theaters were showing pro-German war pictures. The next week, the La Salle started screening the pro-Allies *Fighting For France*, films produced for the French government and presented by Hearst newspapers.[64] These ran for two weeks. With the closing of *On the Fighting Lines with the Germans* on January 14, 1916, no war films played the Loop until the *German War Pictures* opened at the Fine Arts on March 4, 1916, a weeklong engagement sponsored by the German-Hungarian Society. Despite the high profile of *The Battle Cry of Peace*, listings for Chicago theaters reveal that pro-Allies films were less common than pro-German films—and ran for shorter periods.[65]

Around this time, serious questions about Chicago's disjunction from national consensus started to emerge while exhibition and reception practices further underscored local dissent. In August 1915—at the height of post-*Lusitania* preparedness sentiments—an anonymous woman complained to the *Herald* that local movie audiences did not stand for the national anthem, by then associated with pro-Allies sentiment. These reports are noteworthy as there are few stories about audience behavior from this period, underlining the significance of this action. Actually, many Loop theaters had stopped playing it: the Blackstone and Olympic claimed it was because they lacked orchestras (despite providing live musical accompaniment to films), while McVicker's said continuous performances made it difficult to fit it in. Other managers admitted that audiences increasingly opposed nationalist displays that appeared to support anti-German versions of American identity. The Majestic's manager, Fred Eberts, said they stopped playing "The Star Spangled Banner" as it made people leave, while manager Garrity of the Garrick worried that it would "arouse [war] spirit," undermining President Wilson's desire that people remain calm and neutral. Only one manager in the Loop featured the national anthem with any success—George Bowles of the Illinois, then playing *The Birth of a Nation*. He said: "We play the national hymn at all of our performances . . . At the start few people paid any attention to it. Gradually the patriotic response became more general, until today nearly every person in the house comes to his feet."[66] Clearly the choice of film helped recast the anthem's politics; coupled with other movies, it alienated audiences who believed that American identity was leaning too closely toward British partisanship.

Getting Villa

Another major international incident helped the Chicago press reorient preparedness discourses away from Germany. On March 9, 1916, former US ally Francisco "Pancho" Villa raided the New Mexican border town of Columbus, almost leading the United States into war with Mexico, attacking the United States because President Wilson had acknowledged Mexico's military government. Previously, Villa and the US government had fought the Mexican dictator's regime together, but after Villa's brutal defeat at the Battle of Celaya in October 1915, Wilson made peace with Mexico to preserve national security. In January 1916, Villa killed a group of American engineers, who were working in Mexico, to avenge this betrayal. In the context of World War I, Villa's attack had particular resonance—he was a former US ally rumored to be supported by the Kaiser (something not mentioned in Chicago's press).[67] By this time, Wilson himself was now endorsing preparedness, albeit defining it as *"armed* neutrality," while engaging in diplomatic efforts to end the war.[68] Villa's attacks only added to fears that America faced imminent invasion.

Motion pictures were in a unique position to capitalize on this story: before attacking the United States, Villa had worked twice with Christy Cabanne, first in *Life of Villa* (Biograph, 1912), a single-reel documentary/reenactment of the Mexican Revolutionary War, and then on another biopic, *The Life of General Villa* (Mutual, 1914). After this assault, he was in at least one more film, April 1916's *Following the Flag in Mexico*, released by the small Tropical Film Company. Following Villa's US attacks, several smaller producers recorded these border skirmishes and reenacted the invasion. The first such release was a *Chicago Herald* production in collaboration with the C. L. Chester Company, the five-reel *Getting Villa* (1916), which followed American soldiers marching into Mexico on Villa's trail.[69] It premiered in March 1916 at the Auditorium Theater with tickets priced at ten and twenty-five cents "to put them within the reach of everybody."[70]

CHAPTER 7

Chicago papers used the Villa films to deflect preparedness sentiments away from Germany, highlighting the need to focus on the nation's own borders, not a European War. As Louella Parsons noted: "We have watched the other war pictures with perhaps rather indifferent interest, because their fight is not our fight, but this film is different. It is the picture of our own countrymen striving to bring to justice the man who dared defy our flag and our soldiers. It is our own fight, our own soldiers and our own pictures."[71] *Getting Villa* recharged patriotism in Chicago's theaters. For the first time, exhibitors posted military recruiting announcements in case of a war at home. Rookies stationed at Fort Sheridan were invited to see *Getting Villa* free the first Monday of its release. Two days later, naval reserves were given a guest pass, then Colonel Milton J. Foreman and the First Cavalry attended the first Friday night screening. Because they used actuality footage, the Villa movies could claim authenticity, even as they edited their material into a narrative that blurred fiction and reality—as the *Herald* somewhat confusedly noted: "It was so real one looked for a close-up of [movie star] Marguerite Clarke as the girl back home."[72]

Villa gave Chicago's audiences a clear enemy, one who fought for a nation with which few had any allegiance. Patrons no longer left theaters during the national anthem. Spectators at the Ziegfeld even cheered every time they saw the American flag during the late March screening of Vitagraph's pro-Allies war drama *The Hero of Submarine D-2* (Paul Scardon, VLSE, 1916).[73] But these sentiments worried some in Chicago's German American community, especially given rumored links between Villa and Germany. Responding to these fears, Paul Mueller, editor of Chicago's German-language *Abendpost* newspaper, warned America that if they joined the "Kaiser's enemies" they would be defeated, while simultaneously declaring he was proud to be an American citizen.[74] His statement indicates the continued struggles over definitions of American identity—and patriotism—being fought in Chicago (and elsewhere in the United States). Soon after, 25,000 German Americans from Illinois appealed to Washington for peace as part of a campaign organized by the National German-American Alliance, which had more than two hundred thousand members statewide. Its Chicago members sent messages to Illinois senators Sherman and Lewis, and the city's German societies met at Turner Hall on the North

Patriotism and Patronage

Side on May 4 to plan a public demonstration against America entering the war, which took place outside the Auditorium Theater on May 14.[75]

Exhibition and Patriotism: The Eve of War

Still, pro-German sentiments remained resilient citywide. The war-related films that got the most attention from the Chicago press continued to be those linked to the German cause, outnumbering titles sympathizing with the Allies. Similar sentiments marked promotional discourses and exhibition strategies throughout most of the city. As submarines were closely associated with the German war effort, the Chicago press linked the decidedly apolitical *Twenty Thousand Leagues Under the Sea* to German heroism when it played the Studebaker in October 1916. The *Herald* proudly observed that "the German U-Boats were duplicating the story in reality off the American coast," while the *Tribune* also approved, noting, "Universal had the Kaiser for a press agent," even though the film had nothing to do with Germany or the current war.[76] In November, the Playhouse had a hit with *War on Three Fronts* (Frank E. Kleinschmidt, Captain F. E. Kleinschmidt–Selznick, 1916) a nonfiction war picture recorded at the Russian, Balkan, and Italian fronts from the German and Austrian perspective that included footage of Austrian soldiers being killed in the trenches, aerial shots, and scenes from a U-boat, with all proceeds donated to the German Austro-Hungarian Relief Association.[77] It drew large crowds and was particularly popular with German Americans who had helped import it to Chicago. Even Louella Parsons, not a fan of war pictures, liked it, noting that it was that rare thing—a "genuine" war picture because its director was a German Americans, and therefore understood his topic.[78] Significantly, the US government stopped all exhibition of this film after the country entered World War I, and Kleinschmidt was arrested "on the technical charge of the possession of a loaded revolver . . . on information supplied [to] the police by the Naval Intelligence Bureau."[79]

As war seemed imminent by year's end, there was a corresponding upswing in the production of war-related dramas. First-run Loop theaters showed several such features, including the antiwar melodrama *War Brides* (Herbert Brenon, Herbert Brenon Film Corporation–Sel-

273

znick, 1916); the pro-British war romance *The Girl Philippa* (S. Rankin Drew, Vitagraph-VLSE, 1916); the pro-Allies, prowar *Joan the Woman* (Cecil B. DeMille, Paramount–Famous Players–Lasky, 1917); and the preparedness drama *Womanhood: The Glory of the Nation* (J. Stuart Blackton, William P. S. Earle, Vitagraph-VLSE, 1917).[80] While most took the Allies' side, these sentiments reveal more about the politics of film producers—mainstream pro-German features were in short supply.

Although Chicago's censors did not speak for the whole city, their verdicts on war films further revealed the city's dissent from national consensus—as did exhibition practices, audience responses, and protests over war taxes. In many cities and states, pacifist films had problems with censors, but not Chicago where they were welcomed because they were not anti-German. Indeed, the censorship board made a clear political statement in passing *War Brides*, a film banned in Kansas City and Pennsylvania that had problems with the New York and Maryland boards because of its strong antiwar stance—its pregnant lead kills herself to protest war and to prevent her unborn child being used as future cannon fodder. Its producer, Lewis Selznick, even used the support of the Chicago censors to justify keeping it in circulation.[81]

With war on the horizon, different class-based loyalties further fragmented local consensus on national ideals. Surviving reports suggest that many middle- and working-class residents supported Germany, wanted to avoid war, or had no firm opinion on the matter. Meanwhile, Chicago's high society strongly favored the Allies, organizing film benefits to raise funds. In March 1917, a group of society women led by Mrs. W. G. Beale organized a benefit at the Strand for the American Fund for the French Wounded. Upper-class Chicagoans, including Mrs. David R Foraan, Mrs. Arthur Meeker, Mrs. Russell Tyson, and Mrs. L. Hamilton McCormick purchased boxes for a gala performance of the latest official French war pictures, *Heroic France: The Allies in Action* (Merl LaVoy, Rothacker Film Manufacturing Company–Mutual, 1917). Under the supervision of Mrs. Halsted Freeman, local debutantes acted as ushers and admission prices were kept "sky high" to preserve exclusivity and raise as much money as possible for French causes. The spectacle of uniformed students from the Northwestern Military and Naval Academy at Lake Geneva, Wisconsin, marching to the theater

Patriotism and Patronage

accompanied by their band further linked the Allied cause to American patriotism.[82] Throughout this film's run, the theater was decorated inside and out with Allied flags while ushers wore Red Cross uniforms. Students from Highland Park's Deerfield-Shields High School were invited to attend, and its two hundred boys dressed in military uniforms while one hundred female pupils came as Red Cross nurses.[83] After a month at the Strand, *Heroic France* moved to the much smaller Rose on West Madison, where there was no such aplomb.[84] Events soon proved that other Chicagoans had very different ideas about the war, with the middle classes particularly resisting identification with the Allies.

Patriotism and Protests

Even in Chicago, the outbreak of war led to a brief surge in pro-Allies films, all surrounded by nationalist trappings as some exhibitors abandoned their earlier pro-German stance to present a unified national front.[85] Like earlier public proclamations of American sentiment, these screenings largely occurred in the Loop. As the United States went to war in April 1917, the official British War Pictures were held over at the Band Box.[86] A few days later, the Auditorium held a heavily promoted one-day screening of Pathé's *Official British War Films* to "a capacity house totaling $10,000 in paid admissions," netting the theater some $3,000, and even earning the praise of the German-leaning press.[87] To aid recruiting, Vitagraph donated pictures of "a marine corps gun crew manning an anti-submarine gun" to twelve Loop houses and offered them to 250 neighborhood theaters.[88] George Kleine and William Selig donated movies to help navy recruiting and attended the first of a series of weekday night screenings in Grant Park, where their films were accompanied by a one-hundred-piece navy band.[89] Later that month, Jones, Linick and Schaefer, and Captain F. R. Kenney launched a massively promoted army recruitment drive for *Joan the Woman* at the Colonial. Four girls dressed as Joan of Arc in full armor toured the Loop in cars with army officers in attendance, stopping on every block to encourage citizens to enlist.[90] In early May, Jones, Linick and Schaefer's press agent, Ralph Kettering, mailed fifteen thousand letters promoting the film to Chicago teachers, civic organizations, and women's clubs in envelopes headed "he wasn't too proud to fight!" These reinforced the film's message: *Joan's* male protagonist was a reluctant soldier who took on a suicide mission after Joan of Arc takes him back to their past life together.[91]

Perhaps most notably, Essanay joined with the First Illinois Regiment in July 1917, using their Bryant Washburn four-reel feature *The Man Who Was Afraid* (Fred E. Wright, KESE, 1917) for a recruitment drive.[92] The film dealt with a reluctant soldier whose mother persuaded him not to join the National Guard. He finally signs up and accomplishes a dangerous mission on the Mexican border, recalling Villa's attack and playing to current paranoia about national security.[93] George K. Spoor donated the print, and the film was shown free to packed houses between 11 a.m. and 11 p.m. at an unnamed Loop theater, with speeches between shows. During screenings, the "entire First Illinois Regiment paraded the streets of the Loop district carrying banners inviting the public to see *The Man Who Was Afraid*."[94] Between showings, officers urged male viewers to sign up and fight. Booths were placed in the lobby where hundreds of spectators reportedly enlisted. More uniformed men were stationed around the Loop to recruit pedestrians. If they refused, they were handed a movie ticket, stating: "Go see *The Man Who Was Afraid*." Despite this, the regiment's numbers were still not up to required wartime enrollments, indicating lingering ambivalence about America's stance on the war and reticence to fight. The film was subsequently used in the service of recruiting drives through the city, and KESE provided exhibitors nationwide with materials toward these ends.[95]

Theaters also displayed their patriotism through benefits for the armed forces. This strategy was relatively safe as most patriots could support the troops, even if they did not back US intervention in Europe or opposed the Allied cause. Other theaters offered free seats to the military or draft cardholders: in May 1917, the Pastime (West Madison) admitted all uniformed soldiers for free, while the Playhouse (410 South Michigan) gave registration cardholders free admission for a week in late June and early July, provided they were accompanied by one paid admission.[96] This largesse also responded to the decline in paid admissions that had troubled exhibitors all summer, with these promotions filling seats and attracting good publicity.

Still, "the preponderance of movies playing in picture palaces and neighborhood theaters across the land did not tell stories about the war."[97] The war and war themes did not dominate production, nor was it "the most salient historical context for the films produced in the period from 1917."[98] Given that the industry wanted to please its customers, it was not surprising that this topic was avoided, particularly during the first few months of war. Leslie Midkiff DeBauche found "about 14 percent of the 568 available films [in April 1917] were war-related, and half of these were newsreels or documentaries . . . the mainstream film producers . . . were not, at this date, exploiting the war, neutrality, or preparedness in their feature films to any great extent. War-related feature films would not become a significant factor in the 'List of Current Film Release Dates,' until September 1918, two months before the [end] of the war."[99] Even as the production of war-related films increased throughout this conflict, they never constituted more than 23 percent of all titles (still an impressive number, although most were shorts, serials, and documentaries), with specials constituting a slightly larger percentage, hence their visibility in the first-run theaters. The major change in production during war years (other than an increase in fictional features set against or dealing with the war) was a notable reduction in the number of films, a development related to the war and one of enormous consequence.[100] The war was inescapable, however, when it came to publicity, newspapers' motion picture coverage, exhibition strategies, taxes, and other economic matters, framing reception regardless of the title seen on screen. Even the absence of war-related content was often a strategic decision: non-war-related material was variously presented as offering relief to a stressed population and demonstrating cinema's patriotic efforts to elevate morale even as it suggested a lack of interest in the conflict or opposition to it. Exhibitors capitalized on these ambiguities, steering screenings toward their audiences' beliefs.

As DeBauche points out, there were two schools of thought about how films should handle the conflict. "One position held that movies should provide light-hearted escape, while the other argued films ought to show contemporary reality."[101] Some films balanced the two, often by focusing on the home front. An early example was Essanay's highly successful twelve-part war-themed series *Do Children Count?* (Lawrence

CHAPTER 7

C. Windom, KESE, 1917).[102] This title was particularly significant because it pointed to a shift away from characteristically Progressive interests—particularly instructional and sociological ones that involved oversight of private concerns—and toward war-related content. This upbeat educational series was originally focused on childrearing and was a follow-up to the company's popular series *Is Marriage Sacred?* (1916–17), changing to a war series in response to contemporary events.[103] Like many such titles (including *Joan the Woman*, *War Brides*, and *The Little American*), it focused on the home front, eliding nation, femininity, and modern domesticity through its six year-old army "sergeant," Mary McAlister, who played a different role in each installment (the cast for each episode was roughly the same, although each focused on different characters).[104] Advertisements from July 1917 featured her in her army uniform, looking very serious, with the accompanying text: "Little Mary McAlister, The Youngest Sergeant in the US Army now is starring in Essanay's starting series on *Do Children Count?* . . . You will find that this winsome child actress will count with your patrons. Only 6 years old, she has been commissioned recruiting sergeant by Capt. F. R. Kenney, U.S.A., for her Red Cross and Recruiting work. She counts!"[105] McAlister's patriotism is also expressed in a December 1917 *Photoplay* interview where she mentions that her favorite doll, Alice, was made in Germany, "but Mother and I think that it would be better if that were not generally known."[106]

In June 1917, George Spoor announced that Essanay would only produce comedy-dramas or "straight comedy" during wartime "to make the people laugh and forget the sufferings of their relatives in the war zone."[107] Three months later, he asked the rest of the film industry to follow, stating, "Outside of material aid, I know of nothing so much needed, nothing of so great importance, as to furnish the public with enlivening humor . . . especially now that the nation is giving its sons to the battlefields of France."[108] Spoor believed that public fascination with tragedy and drama could only be sustained in times of peace; in wartime, real anguish satiated that desire: "What [the public] wants from the front is facts, what it wants in motion pictures is recreation."[109] It is unclear what effects (if any) Spoor's statement had on film production, but it is nonetheless revealing.[110] He was an undisputed patriot, but he was also a businessman whose company was in financial trouble because of poor bookkeeping rather than unpopular films.[111] While comedies remained popular, war films did not.[112] Embracing comedy as part of patriotism would help Essanay's bottom line while establishing cinema's distractions and pleasures as central to the medium's patriotic mission. Again, patriotism constituted a marketing and exhibition strategy rather than something specifically linked to film content, a tactic seen in both neighborhood theaters and Loop houses of all sizes.

Spoor received support from fan magazines and the trade press. In December 1917, *Photoplay* mentioned that the soldiers at Ford Sheridan, near the Chicago suburb of Highland Park, elected to see a Mary Pickford film after a day of hard training rather than going to a war movie playing nearby. Meanwhile, a group of "mild old ladies" opted for the war film, one marked by inaccuracies like "cavalryman with his hat worn wrong as he steamed along on a charger that wouldn't pass government regulations." The magazine argued: "the fact is indisputable that the soldier of today does not want to see war pictures. Fort Riley, Fort Sheridan, Fort Bliss and other camps corroborate this." Indeed, soldiers' distaste for war films was used as evidence that these were no good for the exhibitor or for the nation.[113] But the article's suggestion that war films attracted small audiences (or maybe drew older spectators) seems closer to the mark. While nonwar films helped maintain morale, both among enlisted men and the home front more generally, war films were made in relatively small numbers because they were often unpopular. Patriotic justifications aside, the film industry did not make films to entertain the troops but to stay in business—and this was a period when box-office receipts were falling.

Although dissent was muted as the nation entered the war, this did not last long. By September 1917, Chicago's exhibitors were again accused of treating the national anthem without respect, using it to accompany pictures, playing it with a ragtime beat, sometimes imbuing it with bathos, and almost always playing it without dignity.[114] This burlesque commented on war policies and their attendant versions of national identity. Local antipathy toward the Allies also shaped the reception of "important" war dramas like *Joan the Woman*: despite the bluster Jones, Linick and Schaefer generated, its box office was poor.[115] In July 1917, Louella Parsons admitted, "*Joan the Woman* [is] one of the best of the big productions [but] was coldly received by many Chicagoans."[116] Although attendance spiked when America entered the war, much of it came from repeat viewers who likely agreed with advertising that proclaimed: "This peasant maid's heroism in France is inspiring to the patriotic Chicagoans."[117] Contested national ideals—as well as Chicago's increasing distance from official sentiments—would be more evident in the censorship of *The Little American* (Cecil B. DeMille, Mary Pickford Company–Paramount, 1917) during summer 1917. Nevertheless Mary Pickford's popularity revealed the strength of celebrity culture, trumping the film's anti-German message, as many patrons were more loyal to cinema and its stars than any nation. Even though many Chicagoans were sympathetic to Germany, they despised Funkhouser. The censorship of *The Little American* became a personality contest he could not win, even with audiences who shared his political views.

The Little American

Funkhouser did not hide his pro-German leanings when it came to *The Little American*, banning it because it was "offensive to German-Americans."[118] It is unclear why this film had more problems with the censors than other anti-German war films, but it was likely singled out because Pickford's popularity might turn audiences against Germany, especially in her new guise as the ideal *American* woman. As DeBauche notes, "It was with the release of the *The Little American* that Famous Players began seriously to promote the tag line 'America's Sweetheart' . . . Artcraft's suggestions for promoting *The Little American* by linking Mary with patriotic action . . . marked a change in Pickford's persona. . . . She was 'Our Mary,' representing an ideal of modern American youth and femininity."[119] If Pickford represented America, then her character's near rape and murder at the hands of German troops made a statement about national allegiances that Chicago's censors hoped to mute. As Funkhouser exclaimed: "I cannot pass this picture BECAUSE it would offend the Germans here, who did not start this war" (emphasis in original).[120] He claimed he would only relent if Artcraft's counsel, Carl Pierce, could get "George Creel and the Department of Public Information in Washington to endorse this picture" and was shocked when Creel called it "as a splendid patriotic subject" and wired his approval.¹²¹ The censor then backtracked, claiming that he had no idea who Creel was and stood by his ban.¹²²

Set in 1914 at the outbreak of war, *The Little American* combined anti-German elements with more complex reflections on national identity. Although it "contained every known anti-German sentiment: the violation of Belgian neutrality, the sinking of the Lusitania, the atrocities against women and children in France, the Prussian goal of world conquest," these were balanced against a more complex configuration of *German American* identity.¹²³ Pickford's character, Angela, is overdetermined as a resolutely patriotic American, born on July 4 and living in Washington DC. The film's prologue features her receiving a box of chocolates arranged in the shape of the flag and likens her to another American Beauty—the rose. She symbolizes a national conscience that is, at first, neutral, seen in her two suitors, the French Jules and her true love, Karl, a German American (with an American mother). In a move that recalls the plots of earlier preparedness films and Civil War reunion dramas, both men are conscripted to fight for different sides in Europe. At the same time, Angela sails to France to care for her ailing aunt. First she survives the German torpedoing of her transatlantic ship, the *Veritania*, then discovers that Germans have invaded her late aunt's chateau. After witnessing the war's atrocities and nearly being murdered, she becomes a strong supporter of the Allied cause—but as an *American*, not a French girl, complete with a strong sense of justice, leadership, and resilience. This characterization was in keeping with Pickford's established star image where, on screen she acted on her strong moral sensibilities, trailblazing paths against injustice and, off screen, sold Liberty Bonds.

If Angela's national identity is secure, Karl's is more fluid, pointing to the film's need to vilify Germany while not alienating German Americans. Although Jules, his somewhat effeminate love rival, is characteristically and comically French from the start, Karl is not initially ethnically marked, revealing the proximity between American and German American identity. His German ancestry only becomes visible after conscription. Crucially, once away from America (and Angela's American influence), he changes. It is only when she recognizes him as one of the Huns trying to rape and kill her that Karl remembers who he really is. Back under her influence, he loses the vicious qualities his

CHAPTER 7

fellow Germans instilled in him and becomes the individual seen at the beginning of the film. With Angela at his side, he works for the Allies, denounces the Kaiser, and is nearly shot. Karl thus represented an object lesson in nationalism for German Americans in the domestic audience—separating German and German American identities and placing them on different sides of the conflict. Karl's transformation (and redemption) indicated the brutality of the German war machine rather than condemning American individuals of German ancestry. It was, perhaps, this very strategy that led one of Evanston's censors, a Mrs. N. S. Rose, to declare: "there was nothing in the picture to hurt the feelings of German-Americans."[124]

In banning *The Little American*, Funkhouser faced an unprecedented problem. His usual defenders in sociology departments, the clergy, reform organizations, social workers, and women's clubs were, for once, not on his side and supported the film as an essential part of the war effort.[125] Once again, such shifts indicated that Progressive Era concerns and affiliations were on the wane. These changes in reformers' sentiments not only revealed their pro-Allies beliefs but also pointed to cinema's changed social function, particularly its new links to significant national interests, something that was evident in a *Herald* editorial titled "Our Country versus Funkhouser": "Straight in the path of a great propaganda movement, utilizing what the President styles the one 'universal language' to spread the truth and shorten the war for humanity's sake and for liberty's sake Funkhouser, a local magnate, obtrudes the stupid foot and imbecile mind of censorship."[126] As was customary, the trade press presented Funkhouser's efforts as treasonable, destroying efforts to raise money and manpower for the war while fracturing national consensus: his ban effectively isolated Chicago as a place unlike the rest of the country when it came to free dramatic expression.[127] During the city's censorship hearings, he was even accused of working against President Wilson's calls for the moving picture industry to unite the American people in the war effort. Still, the censor insisted he had banned the movie because "it is against the German people; objectionable to a *friendly nation*" (my emphasis).[128] He then expressed his frustration with the film industry's refusal to use movies for good, linking their support of the Allies with their continued immorality and seditious intent.[129]

Although some of his allies, including Chief Schuettler, supported him, Funkhouser lost the battle over *The Little American*, which finally opened at the sold-out Studebaker on Saturday, July 30, benefiting from the popularity of its star and the publicity over its censorship.[130] Underscoring the film's patriotism, its opening was preceded by a parade that gathered crowds downtown while prospective spectators waited for over an hour to buy tickets: "Mr. Anderson, assistant manager, said it was the largest and most patriotic crowd he had handled all year."[131] Still, issues of wartime allegiances and definitions of national identity were more volatile than *American*'s reception would suggest, with its much-loved star accounting for much of its success. Despite this film's popularity, pro-German sentiments continued dominating Chicago's neighborhood theaters.

Supporting the Troops, Resisting the War

Although many Chicagoans maintained strong reservations about the war, pageantry, recruitment drives, and collections for soldiers raised patriotic fervor. It was not long before exhibitors and patrons had to contend with the costs of warfare, both economically and socially, leading to an upswing in the city's antiwar sentiments, especially after war taxes positioned cinema *against* nation. Even exhibitors who screened films for war-related charities and offered their theaters for recruiting drives disliked the government's plan to levy a war tax on movie tickets. This policy threatened their business model, altered their relationship with audiences, and challenged their livelihood. War taxes profoundly changed exhibition, raising ticket prices, closing many theaters for good, and threatening many independent exhibitors' livelihoods. These taxes also damaged any fragile consensus regarding the war, causing many Chicago exhibitors to return to their original antiwar stance, abandoning nascent efforts to lure patrons away from any pro-German loyalties, and further complicating ideas of cinema as a national medium.

First floated in October 1914 to help fund the defense of the Mexican border, exhibitors disliked this proposal from the start, seeing little benefit in the proposed $100 tax required from all theaters in cities with populations of over fifteen thousand.[132] The matter was revisited

CHAPTER 7

on the eve of war in February 1917, but this time, opinions were split with Chicago's leading producers and exhibitors insisting that national security was more important than business. But producers like Selig and Essanay and theater chain magnates like Jones, Linick and Schaefer; Alfred Hamburger; Ascher Brothers; Schoenstadt; and Lubliner and Trinz had more extensive resources than smaller independents. In February 1917, just before the United States entered the war—and before any taxes had been proposed—George Spoor boasted, "Business will not be considered, neither will our individual time. Essanay will do its part, that much I personally guarantee, with money and with men." Aaron Jones and J. Trinz even vowed they would fight at the front, while H. Lubliner boasted, "I would take my son and go to war should the call come today. He is not of fighting age but he could help carry water to the troops." Meanwhile, Nathan Ascher promised 10 percent of one day's proceeds from his chain for preparedness.[133] These industry figureheads continued supporting the war over the next few months, differentiating them from the antiwar, antiwar taxes, and, often, pro-German voices of local independent exhibitors who suspected taxes would reduce their box office, offend audiences, and destroy business.

Aware of the war's destructive influence on the European film industry and hoping to avoid this fate at home, major producers and exhibitors started linking cinema to patriotism *before* the war started. As Louella O. Parsons reminded *Herald* readers: "In England the war has made serious inroads on the picture business. The Zeppelin raids have made it necessary to close the picture houses at night. This has cut down on film production abroad and has seriously affected the exportation of American films. The tragedies into which many families have been cast have also greatly decreased the receipts of the picture houses."[134] Led by the trades, the film industry developed a number of incentives to help exhibitors' position their theaters on the front line of patriotism—all at little cost. In February 1917, Selig's twice-weekly newsreel began featuring a large flag over its closing credits, accompanied by a "patriotic and appropriate quotation."[135] William Selig boasted: "The Stars and Stripes first, last and all the time. We want to impress this upon our people. Each edition of the Selig News Reel carries Old Glory, and both of our studios here and in California have a flag flying at full staff.

Our . . . London office is also decked with American flags."[136] In March, the Associated Motion Picture Advertisers campaigned to move the industry "into line for patriotism and preparedness" in order to erase the potentially greater dangers of public apathy or opposition to the war. Posters, films, slides, and movie advertising were designed to stimulate audiences' patriotism and incite them to join the war effort.[137] More importantly, these materials tried to establish cinema as an essential industry, one that should not be shut down or limited during war.

One way the industry could show its essential industry status was by capitalizing on cinema's established community appeal to turn patrons into patriots during wartime. Exhibitors turned their theaters into patriotic institutions, sidestepping more complicated national allegiances by taking on tasks like collecting cigarettes to send to enlisted American men stationed overseas. The *Motion Picture News* coordinated a campaign based on a popular British model where large glass bowls were placed in theater lobbies carrying a sign, "Men: Drop in a cigarette for our boys at the front. If you haven't a cigarette, drop in a penny. It will buy a cigarette."[138] To cut costs, the paper printed free signs for exhibitors, calling this a "a live-wire method of attracting any patron's interest to the theater," as audiences could do something "of actual, direct benefit to the soldiers":

> This is a war of high tension, of highly strung nerves, and cigarettes, according to first-hand observers, are just about as indispensable as bullets. The first question a litter bearer asks of a wounded man is, "Have a smoke?" Invariably the wounded man—unless he is too severely wounded—will reply "Sure!"[139]

The Red Cross agreed to distribute cigarettes for the Motion Picture Division of the Our Boys in France Tobacco Fund. The *News* contributed money so that every twenty-five cents donated would purchase forty-five cents worth of tobacco. For each twenty-five cents, or forty-five cigarettes collected, theaters received a postcard directly from a man in the trenches to display in their lobby.[140] Mutual's Chicago exchanges even released a free 1,500-foot film to be shown only in the city's theaters: *Our Boys at Camp Grant* debuted on November 19, 1917, with all proceeds going to the cigarette fund.[141]

CHAPTER 7

Although exhibitors participated in these festive (and cheap) war-related events (which did not require any changes in programming), their antipathy to the war effort increased exponentially after May 1917, when the federal government proposed adding an emergency 20 percent tax on all seats costing more than five cents. At this time, admission prices in Chicago were stagnant (partly because of overcompetition), with neighborhood houses charging between ten and fifteen cents—still a significant raise from the five cents common just a year or two earlier.[142] The proposed tax alienated exhibitors who were already suffering—Chicago had the worst oversaturation and the largest number of uncompetitive small houses in the nation.[143] It soon became known as the city most opposed to war taxes, both for financial and political reasons.[144] Even luminaries like Jones, Linick and Schaefer now protested, noting that exhibitors would have to absorb the cost of administering taxes while losing audiences.[145] Matters were so bad that exhibitors considered closing for six to eight weeks, a move prompted by "the hot weather conditions experienced in the past and added to by the abnormal and unsure war conditions of the present."[146] Making the situation worse, in late May the city council proposed changing the current uniform tax structure (all Chicago theaters now paid $200 a year) to a graduated system based on theater capacity, starting at $200.[147] Due to the sharp increase in movie theater size, this was potentially devastating. Exhibitors appealed, stressing that they were barely making a living, claiming most revenue went to stars.[148] The city postponed its decision amid rumors that they were leaning toward the uniform tax.[149]

In early June 1917, the federal government's Finance Committee presented a revised bill that would abolish a proposed footage tax and only tax admissions over twenty-five cents—a move designed to safeguard independent and smaller houses that would have helped many Chicago theaters. The *Motion Picture News* rejoiced: "the industry has passed the first trenches of the gravest crisis in its history. Last week we faced a double war tax [on production and exhibition] which would have annihilated the industry."[150] But celebrations were premature, as the revised schedule was rejected. After much debate, President Wilson signed a higher war tax into law on October 3, 1917, active as of December 1. The *Moving Picture World* summarized the bill:

1. Only Theatres Charging Admission Price of 5 Cents Are Exempt.
2. All Amusements, the Proceeds of Which Go to Religious, Charitable or Educational Institutions Are Exempt.
3. All Persons Using Season Passes, Complimentary Tickets, Etc., Must Pay Tax.
4. Only Bona Fide Employees, Municipal Employees and Children Under Twelve Years of Age, Where No Admission Charge Is Made by the Theatre for Such Children, Are Exempt From Paying Admission Tax.
5. Report Must Be Paid in Revenue District, Where Theatre or Principal Place of Business Is Located.
6. Tax Must Be Paid in Revenue District, Where Theatre or Principal Place of Business Is Located.

   ... Tax Placed on Raw Film Product, 1/4 Cent Per Foot; Positive Prints, 1/2 Cent Per Foot; Admission Prices, 1 Cent on Every 10 Cents or Fraction thereof.

   ... Total Amount to Be Raised by Tax on Industry, $53,750,000.

   ... Distributed as Follows: Motion Picture Films, $3,000,000; Amusement Admissions, $50,000,000 (Including All Forms of Amusement); Cameras, $750,000.[151]

The bill increased production costs, and the price of prints, rentals, and equipment (the tax on cameras also extended to projectors). Exhibitors would have to charge taxes to season ticket holders or anyone entering a theater on a complimentary ticket or coupon—including film critics. Although it covered all entertainments, movies suffered most because each stage of the industry was taxed.[152] While patrons knew that the government was responsible and might blame increased costs on overreaching federal powers, exhibitors were not pleased—particularly those in areas of the upper Midwest, like Chicago and Wisconsin, that were home to many German Americans. Wisconsin's exhibitors immediately sent a formal protest letter to the Conference Committee on War Tax, explaining that the tax would put most small theaters out of business.[153]

Although opposed to increased taxation, the trades saw a possible upside. For years, they had argued for higher prices rather than cheaper,

CHAPTER 7

longer programs (often padded with older films and cheap vaudeville). But strong competition in Chicago had kept prices lower than in most American cities—even the rise to ten to fifteen cents was hard earned.[154] As early as 1912, exhibitor Sam Schiller (of the Schiller Theater) had lamented that programs in the city were too cheap, with most exhibitors offering four or five one-reel films and two or three illustrated songs for a nickel when the same price four years earlier had bought two three-hundred-foot films.[155] He soon went out of business. As late as December 1914, the *Defender* observed that almost all the North and West Side neighborhood theaters were showing five reels for five cents, with ten-cent prices dominating only on the South Side, particularly in black neighborhoods—a policy their correspondent considered racially motivated.[156]

With war taxes raising costs of production, distribution, and exhibition, Chicago's theaters—like those in the rest of the country—would have to raise prices. The *Motion Picture News'* editor, William A. Johnston, saw just there were just two options in the face of a 15 percent war tax on tickets:

> The easiest way is to cut prices—or to hold them low and give a lot of poor quality for the money. It has been done before in many lines; but it has never succeeded.
>
> The hardest way is to charge the price and give good quality; but it is the money-making way.
>
> The time has passed when people will come into your theater because you've got film and projection machines. . . . The public will pay for [attractive] entertainment, pay well in round numbers, and if you don't give it someone else will.[157]

Although Johnston recognized "some ten-cent theaters will go out of business," and others would cut prices to a nickel to avoid the tax, he believed these "disastrous results" would fade, producing general uplift.[158] Still, any theater, including five-cent houses, would have to bear the brunt of taxes on producers and distributors. He believed "taxes of all sorts will make it an impossibility to produce subjects for the five-cent house during the coming year. The margin between operating costs and admissions, already of tissue paper width in the five-cent house, will be wiped out completely."¹⁵⁹ This would leave the industry with more high-priced theaters that could afford high-quality entertainment.

At first, it seemed the tax would kill Chicago's five-cent houses. Ticket prices had steadily increased since 1915 and they surged throughout the northeast after the war tax was floated. As the *Motion Picture News* noted, "audiences, as a rule, are awakening to the fact that war conditions in this country make it absolutely necessary to charge even more for amusement and entertainment."¹⁶⁰ During summer and early fall, prices doubled in Newark, New Jersey, increasing by one-third in September 1917 alone. Philadelphia's Stanley chain hiked prices (from fifteen to twenty-five cents to forty cents) with no reported decrease in patronage, while Baltimore exhibitors sweetened hikes with larger orchestras, enlarged programs, and "enhanced presentations."¹⁶¹ A similar picture emerged in New Orleans, where patrons "readily and cheerfully" accepted the tax, with some theaters witnessing surges in attendance. Patronage was slightly higher during the first week of its implementation in Omaha, while in California the only problem was a shortage of pennies for change. In Michigan, the tax was a success "despite the many complaints at the small houses in poorer sections. In better neighborhoods . . . the people understand the reason . . . and are paying it without objection."¹⁶²

Things were different in Chicago, which soon became the center of the antitax movement. There was a marked decline in attendance for the first two days of the tax because many audiences did not support the war and others were unwilling or unable to pay. Ten-cent houses immediately halved admission prices to avoid a one-cent tax—a largely political move that displayed antiwar, anti-Allies sentiment.¹⁶³ Although one exhibitor, Julius E. Franke, complained that these "exhibitor slackers . . . escape the government tax," even at the cost of their profits, others supported these moves.¹⁶⁴ As admissions were taxed if the house charged more than five cents for any performance, the only way to avoid taxes was to reduce *all* ticket prices.¹⁶⁵ Many neighborhood exhibitors cut prices, although it deeply hurt their businesses. Even owners of large chains were now "worried and dubious about the ten per cent amusement tax." Max Ascher now believed it would close many theaters. Lubliner and Trinz believed it would be "hard

CHAPTER 7

at first but that Mr. Public will very soon get used to it," while Aaron Jones alone thought it would not affect business. All three believed separate tickets should be given for admission and taxes, reminding patrons where their money was going.[166] Other exhibitors reportedly increased prices by more than 10 percent, adding a nickel rather than a penny, making Chicago the only city in the nation to be accused of war profiteering.[167]

Some patrons protested the tax. At the State Street Castle (admission twenty cents plus tax), manager Weil reported the occasional "grouch." Two Bijou Dream patrons also objected: "a Polish woman who couldn't understand what we tried to tell her and the other was a Chinaman in the same boat." Its manager, Sigmund Faller, complained that the tax brought in more revenue than his theater: the low profit margin on its ten- and fifteen-cent admissions made it impossible for him to absorb it. George Moore at the Orpheum (fifteen- and twenty-cent prices) received complaints and "a few kicks from people, but I guess they must have been pro-Germans."[168] More significantly, in an early December meeting of the Chicago Motion Picture Theater Owners' Association, representing theaters outside the Loop, some members announced a 35 percent decrease in patronage, while others estimated a 15 percent decline. Only a few stated that the tax had not reduced audiences. Loop businesses were more resilient, partly because they did not rely on a relatively fixed patronage dependent on class and ethnicity and had already successfully capitalized on the war.

Demographics of city neighborhoods strongly affected the reception of the war tax. Tellingly: *"Americans paid the levy less willingly* than foreigners, and . . . theaters in foreign neighborhoods, where the population was mixed, were apparently less hurt by the move than those in high class districts where the inhabitants were all American" (my emphasis).[169] Evidently ethnic audiences did not object as long as they knew where the money was going. One exhibitor, Max Jesselson who owned two theaters in neighborhoods "where as many as a dozen nationalities rub elbows," placed ads in foreign language publications explaining the reasons for the increase. Meanwhile, many fully assimilated American citizens "refused to pay the tax because of pro-German tendencies."[170] Chicagoans who considered themselves Americans (and often were not recent immigrants) were most likely not to share anti-German sentiments and opposed the war tax more than others. These self-regarded "true Americans" now had to pay for a war that threatened their very definition of nation and patriotism, erasing forms of self-definition and historical allegiances (Germany as a friend, Britain as the colonial enemy) for newly created wartime loyalties. In contrast, recent immigrants adhered more closely to current governmental ideals, possibly because they desired to assimilate. In February 1918, *Photoplay* reminded readers that their pennies added up, funding "a good start on a destroyer, enough to fire a big gun several times." While calling the tax a patriotic measure, the article's tone was scolding, with the Chicago-based magazine likely warning its local readers that not paying the tax made them "slackers" and noting that without their patronage both the war and the film industry might be lost.[171]

The war had other deleterious effects on exhibition. A war-related labor shortage forced exhibitors to reduce screenings or temporarily close after many employees were drafted. The Republic on Lincoln Avenue had three men enlist and two drafted on the same day in October 1917, leaving it without a manager, projectionist, pianist, drummer, and stage manager, and causing its owner to contemplate closing for good.[172] Meanwhile, the Auditorium had to postpone its screening of the allegorical drama *The Eyes of the World* (Donald Crisp, Clune Film Producing Company, 1917) in November 1917 as labor shortages made it impossible to renovate the theater in time.[173] Along with unsteady economic conditions, the draft made Jones, Linick and Schaefer delay constructing "the most magnificent motion picture theater in Chicago."[174] Although newly assigned military personnel briefly swelled some takings, particularly in the Loop's all-night houses, regular patronage dropped.[175] War was bad for business, exacerbating the major slump that had hit all Chicago theaters—downtown, in entertainment districts, and in the neighborhoods—throughout summer 1917.

As all this suggests, World War I did not necessarily unify the nation, improve box office, or produce consensus—properties often associated with national cinema during wartime. Instead, in Chicago, the state of local exhibition and censorship demonstrated the persistence of pro-German/anti-British sentiments that rested uneasily with official national discourse, while illustrating profound contestation over

CHAPTER 7

local definitions of national identity. The industry's decision to position film as a national medium thus required more nuanced declarations of American ideals and history that exhibitors could moderate, tailoring them to accommodate audiences' varying beliefs. Consequently, patriotism and war spirit were usually evoked through the promotions, presentations, and discourses surrounding films, rather than motion picture content, as these could be more sensitive to local needs. World War I thus *extended* the importance of supplementary discourses and exhibition strategies in shaping the meanings of motion pictures even as other institutional developments, like the feature film, might ostensibly appear to standardize reception.

Signs of change were afoot, however, both socially and cinematically. The movies' overall success in moderating contentious opinions and in becoming a national and local leader in wartime played a role in resolving the Progressive Era's signature dilemma: the problem of integrating modernity into a functioning society. Movies used the war to reposition their formerly shocking and somewhat jaded novelty in the service of a highly organized and well-oiled society, soothing anxieties and providing information to a nervous populace. War newsreels—reportedly more vital and up-to-the-minute than the printed page—increasingly allowed cinema to present itself as a significant source of information rather than a distraction. Indeed, discourses surrounding early wartime newsreels emphasized how they helped patrons *concentrate* on their work or leisure. Once America entered the war—and more Americans went off to fight—fan magazines and trade papers argued that movies, particularly non-war-related subjects, offered pleasurable diversions that simultaneously uplifted the home front, revived the troops, and maintained morale. Here, distraction could have significant social value, aiding the culture and facilitating a more ordered and well-functioning society. These discourses indicated two different ways to manage modernity—turn distraction into its opposite or, alternately, capitalize on the need for distraction and filter it into socially useful ends. Cinema did both.

War also trivialized other Progressive anxieties about the more mundane changes in American life and the need to control, monitor, and improve them. As the terms of national and social debate shifted during the war, Progressivism lost momentum and the film industry changed. War taxes and 1917's temporary economic downfall fundamentally transformed exhibition, helping create a more streamlined market that required fewer films. Although World War I ultimately did not resolve issues of national identity—a largely impossible task as nations continually change and are marked by their specific discursive conflicts—it nevertheless created a space where cinema could capitalize both on the need for patriotism and the schisms it evoked, exploiting the different niches producers and exhibitors served. These practices again point to the importance of exhibition and the continued role of off-screen pleasures in mediating the on-screen experience, rather than the narrowing down of focus to the screen usually associated with cinema of the late 1910s.

Conclusion

Progressivism provides many insights into this period's cinema. It points to the importance of otherwise neglected institutions like neighborhood cinemas, reveals its understanding of spectatorship as a largely collective phenomenon while highlighting important conceptual structures like oversight, self-awareness, uplift, and the reappraisal of public and private spheres. As a modernist medium, movies were central to many Progressive Era debates about taming and integrating the new, participating in key period discourses on leisure, municipal regulation, and censorship. Similar impulses marked the film industry's interactions with reformers, federal and local government, and neighborhood ideals, as well as the medium's aspirations to national cinema. While Progressivism was wracked by debates, its ideals and practices all evince a shared belief in progress, working toward a better, more cohesive, more community-oriented, and more advanced society.

Often seen as marking the end of Progressivism, World War I challenged many of these suppositions. Most notably, it questioned its structural emphasis on progress, suggesting that the nation had not moved beyond such conflicts despite the many sentiments to the contrary expressed throughout the Civil War's golden anniversary. President Wilson's change of heart and his administration's unpopular decision to enter the war severely undermined Progressive Era faith that government could solve social ills and work for the public good.[1] Despite efforts to link it to patriotism, the war fragmented the nation and many of the community ideals Progressivism held so dear, fundamentally undermining beliefs that public works might produce a better future. Even though the nation was saved from any direct attack, the loss of life and the sense of insecurity arising from a global conflict with no certain cause suggested modernity could not be managed or stabilized, further indicating the limitations of government power.

While elements of Progressivism continued into future decades (as seen in the New Deal), the postwar period saw a move back toward individualism, suspicion of government, and the more laissez-faire business practices responsible for 1920s boom-bust cycles. According to historian Neil Wynn: "the First World War was more than just an historical full stop marking the end of one period and the beginning of another: for America . . . [it] was a complex affair that saw some prewar developments brought to a conclusion, some come to a temporary halt, and others continue, colored by the particular nuances of wartime . . . thus creating the sense and reality of change."[2] In particular, the war fundamentally altered the American public's experience of change, rendering the novelties of the prewar period mundane (while dispelling their newness), emphasizing wartime and the postwar years as times of change and retrenchment. The Progressive Era ideals designed to tame these older novelties seemed quaint and out of touch with new postwar transformations, particularly those focused on internal threats to social order, like the inward gaze associated with self-monitoring and oversight. While Chicago's censors' diminished power resulted more from local politics and the actions of a maverick board, local censorship more generally waned during the postwar years, attesting to shifts away from community ideals and greater suspicions of government power, even at the municipal level.

By war's end in 1918, some of the domestic issues with which Progressive society struggled had been resolved or tabled, like national identity, while others, like the oversight of popular entertainment and its participants, appeared trivial. Concerns with uplift were temporarily rendered moot, partly as this very sentiment evoked a paternalism that was no longer as popular given diminished faith in government power and partly because of cinema's participation in the war effort. Through its work with the Creel office, providing information, conducting recruitment drives, and selling Liberty Bonds, the film industry demonstrated its civic responsibility, proving (at least for a short while) that rigid oversight was not necessary. As movies had instilled patriotism during an unpopular war and helped keep the peace domestically, concerns about their effects on the public and cultural values were temporarily assuaged.

Although the war's immediate effects on cinema were primarily economic, they had significant social and cultural ramifications, although some aspects of film culture remained relatively unchanged. War taxes led to a sharp reduction in the number of theaters, closing many smaller neighborhood establishments and threatening first-run theaters not owned by major studios/distributors. Fewer venues led to decreased film production as the film industry became more streamlined with the increase in mergers and the demise of both older companies (like Selig and Essanay) and newer feature-film-oriented concerns like World setting the stage for future oligopolies. Larger and better-situated neighborhood theaters survived, with growth in this area postwar (as seen in Balaban and Katz's postwar success with even bigger local establishments), but these houses were less intimate, moving away from the now somewhat dated prewar neighborhood ideals. As theaters closed, movies were not necessarily so close to home, and new economies of scale changed patterns of exhibition, as also seen in the greater success of the downtown picture palace postwar. As fewer larger theaters meant higher ticket prices and less frequent admissions, the neighborhood theater's intimacy was somewhat eroded. While surviving houses did not completely renounce more social, theater-oriented activities—pressbooks from the Classical era easily refute such ideas—they were less invested in communal ideals.

Changes in cinema's address correspondingly deemphasized the intimacy that was so important in the prewar years, often evoking something more auratic, as changes in stardom attest. Throughout the Progressive Era, stardom was marked by ideals of the star-as-friend, rooted in the regular screen encounters still-rapid rates of feature and short film production made possible.[3] As production slowed, this ideal gradually diminished and was replaced by something more overtly glamorous—although, again, this process was intermittent and far from conclusive. As 1920s production trends moved away from sentimentality and toward consumerism, urban life, action, and sophistication, the relationship between audience, characters, diegesis, and screen similarly shifted away from the old-fashioned kinship associated with community.[4] Desires to cross the screen may not have changed, nor the strength of affiliation with favorite stars and favorite theaters, but movies were no longer as manifestly engaged with neighborhood ideals.

NOTES

Notes to Introduction

1. The following historians highlight change as a quintessential Progressive Era characteristic: John Whiteclay Chambers II, *The Tyranny of Change: America in the Progressive Era, 1890–1920* (New Brunswick, NJ: Rutgers University Press, 2000); Steven J. Diner, *A City and Its Universities: Public Policy in Chicago, 1892–1919* (Chapel Hill: University of North Carolina Press, 1980); Jackson Lears, *The Rebirth of a Nation: The Making of Modern America, 1877–1920* (New York: HarperPerennial, 2010); Robert H. Weibe, *The Search for Order, 1877–1920* (New York: Hill and Wang, 1966).

2. Ben Singer and Charlie Keil, introduction to *American Cinema of the 1910s* (New Brunswick, NJ: Rutgers University Press, 2009), 1–2.

3. Sean Dennis Cashman, *America Ascendant: From Theodore Roosevelt to FDR in the Century of American Power, 1901–1944* (New York: New York University Press, 1998), 19.

4. Diner, *A City and Its Universities*, 53; Lears, *Rebirth of a Nation*, 197–200, 263–323.

5. Chambers, *Tyranny of Change*; Diner, *A City and Its Universities*; Richard Hofstadter, *The Age of Reform* (New York: Vintage, 1960); Lears, *Rebirth of a Nation*; Daniel Earl Saros, *Labor, Industry, and Regulation during the Progressive Era* (New York: Routledge, 2008).

6. See, for example, Ben Singer, *Melodrama and Modernity: Early Sensational Cinema and Its Contexts* (New York: Columbia University Press, 2001); Leo Charney and Vanessa Schwartz, eds., *Cinema and the Invention of Modern Life* (Berkeley: University of California Press, 1996).

7. Cashman, *America Ascendant*, 6.

8. Rivka Shpak Lissak, *Pluralism and Progressives: Hull House and the New Immigrants, 1890–1919* (Chicago: University of Chicago Press, 1989), 1. John Whiteclay Chambers II also notes that Progressives were often opposed to one another, making reform and change important even as their goals varied wildly. As he notes, it was not only Progressives who sought change but also

NOTES TO INTRODUCTION

"radicals, conservatives, and important nonprogressive movements." Chambers, *Tyranny of Change*, xi–xii, xxi, xxi.

9. Chambers, *Tyranny of Change*, xix–xx.

10. Ibid., 141–42.

11. See, for example, Kathleen D. McCarthy, "Nickel Vice and Virtue: Movie Censorship in Chicago, 1907–1915," *Journal of Popular Film* 5, no. 1 (1976): 37–55; Nancy J. Rosenblum, "Between Reform and Regulation: The Struggle over Film Censorship in Progressive America, 1909–1922," *Film History* 1 (1987): 307–25.

12. June Howard, *Form and History in American Literary Naturalism* (Chapel Hill: University of North Carolina Press, 1985), 127–35.

13. Singer and Keil, introduction to *American Cinema of the 1910s*, 1.

14. Chambers, *Tyranny of Change*, 40–41.

15. Lissak, *Pluralism and Progressives*, 1.

16. Blake McKelvey, *The Urbanization of America, 1860–1915* (New Brunswick, NJ: Rutgers University Press, 1963), 74.

17. Richard Hofstadter, ed., *The Progressive Movement, 1900–1915* (Englewood Cliffs, NJ: Prentice-Hall, 1963), 2–3.

18. Sean Dennis Cashman, *America in the Gilded Age: From the Death of Lincoln to the Rise of Theodore Roosevelt* (New York: New York University Press, 1993), 371.

19. Cashman, *America in the Gilded Age*, 164, 354.

20. Chambers, *Tyranny of Change*, 80–84.

21. Ibid., 12.

22. Ibid., 6.

23. Daniel Eli Burnstein, *Next to Godliness: Confronting Dirt and Despair in Progressive Era New York City* (Urbana: University of Illinois Press, 2006), 52.

24. Diner, *A City and Its Universities*, 64.

25. Warren Susman, *Culture as History: The Transformation of American Society in the Twentieth Century* (Washington, DC: Smithsonian Books, 2003), xix–xxx, 86–103, 251–85.

26. Edward Alsworth Ross, introduction to *Public Recreation*, by Richard Henry Edwards (Madison: Bulletin of the University of Wisconsin, Serial No. 709, General Series No. 513, February 1915), 5.

27. For a detailed discussion of leisure and health movements in the nineteenth and early twentieth centuries, see Harvey Green, *Fit for America: Health, Fitness, Sport, and American Society* (New York: Pantheon, 1986).

28. McCarthy, "Nickel Vice and Virtue," 37–55; Rosenblum, "Between Reform and Regulation," 307–25.

29. Lary May, *Screening Out the Past: The Birth of Mass Culture and the Motion Picture Industry* (Chicago: University of Chicago Press, 1980; rev. ed., 1983), 62–64. Page numbers are from the 1983 edition.

30. May, *Screening Out the Past*, 244.

31. Ibid., 245.

32. Charlie Keil, "1913: Movies and the Beginning of a New Era," in *American Cinema of the 1910s*, 92, 94–96. While agreeing with Keil that Progressivism helped structure these developments, I argue that many of the changes seen in 1913 resulted from developments that started a few years earlier, particularly stars and picture palaces (many of these can more correctly be described as larger neighborhood theaters), and can only be fully understood if seen in this broader historical context, something the format of Keil and Singer's book does not allow, a limitation inherent in the format of the series, as essays cover just a single year in film history.

33. Constance Balides, "Cinema under the Sign of Money: Commercialized Leisure, Economies of Abundance, and Pecuniary Madness, 1905–15," in *American Cinema's Transitional Era*, ed. Charlie Keil and Shelley Stamp (Berkeley: University of California Press, 2004), 288–89, 292.

34. Constance Balides, "Making Ends Meet: 'Welfare Films' and the Politics of Consumption during the Progressive Era," in *A Feminist Reader in Early Cinema*, ed. Jennifer Bean and Diane Negra (Durham, NC: Duke University Press, 2002), particularly 166–83.

35. Ideas of collective spectatorship would have widespread consequence for exhibition and film form. With a few important exceptions, this issue has been largely overlooked, although there are a few important exceptions. Shelley Stamp and Ben Singer's work on serials foregrounds how these films addressed a collective social audience through a scheme that interwove text, context, and tie-ins, while both Robert Sklar and Lee Grieveson have excavated older literature on both the psychic and social aspects of film spectatorship that foregrounds it as an essentially collective experience. But the pervasive influence these concepts had on the period's cinema demands that we attend to them in more detail. They shaped mainstream moviegoing, determined textual address, and motivated more oppressive practices like regulation and censorship. They are also important because they restore an important historical dimension to spectatorship while countering some of our theoretical assumptions, including those that maintain that spectatorship can only be collective (and somehow often inherently resistant) if films are open texts or somehow subordinated to other entertainments (like songs, contests, live drama). Robert Sklar, "'The Lost Audience': 1950s Spectatorship and Historical Reception Studies," in *Identifying Hollywood's Audiences: Cultural Identity and the Movies*, ed. Melvyn Stokes and Richard Maltby (London: BFI, 1999), 81–92; Shelley Stamp, *Movie-Struck Girls: Women and Motion Picture Culture after the Nickelodeon* (Princeton, NJ: Princeton University Press, 2000); Singer, *Melodrama and Modernity*.

36. See, for example, Warren Susman, "'Personality' and the Making of Twentieth Century Culture," in his *Culture as History*, 271–85; and P. David Marshall, *Celebrity and Power* (Minneapolis: University of Minnesota Press, 1997), 30–38.

37. Hugo Münsterberg, *The Photoplay: A Psychological Study* (1916; Mineola, NY: Dover, 1970); Gideon H. Diall, *The Psychology of the Aggregate Mind of an Audience* (Terre Haute, IN: Inland, 1897).

38. Charlie Keil and Shelley Stamp, introduction to *American Cinema's Transitional Era*, 1.

39. Charlie Keil, "'To Here from Modernity': Style, Historiography, and Transitional Cinema," in Keil and Stamp, *American Cinema's Transitional Era*, 51.

40. Keil and Stamp, introduction to *American Cinema's Transitional Era*, 1. Keil's previous work, *Early American Cinema in Transition: Story, Style, and Filmmaking, 1907–1913* (Madison: University of Wisconsin Press, 2001) ends this period at 1913, which would make 1913–17 another separate period. While this latter period is superficially more compelling in terms of film textuality and institutions, there are key similarities between films from 1911–12 and those from 1915–17, including (but not limited to) continuities in film style and narrative and the cinema's cultural status.

41. Keil and Stamp, introduction to *American Cinema's Transitional Era*, 1–2.

42. Lee Grieveson, "Not Harmless Entertainment: State Censorship and Cinema in the Transitional Era," in Keil and Stamp, *American Cinema's Transitional Era*, 266.

43. Keil and Stamp, introduction to *American Cinema's Transitional Era*, 2.

44. Keil, "To Here from Modernity," 51.

45. Ibid., 53.

46. Ibid., 57.

47. Ibid., 58.

48. Ben Brewster, "Periodization of Early Cinema," in Keil and Stamp, *American Cinema's Transitional Era*, 74.

49. Brewster, "Periodization of Early Cinema," 74. Singer adds that the concept of two forms of cinema did not seem strange, given the multiplicity of theatrical entertainments and the coexistence of vaudeville (akin to the film program) and the legitimate theater or single play (the feature). Ben Singer, "Feature Films, Variety Programs, and the Crisis of the Small Exhibitor," in Keil and Stamp, *American Cinema's Transitional Era*, 84.

50. Tom Gunning, "Systematizing the Electric Message," in Keil and Stamp, *American Cinema's Transitional Era*, 17. He also suggests that the term *transitional cinema* implies only one transitional period in American cinema, adding that this also implies that its significance is less than that of the eras it bridges. Besides masking the period's complexity and its own transformations,

Gunning suggests the idea of a transitional cinema leads to an overtly linear periodization, one with clean breaks that oversimplifies film history. Gunning, "Systematizing the Electric Message," 16.

51. Jennifer Bean has stated that her work on the transitional period does not involve features at all. Untitled presentation, Transitional Period workshop at the Society for Cinema and Media Studies Conference, London 2005.

52. Singer, "Feature Films, Variety Programs, and the Crisis of the Small Exhibitor," 77.

53. Four reels was the industry standard for feature films by 1912. See Singer, "Feature Films, Variety Programs, and the Crisis of the Small Exhibitor," 84. Exhibitors had previously constructed their own programs from the short films they booked from local exchanges. The service changed this: now distributors created the program (options were available—the cheaper programs featured older films) for exhibitors, promising specific films or releases from specified companies on certain days. Although the exhibitor lost yet more creative control over his program, he gained a more standardized product that was easier to promote in advance along with advertising materials from the exchange.

54. Eileen Bowser, *The Transformation of Cinema, 1907–1915* (New York: Charles Scribner's Sons, 1990), 215.

55. See, for example, Anthony Slide, *Early American Cinema*, rev. ed. (Metuchen, NJ: Scarecrow Press, 1994), 26; Charles Musser, *The Emergence of Cinema: The American Screen to 1907* (Berkeley: University of California Press, 1994, originally published New York: Scribner's, 1990), 400.

56. See Michael Aronson, "The Wrong Kind of Nickel Madness: Pricing Problems for Pittsburgh Nickelodeons," *Cinema Journal* 42, no. 1 (2002): 71–100.

57. Richard Abel, *Americanizing the Movies and "Movie-Mad" Audiences, 1910–1914* (Berkeley: University of California Press, 2006), 46–48, 86–89.

58. Robert C. Allen, "Motion Picture Exhibition in Manhattan, 1906–1912: Beyond the Nickelodeon," in *Film before Griffith*, ed. John L. Fell (Berkeley: University of California Press, 1983), 162–75; Kathy Peiss, *Cheap Amusements: Working Women and Leisure in Turn-of-the-Century New York* (Philadelphia: Temple University Press, 1986); Ben Singer, "Manhattan Nickelodeon Audiences: New Data on Audiences and Exhibitors," *Cinema Journal* 34, no. 3 (1995): 17–19; William Uricchio and Roberta Pearson, "Manhattan's Nickelodeons New York? New York! William Uricchio and Roberta E. Pearson Comment on the Singer-Allen Exchange," *Cinema Journal* 36, no. 4 (1997): 98–102; Judith Thissen, "Oy, Myopia! A Reaction from Judith Thissen on the Singer-Allen Controversy," *Cinema Journal* 36, no. 4 (1997): 102–7; Ben Singer, "Manhattan Melodrama: A Response from Ben Singer," *Cinema Journal* 36, no. 4 (1997): 107–12.

59. Lauren Rabinovitz, *For the Love of Pleasure: Women, Movies, and Culture in Turn-of-Century Chicago* (New Brunswick, NJ: Rutgers University Press, 1998).

60. The most important of these are Douglas Gomery, *Shared Pleasures: A History of Movie Presentation in the United States* (Madison: University of Wisconsin Press, 1992), which features studies of Chicago exhibition even though it is not a local study per se; Rabinovitz, *For the Love of Pleasure*; Julie Ann Lindstrom, "'Getting a Hold Deeper in the Life of the City': Chicago Nickelodeons 1905–1914" (PhD diss., Northwestern University, 1998). Other important studies can be found in work on black cinema, including Jacqueline Najuma Stewart, *Migrating to the Movies: Cinema and Black Urban Modernity* (Berkeley: University of California Press, 2005); and Mary Carbine, "'The Finest Outside the Loop': Motion Picture Exhibition in Chicago's Black Metropolis, 1905–1928," *Camera Obscura* 23 (May 1990): 9–42.

61. Despite their often spectacular and exotic nature, Selig's films were considered startlingly accurate representations of midwestern life, as W. Stephen Bush notes: "If the future historian, whose duty it shall be to describe the manners, customs and ways of living of the plain American people, has about six well-selected Selig films, his task will be an easy one. No need of excavating the suburbs of Chicago or digging into the ruins of Indianapolis or Omaha or Des Moines. The Selig films do far more than merely tell a story. They portray with a thousand subtle touches of a master hand the manner of life of the great yeomanry of our country, the plain people, especially of the Middle West . . . I believe I could tell, in nine cases out of ten, whether a Selig film is being shown, with my eyes shut. Audiences always take these films seriously. Their interest is aroused in an unusual degree. The film compels such strict attention that it is impossible for the audience to waste any time in whispered comments. The result is an unusually profound silence" (Stephen Bush, "Comments of the Fleeting Hour," *Moving Picture World* 6, no. 14, April 9, 1910, 552).

62. Diner, *A City and Its Universities*, 64.

63. Despite the volume of sociological research conducted at the University of Chicago during this time, few books or papers were published covering this period. Even as late as 1932, social historian Day Monroe highlighted these problems of documentation in relation to social history:

> Even adequate information as to the size of families is lacking . . . basic to these discussions, there must be had such fundamental information as the numbers of households of a given size, the average length of the period during which there are children under seven years of age to be cared for, the average proportion of families maintaining homes, and the relative number of home-makers earning.

NOTES TO INTRODUCTION

Reports on cinema are often less specific. Census data from this period is not particularly unhelpful. While Progressive society believed that leisure and cultural life were important, there was no data or factual information about popular culture of any kind included in U.S. Census publications until the 1920s and 1930s. The 1910 census records industrial, agricultural, and commercial activity, but gives no space to more "private" concerns, save for figures on population growth and distribution. This inattention is surprising since these issues increasingly underpinned reform work and public policy on housing, city planning, wage guidelines, and education. Day Monroe, *Chicago Families: A Study of Unpublished Census Data* (Chicago: University of Chicago Press, 1932; reprint, New York: Arno Press, 1972), 2, 117–18.

64. Charles Edward Merriam, *Chicago: A More Intimate View of Urban Politics* (New York: Macmillan, 1929), 3.

65. Christine Bolt, "The American City: Nightmare, Dream, or Irreducible Paradox?," in *The American City: Literary and Cultural Perspectives*, ed. Graham Clarke (London: Vision Press/St. Martin's Press, 1988), 13–22.

66. Lissak, *Pluralism and Progressives*, 21.

67. Sophonisba P. Breckenridge, *The Child in the City: A Series of Papers Presented at the Conferences Held during the Chicago Child Welfare Exhibit* (Chicago: Department of Social Investigation, Chicago School of Civics and Philanthropy, 1912); Diner, *A City and Its Universities*, 44–47, 106, 123–24, 136, 152, 166–67; Lissak, *Pluralism and Progressives*, 7; Allen Hoben, *The Minister and the Boy: A Handbook for Churchmen Engaged in Boys' Work* (Chicago: University of Chicago Press, 1912); *Who's Who In America*, vol. 8 (Chicago: Albert Nelson Marquis, 1914–15), 2308. Hoben was field secretary of the Juvenile Protective Association between 1910 and 1913, organizing its neighborhood activities, working with communities to establish healthy recreational programs, and often lobbying against motion pictures. Other University of Chicago faculty active in social reform included Nathaniel Butler, professor of education, who helped draw up plans for improved vocational education in conjunction with the Chicago Association of Commerce; political scientist and lawyer Ernst Freund, who composed protective legislation in conjunction with local reform groups, including the Immigrants Protective League, to ensure the health and safety of the weaker and less fortunate members of society and establish the groundwork for a new welfare state; Baptist minister and founding president of the University of Chicago William Harper, who encouraged faculty to engage in public service and helped establish the University of Chicago settlement house; sociologist and another Baptist minister Charles Henderson, who trained social workers, was an active member of the Chicago Vice Commission, and was a leading member of the reform movement who worked in the city's settlement houses; bacteriologist Edwin O. Jordan, who campaigned for improved public hygiene and a purified water supply; head of political science

Harry Judson, a campaigner for charter reform; Divinity School dean Shailer Mathews, a member of the City Club's committee for educational reform; philosopher and leading reformer George Herbert Mead, who worked in the local settlement houses and was involved in constitutional, legal, educational, and social reform; political scientist, board member for the city park's commission, and local politician Charles E. Merriam, who worked for charter and local taxation reform; Baptist minister and founder of the sociology department Albion Small; philosopher James Hayden Tufts, whose career in academia and reform was concerned with the moral and ethical aspects of contemporary social problems, and who worked in the settlement houses and campaigned for housing improvements; and sociologist Charles Zueblin, who worked at Hull House, organized and financed after-school cultural and recreational activities for children, and sat on the board of the city's parks commission. A number of the university's trustees, including Adolphus Bartlett, Frederic Delano, Thomas Donnelley, Wallace Heckman, Charles Hutchinson, Herman Kohlsaat, Franklin McVeagh, and Julius Rosenwald, were also extremely active in reform work. While it played a less pivotal role in social science and philanthropic endeavors, neighboring Northwestern University also included a number of key reformers among their faculty, such as criminologist Robert Gault; legal expert John Gray, who campaigned for electoral reform; president Abraham Harris, who served on the Vice Commission; business school dean William Hotchkiss, who headed the 1911 Cook County investigation into the juvenile court system; and Law School dean and legal aid advocate John Wigmore, who helped establish a new training program for the city's police officers in 1915. See Diner, *A City and Its Universities*, 14–18, 31–44, 86, 90, 94–98, 104–8, 112, 114–17, 123–27, 130–31, 133–36, 138–39, 141–47, 156, 158, 163, 177, 180–90.

68. Robert Grau, *The Theatre of Science: A Volume of Progress and Achievement in the Motion Picture Industry* (New York: Broadway, 1914), 16. Michael Aronson systematically justifies Pittsburgh's claim in *Nickelodeon City: Pittsburgh at the Movies, 1905–1929* (Pittsburgh: University of Pittsburgh Press, 2010).

69. Lee Grieveson, "Why the Audience Mattered in Chicago in 1907," in *American Movie Audiences: From the Turn of the Century to the Early Sound Era*, ed. Melvyn Stokes and Richard Maltby (London: BFI, 1999), 81. Although the nickelodeon era had begun around 1905, movies were still essentially a novelty at this date. Exhibition was transient and unsystematic, mainly designed to satiate audience curiosity as seen in the use of motion pictures in cheap vaudeville, fairgrounds, traveling shows, or short-lived storefront shows. Alternatively, it could be a more specialized form of entertainment whose content and programming was controlled by a skilled operator (examples here include shows in big-time vaudeville). As Charles Musser notes, around 1907 exhibition became a more standardized practice, one that served an increas-

ingly consolidated film industry based on narrative films. Musser, *Emergence of Cinema*, 433.

70. In contrast, films were shown in many converted theaters in New England with capacities up to one thousand, demonstrating the wide variations in exhibition nationwide. Musser, *Emergence of Cinema*, 428–29.

71. "Will G. Barker on Moving Pictures," *Moving Picture World* 1, no. 42, December 21, 1907, 689; Bowser, *Transformation of Cinema*, 6.

72. McCarthy, "Nickel Vice and Virtue," 46–47.

73. William Cronon, *Nature's Metropolis: Chicago and the Great West* (New York: Norton, 1992), 39–46.

74. Louise de Koven Bowen, *Five and Ten Cent Theaters: Two Investigations* (Chicago: Juvenile Protection Association, 1911); Louise de Koven Bowen, *Safeguards for City Youth at Work and at Play* (New York: Macmillan, 1914); Louise de Koven Bowen, *Some Legislative Needs in Illinois* (Chicago: Juvenile Protective Association, 1914).

75. The Edward Alsworth Ross papers at the State Historical Society at the University of Wisconsin-Madison include the famous sociologist's personal notebooks from his field missions to Chicago, where he met with other reformers like Jane Addams, Mrs. Bowen, and Gertrude Howe Britton. He accompanied them on their research trips to working-class factories and places of amusement, like the cinema, but his notes are also vague, essentially just providing his opinions on the degraded state of urban popular culture. Edward Alsworth Ross Papers, Box 26, Files 10 and 12, Ethnological Notes, ca. 1912, vols. 2 and 4.

76. Gustave Le Bon, *The Crowd: A Study of the Popular Mind* (New York: Ballantine, 1969).

77. These ideas drew on aspects of crowd psychology that were more directly concerned with, and influenced by, work on suggestion, imitation, and hypnosis developed by the likes of Alfred Binet, Gabriel Tarde, and Robert Park. Gabriel Tarde, *On Communication and Social Influence: Selected Papers*, edited and with an introduction by Terry N. Clark, Heritage of Society (Chicago: University of Chicago Press, 1969); Gabriel Tarde, *The Laws of Imitation*, translated from the second French edition by Elsie Clews Parsons, with an introduction by Franklin H. Giddings (Gloucester, MA: Peter Smith, 1962; originally published New York: Henry Holt, 1903); Robert E. Park, *The Crowd and the Public and Other Essays* (Chicago: University of Chicago Press, 1972); Alfred Binet, *On Double Consciousness: Experimental Psychological Studies*, new ed. (Chicago: Open Court, 1905).

Notes to Chapter 1

1. As Wilfred Trotter, a leading proponent of crowd psychology observed, "The two fields—the social and the individual—are . . . absolutely continuous; all human psychology, it is contended, must be the psychology of associated man, since man as a solitary animal is unknown to us, and every individual must present the characteristic reactions of the social animal if such exist." Wilfred Trotter, *Instincts of the Herd in Peace and War* (New York: Macmillan, 1915, 1917, 1919), 12.

2. Gerald Stanley Lee, *Crowds: A Moving Picture of Democracy* (New York: Doubleday, Page, 1913), 271, 275, 305.

3. P. David Marshall, *Celebrity and Power: Fame in Contemporary Culture* (Minneapolis: University of Minnesota Press, 1997), 35.

4. Le Bon, *The Crowd*, 20.

5. Lee Grieveson, unpublished paper presented at the Screen Studies Conference, Glasgow, 2000, 3.

6. Le Bon, *The Crowd*, 36.

7. See, for example, Bowen, *Five and Ten Cent Theaters*; Bowen, *Safeguards for City Youth at Work and at Play*; John Collier and Edward M. Barrows, *The City Where Crime Is Play* (New York: People's Institute, 1914); Richard Henry Edwards, *Public Recreation* (Madison: Bulletin of the University of Wisconsin, Serial No. 709, General Series No. 513, February 1915); Allen Hoben, *The Minister and the Boy: A Handbook for Churchmen Engaged in Boys' Work* (Chicago: University of Chicago Press, 1912); and Julia Schoenfeld, "Commercial Recreation Legislation," *Playground* 7, no. 12 (1914): 461–79.

8. Gregory Waller, *Mainstreet Amusements: Movies and Commercial Entertainment in a Southern City, 1896–1930* (Washington, DC: Smithsonian Institution Press, 1995), 136.

9. These observers often rationalized their inability to understand the movies' appeal in terms of their higher and more educated sensibilities. Mary Heaton Vorse stated: "The keener your intellectual capacity, the higher your artistic sensibilities are developed, just so much more difficult it is to find this total forgetfulness." The German sociologist Emilie Altenloh agreed. Based on her observations of audiences in Mannheim during 1913–14, she found "it appears very difficult for the very educated, intellectual people to lose themselves in the separate, often disjunctive, successive plots. Repeatedly, people who are used to dealing with everything in a purely intellectual manner say that it is extraordinarily difficult for them to apprehend the coherence of a film plot." Mary Heaton Vorse, "Some Picture Show Audiences," *The Outlook* (June 24, 1911): 445; Emilie Altenloh, "On the Sociology of Cinema (1914)," in *Red Velvet Seat: Women's Writings on the First Fifty Years of Cinema*, ed. Antonia Lant with Ingrid Periz (London: Verso, 2006), 121.

10. Lee, *Crowds: A Moving Picture of Democracy*, 269, 146.
11. Ibid., 269–75.
12. Patrick Brantlinger, "Mass Media and Culture in *Fin-de-Siècle* Europe," in *Fin de Siècle and Its Legacy*, ed. Mikulás Teich and Roy Porter (Cambridge: Cambridge University Press, 1990), 100.
13. Patrick Brantlinger, *Bread and Circuses: Theories of Mass Culture as Social Decay* (Ithaca, NY: Cornell University Press, 1983), 53–81. Brantlinger provides an excellent and thorough analysis of the relationship between "crowd theories," mass media, modernism, and the distinction of cultural tastes.
14. Marshall, *Celebrity and Power* 31.
15. Ibid., 31.
16. Le Bon, *The Crowd*, 10.
17. Charles Mackay, *Extraordinary Popular Delusions and the Madness of Crowds* (New York: The Noonday Press / Farrar, Straus, and Giroux, 1932; reprint of 1841 and 1852 editions), xvii.
18. Mid-nineteenth-century fiction turned to the urban crowd, revealing it to be a matter of public interest, fascination, and fear. Edgar Allan Poe's "The Man of the Crowd" details the obsession of its unnamed, passive, first-person protagonist, a convalescing invalid who no longer participates in life but instead watches the masses in London's streets. His crowd is a fascinating but dangerous spectacle, without aim, motive, or identity, tempting its observer to lose his remaining vestiges of self to join its collective void. Edgar Allan Poe, "The Man of the Crowd," in *Seven Tales*, ed. W. T. Bandy (New York: Schocken, 1971), 135–37. By the early twentieth century, popular socially oriented novelists like H. G. Wells expressed anxiety about the abstract, synthetic interaction of the modern city. In *Anticipations* (1914), Wells predicted suburbs housing a new class of educated individuals would replace the city and its crowds. He maintained that "a process . . . is at work . . . whereby the great swollen, shapeless, hypertrophied social mass of today must give birth at last to a naturally and informally organized, educated class, an unprecedented sort of people, a New Republic dominating the world." Inspired by Malthus, he believed that mobs would breed themselves out of existence as their gene pool grew progressively weaker. H. G. Wells, *Anticipations of the Mechanical and Scientific Progress upon Human Life and Thought* (London: Chapman and Hall, 1914), 302. Utopian thinker Henry Olerich's 1893 novel, *A Cityless and Countryless World: An Outline of Practical Co-Operative Individualism*, expresses a similar view of the crowd. It features a wise, cultured Martian, Mr. Midith, detailing the practice of communal living in a semiurban, semirural environment on his more advanced planet. Olerich believed that rural life suffocated individual improvement, whereas urban dirt, depravity, and crowds bred depressed and unenlightened masses: "But, as man's intellectual powers continue to unfold, as his sensibilities become more acute, and as he employs more and more

NOTES TO CHAPTER I

machinery to perform his manual toil, he slowly but gradually discovers the evil effects of dividing the population into cities and country; for both are faulty, both are unhealthy, both are inconvenient, and both are useless." Henry Olerich, *A Cityless and Countryless World: An Outline of Practical Co-Operative Individualism* (New York: Arno Press and the *New York Times*, 1917 reprint of 1893 original, Holstein, IA: Gilmore and Olerich), 238.

19. Georg Simmel, "The Metropolis and Mental Life," in *On Individuality and Social Forms*, ed. Donald N. Levine (Chicago: University of Chicago Press, 1971), 324.

20. Simmel, "The Metropolis and Mental Life," 338.

21. Ibid., 334.

22. Georg Simmel, "Fashion," in Levine, *On Individuality and Social Forms*, 295.

23. Le Bon, *The Crowd*, 11–12.

24. Robert E. Park, *The Crowd and the Public and Other Essays* (Chicago: University of Chicago Press, 1972), 47.

25. Richard Lindberg, *Chicago by Gaslight: A History of Chicago's Netherworld, 1880–1920* (Chicago: Academy Publishers, 1996), 211. His figures were taken from the *Daily News* Almanac, 1946.

26. "The Moving Picture and the National Character," *Review of Reviews*, September 1910, 315–16.

27. Walter Prichard Eaton, "The Menace of the Movies," *American Magazine*, September 1913, 55–56.

28. "The Cinematograph Craze," the *Dial* LVI, no. 664, February 16, 1914, 129, 131.

29. Tarde, *On Communication and Social Influence*, 16.

30. Donald N. Levine, "Note on *The Crowd and the Public*," in Park, *The Crowd and the Public*, xxviii.

31. "Movies and the Eyes," *Literary Digest*, July 31, 1915, 209.

32. Lee Grieveson, *Policing Cinema: Movies and Censorship in Early Twentieth-Century America* (Berkeley: University of California Press, 2004), 61–64.

33. "'Movies' In Church and Out," *Literary Digest*, July 4, 1914, 24, citing the *New York Sun*.

34. "The Moving Picture and the National Character," *Review of Reviews*, September 1910, 316.

35. "Little Girls Rob Houses: Blame on Moving Pictures," *Chicago Daily Tribune*, Saturday, January 11, 1913, 14.

36. Grieveson, *Policing Cinema*, 65–66.

37. George Elliott Howard, "Social Psychology of the Spectator," *American Journal of Sociology* 18, no. 1 (1912): 33–36.

38. Howard, "Social Psychology of the Spectator," 34.

39. Richard Henry Edwards, *Public Recreation* (Madison: Bulletin of the University of Wisconsin, Extension Division, Serial No. 709, General Series 513, 1915), 126.

40. Howard, "Social Psychology of the Spectator," 37.

41. Ibid., 37.

42. Lee Grieveson, "Why the Audience Mattered in Chicago in 1907," in Stokes and Maltby, *American Movie Audiences*, 82.

43. Hugo Münsterberg, *The Photoplay: A Psychological Study* (New York: D. Appleton, 1916), 107–11, 220–28.

44. Münsterberg, *The Photoplay*, 222–23.

45. Le Bon, *The Crowd*, 35.

46. Binet, *On Double Consciousness*, 6, 64.

47. Ibid., 69.

48. Tarde, *Laws of Imitation*, xiv.

49. Sociology and criminology both had antecedents in mass psychology: Gabriel Tarde strongly influenced Robert Park and contemporary criminologists particularly with his work on studies of suggestion, imitation, and the formation of the aggregate mind through mass culture. Tarde, *On Communication and Social Influence*, 1, 68.

50. Jane Addams, "The House of Dreams" (1909), reprinted in Lant, *Red Velvet Seat*, 301.

51. Tom Gunning, "An Aesthetic of Astonishment: Early Film and the (In)Credulous Spectator," in *Viewing Positions: Ways of Seeing Films*, ed. Linda Williams (New Brunswick, NJ: Rutgers University Press, 1994), 114–33.

52. An Exhibitor, "The Length of Film Subjects," *Moving Picture World* 5, no. 24 (1909): 6. Also see Keil, *Early American Cinema in Transition*, 134–50.

53. Mary Heaton Vorse, "Some Picture Show Audiences," *The Outlook* (June 24, 1911): 443, 445.

54. These sentiments were not restricted to America either; the French writer and poet Jules Romains's expresses something very similar in his 1911 essay, "The Crowd at the Cinematograph": "The group dream now begins. They sleep; their eyes no longer see . . . They no longer realize they are in a large square chamber, immobile, in parallel rows as in a ploughed field . . . The crowd is a being that remembers and imagines, a group that evokes other groups much like itself—audiences, processions, parades, mobs in the street, armies. They all imagine that it is they who are experiencing all these adventures, all these catastrophes, all these celebrations." Richard Abel has observed this "empathetic, if sometimes sentimental, attitude . . . contrast[ed] markedly with [Le Bon's] classic . . . study of crowd psychology," but it still bears a strong structural resemblance to these reports. All these theories evoked prevailing wisdom that spectatorship was something fundamentally collective (at both

physical and psychic levels) contrasting with the individualism that marked much later academic film studies discourse. Romains's observations account for identification in terms of empathy as well as memory, however, something entirely missing from Le Bon's crowd, possibly because it evoked individuality and the capacity for introspection. These terms link Romains's thoughts to the other dominant way of thinking about the collective in Progressive culture—the community. Jules Romains, "The Crowd at the Cinematograph," in *French Film Theory and Criticism: A History/Anthology*. Vol. 1, *1907–1929*, ed. Richard Abel (Princeton, NJ: Princeton University Press, 1988), 31n99, 53.

55. Olivia Howard Dunbar, "The Lure of the Films," *Harper's Weekly*, no. 57, January 18, 1913, 20.

56. Francis Hackett, "The Movies," *New Republic* (May 1, 1915): 329.

57. Vice Commission of Chicago, *The Social Evil in Chicago* (New York: Arno Press and the *New York Times*), 1970 reprint of 1911 edition, 174, 231. In addition, they believed this darkness damaged patrons eyesight, advocating instead "the use of glass screens with lighted interior[s] . . . to remove moral dangers and eye strain." Vice Commission of Chicago, *Social Evil in Chicago*, 247. Also see Jane Addams, *The Spirit of Youth and the City Streets* (Chicago: University of Chicago Press, 1909), 86. Even the Vice Commission recommended that the city "provide for the presentation of pictures in well-lighted halls, "one of its few suggestions for movie theaters," *Social Evil in Chicago*, 56, 61.

58. A Picture Lover, "Helpful Hints to Exhibitors," *Moving Picture World* 6, no. 3 (1910): 507.

59. New projectors and screens were developed to handle the problem: in March 1911, *Billboard* noted a new projector that could deal with relatively bright ambient light that had been successfully used in Chicago's moving picture and vaudeville houses, including the Majestic, Plaza, and Academy Theaters. "Chicago Film News," *Billboard* 23, no. 9, March 4, 1911, 14.

60. Nonetheless, reformers still protested the relative darkness inside movie theaters, much to the amusement of the trade press. As James S. McQuade recounts in June 1912: "Mrs. Joseph T. Bowen . . . announced that the [JPA] is preparing an ordinance . . . requiring owners of all moving picture theaters to keep their places lighted while pictures are shown. . . . Picture theater owners, the great majority of them, have no reason to fight this ordinance, from the fact that by far the greater number of Chicago picture theaters are lighted while pictures are being shown. . . . The Motion Picture Exhibitors' League of America should fight the dark picture theater as being the worst foe of pictures at the present time. It furnishes overzealous reformers and the ever-ready brand to throw into the exhibitors' camp." Just one month later, Alderman Thompson proposed a "morals ordinance" to the building committee, recommending a "fixed degree" of light in all parts of a movie theater,

conforming to an approved test wherein "a person with normal eyesight must be able to read standard 'test' type at fixed distances, within the theater, while the pictures are being presented" (James S. McQuade, "Chicago Letter," *Moving Picture World* 12, no. 9, June 1, 1912, 809).

61. James S. McQuade, "Chicago Letter," *Moving Picture World* 9, no. 7, August 26, 1911, 527.

62. "Difficulties Encountering M.P. Legislation," *Billboard* 22, no. 13, March 26, 1910, 21.

63. James S. McQuade, "Chicago Letter," *Moving Picture World* 9, no. 7, August 26, 1911, 527.

64. "Chicago Theatres May Close: Situation Tense as Exhibitors Fail to Show Interest in Fight against Unjust Legislation by the Municipal Authorities—Exchanges Threaten to Refuse Service for Our Week," *Motion Picture News* 9, no. 5, February 7, 1914, 15.

65. Waller, *Mainstreet Amusements*, 4.

66. "The Moving Picture and the National Character," *Review of Reviews*, September 1910, 319.

67. Olivia Howard Dunbar, "The Lure of the Films," *Harper's Weekly*, no. 57, January 18, 1913, 20.

68. See, for example, Barbara Klinger, "Digressions at the Cinema: Reception and Mass Culture," *Cinema Journal* 28, no. 4 (1989): 3–19.

69. Miriam Hansen, *Babel and Babylon: Spectatorship in American Silent Film* (Cambridge, MA: Harvard University Press, 1991), esp. 76–89.

70. Francis Hackett, "The Movies," *New Republic* (May 1, 1915): 329. Clearly, the movement toward adaptations of respected literary and dramatic texts during the mid-1910s did not offset all criticism, but instead caused some writers to bemoan the inherent incompatibility between the cinema (a mass form) and literature/drama (as modes inviting individualized contemplation). For some, this combination threatened to implode all culture. The *New Republic*'s Floyd Dell complained the movies censored, "sterilized [and] emasculated" classics: "All the harm, the fever of thought, of doubt, of inquiry . . . is thus eliminated. The husk is preserved and those who have seen it [the movie] will think they have seen Ibsen's *Ghosts*, as advertized [*sic*] outside. Thus is art robbed of its sting, truth of its victory." In 1916, an anonymous writer for *The Outlook* complained that, "as a mass form, motion pictures could have no educational or inspirational value." As a correspondent for *Current Opinion* argued, "whether it is an exaggerated, written-into, and therefore weakened paraphrase of an opera story, or whether it is a presentation of a historical event, the effect upon the young mind is too often an assimilation of facts that are not facts and the acceptance of adulterated versions of literature." "The Immoral Morality of the 'Movies,'" *Current Opinion* 59, no. 4 (1915): 244; "'Movie' Manners and Morals," *The Outlook* (July 26, 1916): 695.

71. "Comments on the Films," *Moving Picture World* 10, no. 7, November 18, 1911, 549.

72. Ernest A. Dench, "Strange Effect of Photoplays on Spectators," *Illustrated World* 27, no. 5 (1917): 788.

73. "Her Temptation," *Moving Picture World* 32, no. 4, April 28, 1917, 636–37.

74. "The Love Girl," *Moving Picture World* 29, no. 2, July 8, 1916, 265.

75. "Hypnotism in 'Crimson Stain,'" *Moving Picture World* 30, no. 1, October 7, 1916, 99.

76. Trotter, *Instincts of the Herd in Peace and War*, 15–23.

77. Ibid., 43.

78. Lissak, *Pluralism and Progressives*, 15.

79. Ibid., 14.

80. Ibid., 15.

81. Ibid., 13–16.

82. Hansen, *Babel and Babylon*, 76–77.

83. Vachel Lindsay, *The Art of the Moving Picture* (New York: Liveright, 1970; reprint of 1922 revision of 1915 original), 77–78.

84. Lindsay, *The Art of the Moving Picture*, 67–68.

85. Ibid., 68, 75.

86. Ibid., 75. Lesley Brill also discusses movies' particular ability to represent crowds in *Crowds, Power, and Transformation in Cinema* (Detroit: Wayne State University Press, 2006).

87. Brill, *Crowds, Power, and Transformation in Cinema*, 3–6.

88. Hansen, *Babel and Babylon*, 84.

89. Ibid., 79–89.

90. Diner, *A City and Its Universities*, 64.

Notes to Chapter 2

1. Susman, *Culture as History*, xxvi–xxxviii, 252–62.

2. The most sophisticated example of this argument appears in Miriam Hansen's seminal and highly influential study, *Babel and Babylon*.

3. Brewster, "The Periodization of Early Cinema," 66–75, esp. 74; Singer, "Feature Films, Variety Programs, and the Crisis of the Small Exhibitor," 76–100; Jennifer Bean, untitled presentation, Workshop on Transitional Cinema, Society for Cinema and Media Studies Annual Conference, London, 2005; Bowser, *Transformation of Cinema*, 212–15.

4. Bowser, *Transformation of Cinema*, 191.

5. Michael Quinn, "Early Feature Distribution and the Development of the Motion Picture Industry: Famous Players and Paramount, 1912–1921" (PhD diss., University of Wisconsin–Madison, 1998), 19. Also see 65–69.

6. Although I do not have the space to discuss it in any detail, exhibitor demands for open booking during 1917 suggested the broader industry-wide crisis that led to the failure of many companies and the consolidation of others, marking the beginning of the oligopoly that helped define the Classical years.

7. Richard Koszarski, *An Evening's Entertainment: The Age of the Silent Feature Picture, 1915–1928* (Berkeley: University of California Press, 1994), 63.

8. As Quinn points out, the GFC could not really accommodate features, because their business model depended on undifferentiated product. He points out that the collapse of the MPPC opens the market for features. While his argument is persuasive, he neglects to consider the ways that Mutual and Universal accommodated feature distribution even before the collapse of the Trust. "Early Feature Distribution and the Development of the Motion Picture Industry," 2, 43–101.

9. Quinn, "Early Feature Distribution and the Development of the Motion Picture Industry," 105–6. There were changes in 1917 as distributors started yielding to exhibitor complaints and some companies like KESE and even Paramount briefly turned to an open booking system.

10. As Quinn notes, Paramount initially adopted the GFC's licensing scheme to prevent its exhibitors using any other service. As before, exhibitors ultimately rebelled, leading to the antitrust case against Paramount in 1921. As Quinn notes further, they had to drop the exclusive licensing as many exhibitors opted for a daily change of program and needed more films than Paramount could provide. "Early Feature Distribution and the Development of the Motion Picture Industry," 142–46.

11. "Many Selig Specials for Early Release," *Motion Picture News* 11, no. 6, February 13, 1915, 41; "In the Picture Playhouses: Tyrone Power Becomes Star in Chicago Photoplay Studio," *Chicago Herald*, November 17, 1914, 11. Early Spectacular Specials included "*The Servant in the House*, the play in which Tyrone Power enacted his world-famous character of 'The Drainsman'; *The Carpet from Baghdad*, in which Kathlyn Williams stars; *The Crisis*, Winston Churchill's noted novel; *A Texas Steer*, Charles Hoyt's best comedy; *The Ne'er-Do-Well*, the principle scenes for which were taken in the Canal Zone; and *The Rosary*, for which an entire Irish village was erected." Not all of these were immediately available—*The Crisis* would not even be produced for at least another year.

12. "Selig Diamond Specials for Release on General," *Motion Picture News* 11, no. 15, April 17, 1915, 47. In April 1915 the list of forthcoming Diamond Specials supported this policy, as it included such fare as *His Father's Rifle*; "a Jungle Zoo wild animal drama"; a Tom Mix western; *Two Boys in Blue*; and an ethnic thriller, *How Callahan Cleaned Up Little Hell*.

13. "William Selig Perfects Strong Organization," *Motion Picture News* 12, no. 4, July 31, 1915, 55, reprinted in Kalton C. Lahue, ed., *Motion Picture Pioneer: The Selig Polyscope Company* (South Brunswick, NJ, and New York: A. S. Barnes, 1973), 220.

14. "Chicago News and Comment: Leaks in the Loop," *Motion Picture News* 15, no. 19, May 12, 1917, 3004. Selig *was* successful with these films, "never having produced a picture that was a failure," but, aside from other extravagances, it seems unlikely that even high-grossing big pictures could support a studio, releases being too few and far between to justify the resources and time they devoured. See *"Garden of Allah* Rights Bought by Sherman," *Motion Picture News* 15, no. 1, January 6, 1917, 65.

15. "Essanay Adds Another 3-Reeler to Weekly Program: Quality Will Not Be Sacrificed in This Increased Production, Declares President Spoor, Whose Company Is Striving for a Well Balanced List of Successes," *Motion Picture News* 12, no. 7, August 21, 1915, 45.

16. "Essanay Adds Another 3-Reeler to Weekly Program," 45.

17. "Essanay Announces Increased Feature Production," *Motion Picture News* 14, no. 23, December 9, 1916, 3674.

18. "Although the screen time of these two special brands is announced as approximately 33 minutes, it was decided to call them features, because it was believed that the merit of the photoplays warranted it, Mr. Spoor's idea being that the merit of the play rather than the screen time should determine whether or not a picture should be called a feature." "Spoor Announces Two Special Lines from Essanay," *Motion Picture News* 14, no. 22, December 2, 1916, 3487.

19. "Spoor Announces Two Special Lines from Essanay," 3487.

20. "Essanay's February Releases on General Program," *Motion Picture News* 15, no. 6, February 10, 1917, 891; "Added Subjects in Essanay's Marriage Series," *Motion Picture News* 15, no. 7, February 17, 1917, 1057.

21. "New Essanay Series, *Do Children Count?*," *Motion Picture News* 15, no. 9, March 3, 1917, 1399.

22. These were all self-contained. Titles included: (1) *The Guiding Hand*, (2) *The Wonderful Event*, (3) *Steps to Somewhere*, (4) *The Yellow Umbrella*, (5) *A Place in the Sun*, (6) *Where Is My Mother*, (7) *When Sorrow Weeps*, (8) *The Uneven Road*, (9) *The Season of Childhood*, (10) *The Little White Girl*, (11) *The Bridge of Fantasy*, (12) *The Kingdom of Hope*. The series increasingly took on wartime content as Little Mary was appointed the youngest sergeant in the US Army after being "commissioned [as] recruiting sergeant by Capt. F. R. Kenney, U.S.A., for her Red Cross and Recruiting work." Advertisement, *Motion Picture News* 16, no. 2, July 14, 1917, 214.

23. "*Do Children Count?* Breaks House Policies," *Motion Picture News* 16, no. 2, July 14, 1917, 239.

24. "Essanay Plan Release of Periodic Specials," *Motion Picture News* 16, no. 22, December 1, 1917, 3820.

25. "Essanay Offers Only Light Subjects during War," *Motion Picture News* 15, no. 23, June 9, 1917, 3597; "Boom Recruiting with *The Man Who Was Afraid*," *Motion Picture News* 16, no. 2, July 14, 1917, 254; "Spoor Organizes Exhibitors in Food Economy," *Motion Picture News* 16, no. 18, November 3, 1917, 3070.

26. Bowser, *Transformation of Cinema*, 255.

27. Ben Brewster, "*Traffic in Souls* (1913): An Experiment in Feature-Length Narrative Construction," in *The Silent Cinema Reader*, ed. Lee Grieveson and Peter Krämer (London and New York: Routledge, 2004), 229. Also see Bowser, *Transformation of Cinema*, 199–200, 203. An interesting—and relatively late—example of a feature predicated on one- and two-reel feature narrativity was the October 1916 Douglas Fairbank's vehicle *Manhattan Madness* (Allan Dwan, Triangle-Fine Arts). A story about a former New Yorker's love for the West (Fairbanks) and his East Coast friends' frustration with his contempt for his home town, the film starts with a prologue where Steve O'Dare (Doug) is seen out West before returning to Manhattan to sell some war horses to Count Wilkie. Following displays of Nevada, New York, and Doug's athleticism, the film alternates between visualizations of the friends' argument about whether East or West is best, which takes up the first fifteen minutes of this forty-seven-minute-long film. Then Steve meets "The Girl" while dining at his friends' country club, but after she leaves, his boredom returns. The next seven minutes set up the plot, where Steve, he hasn't "had a real thrill since I landed," and his friends bet $5,000 that he will. Shortly afterward, Count Wilkie summons Steve to his dark old mansion just outside Manhattan. The next twenty-two minutes are action packed, offering another story that bears a strong resemblance to period serials. With the help of a maid, Steve quickly discovers that Count Wilkie is holding hostage the girl he saw in the country club. He tries to save her, falls through a trapdoor into a basement where he overhears talk about a stolen Vandergold necklace, a sensational case his friends had told him about earlier, and discovers that the girl was kidnapped because she knew about their crime. Freed by a maid, Steve rescues the girl, tackles Wilkie's henchmen, confronts the Count, and fights again while his friends rush to the castle. The girl then disappears only for Steve to realize this episode was a prank, established by his friends to win the bet, featuring Broadway actors. Then Steve turns the table—his western friends arrive as he tells his pals he is the notorious western bank robber and sharp shooter, Black Burke, and rides off with the girl. At the end, he confesses (via letter) that he's not the notorious criminal, and, smiling at the camera, announces the only thing he's stolen is a girl.

NOTES TO CHAPTER 2

The core of *Manhattan Madness*, and the bulk of its action, lasts for less than half its five reels, its tight suspense and action resembling a two-reel film. The first part of the film sets up key elements of the story—Steve's character, his love for his new home out West, his attraction to the girl, the bet with his friends, and the stories of Black Burke and the theft of the Vandergold necklace—to be used later. In itself, this is not remarkable, but the relative length of the set-up—almost half the film—is unusual, especially as it is largely devoid of significant action. This likely happens because the first part of the film represents "reality," whereas its second act, more story-based, is just a trick. The structure of this feature resembles one- and two-reels films in at least two ways: first, the set-up and the action are almost like two related short films, the first comparing and contrasting two ways of life (the East and the West), the other, a fast-paced mystery/suspense/action thriller. Second, the framed narrative uses a device more typically found in one- and two-reelers where a character discovers they have been tricked, had a dream, or mistaken something that was fake for something real and then laughed it all off. In effect, these narratives depend on the illusion of change, not its practice, unlike most stories, a phenomenon that would also account for the long set-up. (Of course, one thing does change here—Steve finds a wife.) While *Manhattan Madness* is feature length, its storytelling techniques are primarily those of shorter films.

28. Brewster, "*Traffic in Souls* (1913): An Experiment in Feature-Length Narrative Construction," 230–31.

29. Ibid., 34.

30. Bowser, *Transformation of Cinema*, 261.

31. Keil, *Early American Cinema in Transition*, esp. 5–6, 55–56, 105–24, 168–69, and 209. Keil notes that toward the end of his transitional period, films start featuring more eyeline matches and point of view, use closer shots for emblematic purposes, and employ more cutting between spaces. As he notes, however, there is limited shot/reverse shot and scene dissection, with eyeline matches primarily used for point of view or to link two proximate spaces. He notes that editing deals with three forms of spatial relations: "Overlap, proximity and alterity. In overlap, the second shot contains some portion of the first, reproduces it in a changed context of scale, or presents it from a different angle. . . . Proximity involves a relationship of relative closeness between two spaces. . . . Because the two spaces are physically distinct, filmmakers must supply cues to suggest proximity, sometimes in combination, such as reciprocated gazes, matching of character movement across spaces, and continuity of décor in shared space. Finally, when the transition from one space to another involves a significant physical distance, alterity comes into play. Note that any type of spatial relationship can enter into an alternating sequence, although cross-cutting typically involves alterity." Keil, *Early American Cinema in Transition*, 105. Early features—like late one-reel narrative films—employ alterity,

proximity, and overlap, but the former two dominate. Proximity takes on many of the functions that scene dissection would later use, with narratively charged contiguous spaces being used and reused to develop the narrative and characters, foreshadow events, and comment on the action. Overlap was primarily found in cut-ins and cut-outs and for inserts and point of view, but in most cases, changes of angle are rare, as was shot/reverse shot.

32. Just a few examples include *The Avenging Conscience* (D. W. Griffith, Majestic-Mutual, 1914); *His Picture in the Papers* (John Emerson, Fine Arts-Triangle, 1916); *Manhattan Madness* (Allan Dwan, Fine Arts-Triangle, 1916); *The Whip* (Maurice Tourneur, Paragon, 1917); *Hell's Hinges* (Charles Swickard, NYMP–Kay Bee–Triangle, 1916); *The Cheat* (Cecil B. DeMille, Jesse L. Lasky–Paramount, 1915); *Carmen* (Cecil B. DeMille, Jesse L. Lasky–Paramount, 1915); *A Fool There Was* (Frank Powell, Fox Film Corporation, 1915); and *Snow White* (J. Searle Dawley, Famous Players–Lasky–Paramount, 1916).

33. Oversight also structures many serials, which explore its potential to protect and endanger. Their adventure-seeking heroines are not only imperiled by their audacity (which often saves them as well) but also by the men who spy on them and plan their death. In *The Perils of Pauline*, Pauline is under threat precisely because Koerner/Owen constantly watches her, and this supersedes Harry's largely ineffective protective gaze, something she in turn tries to evade. In response to these threats, many of these women have suitors who try to protect them, something embodied in their careful oversight. Some cautiously monitor their girlfriends (like *Pauline*'s Harry) while others more actively encourage them, help them in their adventures, like *Patria*'s Donald Parr. As in *Traffic*, oversight is linked both to danger and protection, indicating the importance of its correct use. Many serials apply this gaze to transformations in women's lives and their increased participation in public life, seeking to monitor and regulate it so that it does not get out of hand. This practice recalls Singer's and Stamp's observations that the serial heroine's oscillation between daring feats and entrapment articulates both women's desire for an increasingly active public life and the cultural pressures to contain it. This tension between innovation/modernity and tradition was central to Progressivism.

The role of oversight in these serials was consequently more complex. Given that these are primarily women's films, this look is transformed into a more self-conscious female gaze as feminine audiences not only enjoyed the spectacle of these women's activities but also identified both with the position of looking and being looked at. They likely identified with the serial queen's efforts to elude the controlling gaze of others, be it protective or threatening, while recognizing something else that these films made clear: women's activities were studied by others to some degree, taking on the quality of a performance. This might lead audiences to reflect back on ways in which their own behaviors were received, fostering self-awareness while variously making women question why they were being monitored or alternately turning this into something desirable, influenced by the structure of celebrity culture. Singer, *Melodrama and Modernity*, 222, 225–40; Shelley Stamp, "An Awful Struggle between Love and Ambition: Serial Heroines, Serial Stars, and Their Female Fans," in Grieveson and Krämer, *Silent Film Reader*, 213, 217–23.

34. See, for example, Tom Gunning, "Heard over the Phone: *The Lonely Villa* and the de Lorde Tradition of the Terrors of Technology," *Screen* 32, no. 2 (1991): 184–96.

35. Significantly, Mary not only recommends the use of her father's Dictaphone but also uncovers Trubus's use of bugs and the dictagraph to control his criminal enterprise, linking technology to the young working woman, as is so common at this time.

36. *Photoplay* lamented the negative representation of reformers and child welfare workers in a January 1918 editorial, noting "there is no money in this business of taking care of helpless children, and the men and women who undertake the work would not do so unless they had the interests of the children at heart. Can we not have at least one picture showing the good that is done by child welfare societies?" "Close-Ups: Slander," *Photoplay* 13, no. 2, January 1918, 75.

37. Bowser, *Transformation of Cinema*, 258. She also quotes from a review of *The Prisoner of Zenda* (Hugh Ford, Edwin S. Porter, Famous Players, 1913) where the critic discusses what is clearly its prologue, admiring "the idea of showing each of the principal characters on the screen prior to the first reel, and giving a good purpose in making identities clear." As Bowser notes, this "could not only add spectacle and exploit star value; [it] could also . . . clarify a complex plot" (258).

38. Prologues, perhaps more common at the very start of American feature-length production, are present in 1917 releases. Some stage adaptations, like *The Wishing Ring* (1914), feature them, but others do not (*Carmen* [1915] and *The Squaw Man*). Some fairy tales and fantasy films like *Snow White* (1916) have prologues, while films like *Cinderella* (James Kirkwood, 1914) start in the middle of the action.

39. Bowser, *Transformation of Cinema*, 204.

40. "Play Plus Photoplay," *New York Times*, June 1, 1915, 15.

41. While the presentation was unified around a larger theme, unlike vaudeville or short-film exhibition, it certainly did not invite a disembodied form of spectatorship with its incense, sporadic shouting, reel breaks, and mixture of stage/screen/orchestra/box performances that dispersed meaning throughout various parts of the theater and through a variety of media. James S. McQuade, "Chicago Letter," *Moving Picture World* 16, no. 7, May 17, 1913, 689; "*Quo Vadis* at the Regent," *Moving Picture World* 19, February 7, 1914, 680;

W. Stephen Bush, "Rothapfel Rehearsing," *Moving Picture World* 19, February 14, 1914, 787.

42. "In the Picture Playhouses: Reel Facts," *Chicago Herald*, January 19, 1915, 11.

43. "'The Escape,' a Film Treating of Eugenics and Sex Questions, Exhibited at the Cort Theater," *New York Times*, June 2, 1914, 11.

44. "*A Fool There Was*," *New York Dramatic Mirror*, January 20, 1915.

45. Prologues were not universal, however, although they were remarkably common. *Carmen* (Cecil B. DeMille, Lasky/Paramount, 1915) does not really have a prologue proper. Although all the characters are given relatively lengthy introductions, these are integrated into the narrative. It is unlikely that this was a directorial touch, given that DeMille featured prologues in his subsequent films like *The Cheat* and *Joan the Woman*. It is possible that this is because the only surviving print is a 1918 reissue, and, according to Sumiko Higashi, the film was reedited. *Hell's Hinges* also arguably does not have a prologue, although its opening scenes of the Reverend Robert Henley's early career in the East establish his weaknesses for women and wine well before he ventures West. Sumiko Higashi, *Cecil B. DeMille and American Culture: The Silent Era* (Berkeley: University of California Press, 1994), 1, 15–27, 216–17n41.

46. While mindful that "feature cinema in the teens is not a simple outgrowth from one-reel cinema," Ben Brewster considers prologues a relic of a "reel-based construction." Brewster's argument is quite specific, however, being based upon his close analysis of *Traffic in Souls* (George Loane Tucker, Imp-Universal, 1913), which features an unusually long two-reel prologue. Most prologues are far shorter, making them something quite unlike a single-reel film, and something that one-reelers could not easily accommodate, although they were used for serials, as mentioned below.

Traffic in Soul's prologue establishes the context of the white slavers' work in a way that is more documentary-like than the principal narrative, but is like most prologues in that it is somewhat separate from the main narrative and provides a context for what follows. Ben Brewster, "*Traffic in Souls*: An Experiment in Feature-Length Narrative Construction," *Cinema Journal* 31, no. 1 (1991): 37. Also see 42–43.

47. Tom Gunning, "The Intertextuality of Early Film: A Prologue to *Fantomas*," in *A Companion To Literature and Film*, ed. Robert Stam and Alessandra Raengo (Oxford: Blackwell, 2004), 135.

48. The character's name and nationality were changed for its 1917 release (shift from Japanese to Burmese) as the United States was allied with Japan for World War I. I use the name on the print viewed.

49. Returning to the original framing, he turns off the light so just a spot illuminates him before a cut to the next title introducing Richard Hardy (Jack Dean). This flaunts another one of this film's other characteristics—its expres-

sionist "Lasky lighting." Lea Jacobs, "Belasco, DeMille, and the Development of Lasky Lighting," *Film History* 5 (1993): 405–18.

50. Kathlyn Williams is presented differently, gesturing melodramatically toward the audience, seemingly so enwrapped in her character that she fails to notice us at all. The only other actor who fails to register the presence of the camera/audience is Jack F. McDonald, who plays the rube, Slap Jack, who just scratches his head and smokes a corncob pipe. The first narrative title—"Glenister's break with Cherry"—would seem to suggest a move into the narrative proper, yet this film was alternately promoted as eight reels and a prologue (*New York Times*) or nine reels, indicating that the prologue was significant in its own right and was marked in promotional rhetoric.

51. There is a cut to the first of four titles, introducing the major players and their roles, each followed by a representational vignette introducing us to Sally Martin (the parson's daughter), the Earl of Bateson, his naughty son Giles, a student who prefers parties to studying, and "Gyp Williams, the Orphan," a small terrier in a basket. These four shots and three titles constitute the film's prologue.

52. The opening curtain acknowledges viewer awareness that this is a presentation and sets up a certain distance: *The Wishing Ring* is, after all, as the opening title notes, "An Idyll of Old England."

53. Bowser, *Transformation of Cinema*, 206.

54. The next two titles headed "fact" turn to Jules Verne, noting how his book astounded at the time because of its marvelous inventions and imagination, but notes that he died disappointed because he was not taken seriously, as he was "fifty years ahead of his time." His name, "Jules Verne," and a shot of a photograph of him follows. After establishing links between these two creative forces and their historical accomplishments, a history that privileges the present and modernity's innovations, the prologue moves to fiction. The next two titles (the first headed "Fiction" sets up Verne's tale of sea-monster attacks causing global panic, causing the US government to send an expedition out to rid the seas of this danger. This ends the prologue as the film shifts to telling the story, starting with the distinguished French scientist, Professor Arronax, visiting a Fifth Avenue hotel in New York.

55. Stamp, "An Awful Struggle Between Love and Ambition," 210.

56. Jane Feuer, *The Hollywood Musical*, 2nd ed. (Bloomington: Indiana University Press, 1993), 68.

57. Catherine Fowler, *The European Cinema Reader* (London: Routledge, 2002), 77.

58. Sabine Haenni, "Staging Methods, Cinematic Technique, and Spatial Politics," *Cinema Journal* 37, no. 3 (1998): 97–98.

59. The third title of the MoMA print reads "Not biographical but photodramatic and allegorical, and might apply to the lives and works of many men

of genius, whose failings in private life have been outweighed by their great gifts to humanity."

60. Overall, however, Payne's story (prologue plus epilogue) lasts about two reels, with each shorter episode being about one-reel long, allowing Griffith to sidestep many of the problems of feature film construction by using these more established models.

61. Hansen, *Babel and Babylon*, 130.

62. Ibid., 131.

63. Ibid., 134.

64. Ibid., 139.

65. Münsterberg, *The Photoplay*, cited by Hansen, *Babel and Babylon*, 139.

66. Christian Metz, *Language and Cinema* (The Hague: Mouton, 1974), 77–78, 107–12. Cited in Hansen, *Babel and Babylon*, 134–35.

67. Hansen, *Babel and Babylon*, 138.

68. Tom Gunning, "Weaving a Narrative: Style and Economic Background in Griffith's Biograph Films," *Quarterly Review of Film Studies* 6, no. 1 (1981): 11–25, cited in Hansen, *Babel and Babylon*, 141.

69. Hansen, *Babel and Babylon*, 146–48.

70. Ibid., 162.

71. Ibid., 204, 205.

72. This sequence is so radically different from the rest of the film that one of my graduate students left class briefly, returned, and thought we had started screening another Pickford movie. It is also important to note that Pickford repeatedly toyed with more adult roles, often with less success, even asking the readers of *Photoplay* in 1925 what kinds of parts she should play. Readers overwhelmingly responded with requests for child roles, even though this contest suggests Pickford's (and her management's) desire to test the waters with the hopes of reinventing the star as a more adult player. James R. Quirk, "The Public Just Won't Let Mary Pickford Grow Up," *Photoplay*, September 1925, 36–37.

73. Fowler, *European Cinema Reader*, 77.

74. Hansen, *Babel and Babylon*, 84.

75. Ibid., 44.

Notes to Chapter 3

1. "Youth," *Photoplay* 10, no. 2, July 1916, 23. Over six months, *Photoplay* profiled its finalists and discussed their prize trips to New York to be tested at World Studios in Fort Lee, New Jersey. Finally, the screen tests were published in December 1916, with *Photoplay* announcing that five girls—Lucille Zintheo, Helen Arnold, Lucille Satterthwaite, Alatia Marton, and Peggy Bloom—had signed one-year contracts with Selznick and the Frohman Amusement Cor-

poration. World only offered a contract to one, Zintheo, who turned them down after Selznick offered her more money. There is no evidence that Bloom signed with any studio, and I cannot find any record of her appearing on screen. Two contestants received contracts later: Mildred Lee (under the name Mildred Moore) and Claire Lois Butler Lee known as Lois Lee. "Beauty and Brains: The Successful Finale," *Photoplay* 11, no. 1, December 1916, 27–28.

2. "'Beauty and Brains': The Successful Finale," 29–30.

3. "Eleven Girls Waiting for the Train!" *Photoplay* 10, no. 3, August 1916, 412, 162–63. Letter quoted from Marie Haynes, Chicago, 162.

4. Shelley Stamp, "'It's a Long Way to Filmland': Starlets, Screen Hopefuls, and Extras in Early Hollywood," in Keil and Stamp, *American Cinema's Transitional Era*, 333.

5. Maria Elena Buszek, *Pin-Up Grrrls: Feminism, Sexuality, Popular Culture* (Durham, NC: Duke University Press, 2006), 180.

6. Stamp, *Movie-Struck Girls*, 17, 35–37. Stamp notes that the mirrored foyers in movie theaters encouraged women to display themselves—and check their own performances—before and after movies. In addition, as she notes, exhibitors also provided women with such accoutrements as hatpins and hairpins in the ladies' rooms so they could check up and improve their appearance while at the movies. All this encouraged an ethos of self-presentation and self-display that was analogous to—and, by extension, connected with—the movies and their presentation of celebrities.

7. Richard deCordova, *Picture Personalities* (Urbana: University of Illinois Press, 1990; reprint 2001), 44, 128.

8. Stamp, "It's a Long Way to Filmland," 338.

9. "Close-Ups: The Motion Picture Crisis," *Photoplay* 10, no. 6, November 1916, 63–65. This editorial states: "Of individual evils, the cancerous salary is the most conspicuous and most stupid. Managers highly intelligent have fallen for actors' graft like children" (64).

10. Many of the period's films, including titles as diverse as *What Happened to Mary* (Charles Brabin, Edison, 1912), *Young Romance* (George Melford, Famous Players–Lasky, 1915), and even *Traffic in Souls* dealt with the frustration of working at often dismal jobs that promised little in the way of self-advancement. Their protagonists sought the kind of escape and self-transformation promised in consumption (*Young Romance*) or, alternatively, more glamorous forms of work (as when Mary finds herself suddenly and briefly a stage success), even though these were not without dangers. Even when these protagonists did not succeed in finding happiness and returned to the world of respectable drudgery, their desires captured something that audiences identified with: the hope for transformation, self-improvement, and luxury, something embodied in celebrity.

11. Mark Whalan, *American Culture in the 1910s* (Edinburgh: Edinburgh University Press, 2010), 13; Barbara Miller Solomon, *In the Company of Educated Women: A History of Women and Higher Education in America* (New Haven, CT: Yale University Press, 1986), 130.

12. Whalan, *American Culture in the 1910s*, 13; Nan Enstad, *Ladies of Labor, Girls of Adventure: Working Women, Popular Culture, and Labor Politics at the Turn of the Century* (New York: Columbia University Press, 1999), 19, 108–14.

13. Kathy Peiss, *Cheap Amusements: Working Women and Leisure in Turn-of-the-Century New York* (Philadelphia: Temple University Press, 1987); Whalan, *American Culture in the 1910s*, 57–70, 121–40.

14. Leo Braudy, *The Frenzy of Renown: Fame and Its History* (1986; New York: Vintage, 1997), 29–51, 491, 493–95.

15. Photographs were commonly printed as postcards during the Progressive Era (and beyond), combining practices of self-staging with conventions of celebrity memorabilia. This practice revealed that people were increasingly mindful of their self-presentation, expecting that others were watching them—again, likely the combined result of Progressivism's reform and its valorization of fame. As a form of mimicry, these postcards further indicate how the public staged itself in the guise of fame, literally putting their images into circulation.

16. Marsha Orgeron, *Hollywood Ambitions: Celebrity in the Movie Age* (Middletown, CT: Wesleyan University Press, 2008), 17–29.

17. With this came a number of different stratifications of known film performers—stars from short films, stage stars in features, short-lived personalities (sometimes known from other media or from news or society), eponymous serial players often associated with one role, and a variety of satellite "names."

18. Charles Ponce de Leon, *Self-Exposure: Human-Interest Journalism and the Emergence of Celebrity in America, 1890–1940* (Chapel Hill: University of North Carolina Press, 2002), 42–73.

19. Throughout this period, film companies listed their addresses in fan magazines, for instance, almost encouraging the public to come in and try their luck on screen, even though there was no shortage of aspirants.

20. Ponce de Leon, *Self-Exposure*, 54–55.

21. Ibid., 28–40; Susman, "'Personality' and the Making of Twentieth Century Culture," in his *Culture as History*, 271.

22. Stamp, "It's a Long Way to Filmland"; Orgeron, *Hollywood Ambitions: Celebrity in the Movie Age*, 108–12.

23. Susan A. Glenn, *Female Spectacle: The Theatrical Roots of Modern Feminism* (Cambridge, MA: Harvard University Press, 2000), 3.

24. Glenn, *Female Spectacle*, 7.

NOTES TO CHAPTER 3

25. Liz Conor, *The Spectacular Modern Woman: Female Visibility in the 1920s* (Bloomington: Indiana University Press, 2004), xv.

26. Glenn, *Female Spectacle*, 7.

27. Ponce de Leon, *Self-Exposure*, 12–13, 16–21, 41, 119; Braudy, *Frenzy of Renown*, 5–14, 491–584; Joshua Gamson, *Claims to Fame* (Berkeley: University of California Press, 1994), 40–58, 186–96; Daniel Boorstin, *The Image: A Guide to Pseudo-Events in America*, 25th anniversary ed. (New York: Vintage, 1991), 45–76. As Gamson notes, early forms of fame, especially the premodern, legitimated social hierarchies, with only the elite having the resources and time to chase fame (18).

28. This emphasis on the leisure of the famous characterized celebrity discourse throughout the Progressive Era, perhaps not surprisingly given leisure's increased significance and importance during this time.

29. DeCordova, *Picture Personalities*, 23–87.

30. Abel, *Americanizing the Movies*, 235.

31. Stars endorsed products, engaged them to ghost write books and columns, while magazines and newspapers organized star search contests that drew on the public's own desire to appear on screen. All this attests not only to the extent to which celebrity saturated the culture but also the ways in which members of the public were invited to model themselves in relation to those who had fame. Besides affecting both their expectations and self-presentation, celebrity also ideologically reinforced associations between proper identity construction and fame.

32. Susman, "'Personality' and the Making of Twentieth Century Culture," in his *Culture as History*, 276–78.

33. Ibid., 281–83.

34. Ibid., 280–82.

35. Jennifer M. Bean, "Technologies of Early Stardom and the Extraordinary Body," in *A Feminist Reader in Early Cinema*, ed. Jennifer M. Bean and Diane Negra (Durham, NC: Duke University Press, 2002), 407–8.

36. Jackie Stacey's discussion of the social aspects of identification is important here, explored in *Star Gazing: Hollywood Cinema and Female Spectatorship* (London: Routledge, 1994), 126–223. The tendency toward stars making personal appearances in local theaters also indicates the complexity of identification and the ways in which it plays with multiple registers of the star's performance and on- and off-screen presence.

37. Even the film industry's efforts to hire stage stars revealed the period's interest in fame and its marketability in Progressive Era culture: it was no accident that Adolf Zukor called his company *Famous* Players in *Famous* Plays, emphasizing renown even more than quality. Although these films featured performers who could justifiably be engaged for their talents and expertise,

they also attracted audiences who wanted to see what these players looked like, how they moved, and to experience the phenomenon of their fame more closely. How, for example, did the sixty-eight-year-old Sarah Bernhard look and how did she move in *Queen Elizabeth* (Henri Desfontaines/Louis Mercanton, Famous Players, 1912)? Although film history usually considers these stage imports within the broader context of uplift, not all these performers were highbrow figures. Substantial numbers came from vaudeville or were showgirls rather than accomplished actors. Examples included Olive Thomas, Ann Pennington, and Mae Murray (all Ziegfeld Girls), ballroom dancers Vernon and Irene Castle, and swimmer/vaudevillian Annette Kellerman, none of them the conventional highbrow actors of lore. Movies also featured performers who had reached a high level of success in other media, some of them seemingly unrelated to the stage. As such, cinema increasingly became a site to explore fame more generally, with audiences being able to distinguish between movie stars of various pedigrees and celebrities—those with fame from elsewhere, deserved or not.

38. Nesbit had a minor film career; Ben Lindsey appeared as himself in *Saved by the Juvenile Court* (Otis Thayer, Columbine Film Company, 1913); Milholland Boissevain and Carnegie appeared as themselves in episodes of *Our Mutual Girl* (John W. Noble, Reliance-Mutual, 1913), a serial that featured many celebrity cameos and guest appearances. Villa appeared in a number of films as himself, documenting his exploits around the Mexican border, including films for Biograph and Mutual. Villa's awareness of his fame and his interest in having his exploits recorded reveal his conscious construction of a celebrity image and his efforts to ensure that he helped create his own persona, presumably hoping to shape his own position in history. Unfortunately for him, most of these films are lost.

39. Lee Grieveson, "The Thaw-White Scandal, *The Unwritten Law*, and the Scandal of Cinema," in *Headline Hollywood: A Century of Film Scandal*, ed. Adrienne McLean and David A. Cook (New Brunswick, NJ: Rutgers University Press, 2001), 43.

40. As Lee Grieveson notes, the first film about the Thaw-White murder, *The Unwritten Law: A Thrilling Drama Based on the Thaw-White Case* (Lubin, 1907) was "effectively the first film in the United States to become widely scandalous in itself." As Grieveson points out, this trial, and the scandals around it, rapidly became fodder for all kinds of popular culture, including films and plays. Given this film's original reception, it is a significant sign of the transformation of cinema that Nesbit herself could appear in *Redemption* some ten years later and have her performance heralded in the trades. Grieveson, "The Thaw-White Scandal, *The Unwritten Law*, and the Scandal of Cinema," 29, 35–38.

NOTES TO CHAPTER 3

41. Sidonie A. Smith and Julia Watson, *Before They Could Vote: American Women's Autobiographical Writing, 1819–1919* (Madison: University of Wisconsin Press, 2006), 347.

42. Peter Milne, Review of *Men Who Have Made Love to Me*, *Motion Picture News*, February 2, 1918, 734–35.

43. Ibid.

44. Emily Wortis Leider, *Becoming Mae West* (New York: Da Capo Press, 2000), 96.

45. James S. McQuade, "Seen on the Screen: *Men Who Have Made Love to Me*," *Moving Picture World*, January 26, 1918, 525.

46. Although she was extremely popular, MacLane was widely criticized for her self-obsession. According to critic and playwright Mary Cass Canfield: "Mary MacLane . . . lives in a morass of demoralized and despondent self-interest. All worlds revolve . . . about her Tempestuous, Unsatisfied Ego . . . Her book has such a shut-in atmosphere that one cries out, 'More air,' as one penetrates the labyrinth of her complexities . . . Whether she confesses, 'I am fond of green peas, baseball, and diamond rings,' which *has* humour, or, 'I wear No. 6 gloves, the calf of my leg is a shapely thing,' or 'I do not want of God a passport, a safe conduct into Heaven,' one sees that Miss MacLane makes the mistake of considering *all* self-revelation interesting" (Mary Cass Canfield, from *Grotesques and Other Reflections* [New York: Harper and Brothers, 1927; reprint of 1917 review], 48–60).

47. Lynde Denig, "'How Molly Made Good': Unusual Photoplay Introducing Ten Stage Stars Is Presented by Kulee Features, Inc.," *Moving Picture World* 26, no. 4, October 23, 1916, 626.

48. Keil, *Early American Cinema in Transition*, 81–82, 167.

49. "How Molly Made Good," *New York Times*, October 20, 1915, n.p.

50. This was the peak period for actors to move into films, and one in which high salaries were consistently offered to big stage names.

51. The sole exception is Julia Dean, the only relatively young woman, who is initially too busy to see her. After her sister persuades her to read Molly's letter, she relents and bonds with Molly, displaying the heroine's ability to get along with anybody.

52. This movie demonstrates both her resourcefulness and her ability to negotiate urban and suburban space—something most films suggest that immigrants, particularly female immigrants, are unable to do.

53. Graeme Turner, *Understanding Celebrity* (London: Sage, 2004), 1–27. Turner notes, however, that the cultural pervasiveness of celebrity—and its ability to form communities—challenges this atomization hypothesis.

54. Kenneth McGaffey, "Clothes Do Not Make the Woman," *Photoplay* 13, no. 2, January 1918, 84.

55. Ibid.
56. Ibid., 84–87.
57. Ibid., 87.
58. "Close-Ups: Acting Not One Round of Pleasure," *Photoplay* 13, no. 2, January 1918, 75.
59. Jennifer M. Bean, "Technologies of Early Stardom and the Extraordinary Body," in Bean and Negra, *A Feminist Reader in Early Cinema*, 415–24.
60. Ibid., 413.
61. "Close-Ups: What Is the Secret of Success?" *Photoplay* 13, no. 2, January 1918, 76.
62. Stamp, "It's a Long Way to Filmland," 332–47.
63. As Stamp notes, this led to moral concerns about what would happen to these women. "It's a Long Way to Filmland," 332–39.
64. "How To Get In!," *Motion Picture Classic* 2, no. 5, July 1916, 22. Even then, this series did not answer that other key question: what makes an actor a star? One suggestion was brains and beauty, having a heart and a kind, empathetic personality in real life as well as looks that register well on screen. Another article stressed physical fitness and perfection, seeing acting as a primarily physical job based on posing, strength, and beauty. This did not mean that work was not involved. Quite the contrary: plastic surgery was recommended to fix errant features and maintaining a good physique took physical work. As acting was itself histrionic, actors had to have good self-control and maintain their emotional health, not just look pretty in front of the camera. L. E. Eubanks, "The Actor's Physical Personality," *Motion Picture Classic* 3, no. 4, December 1916, 22–23; "Hints to the Players: The Key to Popularity," *Motion Picture Classic* 3, no. 3, November 1916, 58.
65. It was entirely understandable that fan magazines emphasized that being a star was work, especially as film companies owned several of them (J. Stuart Blackton published *Motion Picture Supplement*, and all the early magazines were affiliated with select film companies). Rather than employing a discourse of professionalism to create something like DeCordova's picture personality, these articles used it to offset the leisure and consumption associated with celebrity discourse. Press agents consequently presented their clients in terms of self-sacrifice, showing that their fame and wealth came at a cost. In April 1917, for instance, the *Chicago Sunday Herald* published Clara Kimball Young's "Ten Commandments" for getting into the movies. She—or, most likely, her publicist—used this opportunity to spin her recent divorce from director James Young as a sacrifice needed to maintain her career, blaming Young's jealousy and negative interference in her work. Her third (and longest) commandment was "Thou Shalt Take Unto Thyself a Good Husband but If He Proves Vexatious and Interferes With Thy Career It Is Better to Rid

Thyself of His Presence." This article painted her life as far from carefree, while foregrounding stars' more general focus on their professional responsibilities at the expense of romance.

66. "How to Get In!," 22.

67. Ibid., 23.

68. It is impossible to provide a full list of star endorsements up to 1917, but the following gives a sense of the scope of this activity. Dorothy Gish, endorsing Ingram's Milkweed Cream and Velveola Souvera Face Powder; Mary Pickford endorsing Pompeian Beauty Products; Pearl White endorsing Sempre Giovine's pink complexion cake soap, diamonds from L. W. Sweet and Co. of New York, and Burson Fashioned Hose; Mary Fuller, Earle Williams, and Lillian Walker all endorsing Deab's Mentholated Cough Drops; Geraldine Farrar endorsing Kosmeo face cream and powder; Kathlyn Williams endorsing Sempre Giovine's pink complexion cake soap; Ruth Roland for Sweet's Diamonds and Ingram's Milkwood Cream; Cleo Ridgely for Ingram's Milkweed Cream, powder, and rouge; Lillian Walker for Sweet's Diamonds.

69. Gordon Gassaway, "'Personality—Plus' on the Screen," *Motion Picture Classic* 1, no. 1, September 1915, 55.

70. Ibid., 58, 67. For Gassaway, the "plus" that made a Mary Pickford or a Marguerite Clark was something in their brains that a director noticed and worked with. He suggests, in effect, that directors not only have the ability to perceive who can be a star, but that their star quality also emerges because of the way they take direction, something that also relates to the interpersonal connection between director and star.

71. Gassaway starts his article by recounting how a beautiful, tall girl, well dressed but with shoes that were slightly too worn, was sent away from the studios because she had the wrong personality for films. Another *Classic* article, this time from May 1916, tells a similar story, this time of a beautiful nineteen-year-old who a director rejected, telling her she had no hope of making it in the movies until she turned sixty, as she had the wrong kind of beauty for the screen. Gassaway, "'Personality—Plus' on the Screen," 55; Arthur Hornblow Jr., "Have You a Camera Face?" *Motion Picture Classic* 2, no. 3, May 1916, 14.

72. Hornblow, "Have You a Camera Face?," 14.

73. Ibid., 64.

74. "Beauty Winners Face the Camera!" *Photoplay* 10, no. 6, November 1916, 126.

75. The contest's relatively low rate of success, despite its panel of experts, underscored its cautionary message about the difficulties of screen success. Four of its six failures refused to go home, continuing to search for a career in movies to no avail. None of the winners had much success either. Lucille Zintheo had the most prominent career, working as Larry Semon's leading

lady under the name Lucille Carlisle for a few years in the late 1910s and early 1920s. Most of the others made brief appearances in a handful of films and were out of the business after their contract expired. Mildred Lee (Mildred Moore) and Lois Lee, neither among the original five winners, had longer careers than most of them, but they were still confined to a few roles of little substance. Louella O. Parsons, "Girls Win Screen Place and Big Future as Screen Contenders," *Chicago Sunday Herald*, October 8, 1916, part 7, 1; "Beauty and Brains: The Successful Finale," *Photoplay* 11, no. 1, December 1916, 30. Claudia Sassen, "Lucille Carlisle: A Leading Lady," http://www.claudia-sassen.net/Larrygallery/lucille/index.html, accessed July 25, 2008.

76. Stamp notes that these female star aspirants "were pursuing a particularly gendered version of the American dream"; "It's a Long Way to Filmland," 333.

77. Allen C. Rankin, "Patrons of Film Plays Start Hunt for Girl Who Will Be a Star," *Chicago Sunday Herald*, November 29, 1914, sec. 6, 6.

78. Carter Harrison II was mayor five times, like his father. The dates given are for the term that included the release of his wife's film and her efforts to establish a career as a screenwriter.

79. Rankin, "Patrons of Film Plays Start Hunt for Girl Who Will Be a Star," 6.

80. Ibid.

81. The paper had initially planned to appoint a board of judges to select ten women from each district, including stars like Francis X. Bushman, but then realized that the interest would be greater if the public could participate.

82. Local theaters carrying Essanay films printed coupons that could be exchanged for free admission if the prospective patron presented votes naming the neighborhood's favored candidate.

83. "Public Is to Decide 'Who Will Be Sue,'" *Chicago Herald*, December 11, 1914, 4. On December 24, the paper reported that the judges had met on December 23, 1914, and reduced the list to forty. "'Who Will Be Sue?' One Out of Forty," *Chicago Herald*, December 24, 1914, 4; Allen C. Rankin, "Judges Announce Selections in the 'Sue' Contest," *Chicago Sunday Herald*, December 27, 1914, sec. 6, 8; "New 'Sue' Song Feature in Motion Picture Shows," *Chicago Herald*, February 10, 1915, 16; "'Sue' Contestants Visit Cement Show at Coliseum," *Chicago Herald*, February 17, 1915, 7; "Winner of Sue Contest to Pose for Sculptor," *Chicago Herald*, February 18, 1915, 9; "Elks to Gather Ballots for Girl in 'Sue' Contest," *Chicago Herald*, February 25, 1915, 4; "Final 'Sue' Vote Coupon in Herald This Morning: Six O'Clock Tomorrow Night Marks Time Limit for Expiration of Ballots," *Chicago Herald*, March 4, 1915, 4.

84. "Twelve 'Sue' Aspirants to Appear in Films," *Chicago Herald*, December 14, 1914, 18 (back page—a.k.a. the *Herald*'s second front page). Martin Johnson's thoughts on local film stardom were of great help here.

NOTES TO CHAPTER 3

85. "Elks to Gather Ballots for Girl in 'Sue' Contest"; Final 'Sue' Vote Coupon in Herald This Morning: Six O'Clock Tomorrow Night Marks Time Limit for Expiration of Ballots"; "All 'Sue' Votes Are In," *Chicago Herald*, March 6, 1915, 5.

86. James S. McQuade's Chicago Letter, "Who Is Sue?" *Moving Picture World* 22, no. 11, December 12, 1914, 1502.

87. James S. McQuade, "Chicago News Letter," *Moving Picture World* 23, no. 9, February 27, 1915, 1272.

88. Stamp, "It's a Long Way to Filmland," 334.

89. The other North Side favorite was May Connery. South Side theaters meanwhile lobbied for Florence Tighe and Gladys Swain. McQuade, "Chicago News Letter," 1272.

90. James S. McQuade, "Chicago News Letter: 'Sue' Contest Will End March 4th," *Moving Picture World* 23, no. 10, March 6, 1915, 1427. McQuade listed the leading candidates vote totals at the time of going to press: "Dorothy Warshauer, 968, 740; Florence Tighe, 594, 800; Gladys Swain, 402, 665; Myrtle Johnson, 350, 975 and Beatrice Brown, 285, 950."

91. "Miss Warshauer Choice as 'Sue,'" *Chicago Sunday Herald*, March 7, 1915, part 2, 1.

92. The featured contest winners were: runner-up, Florence Tighe, Gladys Swain, Myrtle Johnson, Beatrice Brown, Marguerite Foster, Elizabeth Garry, Alice McChesney, June Price, Hazel Daly. The plot of *Sue* was printed just before the contest ended and bore an uncanny resemblance to events surrounding the photoplay—especially as regards the role of the *Herald*—undermining the initial premise behind the contest.

> The play opens in the office of the city editor of the *Herald*. He is swamped with pictures of pretty girls who desire to play the part of Sue. The scene changes to the home of Senator Newland.
>
> Sue Newland, the pretty daughter, is alone in the library. She is bored to death. She picks up a copy of the *Herald* and sees an ad about the contest for "Sue." She decides to enter. She sends her photo to the newspaper and is informed that she has been chosen among a number of others to pose at the Essanay studios for a trial film. Jack Rankin, one of the *Herald*'s star reporters, is assigned to cover the story at the Essanay plant.
>
> He goes about it very peevishly. J. Mortimer Rose, son of a millionaire, is a suitor for Miss Newland's hand. He learns she has entered the contest and is very angry. He accompanies Jack to the studios, where he remonstrates with her. Jack falls in love with her at first sight. Rose is given the cold shoulder. Later Rose enters the newspaper office and fights with Jack. The next evening Rose is taken in a gambling raid. Jack, because of Sue, gets the police captain to let him go. Rose leaves the

city, and the next morning the *Herald* announces Miss Newland has won the contest. Jack hurries to tell her the good news. There is a happy love scene and the play ends.

Louella O. Parsons, "Synopsis of Photoplay 'Sue,'" *Chicago Sunday Herald*, February 28, 1915, sec. 7, 7.

93. Ibid.

94. It goes without saying that this is a pattern replayed in much contemporary reality television.

95. Irene O'Connor and runner-up Anna Nessel were chosen to represent Chicago, and Champaign's Gwendolyn Morgan represented the state. None of these girls won the nationwide contest, and the competition was overshadowed by Sue, lacking its carefully orchestrated suspense and use of local loyalties. Over two hundred candidates entered—a fraction of its predecessors—and far less space was devoted to it. Advertisement, *Chicago Sunday Herald*, April 4, 1915, part 1, 1; "Winners Named in Beauty Race," *Chicago Herald*, Tuesday, May 25, 1915, 5.

96. Local contests interested Chicagoans more than the Universal competition, possibly because the odds of winning were higher, possibly because of the appeal of a local girl becoming a star, something that linked celebrity, local community, and the neighborhood theater.

97. "Here's Chance to Star in Movies," *Chicago Herald*, Monday, September 11, 1916, 13.

98. "Fill Out First Movie Star Coupon in Contest Today," *Chicago Sunday Herald*, September 17, 1916, part 7, 3

99. "Here's Chance to Star in Movies," 13.

100. BAB, "Rush to Enter Movie Contest," *Chicago Herald*, Saturday, September 16, 1916, 11; BAB, "Boy off First in Movie Race," *Chicago Herald*, Tuesday, September 19, 1916, 11.

101. "Join Herald Contest and Pick Your Film Favorite," *Chicago Sunday Herald*, September 10, 1016, part 7, 3.

102. Louella O. Parsons, "Contest Girl," *Chicago Sunday Herald*, September 26, 1916, 4; advertisement, "You—Too—May Take Her Path to Glory," *Chicago Sunday Herald*, September 17, 1916, part 7, 6.

103. Advertisement featuring Anita Stewart, *Chicago Herald*, Monday, October 2, 1916, 11; advertisement featuring Mae Marsh, *Moving Picture World*, October 21, 1916, 359.

104. Advertisement featuring Mae Marsh, 359.

105. BAB, "Boy off First in Movie Race," 11; "Poll Heavy Vote in 'Movie' Race," *Chicago Herald*, Friday, November 24, 1916, 16 (back page).

106. BAB, "Another Week to Join Herald Movie Star Contest," *Chicago Sunday Herald*, October 1, 1917, part 7, 1.

107. BAB, "'BAB' Has Good News for Movie Star Candidates," *Chicago Sunday Herald*, October 22, 1916, part 7, 3.

108. BAB, "Another Week to Join Herald Movie Star Contest," *Chicago Sunday Herald*, October 1, 1916, part 7, 1; "More Free Tickets in Big Contest," 1.

109. "Film Race Vote Hits High Mark," *Chicago Herald*, Thursday, November 9, 1916, 12.

110. Louella O. Parsons, "Stop, Look and Listen," *Chicago Herald*, Wednesday, September 20, 1916, 7.

111. "Bab's Tips to Live Ones in Movie Contest," *Chicago Sunday Herald*, October 15, 1916, part 7, 2.

112. "Rivalry Keen in Herald Contest," *Chicago Herald*, Thursday, September 21, 1916, 11.

113. BAB, "Love, Ambition and Thrills in Movie Race Letters," *Chicago Sunday Herald*, October 8, 1916, part 7, 2.

114. BAB, "Another Week to Join Herald Movie Star Contest," 1; advertisement for the Movie Star Contest, *Chicago Sunday Herald*, October 8, 1916, part 7, 2.

115. Louella O. Parsons, "Essanay President Will Coach Winners of Contest," *Chicago Sunday Herald*, December 3, 1916, part 7, 3.

116. BAB, "All the Contest Winners and Who They Are," *Chicago Sunday Herald*, December 10, 1916, part 7, 6. The winners were Frances Boyle, Elmhurst (young woman); Marian Rice, Chicago (little girl); O. Henry Fisher, Chicago (young man); Harry Moir Jr., Chicago (little boy).

117. BAB, "Assign Roles in Big Photodrama for Winners in the Herald Contest," *Chicago Sunday Herald*, December 16, 1917, sec. 7, 6.

118. Louella O. Parsons, "Big Scenes in Herald Contest Film are Completed," *Chicago Sunday Herald*, February 11, 1917, part 7, p. 6.

119. BAB, "Assign Roles in Big Photodrama for Winners in the Herald Contest," 6.

120. Ibid.

121. Louella O. Parsons, "The Day," *Chicago Herald*, Tuesday March 13, 1917, 4.

122. "Today's Programs in Moving Picture Theaters," *Chicago Herald*, Monday, March 26, 1917, 7.

123. Louella Parsons, "Beautiful Stars of the Screen to Open Movie Exposition Today"; "Here's the Program for Movie Show and Convention Week"; "Exhibitors' Election to Be Lively; Chicagoan in Race for Presidency," *Chicago Herald*, Saturday, July 14, 1917, Special Movie Exposition Section, 1; "Potential Star at Movie Show," *Chicago Herald*, Thursday, July 19, 1917, 14.

124. Louella O. Parsons, "Film Exposition 'Riot of Color,'" *Chicago Sunday Herald*, July 15, 1915, 3; Louella O. Parsons, "Crowds Storm Film Exposition," *Chicago Herald*, Friday, July 20, 1917, 14.

125. "Here's Your Chance to Get into Movies," *Chicago Herald*, Saturday, July 14, 1917, Special Movie Exposition Section, 1.

126. "Here's Chance as Film Hero," *Chicago Sunday Herald*, July 15, 1917, 3.

127. In 1916, he opened an East Coast studio for her productions, as the actress disliked the West.

128. See, for example, Hansen, *Babel and Babylon*, 86–87, 243–98; Richard Dyer, *Stars* (London: BFI, 1979), 8.

129. It is thus not surprising that, as Shelley Stamp notes, so many star aspirants were women, as these are impulses already foregrounded in feminine culture. Stamp, "It's a Long Way to Filmland," 332–33, 342–47.

130. Julian Johnson, "The Shadow Stage," *Photoplay* 11, no. 1, December 1916, 76.

131. He notes an absence of European actors (with exception of Max Linder and, briefly, Asta Nielsen in 1912) in star polls and, it might be added, fan magazines (the occasional import like Mlle Valkrien, might get some press, but this was only because of their appearance in American films). Abel also acknowledges that most of the foreign films advertised around 1910, largely Pathé releases, generally didn't promote their stars in newspaper ads presented by exhibitors. Abel, *Americanizing the Movies*, 232, 237, 239.

132. "Eleven Girls Waiting for the Train," *Photoplay* 10, no. 3, August 1916, 41; "Sue Contest Will End March 4th," *Moving Picture World* 23, no. 10, March 6, 1915, 1427; "Youth" (Eulogy to the eleven winners of the Beauty and Brains contest), *Photoplay* 10, no. 2, July 1916, 23.

Notes to Chapter 4

1. This focus on community further corresponded with changes occurring in films at this time, including the more developed narratives, greater scene dissection, and depth of field that provided more dynamic and three-dimensional space, as well as the increasing length of films that produced more detailed and psychologized narratives. Like these films, neighborhood theaters emphasized identification with other people/characters and the sense that other individuals—even if strangers—were knowable and thus part of a community. This approach contrasts with the earlier modernist tendencies of pre-1907 and especially pre-1905 attractions and their somewhat atomized exhibition contexts. Tom Gunning, "From the Opium Den to the Theater of Morality: Moral Discourse and the Film Process in Early American Cinema," in Grieveson and Krämer, *Silent Cinema Reader*, 145–54.

2. For example, in 1911 the *Moving Picture World* praised A. M. Gollos of the Jefferson Theater, 55th and Lake Streets, for his "lively interest in the comfort and welfare of his patrons." "The Jefferson Theater Breaking Records," *Moving Picture World* 9, no. 3, July 29, 1911, 196.

3. Gomery, *Shared Pleasures*, 40–56.

4. Horace Plimpton, *New York Dramatic Mirror*, February 2, 1915, quoted in Koszarski, *An Evening's Entertainment*, 163.

5. Epes Winthrop Sargent, *Picture Theatre Advertising* (New York: Moving Picture World/Chalmers, 1915), 3.

6. McKelvey, *Urbanization of America*, 184

7. Daniel Horowitz, *The Morality of Spending: Attitudes toward the Consumer Society in America, 1875–1940* (Baltimore: Johns Hopkins University Press, 1985), xxvi–xxvii and 30; Mark Seltzer, *Bodies and Machines* (New York: Routledge, 1992), 12–21.

8. Horowitz, *The Morality of Spending*, xxiii.

9. Other developments that testified to the importance accorded leisure in Progressive Era America include the increased role of local government and the development of leisure professionals. Believing leisure was too important to be left to private enterprise, many reformers recommended local government handle it instead. This led to the growth of recreation departments that tried to establish "healthy amusements." Like many municipalities, Chicago employed leisure professionals (whose specialty combined social work, education, reform, and urban planning) who recommended the installation of public parks, swimming pools, golf courses, recreation centers, beaches, and playgrounds. In 1915, J. R. Richards, superintendent of recreation for Chicago's South Park Commission, recommended the city regulate *all* entertainments to temper the "wicked" commercial impulse that threatened to pervert the "play instinct." Like all good Progressives, he believed government investment in municipal recreation would ultimately enrich American stock. He regretted that Chicago was "without a central and controlling organization to shape and determine public recreational service. . . . [Consequently] the public agencies and workers therein are without a common conception of the purposes of public recreation." As recreation studies became more professionalized during the Progressive Era, organizations like the Playground and Recreation Association of America flourished, publishing their own journal, *The Playground*. Its members studied recreation "scientifically," campaigned for improved recreational facilities, and composed model leisure ordinances for city councils. They envisaged cities where all entertainments would be healthy, many would take place outdoors, and few would be commercial. As fresh air was highly valued for its capacity to improve spectators' minds and morals, these professionals believed it could combat problems they associated with the interiors of cheap theaters, something that clearly affected some forms of movie exhibition. In keeping with this, municipal leisure officials organized well-supervised screenings in public parks, like those held in Chicago's Holstein Park during summer 1913. These served the public interest, not individual entrepreneurs' bottom line, and, most importantly suggested that films had redeeming quali-

ties if exhibited properly, unlike many other cheap amusements. "Municipal Recreation for All the People," *American City* 13, no. 6, December 1915, 467; J. R. Richards, "Chicago's Recreational Problem as Related to a City-Wide Organization," *American City* 13, no. 6, December 1915, 469–71; Harvey C. Carburgh, ed., *Human Welfare Work in Chicago* (Chicago: McClurg, 1917), particularly, 89–94, 99–108, 123–24; Bowen, *Safeguards for City Youth at Work and at Play*, 33; "Movies Rival Band Concerts," *Chicago Daily Tribune*, Monday, August 4, 1913, 11.

10. Bowser, *Transformation of Cinema*, 123.

11. Richard Henry Edwards, *Public Recreation* (Madison: Bulletin of the University of Wisconsin, Extension Division, Serial No. 709, General Series No. 513, 1915), 131.

12. Moya Luckett, "Advertising and Femininity: The Case of *Our Mutual Girl*," *Screen* 40, no. 4 (1999): 373; Strand advertisement, *Chicago Sunday Herald*, October 24, 1915, part 6, 3.

13. Bowser, *Transformation of Cinema*, 123.

14. Walter Prichard Eaton, "Class-Consciousness and the 'Movies,'" *Atlantic Monthly* 115, no. 1 (1915): 51.

15. Chicago's urban planners steered the city's growth, drafting zoning laws that shaped urban geography. Planning regulations were initially designed to preserve downtown for business and to keep it safe from fire—while keeping out vice (as seen in its Segregated Vice District or Levée, which was abolished in 1911). The fire started in a barn behind 137 De Koven Street, a working-class Irish section southwest of the Loop, and consumed an area four miles long and two-thirds of a mile wide, killing nearly three hundred people, destroying almost $200 million in property, and leaving ninety thousand homeless. As William Cronon notes, "The entire downtown—the great department stores, wholesale warehouses, Board of Trade, hotels, the very heart of the city—was laid waste in a single night." Fortunately, much of the city's infrastructure was preserved—rail links, grain elevators, stockyards, and factories. Although the city's most valuable buildings as well as the wooden homes of the working poor were destroyed, wealthier dwellings farther afield were undamaged. Its first, largely ineffective, building code was implemented in 1898 but did not have much power and was largely neglected, even after its 1902 revision.

Other plans and regulations had more force, including Daniel Burnham's never implemented City Plan of 1909. The city's history made regulation a priority: its rapid unregulated expansion had ended with the Great Fire of October 9, 1871, that destroyed almost a third of the city and led to its first planning regulations that shaped the city's subsequent development. After the fire engulfed the city's central, north, and west side, new regulations prohibited wooden buildings downtown. Because many workers could only afford

NOTES TO CHAPTER 4

to live in such premises, most migrated to outer districts free of fire restrictions. This effectively put an end to residential neighborhoods within the inner city, particularly for low-income residents, stripping downtown (particularly the Loop) of the kind of community socially and economically necessary for motion picture exhibition in the 1910s. As land values escalated downtown, skyscrapers were developed to deal with its limited space, as Cronon has observed. This turned the Loop into an almost exclusively business and shopping district, forcing out many of the remaining low-rise properties, factories, warehouses, private homes, and cheap theaters. McKelvey, *Urbanization of America*, 121–24; William Cronon, *Nature's Metropolis: Chicago and the Great West* (New York: Norton, 1992), esp. 178–80, 345–46; Witold Rybczynski, *City Life: Urban Expectations in a New World* (New York: Scribner, 1995), 116–19; Homer Hoyt, *One Hundred Years of Land Values in Chicago: The Relationship of the Growth of Chicago to the Rise in Its Land Values, 1830–1933* (1933; New York: Beard Books, 2000), 101–7.

16. "Moving Pictures Past and Present: A Resume of the Growth and Development of the Film Industry from Its Inception to the Present Time," *Billboard* 20, no. 26, June 27, 1908, 6.

17. "The Financial Situation" (editorial), *Billboard* 19, no. 48, November 30, 1907, 12.

18. McKelvey, *Urbanization of America*, viii–ix, 10–11, 49–51, 75–76, 115–16, 84.

19. Cronon, *Nature's Metropolis* 346; McKelvey, *Urbanization of America*, 120.

20. "Fight for Decency On: Women's Clubs Launch State Campaign Covering Unusually Wide Range," *Chicago Record-Herald*, February 7, 1908, 7.

21. McKelvey, *Urbanization of America*, 124.

22. "Trade Notes," *Moving Picture World* 1, no. 43, December 28, 1907, 706. The article states: "Five-cent theaters located in brick buildings will be required to have fireproof ceilings constructed of steel and asbestos; those in frame buildings will be obliged to have both fireproof ceilings and walls. . . . The boxes inclosing [sic] the machines must also be fireproof."

23. "Notes from Chicago," *Moving Picture World* 1, no. 38, November 23, 1907, 614.

24. "Film News: Moving Picture Shows," *Billboard* 20, no. 29, July 18, 1908, 9.

25. These were H. J. Daniels's Park Theater at 492 East North; C. E. Hynds's theater at 543 South Lincoln Street; Anna Hunkler's at 422 Larrabee; Joseph Vinci's at 234 Division; and Samuel Schiller's Crystal Theater, 1629 North Clark Street. Daniels had theaters at 115 East North Avenue; the Lincoln at 156 East North Avenue; the Park at 490 East North Avenue; theaters at 1561 1/2 West North Avenue; 1031 Lincoln Avenue; 3124 Lincoln Avenue, and

3835 South State Street. "Electric Theatres and Nickelodeons: Comprehensive List for the Use of Film Makers, Dealers and Agents: Moving Picture Machine Dealers: Electric Theatre Attractions: Music Publishers, Etc.," *Billboard* 19, no. 11, March 16, 1907, 113; "Electric Theatres and Nickelodeons: Comprehensive List for the Use of Film Makers, Dealers and Agents: Moving Picture Machine Dealers: Electric Theatre Attractions: Music Publishers, Etc.," *Billboard* 19, no. 49, December 7, 1907, 52; and "Electric Theatres and Nickelodeons: Comprehensive List for the Use of Film Makers, Dealers and Agents: Moving Picture Machine Dealers: Electric Theatre Attractions: Music Publishers, Etc," *Billboard* 20, no.12, March 21, 1908, 95–96. Note these are all old street numberings.

26. "Safety and Morals in 5-Cent Theaters" (editorial), *Chicago Record Herald*, November 14, 1907, 6.

27. These laws established safety protocols for motion picture storage and operation and mandated bimonthly inspections by the city's fire marshal to eliminate risk to theaters and adjacent properties. *General Ordinances*, 558–60.

28. "Five Chicago Theaters Closed," *Moving Picture World* 2, no. 12, March 21, 1908, 234.

29. "Chicago Enforces Licensed Operators," *Moving Picture World* 4, no. 5, January 30, 1909, 119.

30. F. H. Richardson, "What Is in the Future," *Moving Picture World* 5, no. 9, August 28, 1909, 280. Two months later, he pronounced, "the end of the day of the Chicago store-room theater draweth nigh. Beautiful new houses seating from 500 to a thousand are going up all over the city. They can . . . give more for the money than . . . the small place, with its limited seating capacity. . . . It really is wonderful what a strong bill they put up for a nickel or a dime. Most of them are ten cents, some ten, twenty and thirty."

Although the nickelodeon is synonymous with early cinema, its longevity may have been overestimated. By August 1909, the *Moving Picture World* predicted the nickelodeon's imminent demise, something that was well underway, as was the development of neighborhood theaters: "The 'store room theater' will gradually disappear . . . but their place will be taken by especially built theaters, seating from five hundred to a thousand, most of them giving a mixed bill of motion pictures and vaudeville at ten cents admission. Many of these are already built and more are projected here in Chicago. *Some of them are beautiful and costly houses and all are creditable in appearance*. They put up a good show, too, which as compared to the ordinary nickel house is normally worth at least three times as much, aside from *the superior comfort and beauty of the surroundings*. Such houses have almost invariably been found to be a paying investment and in the nature of things the smaller, less comfortable house cannot successfully compete with them, other things being equal (my emphasis)." Although the nickelodeon was undeniably important, it was a

NOTES TO CHAPTER 4

transitional phenomenon, its function largely completed by 1908–1909. As the *World's* commentary suggests, the uplift-minded trade press, and most likely the film industry, welcomed these changes. F. H. Richardson, "Among the Chicago Theaters," *Moving Picture World* 5, no. 17, October 23, 1909, 575.

31. "Motion Picture News," *Billboard* 21, no. 44, October 30, 1909, 14.

32. "License Ordinance Held Up Again," *Billboard* 22, no. 4, January 22, 1910, 13. *Billboard* further noted: "All five-cent moving picture theaters with a seating capacity of less than 300 shall pay an annual license fee of $250, more than 300, $400 and all theaters charging ten cents admission, $500. It also provides that children under sixteen years of age unaccompanied by parent or guardian shall not be admitted to moving picture theaters" ("City Fathers Confer: Licenses and Ordinances Discussed In Chicago," *Billboard* 21, no. 44, October 30, 1909, 14). At this time, Illinois law prevented children from performing in theaters. "Nickelodeon Licenses: The Cause of High Licenses Explained and Methods Suggested for Their Reduction—A National Association of Picture Theatre Managers Advocated," *Billboard* 22, no. 21, May 21, 1910, 24.

33. "Nickelodeon Licenses: The Cause of High Licenses Explained," *Billboard* 22, no. 21, May 21, 1910, 24.

34. "Swanson's Moving Picture Theater, Chicago," *Moving Picture World* 4, no. 11, March 13, 1909, 299. This report notes that the theater employed around twenty people and was well attended by women and children.

35. The Swanson also vividly indicates how rapidly a state-of-the-art theater could lose its way. In August 1910, the *Moving Picture World* condemned it for showing old, worn licensed films while its use of cheap, unframed posters ruined "what at one time was considered the best decorated lobby." By September 1910, it was in the hands of the receiver, with Swanson blaming poor management. J. M. B., "Chicago Notes," *Moving Picture World* 7, no. 9, August 27, 1910, 465; J. M. B., *Moving Picture World* 7, no. 10, September 3, 1910, 526.

36. James S. McQuade, "Chicago Letter," *Moving Picture World* 13, no. 3, July 20, 1912, 229. According to this article, the charges brought against the other owners included, "Failure to provide sufficient exits, failure to mark exits properly, crowding of seats, blockading of exits, reduction of aisle space, insufficient stairway and fire escape widths, blockading of aisles and faults in material used in construction and repairs." From 1908, new theaters could not be opened above the ground floor, although older establishments would be allowed to continue operating providing they were in brick buildings with multiple exits. "Chicago Gets It Also," *Moving Picture World* 2, no. 5, February 1, 1908, 78.

37. The ordinance read as follows:

> That it shall be and it is hereby declared to be a nuisance to conduct a public theater in a room located on any floor above the first floor level of

a building of other than fireproof construction or a building which does not comply with the ordinances of the city of Chicago with reference to fireproof construction in force at the time such building was built, and that all such public theaters now being conducted in rooms on any floor above the first floor level of a building of other than fireproof construction, or a building which does not comply with the ordinances of the city of Chicago with reference to fireproof construction in force at the time such buildings are built, with a seating capacity of more than three hundred, shall be and they are hereby declared to be nuisances; and it shall be unlawful to continue to use such rooms for public theatrical purposes whether the same are equipped with a stage and scenery or are used for moving picture shows only.

Ericsson, his deputy, Fire Department Inspector John C. McDonnell and the alderman on the building committee claimed their inspection of the city's the eight second- and third-story theaters reinforced their action: "With possibly the exception of the west side place, every theater we visited should be put out of business . . . [They] are in buildings which are not even near fireproof . . . no theater should have its main floor above ground level. Every balcony in these theaters is a fire trap of itself."

James S. McQuade, "Chicago Letter: Ordinance against Second and Third Floor Picture Houses," *Moving Picture World* 13, no. 5, August 3, 1912, 425; James S. McQuade, "Chicago Letter," *Moving Picture World* 13, no. 3, July 20, 1912, 229.

38. McQuade, "Chicago Letter: Ordinance against Second and Third Floor Picture Houses," 425; "Dangerous Loft Theaters Closed," *Moving Picture World* 15, no. 8, February 22, 1913, 764.

39. A well-publicized theater collapse further strengthened standards. On December 9, 1912, the roof of the brand-new, purpose-built 1,000-seat Home Theater (1539–41 Milwaukee Avenue at the busy intersection with Robey—now Damen Avenue) caved in. Fortunately, the theater was empty, although Hearst's sensational *Evening American* claimed that hundreds of children *could* have died had it happened at a matinee. The press soon revealed that the city's chief building inspector had ignored two reports about its danger, while its owner, Mr. Goldstein, had disregarded an architect who warned him, "your building is absolutely unsafe and . . . should be closed by the police . . . you are assuming a fearful financial responsibility personally in permitting this building to be occupied." Three city building inspectors were fired: two for taking bribes to cover up violations and a third "for inattention to duty." Final responsibility lay with Goldstein and the theater's supervising architect, David Saul Klafter, who had been tried before the state Board of Examiners of Architects three times and had tried to bribe city officials. After this, roof tests were re-

quired of all theaters and the city and the film industry openly supported a stricter building code. As James S. McQuade noted, all parties were "fortunate the house was empty at the time of collapse, both for the good name of the city and for the interests of the moving picture!" "Ordered Closed—Theater Falls," *Chicago Evening American*, December 10, 1912, 8; James S. McQuade, "Chicago Letter," *Moving Picture World*, 15, no. 2, January 11, 1913, 141; editorial, *Chicago Evening American*, December 10, 1912, 8; "Aldermen See Wreck of Theater," *Chicago Evening American*, December 12, 1912, 1; James S. McQuade, "Final Disposition of Home Theater Collapse," *Moving Picture World* 15, no. 8, February 22, 1913, 764.

40. "Ventilation Problems," *Motography* 10, no. 3, August 9, 1913, 82; "Fifteen Hundred Cubic Feet," *Motography* 10, no. 11, November 29, 1913, 377–78.

41. "Theater Ventilation Discussed," *Motography* 10, no. 10, November 15, 1913, 367.

42. "Theater Ventilation Discussed," 367–68.

43. "Chicago Show Stops: Neighborhood Theaters Profitable," *Billboard* 19, no. 11, March 16, 1907, 131.

44. "Trade Notes," *Moving Picture World* 2, no. 19, May 9, 1908, 416.

45. "Hallowe'en Opening, Hamlin Avenue Theatre," *Billboard* 22, no. 45, November 5, 1910, 9.

46. Ironically, some neighborhood theaters became so successful that they attracted patrons from elsewhere in the city. As some of these had cars—very much a status symbol at the time—the trades looked on approvingly, pleased that the industry had extended its reach to wealthier residents. As early as May 1913, James M. McQuade counted twenty-seven cars parked outside the Parkway on North Clark. By 1917, neighborhood theater magnate, Alfred Hamburger, noted that it was a "common thing to see many of the neighborhood houses with ten to a hundred automobiles parked in front." James S. McQuade, "Chicago Film Brevities," *Moving Picture World* 16, no. 6, May 10, 1913, 581; Alfred Hamburger, "Neighborhood Theater a Powerful Agent for Good," *Motion Picture News*, August 11, 1917, 975.

47. Orrin G. Cocks, "Moving Pictures as a Factor in Municipal Life," *National Municipal Review*, October 1914, 709–11; Walter Prichard Eaton, "Class-Consciousness and the 'Movies,'" *Atlantic Monthly* 115, no. 1 (1915): 51.

48. Luckett, "Advertising and Femininity," 372–73.

49. Epes Winthrop Sargent, "Advertising for Exhibitors," *Moving Picture World* 15, no. 5, February 1, 1912, 457.

50. James S. McQuade, "Proposed Increase of Chicago Licenses," *Moving Picture World* 32, no. 13, June 30, 1917, 1004.

51. Gomery, *Shared Pleasures*, 18.

52. "The Jefferson Theater Breaking Records," *Moving Picture World* 9, no.

3, July 29, 1911, 196; James S. McQuade, "Chicago Letter: Chicago Film Brevities," *Moving Picture World* 12, no. 7, May 18, 1912, 612; James S. McQuade, "Chicago Letter: Chicago Film Brevities," *Moving Picture World* 11, no. 12, March 23, 1912, 1057.

53. Louella O. Parsons, "Seen on the Screen: Exhibitor's Notes," *Chicago Herald*, August 10, 1915, 8.

54. All these theaters advertised in the *Chicago Herald* during the week of October 14–21, 1914, most with box or display ads.

55. For example, the Broadway-Belmont Building on the north side (constructed in 1914) contained a movie theater, stores, offices, lodge rooms, and an assembly hall. In 1915, Walter W. Ablschlager erected a 1,000-seat movie house, twelve stores, and eighteen four-room apartments at 2636–64 Milwaukee Avenue, decorated by three hundred electric lights. The same year's South Shore Building at 6836–50 Stony Island Boulevard, on the south side, contained a 1,000-seat cinema (to meet local demand), eight apartments, and eight stores, while a 1916 building at the northeast corner of Garfield Boulevard and Michigan Avenue featured a 1,400-seat Lubliner & Trinz theater, eighteen apartments, five stores, seven shops, and three offices. These structures appeared throughout the city, unifying neighborhoods stylistically and socially. Their architecture linked various spheres of social activity (work, leisure, home) while branding each neighborhood as a distinctive entity. "Two New Theater Buildings Which Are Now under Construction on the North Side," *Chicago Herald*, Sunday, June 21, 1914, sec. 1, 4; "Theater and Business Blocks Being Built on North and Northwest Sides," *Chicago Sunday Herald*, June 13, 1915, sec. 7, 6; "New Synagogue, Theater and Apartment Building under Construction on South Side," *Chicago Sunday Herald*, July 25, 1915, sec. 7, 6; "New High Class Flat and Theater Buildings Going Up in Chicago," *Chicago Sunday Herald*, March 26, 1916, sec. 8, 8.

56. Savoy flyer, July 31–August 2, 1915, Miscellaneous Program Collection, Chicago Historical Society. Historians noting the importance of theater decoration and lavish, attractive amenities include Tino Balio, *The American Film Industry* (Madison: University of Wisconsin Press, 1976); Bowser, *Transformation of Cinema*; Gomery, *Shared Pleasures*; Hansen, *Babel and Babylon*; Garth Jowett, *Film: The Democratic Art* (Boston: Little, Brown, 1976); Koszarski, *An Evening's Entertainment*; May, *Screening Out the Past*; Robert Sklar, *Movie-Made America: A Cultural History of American Movies* (New York: Random House, 1975).

57. "Motion Picture Theatre Construction Department," *Motion Picture News* 8, no. 21, November 29, 1913, 35.

58. Stamp, *Movie-Struck Girls*, 10–24.

59. Louella O. Parsons, "Seen on the Screen: Exhibitor's Notes," *Chicago Herald*, August 10, 1915, 8.

NOTES TO CHAPTER 4

60. T. S. Mead, "The Theatre Beautiful Is Big Asset to Good Pictures," *Motion Picture News* 12, no. 11, September 18, 1915, 140.

61. Neighborhood theaters even provided the illusion of greenery in some of the city's crowded neighborhoods. For example, the 1,400-seat Harper (53rd and Harper), one of the largest South Side theaters, installed a screen set in a faux Italian garden, emulating a trend usually confined to the more prestigious downtown movie theaters in the nation's largest cities. Louella O. Parsons, "Exhibitors' Notes," *Chicago Herald*, August 10, 1915, 8.

62. James S. McQuade, "Chicago News Letter: Clean Pictures of Good Quality in High Demand," *Moving Picture World* 29, no, 14, September 30, 1916, 2119.

63. Sargent, *Picture Theatre Advertising*, 1.

64. Ibid., 3.

65. W. Stephen Bush, "Constructive Work Needed," *Moving Picture World* 29, no. 4, July 22, 1916, 611.

66. James S. McQuade, "Chicago News Letter: Chicago Film Brevities," *Moving Picture World* 10, no. 11, December 16, 1911.

67. "Flood Benefit Tomorrow at the Vaudette Theater," *Daily Calumet*, April 1, 1913, 1; "Here's a Live One," *Chicago Herald*, October 6, 1914, 9; "'Movie' Theater Offers to Aid Christmas Ship," *Chicago Sunday Herald*, October 25, 1914, part 1, 7; "Hamburger's Benefit Day," *Chicago Herald*, July 27, 1915, 10.

68. "More Theater Owners Join to Aid Eastland," *Chicago Herald*, July 29, 1915, 6.

69. "A Novel Advertisement," *Motography* 12, no. 18, October 31, 1915, 596.

70. Sargent, *Picture Theater Advertising*, 177–79, 185–87, 198–99.

71. James S. McQuade, "Chicago News Letter," *Moving Picture World* 14, no. 11, December 14, 1912, 1067; Kathryn Fuller-Seeley, "Dish Night at the Movies: Exhibitor Promotions and Female Audiences during the Great Depression," in *Looking Past the Screen: Case Studies in American Film History and Method*, ed. Jon Lewis and Eric Smoodin (Durham, NC: Duke University Press, 2007), 246–75.

72. Midwest Special Service, Illinois News, *Moving Picture World* 20, no. 8, May 30, 1914, 1283; *Moving Picture World* 21, no. 9, September 5, 1914, 1394; *Moving Picture World* 22, no. 6, November 6, 1914, 806.

73. James S. McQuade, "Chicago News Letter: Chicago Film Brevities," *Moving Picture World* 31, no. 1, January 6, 1917, 84.

74. W. Stephen Bush, "The Kinematographic Grocery," *Moving Picture World* 18, no. 10, December 6, 1913, 1124; Epes Winthrop Sargent, "Advertising for Exhibitors: The Country Store," *Moving Picture World* 18, no. 4, October 25, 1913, 371.

75. Luckett, "Advertising and Femininity," 364–70.

76. Advertisement for the Universal Movie-Game, *Moving Picture World* 26 no. 2, October 9, 1915, 176–77.

77. Robert Grau, *The Theatre of Science: A Volume of Progress and Achievement in the Motion Picture Industry* (New York: Broadway, 1914), 343.

78. The Haltons, "Theater Managers Optimistic," *Chicago Herald*, November 7, 1914, 8.

79. "In the Picture Playhouses," *Chicago Sunday Herald*, October 11, 1914, part 2, 8.

80. Hamburger, "Neighborhood Theater a Powerful Agent for Good," 975.

81. "From Office Boy to Film Monarch: Alfred Hamburger," *Chicago Herald*, August 7, 1915, sec. 2, 4.

82. "Chicago News and Comment: Leaks in the Loop," *Motion Picture News* 15, no. 17, April 28, 1917, 2670. Also see Jane Gaines, "From Elephants to Lux Soap: The Programming and 'Flow' of Early Motion Picture Exploitation," *Velvet Light Trap* 25 (Spring 1990): 29–43; Janet Staiger, "Announcing Wares, Winning Patrons, Voicing Ideals: Thinking about the History and Theory of Film Advertising," *Cinema Journal* 29, no. 3 (1990): 3–31.

83. "From Office Boy to Film Monarch," 4.

84. Louella O. Parsons, "Seen on the Screen: Hamburger Adds Two More to List of His Theaters," *Chicago Herald*, July 2, 1915, 8.

85. Louella O. Parsons, "Seen on the Screen," *Chicago Herald*, August 5, 1915, 7; "From Office Boy to Film Monarch," 6.

86. Hamburger Theaters advertisement, *Chicago Herald*, June 24, 1914, 2; Louella O. Parsons, "Seen on the Screen: New Hamburger Theater," *Chicago Herald*, October 8, 1915, 8; "Directory of New Theatres: Illinois," *Motion Picture News* 12, no. 20, November 20, 1915, 155; Louella O. Parsons, "Seen on the Screen: Another Hamburger Theater," *Chicago Herald*, Friday, March 3, 1916, 6.

87. Advertisement for Alfred Hamburger's theaters, *Chicago Herald*, August 7, 1915, part 2, 3; Louella O. Parsons, "Seen on the Screen," *Chicago Herald*, June 26, 1915, 8; Louella O. Parsons, "Hamburger Adds Two More to List of His Theaters," 8.

88. "Notes of the Trade," *Moving Picture World* 5, no. 2, July 10, 1909, 55.

89. James S. McQuade, "Chicago Letter," *Moving Picture World* 9, no. 10, September 16, 1911, 782.

90. James S. McQuade, "Chicago Letter: No 'Franchise' in Booking of Licensed Films," *Moving Picture World* 14, no. 9, November 30, 1912, 865–66.

91. "In the Picture Playhouses," *Chicago Sunday Herald*, September 20, 1914, part 2, 4.

92. "Chicago News and Comment," *Motion Picture News* 15, no. 13, March 31, 1917, 2024.

NOTES TO CHAPTER 4

93. "Chicago News and Comment: Leaks in the Loop," *Motion Picture News* 15, no. 17, April 28, 1917, 2670; William J. McGrath, "Leaks in the Loop," *Motion Picture News* 16, no. 20, November 17, 1917, 3460.

94. Hamburger made this move: "to broaden the scope of the business and improve the bookings . . . The attorney in charge of the reorganization said: 'It is not only our plan to improve our properties in Chicago and secure the highest class bookings, but we have in mind the building of two additional theaters within the Loop section. We also plan to build or take over other theater buildings throughout the Middle West.'"

There is no evidence that this expansion ever occurred but the theatrical recession of 1917 makes is unlikely. "Hamburger Interests to Be Absorbed by New Corporation," *Motion Picture News* 16, no. 15, October 13, 1917, 2578.

95. "In the Picture Playhouses: Gossip of the Photo Theaters," *Chicago Sunday Herald*, October 11, 1914, sec. 2, 8.

96. "In the Picture Playhouses: Reel Facts," *Chicago Herald*, October 5, 1914, 12; "Land Deal Tops Chicago Record," *Chicago Herald*, March 30, 1915, 5.

97. "Latest News from Chicago: Hamburger Presents Kellerman Film," *Motion Picture News* 9, no. 21, May 30, 1914, 28; "In the Picture Playhouse," *Chicago Sunday Tribune*, July 26, 1914, part 2, 4.

98. Louella O. Parsons, "Seen on the Screen," *Chicago Herald*, January 17, 1916, 8. Coupon, *Chicago Herald*, Tuesday August 4, 1914, 4.

99. Louella O. Parsons, "Seen on the Screen," *Chicago Herald*, March 20, 1915, 7.

100. "New Stars and Old in Movies This Week," *Chicago Sunday Herald*, April 30, 1916, part 6, 7.

101. "Chicago News and Comment," *Motion Picture News* 15, no. 11, March 17, 1917, 1709.

102. Born in Minneapolis, Bayne moved to Chicago at age six and was considered a local star.

103. Louella O. Parsons, "Seen on the Screen," *Chicago Herald*, June 26, 1915, 8.

104. Louella O. Parsons, "Seen on the Screen," *Chicago Herald*, June 1, 1915, 12.

105. F. C. McGarahan, "Chicago Amusements: New Five Cent House," *Billboard* 19, no. 22, June 1, 1907, 7.

106. Untitled, *Moving Picture World* 1, no. 16, June 22, 1907, 250.

107. Ibid.

108. "All Night Picture Show for Chicago," *Moving Picture World* 8, no. 9, March 4, 1911, 471; F. H. Richardson, "Projection Department," *Moving Picture World* 14, no. 2, October 12, 1912, 147.

109. Gene Morgan, "A Night at the All-Night Movie," *Chicago Sunday Herald*, February 14, 1915, part 6, 6.

110. Scott A. Newman, "Jazz Age Chicago: Smaller Loop Movie Theaters," http://chicago.urban-history.org/ven/ths/loop_th.shtml, accessed July 9, 2007.

111. Eric Schaefer, *Bold! Daring! Shocking! True!: A History of Exploitation Films, 1919–1959* (Durham, NC: Duke University Press, 1999), 125–26, 131–35.

112. Movies seemed to have one important advantage over the legitimate stage—they were not seasonal. Any theater devoted to drama had to close down over the summer (the theatrical off season), or find alternate attractions like the earliest high-class imported features. Opera had an even shorter season, lasting for only part of the winter, whereas films based on operas and starring leading soloists, like Paramount's 1915 *Carmen* starring Geraldine Farrar, could be shown at any time of year. "In the Loop Theaters," *Chicago Sunday Herald*, October 31, 1915, part 6, 3.

113. As late as 1915, many of Chicago's newspapers only had detailed daily coverage of the cinema during the summer.

114. "Gossip of Photoplay Theaters and the Films to Be Seen There," *Chicago Sunday Herald*, July 5, 1914, part 2, 2.

115. "In the Picture Playhouses," *Chicago Sunday Herald*, August 2, 1914, part 2, 2.

116. "In the Picture Playhouses," *Chicago Sunday Herald*, August 16, 1914, part 2, 7.

117. "Reel Facts," *Chicago Herald*, August 28, 1914, 12.

118. "In the Picture Playhouses," *Chicago Sunday Herald*, August 30, 1914, part 2, 4.

119. "In the Picture Playhouses," *Chicago Sunday Herald*, October 4, 1914, part 2, 4; "Reel Facts," *Chicago Herald*, October 31, 1914, 13; "In the Picture Playhouses," *Chicago Sunday Herald*, November 1, 1914, part 2, 4; "Reel Facts," *Chicago Herald*, December 4, 1914, 11.

120. Advertisement for the Fine Arts Theater, *Chicago Herald*, April 3, 1915, 2.

121. "Reel Facts," *Chicago Herald*, September 17, 1914, 11.

122. "In the Picture Playhouses," *Chicago Sunday Herald*, November 1, 1914, part 2, 4.

123. Still, with the emergence of big-budget features, Loop openings became essential, especially for road-showed epics, states rights films, or big features that contractually required large openings in each territory. But big Loop theaters could not show expensive first-run features all year round and survive unless they were part of a larger chain or affiliated with other income-generating enterprises, like film distribution. By the mid-1910s, many popular films opened directly in neighborhood theaters, with only the largest, most prestigious/expensive films debuting in the Loop, including road-showed films like *The Birth of a Nation* (1915), the most expensive features from Paramount,

NOTES TO CHAPTER 4

VLSE, KESE, and Selig and vehicles for Theda Bara, Mary Pickford, and Clara Kimball Young, three of the era's biggest stars.

124. Louella O. Parsons, "Seen on the Screen: Notes of the Screen," *Chicago Herald*, October 18, 1915, 7.

125. "In the Picture Playhouses: Gossip of Photoplay Theaters," *Chicago Sunday Herald*, November 1, 1914, sec. 2, 4.

126. Ibid.

127. "In the Picture Playhouses: Where They Are Showing," *Chicago Herald*, October 14, 1914, 12.

128. "In the Picture Playhouses: Gossip of Photoplay Theaters," *Chicago Sunday Herald*, November 1, 1914, sec. 2, 4.

129. Features in downtown theaters attracted tourists and visitors, but this trade was seasonal, mainly summer and Christmas. This was the case in 1914 when big features were not available nationwide in such luxurious surrounding. As the *Herald* noted: "At the Fine Arts and the Ziegfeld, Annette Kellerman [in *Neptune's Daughter*] and *Cabiria* respectively continue to draw well enough to hold their places despite the wonderfully long runs they both have had. This is in part a testimonial to the metropolitan character of Chicago, to the fact that there are weekly thousands of visitors here who have not previously visited the city for months and naturally a vast number of these seek the two plays which have made such a wide reputation in the movie world." Even a year later, Louella Parsons stated that Chicago's "motion picture theaters are a magnet to the visitor tarrying in this city on his vacation." But tourism alone could not support the cost of high-end exhibition, especially as road-showed features spread across the country. Dominic A. Pacyga and Ellen Skerrett, *Chicago: City of Neighborhoods* (Chicago: Loyola University Press, 1986), 9. "In the Picture Playhouses: Gossip about the Films, The Players and Producers," *Chicago Sunday Herald*, September 27, 1914, sec. 2, 8. Louella O. Parsons, "Chicago 'Movie' Shows Mecca for the Visitor," *Chicago Herald*, August 7, 1915, part 2 (Amusement Special), 1–2.

130. "In the Picture Playhouses: Reel Facts," *Chicago Herald*, September 10, 1914, 14.

131. Bowser, *Transformation of Cinema*, 132. For a discussion of Rothapfel's career, see Robert C. Allen, *Vaudeville and Film, 1895–1915: A Study in Media Interaction* (New York: Arno Press, 1980; Dissertations on Film, Ayer, 1977), 294–95.

132. Travelogues of Florida, a color film of kittens, an animated weekly, a newsreel, and the comedy *Her Friend the Milkman* preceded the feature—David Belasco's *The Woman*, a Jesse Lasky Company production. Songs from the Strand Quartette and overtures performed by a thirty-piece orchestra ("the largest . . . ever used in a theater for anything but grand opera") preceded the films, which were accompanied by a pipe organ. Gene Morgan, "As to That

Tired and Overworked Man—Mr. D. Luxe," *Chicago Sunday Herald*, April 25, 1915, part 6, 6; Louella O. Parsons, "Seen on the Screen," *Chicago Herald*, May 1, 1915, 12.

133. Strand advertisement, *Chicago Herald*, October 13, 1915, 6.

134. Advertisement, *Chicago Sunday Herald*, September 26, 1915, sec. 6, 6; Louella O. Parsons, "Seen on the Screen: At Orchestra Hall," *Chicago Herald*, October 8, 1915, 8.

135. Louella O. Parsons, "Seen on the Screen," *Chicago Herald*, October 16, 1915, 8.

136. Louella O. Parsons, "Seen on the Screen," *Chicago Herald*, March 24, 1916, 8.

137. The theater was just one month old and was supposedly completely fireproof. Julia Skinner Sawyers, *Chicago Sketches: Urban Tales, Stories, and Legends from Chicago History* (Chicago: Loyola University Press, 1995), 175–76.

138. Rothapfel condemned the city, establishing a history of mutual animosity. He had little luck in the city, with the local press celebrating his mistakes and minimizing his success elsewhere. James S. McQuade, "Chicago Letter: Chain of First-Class Houses for De Luxe Pictures," *Moving Picture World* 12, no. 11, June 15, 1912, 1012; James S. McQuade, "Chicago Letter: Chicago Film Brevities," *Moving Picture World* 13, no. 1, July 6, 1912, 27.

139. Louella O. Parsons, "Seen on the Screen," *Chicago Herald*, March 24, 1916, 8.

140. Louella O. Parsons, "Seen on the Screen," *Chicago Herald*, February 28, 1916, 6.

141. Louella O. Parsons, "Seen on the Screen," *Chicago Herald*, April 21, 1916, 10.

142. Gene Morgan, "As to That Tired, Overworked Man—Mr. D. Luxe," part 6, 6; Louella O. Parsons, "Seen on the Screen," *Chicago Herald*, August 21, 1915, 7; half-page advertisement for *The Birth of a Nation* at the Illinois Theater, *Chicago Sunday Herald*, June 6, 1915, 7; "Plans for the Studebaker," *Chicago Herald*, August 23, 1915, 10; Louella O. Parsons, "Seen on the Screen," *Chicago Herald*, October 16, 1915.

143. Louella O. Parsons, "Seen on the Screen," *Chicago Herald*, February 26, 1916, 6.

144. Sargent, *Picture Theatre Advertising*, 3.

145. The twenty-six proprietors were Edward Morris, 34 South Halsted; Louis Elsman, 112 and 126 South Halsted; Emanar Amusement Company, 320 South Halsted; John Voumvakes, 527 South Halsted; Joe Vicedomini, 914 South Halsted; Mrs. Amalio Padrocello, 1009 South Halsted; Abraham Rafilson, 1302 South Halsted; Isadore Natkin, 1310 South Halsted; Solovitzik Bros., 1348 South Halsted; Marks and Goodman, 1350 South Halsted; Carl Rademacher, Frank Scott, 1828 South Halsted; Joseph Weiler, 3214 South Halsted;

NOTES TO CHAPTER 4

3520 South Halsted; August Vogel, 4303 South Halsted; Max Schwartz, 5451 South Halsted; J. Shapiro, 5527 South Halsted; Louis Frank, 6204 South Halsted; the National Theatre, 6221 South Halsted; Harry Myers, 6435 South Halsted; Bruce Goldshaw, 7038 South Halsted; Louis Canton, 7052 South Halsted; William Campbell, 7431 South Halsted; Edward Rothe, 7813 South Halsted; Julius Asher, 7833 South Halsted; Isaac Bergson, 6811 South Halsted. Once again, three "Theaters" were listed: the Academy, Bijou, and the Empress (6230 South Halsted)—the National having been downgraded to a five- and ten-cent house.

146. The availability of Independent films after 1909 added to the success of picture theaters in entertainment districts. In October 1910, the Boston (managed by Guy Morville) became the first house in the Loop to show Independent films, about one year after the movement first gathered momentum. A year later, the *Moving Picture World* commented,

> I don't know if it is that the pictures are far superior or if it is a question of novelty, but the fact is that I could not enter the Boston Theater on account of a crowd of visitors waiting their turn. This was at 8.30 on Friday evening and when I made the second attempt at 9.30 I met another crowd, while at the [nearby] Alcazar, Pastime and Casino you could find plenty of seats.

Independent films made it possible for more theaters to distinguish themselves through *content*, making it possible for a greater number to compete within a limited area after the novelty of the nickelodeon boom subsided. "Chicago Notes," *Moving Picture World* 7, no. 18, October 29, 1910, 1000; J. M. B., "In the Loop of Chicago," *Moving Picture World* 7, no. 19, November 5, 1910, 1045.

147. John Anson Ford, "Sunday in a Great City," *World To-Day*, 19, no. 4, October 1910, 1115–16.

148. Clarence J. Perfitt, "Chicago Notes," *Moving Picture World* 6, no. 18, May 7, 1910, 732.

149. "A Picture Lover," "Helpful Hints to Exhibitors," *Moving Picture World* 6, no. 13, April 2, 1910, 507.

150. Scott A. Newman, "Jazz Age Chicago: Small Loop Movie Theaters," http://chicago.urban-history.org/ven/ths/loop_th.shtml, accessed July 10, 2007.

151. "Managers Laud Herald 'Movies,'" *Chicago Herald*, June 26, 1914, 6.

152. Q. David Bowers, *Nickelodeon Theaters and Their Music* (New York: Vestal Press, 1986), 125.

153. Ibid., 168.

154. Advertisement, *Chicago Sunday Herald*, September 23, 1917, part 6, 10;

"Among the Chicago Shows," *Moving Picture World* 5, no. 13, September 25, 1909, 412. Like the many other smaller loop theaters that survived well into the 1910s—including the Casino (58 West Madison, seating capacity 288); the Castle (State at Madison, seating capacity 300); Kozy (40 South Clark, seating capacity 275); Pastime (66 West Madison, seating capacity 390) and the Star (68 West Madison)—these theaters moved from showing programs of one- and two-reelers to becoming subsequent run houses.

155. Gene Morgan, "A Night at the All-Night Movie," *Chicago Sunday Herald*, February 14, 1915, part 6, 6; Susie Sexton, "With the Sun Dodgers on Celluloid Row—Our New Rialto," *Chicago Sunday Herald*, June 13, 1915, part 6, 2.

156. Lewis Erenburg, "Ain't We Got Fun?: Popular Entertainment in Chicago, 1893–1929," *Chicago History* 14 (Winter 1985–86): 14–15; McCarthy, "Nickel Vice and Virtue," 40–43. Reformers also attacked theaters located in the "lower-class" entertainment districts in the poorer parts of the Loop and farther out along major roads like West Madison Street. The *Lakeside Classified Directory* for 1913 lists clusters of five- and ten-cent theaters at intervals along the outlying reaches of West Madison Street (note that this directory gives the operator's name, not that of their business). Two theaters practically faced each other on the 1400 block—James Shaw's at 1418 and Shafer Bros on 1421—as did two on the 2100 block: William H. Bell at 2126 and Fanny Schmidt at 2125. Otto Treulich (2004 West Madison), Kaufman and Lasdon (2342 West Madison), and the Imperial Theater (2329 West Madison). Similar clusters existed farther out as Charles Schaefer (2844 West Madison), the Francisco Theater (2917 West Madison), Clarence Poull (3022 West Madison), Henry Burdorf (3050 West Madison), and the Kedzie Amusement Co. (3202 West Madison) vied for audiences around the 3000 block.

157. Valeria D. McDermott and Annie Elizabeth Trotter, *Chicago Social Services Directory* (Chicago: Burmeister, 1915, 1918), 75, 129, 169, 227.

158. McCarthy, "Nickel Vice and Virtue," 43. As she notes: "On one occasion, the theater, which had a capacity of three hundred, drew an audience of only thirty-seven. Potential customers were siphoned off by neighboring theaters. . . . As one small neighborhood resident explained, 'Oh its a good show, all right, but it ain't lively enough. People like to see fights and fellows getting hurt and robbers and all that stuff.'"

159. Carl W. Condit, *Chicago, 1910–29: Building, Planning, and Urban Technology* (Chicago: University of Chicago Press, 1973), 75.

160. Condit, *Chicago, 1910–29*, 76.

161. Daniel Burnham and Edward Bennett, *The Plan of Chicago* (Chicago: Commercial Club, 1909), 108.

162. Edith Wyatt, "Chicago's Melting Pot: More Miles of Halsted Street

Below the Haymarket—Hull House and Its Meaning," *Colliers* 45, August 27, 1910, 21–22.

163. Humbert S. Nelli, *Italians in Chicago, 1880–1930: A Study in Ethnic Mobility* (New York: Oxford University Press, 1970), 28–97.

164. Wyatt, "Chicago's Melting Pot," 22.

165. Ibid., 21.

166. Ibid.; The Chicago Association of Commerce, *A Guide to the City of Chicago* (Chicago: Rand McNally, 1912), 53–54.

167. C. Y., "Chicago Notes," *Moving Picture World* 7, no. 2, July 9, 1910, 92.

168. When a Mrs. Newton, a reformer and council member, proposed raising the age at which unescorted children could be admitted to movies from fourteen to sixteen in February 1912, she raised the possibility of creating two different movie audiences—adults and general admission. James S. McQuade, "Chicago Letter," *Moving Picture World* 11, no. 9, March 2, 1912, 761.

169. The Adult Ordinance of 1914, *The Chicago Code of 1915*, Section 1, states the bill "provided such picture or series of pictures are not of such character as to tend to create contempt or hatred for any class of law abiding citizen." The meeting was attended by censors and members of local reform organizations including Gertrude Howe Britton, Harriet Vittum, Sophonisba Breckenridge, Mrs. David Lyman Jr., Mrs. Herman Landauer, Mrs. M. L. Purvin, Mrs. Henry Sullivan, Mrs. Charles Stirling, Miss Alice Brackett, and Mrs. Charles Henrotin. "'Adults Only' Ordinance Will Be Carried," *Moving Picture World* 21, no. 2, July 21, 1914, 227.

Notes to Chapter 5

1. Grieveson, *Policing Cinema*, 5.

2. Ibid., 88–120.

3. On May 2, 1907, for example, the City Club endorsed Jane Addams's recommendation that "instead of suppressing these places [movie theaters], they be placed under proper supervision and regulation." The city's reformers discussed the topic for several months, but did not come up with any coherent plan other than recommending the city terminate Sunday shows, something that was doomed to failure in Chicago, a city without Blue Laws. "Vice, Police Herded, Held as Youth's Foe," *Chicago Record Herald*, November 11, 1907, 3; "A Clean Nickelodeon," *Moving Picture World* 1, no. 13, June 1, 1907, 195.

4. "William Lord Wright's Page," *Moving Picture News* 7, no. 13, March 29, 1913, 12. See also Allen Hoben, *The Minister and the Boy: A Handbook for Churchmen Engaged in Boy's Work* (Chicago: University of Chicago Press, 1912); Lissak, *Pluralism and Progressives*, 19.

5. Chicago's board has been the subject of important work. See Grieveson, *Policing Cinema*, 11–120; Lee Grieveson, "Why The Audience Mattered in Chicago in 1907," in *American Movie Audiences: From the Turn of the Century to the Early Sound Era*, ed. Melvyn Stokes and Richard Maltby (London: BFI, 1999); McCarthy, "Nickel Vice and Virtue," 37–55.

6. See Charlie Keil's discussion of verisimilitude in transitional cinema. Keil, *Early American Cinema in Transition*, 127–34, 208.

7. As Grieveson points out, censorship was not just about sanitizing cinema but about putting it in its place—and thus giving it a role that did not involve social leadership. *Policing Cinema*, 151–91.

8. James Gilbert, *Perfect Cities: Chicago's Utopias of 1983* (Chicago: University of Chicago Press, 1991), 125.

9. Lauren Rabinovitz, *For the Love of Pleasure: Women, Movies, and Culture in Turn-of-the Century Chicago* (New Brunswick, NJ: Rutgers University Press, 1998), 106.

10. Testimony of Reverend Frederic Siedenburg, *Report of the Chicago Motion Picture Commission* (Chicago, September 1920), 74.

11. One twelve-page report from 1914 found that most escorted and unescorted women drank alcohol, many to excess, and that most bars had back rooms where women could engage in prostitution. Only twenty-seven of the bars visited "did not contribute to the demoralization of women," with the authors observing that as "the women are started in the idea that they are privileged to drink, and they soon drift into less reputable, and finally disreputable, resorts." The study covered the area from "North Clark Street from the River to the City limits, on Madison Street to the Lake to the City Limits, on Wabash Avenue from the River to Twenty-Second Street, on Twenty-Second Street from Wabash Avenue to Cottage Grove Avenue, and on Cottage Grove Avenue to Seventy-Seventh Street." *The Survey of Conditions Demoralizing to Women and Girls in the Saloons of Chicago* (Chicago South Side Club, 1914), 3, 6–11.

12. The larger, centrally located theaters in the Loop bothered local officials, reformers, and dignitaries far less than their smaller counterparts or the local neighborhood houses—and not just because those establishments had higher cultural aspirations and more expensive ticket prices. They did not have regular patronage and thus did not use cinema to create the kind of community that threatened establishment visions of local identity. On the one hand, this made them easier to attack: they were without loyal supporters and thus acquired an aura of anonymity, offering transitory pleasures to migrating audiences. As such, they could be depicted as places representing the breakdown of modern society, potentially offering cover to all manner of social misfits and criminals. But these establishments were not the city's biggest concern. Their social influence was limited, and most of them were short-lived, closing

down before the city tightened up its censorship and regulation ordinances in 1910 after the Vice Commission report. Attacking them first was tactical, allowing censors and their allies to build support for their main targets: the more reputable neighborhood houses and the longer, more narrativized and illusionistic films that began to dominate the market around 1910, representing the film industry's own efforts at uplift.

13. Grieveson, *Policing Cinema*, 65.

14. Ibid.

15. *Chicago Tribune*, April 10, 1907, 10; *Chicago Tribune*, April 13, 1907, 3; *Chicago Tribune*, April 14, 1907, sec. 1, 5; *Chicago Tribune*, April 15, 1907, 4.

16. Grieveson, *Policing Cinema*, 61–63, 65–67.

17. Ibid., 61–63, 64–65, 67.

18. *Report of the Chicago Motion Picture Commission* (Chicago, September 1920), 54.

19. "Curb Cheap Theaters," *Chicago Record-Herald*, May 2, 1907, 5.

20. "Regulation of Cheap Theaters" (editorial), *Chicago Record-Herald*, May 2, 1907, 8. The editorial notes that Shippy had developed his plan in conjunction with "probation officers, anti-crime workers, relief and aid officers."

21. "Curb Cheap Theaters," 5.

22. JPA Papers, Jane Addams Collection, University of Illinois–Chicago. It would seem to me, at least, that one reason for the popularity of performers like Mary Pickford and Marguerite Clark, for instance, was precisely their capacity to evoke childhood although they were clearly adults. As such, they offered the pleasure of looking at a child without violating the period's social pressures and taboos that clearly sought not only to protect the child from the exploitation of work but also to preserve innocence through removing the child from adult conversations and knowledge. Furthermore, the unspoken interdiction against looking at a child while, simultaneously, valorizing and being attracted to its innocent look, also implies a certain eroticism in the act of looking that threatens the very innocence—and its attraction—for audiences. Also see Gaylyn Studlar, "Oh, 'Doll Divine!': Mary Pickford, Masquerade, and the Paedophilic Gaze," in Bean and Negra, *A Feminist Reader in Early Cinema*, 349–373.

23. "Trade Notes," *Moving Picture World* 1, no. 10, May 11, 1907, 152.

24. "Trade Notes," *Moving Picture World* 1, no. 16, June 22, 1907, 248.

25. Editorial, *Chicago Tribune*, May 3, 1907, 2.

26. "The Electric Theatre Controversy" (editorial), *Billboard* 19, no. 23, June 8, 1907, 20.

27. Abel, *Americanizing the Movies*, 215–27.

28. "Regulation of Cheap Theaters" (editorial), *Chicago Record-Herald*, May 2, 1907, 8.

29. Grieveson provides a more detailed account of this bill and its path through committee. *Policing Cinema*, 72–73.

30. "Trade Notes," *Moving Picture World* 1, no. 29, September 21, 1907, 454.

31. This plan united visual improvement influenced by the City Beautiful movement ("Making Chicago more artistic to the eye and more attractive to the visitor; borrowing a leaf from Paris in this respect"); greater cleanliness (new cleaning technologies and removing politics and corruption from street cleaning); healthier recreations (more parks, school buildings used for recreation and as neighborhood centers); and greater police efficiency. Together these plans and regulations were aimed at establishing a firmer sense of national identity aided by plans to encourage "a distinctly American art and architecture" and increase civic education in schools. This extensive campaign reveals the widespread nature of local government intervention into hitherto private concerns, like leisure and social life, during the Progressive Era, as well as the period's investment in shoring up American national identity. "Plan Big Civic Body to Beautify Chicago," *Chicago Record Herald*, November 11, 1907, 1.

32. Grieveson, *Policing Cinema*, 72, 73.

33. *Report of the Chicago Motion Picture Commission*, 33.

34. Testimony of Major M. L. C. Funkhouser, *Report of the Chicago Motion Picture Commission*, 90.

35. "Trade Notes," *Moving Picture World* 2, no. 23, June 6, 1908, 492. Also see Grieveson, *Policing Cinema*, 74.

36. For a more detailed discussion of the *Block* case, see Grieveson, *Policing Cinema*, 74–76.

37. *Report of the Chicago Motion Picture Commission*, 5.

38. *Jake Block, Nathan Wolf, et al., v. The City of Chicago*, 239 Illinois Supreme Court Reports, 1909, 251; *Report of the Chicago Motion Picture Commission*, 12.

39. *Report of the Chicago Motion Picture Commission*, 79–80.

40. Testimony of George Kleine, *Report of the Chicago Motion Picture Commission*, 41; McCarthy, "Nickel Vice and Virtue," 45.

41. Richard Abel, *The Red Rooster Scare: Making Cinema American, 1900–1910* (Berkeley: University of California Press, 1999), xviii, 88–90. As he demonstrates, one factor behind the trade battles and the formation of early (1907–10) protective organizations like the United Film Service Protective Association and the Film Service Association was the need to protect American production companies against foreign competition, particularly Pathé—the dominant international company at the time.

42. As Abel notes, anti-European, and anti-Pathé, sentiment increased after the *Chicago Tribune*'s 1907 exposé of the city's South Side nickelodeons, even though Philadelphia-based Lubin's *Unwritten Law* (about the all-American Thaw-White scandal) was the most criticized film. Abel, *Red Rooster Scare*, 97–98.

NOTES TO CHAPTER 5

43. C. Y., "Chicago Notes," *Moving Picture World* 7, no. 2, July 9, 1910, 92. Abel notes that Pathé's films also had often "incomprehensible" narratives and characteristically nonrealist aesthetics (often compounded through hand coloring), unlike American films that were narrative-driven, realist, character-centered, and action-oriented, culminating in happy endings (which can be linked to the national and Progressive emphasis on uplift). Abel, *Red Rooster Scare*, 122–26.

44. Abel, *Red Rooster Scare*, 8.

45. Ibid., 94–101.

46. "Bard of Avon Gory? Police Censor of Moving Pictures Tells How to Edit Shakespeare," *Chicago Record-Herald*, June 4, 1908, 3.

47. Ibid.

48. Ibid.

49. Lizabeth Cohen, *Making a New Deal: Industrial Workers in Chicago, 1919–1939* (Cambridge: Cambridge University Press, 1991), 136, 158.

50. "Vice in Nickel Shows: Cheap Theaters Called Sink Holes for Children by Rev. J. E. Powers," *Chicago Sunday Record-Herald*, May 17, 1908, 2.

51. "Skating Rink a Lure: Nickel Show Bad Too," *Chicago Record-Herald*, May 25, 1908, 9.

52. Ibid.

53. Not all clergy agreed: some even used motion pictures to increase their congregations. These were mostly Protestants like the Reverend Johnston Myers who, in June 1913, dubbed moving pictures "a source of joy and helpfulness to the people," and the Reverend Oscar C. Helming who used cinema to teach the Bible, turning his chapel and Sunday School room into a motion picture theater. These sermons and protestations demonstrate how concerns like national identity, civic duty, religion, and patriotism were inseparably linked to the question of censorship and cinema's capacity to form community and instill values in its public—traits that again displayed cinema's ability to influence the society, threatening these local leaders' authority. "Teaches Bible by 'Movies,'" *Chicago Daily Tribune*, Monday, June 23, 1913, 3; "Pastor Praises 'Movies'; Admits He's a Film Fan," *Chicago Daily Tribune*, June 16, 1913, 10.

54. "The Censorship in Chicago," *Moving Picture World* 5, no. 15, October 9, 1909, 487.

55. Ibid.

56. Ibid.

57. "Notes of the Trade," *Moving Picture World* 4, no. 10, March 6, 1909, 267.

58. The first censorship case ever to come to court, *Block v. the City of Chicago*, was brought by a group of exhibitors who rejected the city's power to remove their license for screening films rejected by the city's censors as too violent, including *The James Boys in Missouri* (1908) and *Night Riders* (1908). As

these stories about the James brothers were still circulating in other media, Jake Block and the other exhibitors involved in the suit claimed that the city's actions were unconstitutional and oppressive. The Supreme Court of Illinois supported the city, upholding the censors' power, finding no discrimination against Block as all films would be treated the same, regardless of whether the material circulated elsewhere. Indeed, in the eyes of the court, cinema's power and influence, especially on young minds, demanded careful regulation and monitoring. Stephen Prince, *Classical Film Violence: Designing and Regulating Brutality in Hollywood, 1930–1968* (New Brunswick, NJ: Rutgers University Press, 2003), 13–17.

59. Grieveson, *Policing Cinema*, 100.

60. For a more detailed explanation of the workings of the Board of Censorship, see Robert Fisher, "Film Censorship and Progressive Reform: The National Board of Censorship of Motion Pictures, 1909–1922," *Journal of Popular Film and Television* 4, no. 2 (1975): 143–56.

61. Roberta Pearson, *Eloquent Gestures: The Transformation of Performance Style in the Griffith Biograph Films* (Berkeley: University of California Press, 1992), 130–31.

62. Grieveson, *Policing Cinema*, 101.

63. "The Censorship in Chicago," *Moving Picture World* 5, no. 15, October 9, 1909, 487. The Chicago board had initial and brief links to the city's rival Independent producers and distributors (especially William Swanson).

64. Their follow-up 1911 investigation found considerable improvement in theater conditions and film quality, despite the presence of too many "lurid" melodramas and "silly" comedies. They credited the combination of tighter censorship and the increased cost of theater licenses (raised from $100 to $200 in 1909) that helped reduce the number of licensed five- and ten-cent houses from 425 in 1909 to 298 in 1912. (Clearly, however, this does not deal with the number of unlicensed premises that continued to operate away from the city's guidelines.) Still, the reformers were not entirely satisfied and continued lobbying for poster censorship; stricter theater licensing; improved lighting inside theaters; stronger zoning laws; and, most importantly, the continued vigilance of movie censors. Bowen, *Five and Ten Cent Theaters*, 6.

65. Bowen, *Five and Ten Cent Theaters*, 1.

66. Ibid., 1–2.

67. Ibid., 3–4.

68. "Notes of the Trade," *Moving Picture World* 5, no. 26, December 25, 1909, 919.

69. Although the Association of Commerce strongly recommended that they study housing conditions, the commission largely ignored the consequences of urban deprivation on slum residents. The sole exception was juvenile delinquency, which investigators attributed to "home conditions" to be a

cause for concern, although much of the blame was attributed to parents for keeping a poor and morally corrupt home rather than exploring causes of poverty and overcrowding: "Bad Home conditions often drive the daughters of the family into prostitution and the sons into lives of crime. In such cases the parents are indifferent or ignorant. They allow their children to seek improper amusements without question or guidance. . . . Many families in the congested districts take in boarders who sleep in the same room with members of the family. This accustoms children to the presence of strangers and it is no wonder that they lose their moral sense and easily accept the improper attentions of others. The time has come in Chicago when better housing conditions should be studied and applied. The population in certain quarters of the city is becoming more and more congested. Aside from the dangers resulting from insanitary conditions, bad housing breeds vice and crime" (Vice Commission of Chicago, *Social Evil in Chicago*, 1, 55–65, at 245).

These beliefs were in keeping with Progressivism's belief that the shared and more "public" aspects of life determined social, moral, and civic order—a radical departure from the Victorian emphasis on the private sphere. This omission was significant, given that it was their overcrowded tenements and urban slums that led many residents to venture into public places for relaxation in the first place. Movie theaters, amusement parks, saloons, dance halls, vaudeville theaters, and cafés offered the pleasures, diversion, and escape their homes could not offer. Many tenements scarcely offered space for even close family to interact comfortably. This situation troubled reformers, politicians, and their supporters because this "new" public sphere not only allowed urban residents to congregate and mingle without supervision, but also because its entertainments threatened to overturn the values, morals, and behaviors they hoped to instill in the urban masses. As new forms of socialization uninfluenced by established authorities, they were all the more threatening. This problem was magnified with the introduction of cinema, which had become the nation's leading entertainment by 1907, reaching unprecedented numbers of immigrants, children, women, and the working classes. Jane Addams, *The Spirit of Youth and The City Streets* (Chicago: University of Chicago Press, 1909). See also Grace Abbott, *The Immigrant and the Community* (New York: Century, 1917); Sophonisba P. Breckenridge, ed., *The Child in the City: A Series of Papers Presented at the Conferences Held during the Chicago Child Welfare Exhibit* (Chicago: Department of Social Investigation, Chicago School of Civics and Philanthropy, 1912); Harvey C. Carbaugh, *Human Welfare Work in Chicago* (Chicago: McClurg, 1917); John Collier and Edward M. Barrows, *The City Where Crime Is Play* (New York: People's Institute, January 1914); Richard Henry Edwards, *Christianity and Amusements* (New York: Association Press, International Committee of the Young Men's Christian Association, 1915).

70. This book investigated all the renowned causes of vice—working-class leisure, the saloons, neighborhood streets, cheap movies and live theater, corrupt policing, and poor education—and suggested corrective measures, including an improved park system, better supervision of children's recreation, greater safeguards for working women to protect them from "white slavery"; and argued for improved laws governing working conditions, stronger child labor laws, tougher drug laws, and better treatment for venereal disease.

71. *Testimony and Addresses on Segregation and Commercialized Vice Presented before the City Council's Committee of Nine* (Chicago: American Vigilance Association, November 1912), Pamphlet No. 2; Hoyt, *One Hundred Years of Land Values in Chicago*, 230, 312.

72. Its other duties included social work, public health, policing, and litigation. To these ends, it employed five elected officials and a chief clerk, assistant clerk, attorney, assistant attorney, medical inspector, assistant medical inspector, and "such other help as may be necessary": "To take all legal and necessary steps towards the effectual suppression of bawdy and disorderly houses, houses of ill-fame or assignation within the limits of the City of Chicago, and within three (3) miles of the outer boundaries of the city; to collect evidence of the violation of any state laws and city ordinances concerning such houses, and the keepers, inmates and patrons of the same; and to institute and carry on prosecutions in the name of the City of Chicago against any of said houses, said keepers, inmates and patrons." The court was intended as both a philanthropic and criminal institution, supposedly offering fallen women a new beginning while punishing any individual or institution promulgating vice, but it concentrated on punishment more than rehabilitation. Despite sparing offenders contact with the criminal system, the Morals Court publicized its cases more than the city's other courts, often ruining defendants' lives. *The New World*, a Chicago-based Catholic newspaper, noted that its actions prevented at least one girl from returning home after her trial. Vice Commission of Chicago, *Social Evil in Chicago*, 52; article from *The New World*, undated, no page number given, cited in "Chicago's Morals Court," *Literary Digest* 56, no. 22, May 31, 1913, 1229.

73. "Discovers New Vice Districts," *Chicago Sunday Tribune*, January 19, 1913, 3.

74. Vice Commission of Chicago, *Social Evil in Chicago*, 230, 246–47, 266–68.

75. Ibid., 247–48.

76. Lindberg, *Chicago by Gaslight*, 214.

77. Ibid., 116–18, 136.

78. Ibid., 136–39.

79. Ibid., 140.

80. James S. McQuade, "Chicago Letter," *Moving Picture World* 11, no. 8, February 24, 1912, 665.

81. James S. McQuade, "Chicago Letter," *Moving Picture World* 11, no. 5, February 3, 1912, 390.

82. James S. McQuade, "Chicago Letter," *Moving Picture World* 11, no. 11, March 16, 1912, 954.

83. James S. McQuade, "Chicago Letter," *Moving Picture World* 11, no. 8, February 24, 1912, 665.

84. "Odd Censorship of 'American' Pictures," *Moving Picture World* 11, no. 10, March 9, 1912, 858. The report gave the following specific examples:

> One day recently, the American Film Mfg. Co . . . showed to the visiting inspector a film scheduled for release Thursday, March 7, titled *The Broken Ties*. The central thought in this picture swings about a heartless stepmother who in one scene gathers her effects together and with her son appropriates the husband's pocketbook and leaves.

The police censor took objection to this scene, claiming that it smacked of robbery, despite legal railings to the effect that a wife cannot steal from her husband.

> *From the 400 to the Herd* is the name of another coming "American" which also came in for some remarkable criticism on behalf of the police. This picture, which, it is believed, will make a genuine sensation for its cleverness of plot and astonishing backgrounds, was criticized for an actual sale of property where the deed was shown, a part of the scene action on which the entire story pivoted. There was no suggestion of fraud or attempted fraud, but merely the sale of a big ranch by one man to another.

85. "Moving Pictures as Crime Instigators" (editorial), *Chicago Examiner*, cited in James S. McQuade, "Chicago Letter," *Moving Picture World* 11, no. 11, March 16, 1912, 954.

86. Section 1914, Chicago City Ordinance, 1912; *Report of the Chicago Motion Picture Commission*, September 1920, 5.

87. *Report of the Chicago Motion Picture Commission*, 5.

88. James S. McQuade, "Chicago Letter," *Moving Picture World* 16, no. 4, April 26, 1913, 366.

89. The *Moving Picture World* called him "a man . . . who takes pride in his work and strains himself to the utmost to do it well." James S. McQuade, "Chicago Letter," *Moving Picture World* 16, no. 4, April 26, 1913, 366.

90. James S. McQuade, "Chicago Letter," *Moving Picture World* 16, no. 4, April 26, 1913, 366. McQuade cites the *Tribune*'s writer who called Maeterlink "one of the greatest living writers" while dubbing O'Connor "a policemen enthroned in the high seat of judgment."

91. James S. McQuade, "Chicago Letter," *Moving Picture World* 16, no. 4, April 26, 1913, 366.

92. Mabel Condon, "How the Chicago Censor Board Works," *Motography*, March 15, 1913, 197.

93. O'Connor noted: "Some of the reasons for the rejection of [recent] films were: killing of women and setting house on fire; shooting of man; abuse of children; shooting and burglary; murder and suicide; immorality, brutality and blowing of man to death; abuse of children and stabbing; bribery and intimidation; murder and poisoning of man; robbing house; immoral scenes and boy stealing; woman becomes a drunkard; robbery and assault; kidnapping boy and girl and sub-title of '$25,000 reward, dead or alive.' Causes for ordering cut-outs were very similar and in most cases they were short scenes that were merely incident to the film, while the films rejected were ordered so on account of the objectionable tone permeating them throughout."

94. James S. McQuade, "Chicago Letter," *Moving Picture World* 16, no. 5, May 3, 1913, 473.

95. Ibid.

96. "Vice Inquirers Doom Zoo Dances and Smut Songs," *Chicago Sunday Tribune*, April 13, 1913, 1.

97. On the night of the ban, Chicago's cafés responded with tango "funeral parties," beginning at 11 p.m. and progressing past midnight. Some events took the form of mock interments as patrons staged elaborate performances complete with casket bearers, candles, and funeral music, while others featured frantic dancing into the early hours of the morning. Proprietors stated that the tango and other dances would not die, however, citing a loophole in the hastily drafted ordinance forbidding dancing by patrons, not hired professionals. A café owner cited in the *Tribune* commented that most downtown restaurants would start featuring shows by professional dancers "beginning probably tonight," preventing the death of the tango and the other new "animal dances" at the hands of the city's morality censors. Attempts at lip service were abandoned by September, with many cafés completely ignoring the law, leading Funkhouser to lament that there was indeed "a loophole in the cabaret ordinance." Condemning animal dances as "morality's worst enemy," Funkhouser started prohibiting professional dancing in the city's restaurants. "Exit of Tango Lively in Cafés: Ordinance Goes into Effect at Midnight, but the Dance Goes Merrily On," *Chicago Daily Tribune*, August 30, 1913, 1; "Tango Danced In Cafés Despite Prohibitory Law," *Chicago Daily Tribune*, September 2, 1913, 10; "'Animal Dances' Called Danger," *Chicago Daily Tribune*, October 17, 1913, 8; "Start Fight to Save Tango: Restaurants Seek to Evade Law through Dance Hall Permits," *Chicago Daily Tribune*, September 4, 1913, 3.

98. "Modesty in Clothes" (editorial), *Chicago Sunday Tribune*, September 7, 1913, part 5, 4; "Has Fashion at Last Reached Its Limit?" *Chicago Sunday*

Tribune, August 10, 1913, part 7, 4; "Slit Skirts? Not for Mrs. Gould," *Chicago Daily Tribune*, August 4, 1913, 5. University of Chicago professor Allen Hoben called the new dresses "a menace to the city's morals," because they revealed enough flesh to excite young men's libidos and might encourage women "to regard the street as a stage on which to display their charms." He asked for municipal intervention to counter these "problems," calling for laws to protect the streets, to restore them as to their rightful place as the city's "parlor and . . . playground." Meanwhile, Dr. C. T. Ewart, a self-appointed (male) expert on women's dress, even proclaimed that women's current obsession with fashion was a form of insanity, albeit a "slight, neglected, form." Nevertheless, he recommended treatment for women's nerves and prescribed complete change and bed rest to arrest the progress of this form of insanity and to protect the whole of society. "Calls Fashionable Gowns Menace to City's Morals," *Chicago Daily Tribune*, August 7, 1913, 7; "Are Women Crazy about Clothes?" *Chicago Sunday Tribune*, September 7, 1913, part 7, 2.; "Fashions Not Degrading Women, Jane Addams Says," *Chicago Daily Tribune*, September 26, 1913, 9.

99. "Funkhouser as Morals Guardian," *Chicago Daily Tribune*, March 21, 1913, 2.

100. Testimony of Major M. L. C. Funkhouser, *Report of the Chicago Motion Picture Commission*, 83; Henriette Greenebaum Frank and Amalie Hofer Jerome, *The Annals of the Chicago Women's Club for the First Forty Years of Its Organization, 1876–1916* (Chicago: Chicago Women's Club, 1916), 297–98.

101. This committee consisted of John Pribyl (Selig Polyscope); V. R. Day (Essanay); R. H. Nehls (American Film Manufacturing); Harry Cohen (General Film); F. A. Farnhum (Mutual); Joseph Hopp (Standard Film Exchange); and exhibitors R. R. Levy, W. J. Sweeney, and John Duffin. James S. McQuade, "Chicago Letter," *Moving Picture World* 16, no. 6, May 3, 1913, 473. "Police Censors Unchanged," *Motography* 9, no. 9, May 3, 1913, 332.

102. "Attendance at Chicago Theatres Have Increased since Only Clean Pictures Are Allowed," *Moving Picture News* 7, no. 26, June 28, 1913, 31.

103. Ibid.

104. Ibid.

105. Testimony of Major M. L. C. Funkhouser, *Report of the Chicago Moving Picture Commission*, 83–85.

106. Ibid., 83.

107. George D. Proctor, "Oh, It's an Interesting Life!" *Motion Picture News* 8, no. 23, December 13, 1913, 17.

108. "Latest News from Chicago: Exchangemen Discuss Chicago Censorship," *Motion Picture News* 8, no. 20, November 22, 1913, 31.

109. "Latest News from Chicago: Interests Band to Fight Censorship," *Motion Picture News* 8, no. 21, November 29, 1913, 48. The paper gave one example of this extreme censorship: "Let's give a little instance of how far these

censors have gone with their power. Not long ago the Vitagraph released a subject in which a child while roller skating is picked up on the fender of a street car. The accident had to be cut out. Now, this was a film that taught a strong lesson, nevertheless, it could not be shown."

110. "Police Censors Unchanged," 332.

111. James S. McQuade, "Chicago Letter," *Moving Picture World*, January 3, 1914, 53, 54; James S. McQuade, "Chicago's Deputized Censors," *Moving Picture World*, February 2, 1914, 959.

112. James S. McQuade, "William A. Brady and 'Butcher-Actors,'" *Moving Picture World* 19, no. 1, January 3, 1914, 53.

113. "Chicago Film Brevities," *Moving Picture World*, January 3, 1914, 54.

114. "More about Chicago Censorship," *Moving Picture World*, March 7, 1914, 1244.

115. "More about Chicago Censorship," *Moving Picture World*, March 28, 1914, 1684; Allan H. Spear, *Black Chicago: The Making of a Negro Ghetto, 1890–1920* (Chicago: University of Chicago Press, 1967), 124.

116. "Censorship News from Everywhere: Chicago Mayor Appoints Negro," *Motion Picture News* 9, no. 12, March 28, 1914, 24.

117. "More about Chicago Censorship," *Moving Picture World*, March 7, 1914, 1244.

118. McCarthy, "Nickel Vice and Virtue," 45–46.

119. This new board featured Effie D. Siegler, Eva J. Loeb, Benita E. McGinnis, Edith E. Kerr, George H. Emanuel, Louis L. Prior, Selina Brennan, Theodore N. Phillip, Wilbur F. Willis, and Samuel L. Block. "Chicago's New Movie Censors at Work Inspecting Films," *Chicago Herald*, September 3, 1914, 14; "With the Censors," *Chicago Herald*, August 14, 1914, 14. The following persons passed the exam: Effie D. Sigler, Eva J. Loeb, Benita E. McGinnis, Selina Brennan, Geneva K. Bateman, Edith E. Kerr, Louis L. Prior, George H. Emanuel, Delphi M. Culver, Juliette L. Stuart, Theodore M. Phillip, Geraldine F. Karr, Wilbur F. Willis, Samuel A. Block, Martha E. Abt, Florence B. Kirk, Gertrude Cohn, Juliette A. McKay, Alonzo J. Bowling, Mary E. Rockford, Tillie L. Stein, and Verne W. Langford.

120. "Chicago's New Movie Censors at Work Inspecting Films," 14.

121. Testimony of Major M. L. C. Funkhouser, *Report of the Chicago Motion Picture Commission*, 92.

122. James S. McQuade, "Chicago Letter," *Moving Picture World* 18, no. 3, October 18, 1913, 249; James S. McQuade, "White Slave Film Forbidden in Chicago," *Moving Picture World* 19, no. 1, January 3, 1914, 53; Testimony of Major M. L. C. Funkhouser, *Report of the Chicago Motion Picture Commission*, 82.

123. Testimony of Major M. L. C. Funkhouser, *Report of the Chicago Motion Picture Commission*, 84–87.

124. Mabel Condon, "How the Chicago Censor Board Works," 197; Testimony of Major M. L. C. Funkhouser, *Report of the Chicago Motion Picture Commission*, 85.

125. In May 1908, assistant district attorney Robert W. Childs prohibited all scenes showing the production of counterfeit money, claiming these violated federal statutes. "Government Bars Moving Pictures Showing Making of Bogus Coins," *Moving Picture World* 2, no. 21, May 23, 1908, 458.

126. "Weird Stunts of Our Censor Board: A Growing Menace," *Motography* 12, no. 5, August 1, 1914, 151–53; "Chicago Kills and Cutouts," *Motography* 12, no. 5, August 1, 1914, 160; "Pictures Which Show Money," *Motography* 12, no. 8, August 22, 1914, 274; "Growing Menace of Chicago Censors: More Films Cut," *Motography* 12, no. 14, October 3, 1914, 459–62.

127. *Report of the Chicago Motion Picture Commission*, 5.

128. "Notes of Interest from Chicago," *Motion Picture News* 9, no. 1, January 10, 1914, 25. These grounds were violations of the First Amendment, the 1787 ordinance of the Northwest Territory, and the 1870 Constitution of the State of Illinois with regard to the right to free speech; the illegality of the inspection tax being leveled on films brought into Chicago and Illinois; and the removal or confiscation of property through censorship without compensation or trial by jury. "Chicago Censorship Attacked," *Motography* 11, no. 1, January 10, 1914, 28–29.

129. "Film Companies Lose Injunction Suits," *Moving Picture World* 20, no. 11, June 13, 1914, 1546.

130. "Notes of Interest from Chicago," *Motion Picture News* 9, no. 1, January 10, 1914, 25.

131. "Latest News from Chicago: Mutual Sues Funkhouser," *Motion Picture News* 9, no. 9, March 7, 1914, 33. Mutual was at the vanguard of the fight on censorship, losing the landmark 1915 *Mutual v. Ohio* case that permitted film censorship.

132. "In the Picture Playhouses: Reel Facts," *Chicago Herald*, November 26, 1914, 13.

133. "Chicago Censor Fight Active: Ordinances Now before Board of Aldermen Would Work Much Damage to Exhibitors," *Motion Picture News* 9, no. 7, February 21, 1914, 28.

134. "Funkhouser Denounced," *Motography* 11, no. 3, February 7, 1914, 97.

135. "Chicago Censor Fight Active: Ordinances Now before Board of Aldermen Would Work Much Damage to Exhibitors," 28.

136. "More Chicago Vandalism," *Motography*, 12, no. 14, October 3, 1914, 467. For a detailed discussion of Chicago's role as a "gateway" city for trade, see William Cronon, *Nature's Metropolis: Chicago and the Great West* (New York: Norton, 1991).

137. James S. McQuade, "Funkhouser's Powers Shorn by Chief," *Moving Picture World* 20, no. 3, April 18, 1914; "Curb by Healey for Funkhouser," *Chicago Herald*, May 4, 1915, 3; "Warfare on Vice Schuettler's Job: First Deputy Reinforced by Funkhouser Squad, to Sit on 'Lid,'" *Chicago Herald*, March 5, 1915, 22 (back page); "Thompson Changes Mind: Funkhouser Keeps Office," *Chicago Herald*, May 6, 1915, 3.

138. Testimony of Major M. L. C. Funkhouser, *Report of the Chicago Motion Picture Commission*, 85–87.

139. "Freedom for the Picture," *Motography* 11, no. 4, February 21, 1914, 127–28.

140. The Goat Man, "On the Outside Looking In," *Motography* 11, no. 3, February 7, 1914, 86.

141. Under this new system, an assistant censor would rescreen the offending film/scene and if (s)he found it acceptable, it would pass. If there was any uncertainty, the complete board would review the film and their decision would be final. James S. McQuade, "The Change in the Censorship Plan," *Moving Picture World*, March 7, 1914, 1245.

142. "Chicago Kills and Cutouts," *Motography* 12, no. 5, 160. Joseph Hopp, president of the Amusement Protective League, also stated, "Major Funkhouser has added things to the list forbidden by the ordinance and has judged films arbitrarily." James S. McQuade, "Third Meeting of Amusement Protective League," *Moving Picture World* 19, no. 9, February 28, 1914, 1092–93.

143. "Chicago Censorship under Fire," *Moving Picture World* 22, no. 6, November 6, 1914, 772.

144. "To Censor or Not," *Motography* 10, no. 10, November 15, 1913, 339–40; James S. McQuade, "Strange Objection to *Merchant of Venice*," *Moving Picture World*, March 7, 1914, 1245; "Chicago Film Brevities," *Moving Picture World*, March 14, 1914, 1389; "Weird Stunts of Our Censor Board: A Growing Menace," *Motography* 12, no. 5, August 1, 1914, 151–53; "Chicago Kills and Cutouts," *Motography* 12, no. 5, August 1, 1914, 160; "Growing Menace of Chicago Censors: More Films Cut," *Motography* 12, no. 14, October 3, 1914 459–62; "More Chicago Vandalism," *Motography* 12, no. 14, October 3, 1914, 467.

145. James S. McQuade, "Chicago Letter," *Moving Picture World* 20, no. 5, May 2, 1914, 656.

146. Lindberg, *Chicago by Gaslight*, 149. Harrison lost the Democratic mayoral primary to Robert A. Sweiter, an Irish German Catholic who won many of the immigrant votes that had formerly gone to Harrison—significantly a group who were heavy moviegoers.

147. Herman Kogan and Lloyd Wendt, *Chicago: A Pictorial History* (New York: Bonanza, 1958), 193–95; Lindberg, *Chicago by Gaslight*, 150–52, 204. Black electors turned on Thompson in 1919, though, for his slow response to the Chicago race riots.

NOTES TO CHAPTER 5

148. "Thompson Tells of Plans for City," *Chicago Herald*, April 12, 1915, 5.

149. "Warfare on Vice Schuettler's Job: First Deputy, Re-Enforced by Funkhouser Squad to Sit on 'Lid,'" *Chicago Herald*, May 5, 1915, 22.

150. "Curb by Healey for Funkhouser," *Chicago Herald*, May 4, 1915, 3.

151. "Oppose New State Law For 'Movie' Censors," *Chicago Herald*, May 17, 1915, 7.

152. Louella O. Parsons, "Seen on the Screen," *Chicago Herald*, Tuesday, February 8, 1916, 8.

153. Louella O. Parsons, "Seen on the Screen," *Chicago Herald*, Wednesday, February 9, 1916, 8.

154. The *Herald* described the production of the film and the subsequent controversy as follows:

> The purring of movie cameras in city hall yesterday led to an inquiry. The inquiry led to a discovery that, on authority of the State of Illinois, in accordance with a resolution passed by the state senate, the report of the O'Hara vice commission is being made into a $100,000 eight-reel movie, in which the principal scenes described in the testimony of the girl witnesses will be enacted and corporated into a connected plot.
>
> It appears that the resolution accepting the O'Hara report carried a "rider" recommending that a moving picture be made to show the people far more vividly than could a printed report, what the commission heard and found.
>
> Blair Coan, chief investigator for the commission, was ordered to make a contract for the picture, and he closed it with Essanay, the Chicago producing firm. Work was begun before the session adjourned and is now in heated progress. The picture is to be released in a fortnight and will probably appear first at a loop theater under the title of *Vice*.
>
> Yesterday pictures were taken of Mayor Thompson, Chief Healey, Corporation Counsel Ettelson and Health Commissioner Robertson. Pictures had been made earlier of the senate in session and the commission. Lieutenant Governor O'Hara presiding, conducting a hearing. Scenes were taken in Washington and Springfield where the commission sat, and Congressman Mann, Speaker Clark, Vice President Marshall, Governor Dunne and other famous officials will be shown.
>
> Professional players are enacting the stories told by the girls, from a scenario standing closely by the sworn testimony. In a few instances, the girls themselves have been engaged to pose in the scenes they described, though their names are not made known.
>
> Most of the scenes are laid in Chicago, in skyscrapers, stores, the old vice district and cabarets.

Though the purpose of the legislature was to show Illinois what the commission had found, Essanay will make an international release of the eight-reeler, having assigned the scenario to Charles Michelson and the direction to Richard Baker, and ordered that nothing be spared in turning out a powerful work of general interest.

"Vice Testimony Basis of 'Movie,'" *Chicago Herald*, February 17, 1916, 3.

155. "Ettelson Puts O.K. on *Little Girl Next Door*," *Chicago Herald*, April 21, 1916, 3.

156. Louella O. Parsons, "Seen on the Screen," *Chicago Herald*, Saturday, April 22, 1916, 10.

157. Louella O. Parsons, "Seen on the Screen," *Chicago Herald*, Tuesday, April 25, 1916, 8.

158. "Seems to Need Investigation" (editorial), *Chicago Herald*, April 26, 1916, 4.

159. Ibid.

160. It was widely reported that Igle had recently given Willis a desk, which led to charges of bribery although Igle claimed it was old and only worth $1.50. "How Dare You, Mr. Funkhouser," *Chicago Herald*, March 17, 1916, 7.

161. "Respect the Law!" (editorial), *Chicago Herald*, March 18, 1916, 4.

162. "How Dare You, Mr. Funkhouser," 7.

163. "Chicago Women Issue Warning to City Hall," *Chicago Sunday Herald*, March 18, 1916, 1.

164. "Healey Halts Plan to Drop Funkhouser," *Chicago Herald*, March 22, 1916, 7.

165. *Report of the Chicago Motion Picture Commission*, 74.

166. "Seems to Need Investigation" (editorial), *Chicago Herald*, April 26, 1916, 4.

167. "Women Report Immoral Films Shown in City," *Chicago Herald*, February 15, 1916, 1.

168. During February and March 1916, the following films played the city's first-run Loop theaters (all data from listings in the *Chicago Herald*):

Date	Theater	Films
February 6–19, 1916	Colonial	*The Dumb Girl of Portici* starring Anna Pavlowa
February 6–12, 1916	Ziegfeld	*The Upstart, Love's Crossroads,* a Musty Suffer comedy, and a single reel Kleine comedy
February 6–12, 1916	Strand	*Pudden'head Wilson* until 2/6; starting Monday, 2/7, *Nearly a King* with John Barrymore

NOTES TO CHAPTER 5

February 6–12, 1916	Studebaker	*Peggy* until Wednesday, 2/9 then *Hell's Hinges*
February 6–11, 1916	La Salle	Changed its program daily: Monday, *My Lady's Slipper;* Tuesday, *The Other Side the Door;* Wednesday, *The Fruits of Desire;* Thursday, *The Gods of Fate,* Friday, *The Dragon;* Saturday, *The Snow Trail;* and Sunday, *The Upstart*
February 13–19	Ziegfeld	Mary Miles Minter in *Dimples Thou Shalt Not Covet* (Selig) with a Musty Suffer comedy
February 12–March 4	La Salle	*Poor Little Peppina* starring Mary Pickford
February 13–19	Strand	*The Trail of the Lonesome Pine*
February 13–20	Studebaker	Dorothy Gish in *Betty of Greystone* Monday–Wednesday, Thursday to Sunday, TBA
February 19–March 3	Fine Arts	*The Adventures of Kathlyn*--condensed into eight reels
February 20–26	Strand	Blanche Sweet in *The Blacklist*
February 21–26	Studebaker	Bessie Barriscale in *Bullets and Brown Eyes* and the Keystone comedy *Cinders of Love*
February 20–26	Ziegfeld	*The Clarion, The Witch,* and a comedy
February 27–March 4	Ziegfeld	*Kennedy Square, The Soul Market,* and a Musty Suffer comedy
February 27–March 4	Colonial	Triangle program: Lillian Gish in *Daphne and the Pirate,* Fatty and Mabel in *The Bright Lights,* a newsreel, and the western short *The Stampede*
February 28–March 5	Strand	Frederick Ward in *Silas Marner*
March 4–10	Studebaker	*To Have and To Hold*
March 4–10	Fine Arts	German War Pictures sponsored by the German Hungarian Society
March 5–11	Ziegfeld	*For a Woman's Fair Name, The Price of Happiness,* plus a Musty Suffer comedy

March 5–11	Strand	*A Law unto Himself*
March 5–11	La Salle	*Diplomacy*
March 5–11	Colonial	*The Moral Fabric* and the Keystone comedy *Cinders of Love*
March 12–19	Ziegfeld	*Toys of Destiny, The Blindness of Love,* and a Musty Suffer comedy
March 12–19	Colonial	*The Raiders* plus a Keystone
March 12–19	Studebaker	*For the Defense*
March 12–19	La Salle	*Ben Blair*
March 12–19	Strand	*True Nobility*

169. The theaters in question were the Royal, 408 South State; Trocadero, 414 South State; Gem, 450 South State; Omar, 532 South State; National, 608 South State, and the Chicago, 614 South State. "7 State Street Shows Closed by Chief Healey," *Chicago Sunday Herald*, February 20, 1917, 7 (main section, final edition).

170. "Jury Upholds Barring of *Birth* by Censor," *Motion Picture News* 16, no. 4, July 28, 1917, 573.

171. "Chicago's Censor Head Rebuked in Courtroom," *Motion Picture News*, 15, no. 10, March 10, 1017, 1560.

172. "Echo of Censor Criticism by Judge David Heard," *Motion Picture News* 15, no. 11, March 17, 1917, 1709.

173. William J. McGrath, "Funkhouser in Wrong Again," *Motion Picture News* 16, no. 1, July 7, 1917, 106.

174. "Court Reverses Major 'Funkie,' Who Is Twice Sued," *Motion Picture News* 16, no. 11, September 15, 1917, 1799.

175. "Vitagraph Grapples 'Major Funkie,' September 12," *Motion Picture News* 16, no. 12, September 22, 1917, 1979.

176. "Chicago Censor Loses Round with Vitagraph," *Motion Picture News* 16, no. 14, October 6, 1917, 2397. The explanation of Funkhouser's nickname was "based on the incident in *Pickwick Papers* when the judge at the breach of promise trial misunderstood the name of the widow's lawyer and said to him, 'Yes, Mr. Monkey.' 'Not Monkey—Funkie, the lawyer hastened to put in." "Court Reverses Major 'Funkie,' Who Is Twice Sued," *Motion Picture News* 16, no. 11, September 15, 1917, 1799.

177. *Tribune* quoted in "Funkhouser's Ire Aroused and He Fights Back," *Motion Picture News* 16, no. 15, October 13, 1917, 2578; "City Amendment Proposed to Curb Censor's Power," *Motion Picture News* 16, no. 15, October 13, 1917, 2578.

178. "Funkhouser's Ire Aroused and He Fights Back," *Motion Picture News* 16, no. 15, October 13, 1917, 2578; "Funkhouser Appeals to Women for Aid," *Motion Picture News* 16, no. 20, November 17, 1917, 3461.

179. "Fund Raised to Finance Fight on Funkhouser," *Motion Picture News* 16, no. 13, September 29, 1917, 2151.

180. "Censorship Holds Stage in the Windy City Loop," *Motion Picture News* 16, no. 23, December 8, 1917, 4022.

181. "William Fox Gives Special Showing of *Cleopatra*," *Motion Picture News* 16, no. 22, December 1, 1917, 3848.

182. *Report of the Chicago Motion Picture Commission*, 4.

183. Ibid.

184. Ibid., 5.

185. Ibid., 182.

186. Ibid., 59, 182.

187. Ibid., 31–33.

188. Ibid., 16–28, 33.

189. Andrew Higson, *Waving the Flag: Constructing a National Cinema in Britain* (Oxford: Clarendon Press, 1995), 4–5.

Notes to Chapter 6

1. Lissak, *Pluralism and Progressives*, 1.
2. Ibid., 2.
3. Ibid.
4. Linda Williams, *Playing the Race Card: Melodramas of Black and White from Uncle Tom to O. J. Simpson* (Princeton, NJ: Princeton University Press, 2001), 128.
5. Some writers on the topic suggest that *Birth* spurred black filmmakers into action. Valerie Smith considers *Birth* the "inaugural moment of African-American cinema," Larry Richards states that *Birth* shocked the black film industry into being, while Donald Bogle notes it was a catalyst for a number of black artisan films responding to its racist claims. More recent scholarship, in particular the work of Anna Everett and Jacqueline Stewart, refutes these claims, noting that black filmmaking and film criticism predate *Birth*. In the process, they also stress how blackness is not defined solely in relation to white discourses and filmmaking practices, indicating that black filmmaking was an important cultural enterprise in its own right, designed primarily to serve the black community, not just to counter white (racist) discourses. Stewart, *Migrating to the Movies*, 24, 27–28; Anna Everett, *Returning the Gaze: A Genealogy of Black Film Criticism, 1909–1949* (Durham, NC: Duke University Press, 2001), 1, 8, 34–35, 59–106; Valerie Smith, introduction to *Representing Blackness: Issues in Film and Video*, ed. Valerie Smith (New Brunswick, NJ: Rutgers University

Press, 1997), 1; Larry Richards, *African American Films through 1959: A Comprehensive Illustrated Filmography* (Jefferson, NC: McFarland, 1998), 5; Donald Bogle, *Toms, Coons, Mulattoes, Mammies, and Bucks: An Interpretative History of Blacks in American Film*, new 3rd ed. (New York: Continuum, 1994), 101.

6. Williams, *Playing the Race Card*, 111–12.

7. As Everett and Stewart observe, black film criticism, reception, and production need to be examined on their own terms and not just read under the shadow of *The Birth of a Nation*. Doing so risks reducing black film to a response to Griffith and consequently recentering his work for constructions of race and national cinema. Stewart, *Migrating to the Movies*, 119; Everett, *Returning the Gaze*, 8, 34, 57–106.

8. The most important of these are Stewart, *Migrating to the Movies*; Everett, *Returning the Gaze*; and Mary Carbine, "The Finest Outside the Loop: Motion Picture Exhibition in Chicago's Black Metropolis, 1905–1928," *Camera Obscura* 23 (May 1990): 9–41.

9. These very issues of belonging and community values were central to cinema's address, both in terms of textuality and exhibition. As Stewart notes, many early films were addressed primarily to white audiences, dealing with white culture, white bodies/characters, and establishing norms against which black bodies, where seen, could function as an attraction that might stabilize more marginal immigrant forms of identity as white. Stewart, *Migrating to the Movies*, 1–6, 23–90.

10. In Chicago alone, there were a number of well-established black vaudeville booking circuits that placed acts in major houses like McVickers and the Majestic. One of these was the Central Vaudeville Circuit, which, as Gregory Waller notes, served black theaters in Chicago and other midwestern cities. *Mainstreet Amusements: Movies and Commercial Entertainment in a Southern City, 1896–1930* (Washington, DC: Smithsonian Institution Press, 1995), 172. Another was the Theater Owners Booking Association (TOBA) that served black theaters like Chicago's Monogram and Grand, but was white owned and had a reputation for unfair treatment and corruption. Carbine, "The Finest Outside the Loop," 21–22.

11. Stewart, *Migrating to the Movies*, 196–202.

12. Ibid., xix, 100, 105–7, 110–11.

13. Ibid., 108, 151–54.

14. Ibid., 93–113.

15. Howard B. Furer, *Chicago: A Chronological and Documentary History, 1784–1970* (New York: Oceana, 1974), 30, 39–40.

16. "The Test" (editorial), *Chicago Defender* 9, no. 16, April 18, 1914, 8.

17. Ibid.

18. For a more detailed discussion of the New Negro, see Stewart, *Migrating to the Movies*, 36, 194–95.

NOTES TO CHAPTER 6

19. Ibid., 34.
20. Ibid., 122.
21. Ibid., 116–27.
22. Ibid., 2–3, 89, 93, 102–4, 140–44, 148–53.
23. Ibid., 153.
24. Ibid., 131.
25. Ibid., 149.
26. Carbine, "The Finest Outside the Loop," 12.
27. Stewart, *Migrating to the Movies*, 117. The film theaters were the States, Lincoln, Owl, Elba, Fountain, Phoenix, Pickford, Washington, Atlas, Star, and Vendome.
28. Data compiled from the *Chicago Defender* and http://cinematreasures.org/.
29. Stewart, *Migrating to the Movies*, 114–15.
30. Ibid., 127–31.
31. Sylvester Russell, "Musical and Dramatic," *Chicago Defender*, November 5, 1910, n.p.
32. Stewart, *Migrating to the Movies*, 96.
33. Ibid., 97.
34. "Found in the Pictures," *Chicago Defender*, April 8, 1911, n.p.
35. Stewart, *Migrating to the Movies*, 96.
36. Ibid., 94.
37. Everett, *Returning the Gaze*, 36–37, 40–41.
38. Ibid., 40.
39. Sylvester Russell, "Musical and Dramatic: A Quarterly Review," *Chicago Defender*, April 9, 1910, 3.
40. Sylvester Russell, "Musical and Dramatic: Phoenix Theater Does Good Business," *Chicago Defender*, June 10, 1911, n.p.
41. Everett, *Returning the Gaze*, 42. Also see Minnie Adams, "Musical and Dramatic: Information Theatrically," *Chicago Defender*, November 2, 1912, 8. The only time Addams mentioned movies was in October 1911, when she noted that the Phoenix's "pictures are well worth the admission [even] without the music." Minnie Adams, "Musical and Dramatic: The Phoenix," *Chicago Defender*, October 28, 1911, n.p.
42. Tony Langston, "Theatrical Review: The Star Theater," *Chicago Defender* 10, no. 28, July 10, 1915, 6.
43. Stewart, *Migrating to the Movies*, 178.
44. Advertisement for the Phoenix Theater, *Chicago Defender*, June 3, 1911, n.p.
45. T. Langston, "Musical and Dramatic: The Washington," *Chicago Defender*, March 1, 1913, n.p.; T. Langston, "Musical and Dramatic: The Merit," *Chicago Defender*, March 1, 1913, n.p.

46. "Musical and Dramatic," *Chicago Defender*, October 18, 1913, n.p.; "Musical and Dramatic: The Movies," *Chicago Defender*, August 16, 1913, n.p.; "Musical and Dramatic: The State Theater," *Chicago Defender*, July 19, 1913, n.p.; "Musical and Dramatic," *Chicago Defender*, October 25, 1913, n.p.

47. J. Hockley Smiley, "State Street 'The Great White Way,'" *Chicago Defender*, May 11, 1912, 8.

48. "State Street: Its Pains and Pleasures," *Chicago Defender* 9, no. 18, May 2, 1914, 7.

49. Stewart notes, *"Defender* coverage of the States emphasizes its status as a classy establishment, bringing the finest films to Black Belt audiences at reasonable prices." She adds that "the Lincoln and Owl theaters also sought to present themselves as 'high-class' establishments." *Migrating to the Movies*, 176.

50. T. Langston, "Musical and Dramatic: Lux Theater," *Chicago Defender*, March 1, 1913, n.p.; "Screen Houses," *Chicago Defender*, December 22, 1917, n.p.; "The New Owl," *Chicago Defender*, February 3, 1917, n.p.; "Musical and Dramatic: The State Theater," *Chicago Defender*, Saturday, July 19, 1913, n.p.

51. "Atlas Theater Opens: Great Crowds Attend Opening of New Moving Picture House at 47th and State Street," *Chicago Defender* 9, no. 40, October 3, 1914, n.p.

52. Stewart, *Migrating to the Movies*, 182.

53. "Among the Movies," *Chicago Defender*, December 22, 1917, n.p.; "Among the Movies: The Fountain," *Chicago Defender* 11, no. 17, April 29, 1915, 6; "Musical and Dramatic: The Lux," *Chicago Defender*, November 1, 1913, n.p.

54. Sylvester Russell, "Musical and Dramatic: The Phoenix Theatre Shows Good Pictures," *Chicago Defender*, July 8, 1911, n.p.; Sylvester Russell, "Musical and Dramatic: The Phoenix Theater Has Good Houses," *Chicago Defender*, March 18, 1911, n.p.

55. "Among the Movies," *Chicago Defender* 10, no. 33, August 14, 1915, 6. Evidently, "among its patrons are numbered a great many of Chicago's most prominent people of color."

56. "Screen Houses," *Chicago Defender*, December 22, 1917, n.p.

57. Carbine, "The Finest Outside the Loop."

58. "Musical and Dramatic: The States," *Chicago Defender*, August 2, 1913, n.p.; "Musical and Dramatic: The States," *Chicago Defender*, August 9, 1913, n.p.

59. "Theatres, Music and Art, Society and Women's Clubs: The Lincoln," *Chicago Defender* 10, no. 19, May 8, 1915, 6.

60. "Walkin' the Dog," *Chicago Defender* 11, no. 22, May 27, 1916, 6; "Among the Movies," *Chicago Defender*, March 31, 1917, n.p.

61. "Walkin' the Dog," 6; "Among the Movies," n.p.

62. "Among the Movies," *Chicago Defender* 10, no. 34, August 21, 1915, 6; Tony Langston, "Theatrical Review: The Star," *Chicago Defender* 10, no. 35, August 28, 1915, 6.

NOTES TO CHAPTER 6

63. "Musical and Dramatic: New Star Theater," *Chicago Defender*, November 22, 1913, n.p.

64. Ibid.

65. "Musical and Dramatic: The Star," *Chicago Defender*, December 6, 1913, n.p.

66. Tony Langston, "Theatrical Review: The Star Theater," *Chicago Defender* 10, no. 28, July 10, 1915, 6.

67. "Among the Movies," *Chicago Defender* 10, no. 32, August 7, 1915, 6.

68. "Screen Houses," *Chicago Defender*, December 22, 1917, n.p.; Stewart, *Migrating to the Movies*, 183–85. According to Allan H. Spear, the Alabama-born Henry "Teenan" Jones grew up in downstate Illinois and came to Chicago as a drifter in his teens. He then turned to business, establishing a Hyde Park saloon/gambling house in 1895. His enterprises were initially aimed at whites until reformers forced his Lakeside Club out of business and he moved his interests over to South State Street, "where his two . . . saloons, the Elite #1 and the Elite #2, became centers of Negro night life between 1910 and 1915. Like his predecessors [including Mott], he was active in civic and political affairs. He patronized Negro cultural and athletic enterprises and used both his influence and his financial resources to help aspiring Negro politicians." Spear acknowledges his background in gambling and associations with the black underworld but also notes that he had a reputation as a successful entrepreneur, particularly in the local world of black amusement, so his ownership of the Star did not affect the theater's good reputation. Spear, *Black Chicago*, 77.

69. Stewart, *Migrating to the Movies*, 162.

70. "Musical and Dramatic: The Phoenix," *Chicago Defender* 10, no. 3, January 16, 1915, 8.

71. "Additional Dramatic News: New Owl Theater," *Chicago Defender*, January 20, 1917, n.p.

72. "The New Owl," *Chicago Defender*, February 3, 1917, n.p.

73. "Two Years," *Chicago Defender*, June 23, 1917, 4.

74. Sylvester Russell, "Musical and Dramatic: The Development of Actors, Managers, Playwrights and Composers," *Chicago Defender*, September 10, 1910, n.p. Motts's Pekin Theater was founded and run by Robert Motts in 1905, and billed as "the only Negro owned theater in the world," but he died in 1911 and his theater was not under black ownership at this time. After his death, its fate was mixed, with it opening in various guises with intermittent success. Spear, *Black Chicago*, 76–77.

75. Russell, "Musical and Dramatic: The Development of Actors, Managers, Playwrights and Composers," n.p.

76. T. Langston, "Musical and Dramatic: Lux Theater," *Chicago Defender*, March 1, 1913, n.p.

77. Stewart, *Migrating to the Movies*, 119, 151–53.

78. A. D. Smith, *National Identity* (London: Penguin, 1991), 14, cited in Gertjan Dijkink, *National Identity and Geopolitical Visions: Maps of Pride and Pain* (London: Routledge, 1996), 11.

79. Stewart, *Migrating to the Movies*, 151.

80. Frank S. Helton, "Hon E. H. Morris Wins Color-Line Suit against Colonial Theater: Negroes to Have Seats in Any Part of Theaters in Illinois," *Chicago Defender*, June 11, 1910, 1.

81. "American Music Hall Fined $75 for Drawing Color Line," *Chicago Defender*, February 11, 1911, 1.

82. Frank S. Helton, "Hon E. H. Morris Wins Color-Line Suit against Colonial Theater: Negroes to Have Seats in Any Part of Theaters in Illinois," 1.

83. "Abbie Mitchell Refused Seat at the Majestic," *Chicago Defender*, April 26, 1913, 1.

84. "White Man Insults Woman in Merit Theater," *Chicago Defender*, July 19, 1913, 1.

85. Stewart, *Migrating to the Movies*, 151.

86. The Avenue's management claimed that segregation was a condition for a license, a claim that was clearly false. "Avenue Theater Draws Color Line," *Chicago Defender*, September 6, 1913, 1. While suing the management, Hall praised the Grand, the Avenue's nearest rival, suggesting that they might have financed his case.

87. "Avenue Theater Draws Color Line," 1.

88. "Avenue Theater Erases Color Line: You May Now Sit Any Old Where in the House," *Chicago Defender*, September 13, 1913, n.p.

89. "Municipal Court Judge O.K.'s Theater Jim Crow Rule," *Chicago Defender*, October 11, 1913, 1.

90. Ibid.

91. Louella O. Parsons, "Seen on the Screen: Finds *The New Governor* Superior to Stage Version," *Chicago Herald*, May 20, 1915, 8; "The Nigger" (editorial), *Chicago Defender* 10, no. 22, May 29, 1915, 8. The film played for two weeks in the Loop at the Ziegfeld, from May 23 to June 5, 1915.

92. "The Nigger" (editorial), 8.

93. Untitled editorial, *Chicago Defender* 9, no. 9, February 28, 1914, 4.

94. "*Hit the Nigger* New Film Insult," *Chicago Defender* 9, no. 9, February 28, 1914, 1.

95. "More about Chicago Censorship," *Moving Picture World*, March 28, 1914, 1684; Spear, *Black Chicago*, 124.

96. Stewart, *Migrating to the Movies*, 100.

97. Ibid., 101.

98. Ibid., 104.

99. Ibid., 109–10.

100. Everett, *Returning the Gaze*, 59–106.

NOTES TO CHAPTER 6

101. "Musical and Dramatic: *Satan*," *Chicago Defender*, September 20, 1913, n.p.

102. "Musical and Dramatic: The Lux," *Chicago Defender*, November 1, 1913, n.p.

103. Tony Langston, "Theatrical Review," *Chicago Defender*, June 13, 1914, 6.

104. Advertisement for the Fountain, *Chicago Defender*, October 9, 1915, 6; advertisement for the States, *Chicago Defender*, July 1, 1916, 6.

105. Advertisement, *Chicago Defender* 11, no. 3, January 15, 1916, 6.

106. "Teenan Jones," *Chicago Defender* 11, no. 38, September 16, 1916, 4.

107. Advertisement for *Intolerance*, *Chicago Defender*, November 24, 1917, n.p.

108. See, for instance, advertisements in *Chicago Defender*, August 25, 1917, 4.

109. Stewart, *Migrating to the Movies*, 219; Sylvester Russell, "Musical and Dramatic: Phoenix Continues to Draw Well," *Chicago Defender*, August 5, 1911, n.p.

110. T. Langston, "Musical and Dramatic," *Chicago Defender*, March 1, 1913, n.p.; Sylvester Russell, "Musical and Dramatic: The Phoenix Fares Well with Pictures," *Chicago Defender*, July 1, 1911, n.p.; Sylvester Russell, "Musical and Dramatic: Incidental Music with Pictures at the Phoenix," *Chicago Defender*, June 17, 1911, n.p.; Sylvester Russell, "Musical and Dramatic: The Phoenix Theatre Shows Good Pictures," *Chicago Defender*, July 8, 1911, n.p.

111. T. Langston, "Musical and Dramatic: The Washington," *Chicago Defender*, March 1, 1913, n.p.

112. Abel, *Americanizing the Movies*, 107.

113. Stewart, *Migrating to the Movies*, 204, 207–8, 219–23.

114. Abel, *Americanizing the Movies*, 109–12.

115. The Carrizal Incident took place in June 1916, between General Pershing's American troops and the Mexican Army. US troops C and K were at the border looking for General Villa and were ordered to attack the Mexican soldiers anyway. One of the units involved was the African American 10th Cavalry.

116. Stewart, *Migrating to the Movies*, 207.

117. Abel, *Americanizing the Movies*, 112–14.

118. Ibid., 115.

119. Ibid., 116.

120. Ibid., 117.

121. Stewart, *Migrating to the Movies*, 219. Pearl Bowser and Louise Spence, "Oscar Micheaux's *Body and Soul* and the Burden of Representation," *Cinema Journal* 39, no. 3 (2000): 2–5.

122. Shelley Stamp points out this was "the industry's first sustained, deliberate attempt to cultivate (and cater to) female patronage on a national

scale." Richard Abel discusses shifts in the western's popularity with white audiences from summer in 1913. Stamp, *Movie-Struck Girls*, 102. Also see Singer, *Melodrama and Modernity*, 222–24; and Abel, *Americanizing the Movies*, 120–22.

123. Abel, *Americanizing the Movies*, 73–74, 117–19.

124. Tony Langston, "Theatrical Review," *Chicago Defender*, June 13, 1914, 6.

125. Singer, *Melodrama and Modernity*, 202.

126. Ibid., 203.

127. Stamp, *Movie-Struck Girls*, 102.

128. "Film Business Conditions Reported from All Sections: Chicago Outlook Is Sanguine," *Motion Picture News* 16, no. 4, July 28, 1917, 635.

129. "Among the Movies," *Chicago Defender*, January 20, 1917, n.p.

130. "Among the Movies," *Chicago Defender*, January 13 (?), 1917, n.p.

131. "Among the Movies," *Chicago Defender*, May 19, 1917, n.p.

132. While Patria is frequently accompanied by her fiancé Donald Parr, who protects and sometimes rescues her, he does not try to restrict her activities like other suitors in serial films, such as Harry in *The Perils of Pauline*, likely because her adventures served a higher national cause—preparedness.

133. Stamp, *Movie-Struck Girls*, 129.

134. Ibid., 137–40.

135. Patrons may have also appreciated serials' representations of white male villainy, transforming them into expositions of the follies and weaknesses of the ruling classes. Serials about lost inheritances or sudden changes in fortune might also have offered the thrill of seeing the social elite occupying a precarious position, evoking other kinds of social mobility. Still, it is unlikely that these would be dominant readings or the sole interpretations, especially given the prolonged engagement serials demanded, with audiences returning week after week, revealing some sympathy with even elite protagonists.

136. Singer, *Melodrama and Modernity*, 8–9.

137. Ibid., 11. He notes, "With few, if any, exceptions all film serials were sensational melodramas. They covered a range of subgenres (such as detective, western, gothic, patriotic, and working-girl melodramas), but they all concentrated on violence and intense action—abductions, entrapments, brawls, hazardous chase sequences, and last-minute rescues—in narratively stark conflicts between a heroine or hero-heroine team and a villain and his criminal accomplices. Film serials represent an immediately recognizable and iconographically faithful descendent of the 10-20-30 and its literary cousins." Singer, *Melodrama and Modernity*, 198.

138. Ibid., 90.

139. Ibid., 198.

140. "Among the Movies," *Chicago Defender*, May 5, 1917, n.p.

NOTES TO CHAPTER 6

141. "Among the Movies: The States," *Chicago Defender* 11, no. 1, January 1, 1916, 6; "Among the Movies," *Chicago Defender* 11, no. 27, July 1, 1916, 4 (?). "Among the Movies," *Chicago Defender*, January 13, 1917, n.p.

142. Advertisement for the States Theater, *Chicago Defender*, November 24, 1917, n.p.

143. "Screen Houses," *Chicago Defender*, December 22, 1917, n.p.; "The New Owl," *Chicago Defender*, February 3, 1917, n.p.

144. "In April 1916, the *Defender* called her 'the great Theda Bara' as they announced her appearance at the Fountain in *The Two Orphans*." "Among the Movies: The Fountain," *Chicago Defender* 11, no. 17, April 29, 1915, 6; "Among the Movies: The Phoenix," *Chicago Defender* 10, no. 40, October 2, 1915, 6; "Among the Movies," *Chicago Defender*, January 13 (?), 1917, n.p. [this issue is filed under this date in the microfilm copy but evidence suggests it is probably from a few months earlier]. Also see Stewart, *Migrating to the Movies*, 111. Young was so popular that her 1914 film, *Goodness Gracious* (James Young, Vitagraph, 1914), was part of a double bill with *Her Hour* at the States in December 1917. Advertisement for the States Theater, *Chicago Defender*, November 24, 1917, n.p.

145. Stewart, *Migrating to the Movies*, 111.

146. Mae Tinée, *Life Stories of the Movie Stars: Real Facts about the Reel Folks*, vol. 1 (Hamilton, OH: Presto, 1916), 9, 64.

147. Greta de Groat, "America's First Lady of the Screen: The Life and Career of Clara Kimball Young," http://www.stanford.edu/~gdegroat/CKY/cky.htm, accessed September 13, 2008.

148. Bram Dijkstra, *Evil Sisters: The Threat of Female Sexuality and the Cult of Manhood* (New York: Knopf, 1996), 1–17.

149. Early cinema was never all white. Black players were generally cast in marginal roles varying from attractions, as jokes, occasionally as villains, or as servants/slaves. Many early narrative films, including some early features, used the screen to explore difference (whether racial, ethnic, gender, or class difference) as seen in the appeal of Native Americans in western films, the vogue for Selig-style "oriental exotica," as well as immigrant and working-class dramas and narratives of social mobility or physical migration. While these films usually traded in fantasies and stereotypes, they displayed the play with difference that characterized period cinema. Stewart, *Migrating to the Movies*, 1–92.

150. Everett, *Returning the Gaze*, 165.

151. Stewart, *Migrating to the Movies*, 111–13; Bowser and Spence, "Oscar Micheaux's *Body and Soul* and the Burden of Representation," 2–5.

152. Everett, *Returning the Gaze*, 15–18.

153. "Told at Twilight," *Chicago Defender*, April 7, 1917, n.p.

154. "Movie Gleanings," *Chicago Defender* 11, no. 37, September 9, 1916, 4.

"Noble Johnson," The Silents Majority: The Silent Artists Index, 1997, http://www.silentsmajority.com. As of 2012, this site is no longer available. Stewart notes that there is some ambiguity over Johnson's resignation. "Minutes from a Lincoln board meeting indicate that Noble Johnson resigned . . . because the company was not proving profitable. However, George P. Johnson writes elsewhere that Noble was forced to quit Lincoln because owners of theaters catering to Black audiences (particularly Black Belt theaters in Chicago) complained about Johnson's appearance as leading man in Lincoln films, which were drawing Black viewers away from theaters playing Universal films in which he played smaller roles." Stewart, *Migrating to the Movies*, 301n51.

155. "Realization," *Chicago Defender* 11, no. 40, September 30, 1916, 3; "The Lincoln Co.," *Chicago Defender*, January 20, 1917, n.p.

156. As Mark A. Reid points out, the use of a light-skinned hero corresponded "to contemporary black theatrical conventions that gave the more inspirational roles to fair-skinned . . . actors." *Redefining Black Film* (Berkeley: University of California Press, 1993), 10.

157. Stewart, *Migrating to the Movies*, 112–13.

158. Significantly, the front page of the *Defender* reports Oscar Micheaux's 1911 visit to Chicago well before he was a filmmaker, revealing him already to be a black pioneer: "He is the only colored farmer in his country and stands well with the business world of that section, so much so that the United States government has appointed him to an office for that section of the state. He is worth $150,000, all told." "Mr. Oscar Micheaux in City," *Chicago Defender*, April 29, 1911, 1.

159. Pearl Bowser, Louise Spence, and Jacqueline Najuma Stewart all use the same reports that I cite here.

160. Pearl Bowser and Louise Spence, *Writing Himself into History: Oscar Micheaux, His Silent Films and His Audiences* (New Brunswick, NJ: Rutgers University Press, 2000), 98; Stewart, *Migrating to the Movies*, 201–2.

161. Stewart, *Migrating to the Movies*, 193.

162. Bowser and Spence, "Oscar Micheaux's *Body and Soul* and the Burden of Representation," 6.

163. Stewart, *Migrating to the Movies*, 195.

164. Henry Louis Gates Jr., *The Signifying Monkey: A Theory of African-American Literary Criticism* (New York: Oxford University Press, 1988), particularly 3–41, 89–126.

165. "Ebony Films," *Chicago Defender* 11, no. 27, July 1, 1916, 4 (?). Stewart also discusses this article. See *Migrating to the Movies*, 202.

166. "Realization," *Chicago Defender* 11, no. 42, October 14, 1916.

167. Stewart, *Migrating to the Movies*, 202.

168. Ibid., 93.

NOTES TO CHAPTER 6

169. Other than one brief item in the *Motion Picture News*, there are no other traces that Trykay existed.

170. "Trykay Film Company to Make Negro Comedy," *Motion Picture News* 16, no. 13, September 29, 1917, 2145.

171. J. Ronald Green, *Straight Lick: The Cinema of Oscar Micheaux* (Bloomington: Indiana University Press, 2000), 133. One company that received the *Defender*'s ire was Ebony. In July 1916, the *Defender* published a letter from a Mrs. J. H., who complained that two of the company's comedies, *Aladdin Jones*, *Money Talks in Darktown*, and *Two Knights of Vaudeville*, made "an exaggerated display of the disgraceful actions of the lowest element of the race. It was with abject humiliation that myself and many of my friends sat through the scenes of degradation . . . and if they were meant for comedy, the meaning certainly miscarried. When the beastly actions of the degraded of our people are flaunted before our eyes in places of amusement it is high time to protest in the name of common decency."

A similar incident occurred the next year when the Phoenix refused to show *A Natural Born Shooter*, an old film that the *Defender* had previously lambasted that had been retitled. A white Ebony agent was evidently to blame. Rather than the new release they thought they had booked, the film was one of the "low, degrading comedies that was made two years ago, and which featured Bert Murphy and Frank Montgomery."

Ebony was a white-owned company that primarily marketed its all-black comedies as novelties to white audiences. In 1917, they changed management, and there was reportedly some improvement, but their films, like *A Black Sherlock Holmes*, continued to be "very stereotypical." They had an advantage over their black owned and operated rivals as their two-reel slapstick and chase comedies were distributed by the (now waning) General Film Company from 1917 onward, and reviewed in the mainstream trade press, albeit badly: the *Moving Picture World* felt that one title, *Some Baby* (1917), was only fit for "those who do not want to think," while they noted that *Wrong All Around* (1917) had a not entirely dignified comic hero. Stewart suggests that Ebony was perhaps unfairly maligned. She points out the films listed above were not their productions, but titles they purchased from the Historical Feature Film Company, but they sullied the Ebony name perhaps irreparably. In July 1916, Tony Langston defended Ebony, explaining that the films were old and had been dumped after they failed to gain any bookings when released a year earlier (1915). Stewart notes that Luther Pollard, Ebony's only black officer and one of the company's major creative employees, had hoped to build demand for his company's films in the black community without alienating their white clientele and sought to avoid offensive stereotypes. She points out that extant Ebony films seem to conform to Pollard's intentions, despite using stereotypes like Rastus and Sambo Sam, "construct[ing] contemporary scenarios in which to parody Black character types, particularly city dwellers." "Ebony Film Cancelled: Phoenix Theatre Manager Refuses to Use Degrading Movie," *Chicago Defender*, May 12, 1917, n.p. "Ebony Films," *Chicago Defender* 11, no. 27, July 1, 1916, 4 (?); Richards, *African American Films through 1959*, 21; *Moving Picture World*, December 8, 1917, cited in Richards, *African American Films through 1959*, 21. Stewart, *Migrating to the Movies*, 196–97, 201.

172. Most historians consider Foster the father of black film. Stewart notes his first film, *The Railroad Porter*, was "widely regarded as the first film made by an African-American producer." Mark A. Reid considers Foster Film the first African American–run film company, while Larry Richards not only considers him the father of black filmmaking, but even goes as far as calling him the inaugurator of chase comedy—a genre that predates Foster's work by over a decade. Stewart, *Migrating to the Movies*, xvi; Reid, *Redefining Black Film*, 7; Richards, *African American Films through 1959*, 5, 138.

173. Gregory Waller, *Mainstreet Amusements: Movies and Commercial Entertainment in a Southern City, 1896–1930* (Washington, DC: Smithsonian Institution Press, 1995), 162; Bogle, *Toms, Coons, Mulattoes, Mammies, and Bucks*, 101–2; LaVeta Hewlett, "William Foster," http://www.temple.edu/fma/laveta/t12.html. Foster would reenter films with seven 1929 releases. Hewlett, "Black Film Memorabilia Website: William Foster Filmography," www.temple.edu/fma/laveta/t12.html.

174. Jane Gaines, *Fire and Desire: Mixed-Race Movies in the Silent Era* (Chicago: University of Chicago Press, 2001), 95.

175. Lynn Kirby, *Parallel Tracks: The Railroad and Silent Cinema* (Durham, NC: Duke University Press, 1996), 81. Stewart suggests that his firm opened in 1913, the year he started releasing motion pictures, although he was making films before this time. Stewart, *Migrating to the Movies*, 194.

176. Mark A. Reid states that *Porter* debuted at the Grand in July 1917, but according to the *Defender* it premiered at the States in August—they do not mention anything about it playing in July and have Foster's film playing the Grand *after* the States. Reid, *Redefining Black Film*, 7; "Musical and Dramatic: The States Theater," *Chicago Defender*, August 9, 1913, n.p.

177. See Everett's discussion of Foster's self-promotion, in *Returning the Gaze*, 128–29.

178. LaVeta Hewlett's Foster filmography seems to be the most complete. It lists eighteen titles, including works from 1911 that are never referred to in the *Defender*, which lauds *The Railroad Porter* as his first effort. Hewlett lists the following—she does not separate director, producer, or other roles so it is possible that these are not all directed by Foster, although she does include his actuality work. *Birth Mark* (1911), *The Butler* (1911), *The Railroad Porter* (1912), *The Grafter and the Maid* (1913), *The Fall Guy* (1913), *Colored Championship Baseball Game* (1914), *Mother* (1917), *Brother* (1918), *Fool and Fire* (1918), *A Woman's*

NOTES TO CHAPTER 6

Worst Enemy (1918), *Florida Crackers* (1921), *Black Narcissus* (1929), *Dark Town Follies* (1929), *Darktown Blues* (1929), *Fowl Play* (1929), *High Toned* (1929), *Honest Crooks* (1929), *In and Out* (1929).

179. "Foster and Shoecraft Make Movies," *Chicago Defender*, June 21, 1913, 2. The article notes: "Messrs. William Foster and Joe Shoecraft have gone into the moving picture business [sic]. These progressive young men have installed expensive equipments [sic] and intend to supply the public with high class films in an endeavor to offset the malicious ones produced by other companies. Their first endeavor was at the Y.M.C.A. dedication on Sunday. They also took the ball game."

Five weeks later, the *Defender* reported on the first screening of these pictures. "Mr. Foster's moving pictures of the Y.M.C.A. parade were shown to 4,000 people on Thursday evening and will be the attraction every night next week." "Foster's Movies Make Big Hit," *Chicago Defender*, July 26, 1913, n.p.

180. It offered uplifting recreations, classes, and physical exercise, and tried, largely unsuccessfully, to attract recent migrants, hoping to help them adjust to the big city. Stewart, *Migrating to the Movies*, 141, 143, 287–88n78.

181. "Musical and Dramatic: Foster's Movies Make Big Hit," *Chicago Defender*, July 26, 1913, n.p. Hewlett lists these films, however, as 1912 and 1914 productions, highlighting the confusion around his work. Hewlett, "William Foster," www.temple.edu/fma/laveta/t12.html.

182. "Musical and Dramatic: Foster's Movies Make Big Hit," *Chicago Defender*, July 26, 1913, n.p.

183. *Colored Championship Baseball Game* is listed as a 1914 production in both Hewlett and Richards, again suggesting the problems cataloging Foster's work. It is possible he returned to make a second version of this film the next year, although there is no mention of such a title in the *Defender*. Hewlett, www.temple.edu/fma/laveta/t12.html; Richards, *African American Films through 1959*, 39.

184. "Musical and Dramatic: Foster's Movies Make Big Hit," *Chicago Defender*, July 26, 1913, n.p.

185. "Musical and Dramatic: The States Theater," *Chicago Defender*, August 9, 1913, n.p. The black weekly, the *New York Age*, reviewed the film as follows: "The story deals with a young bride who, thinking her husband had gone out on "his fun," invited a fashionably dressed chap, who was a waiter at one of the colored cafes on State Street, to dine. However, the husband did not go out and, upon returning home, found wifey sitting at the table serving the waiter all the delicacies of the season. Mr. Husband proceeds to get his revolver, which he uses very carelessly, running the unwelcome visitor to his home. Then the waiter gets his revolver and returns the compliment. However, nobody is hurt, despite all the shooting and all ends happily" (*New York*

Age, September 25, 1917, cited in Richards, *African-American Films through 1959*, 136–37).

186. Bernard L. Peterson, *The African American Theater Directory, 1816–1960* (Westport, CT: Greenwood, 1997), 111.

187. Susan Curtis, *The First Black Actors on the Great White Way* (Columbia: University of Missouri Press, 2001), 31–32.

188. "Musical and Dramatic: The States Theater," *Chicago Defender*, August 9, 1913, n.p.

189. "Musical and Dramatic: The Grand," *Chicago Defender*, August 23, 1913, n.p.

190. "Musical and Dramatic: The Movies," *Chicago Defender*, August 16, 1913, n.p.; "Musical and Dramatic: Foster's R. R. Porter," *Chicago Defender*, November 22, 1913, n.p.

191. "Among the Movies: The Star," *Chicago Defender*, July 7, 1917, n.p.

192. Stewart, *Migrating to the Movies*, 195.

193. Ibid.

194. Ibid.

195. "Musical and Dramatic: The Stroll," *Chicago Defender*, August 30, 1913, n.p.

196. Peterson, *African American Theater Directory*, 12–13.

197. "Musical and Dramatic: States Theater," *Chicago Defender*, September 20, 1913, n.p. The *Indianapolis Freeman*, cited in Richards, praised it, noting that "the railroad scene, dancing in the hay, and the automobile ride were ample in variety. William Foster now has the best colored photoplays that the market can supply." Richards notes that the Soundies Distributing Corporation distributed this film, not Foster Films unlike its predecessors, although I have not been able to determine any relationship between these two companies. Its cast included Lottie Grady, Jerry Mills, Richard B. Harrison, Judy Moore, Barie Burton-Huyrain and her baby child, Kandy Kids, Burt and Grant, Kid Brown, Kinky Cooper. Again it was produced and directed by William Foster, this time from a script by Jerry Mills and Jesse Shipp. Richards, *African American Films through 1959*, 72.

198. "Musical and Dramatic: States Theater," *Chicago Defender*, October 18, 1913, n.p.

199. "Musical and Dramatic: Foster's R. R. Porter," n.p.

200. Ibid. I cannot find any information about the Soundies Distributing Company. It may have been another concern linked to Foster or possibly another short-lived corporation seeking to fill a hole in the black film market but without the capital to do so effectively.

201. "Foster the Moving Picture Man Returns," *Chicago Defender* 9, no. 25, June 20, 1914, 4.

202. Richards, *African American Films through 1959*, 27, 61, 117, 187.

NOTES TO CHAPTER 6

203. Reid, *Redefining Black Film*, 8.
204. "Foster the Moving Picture Man Returns," *Chicago Defender* 9, no. 25, June 20, 1914, 4.
205. Everett, *Returning the Gaze*, 54, 113–14, 319n9.
206. Stewart, *Migrating to the Movies*, 158–59, 183–85.
207. "Foster Film Co.," *Chicago Defender* 11, no. 31, July 30, 1916, 4.
208. The *Defender* printed Foster's scenario for *The Barber* in its entirety:

> John Willis, society man, has a beautiful wife, who is crazy over Spanish music. He decides to engage a Spanish teacher for her and mentions his intentions while having work done in a barber shop. The barber on chair No. 1 overhears the conversation, disguises himself with a false mustache, white suit and Mexican sombrero, has cards printed reading, "Alfonso Gaston, Spanish music taught," and heads for the Willis home.
>
> On reaching there he sees several beautiful young ladies. He plays a beautiful piece on his mandolin and the girls surround him enthusiastically. He has been shadowed by a friend who had penetrated his disguise, but slams the door in his face on accepting an invitation to enter the Willis home. All the time the barber is talking in broken English. Mr. Willis returns home unexpectedly while joy was at its height. His wife shows him Alfonso's card, telling him she had found a Spanish music master. Mr. Willis, being able to speak Spanish, questioned the musician, but of course, the barber could not understand. Mr. Willis thought the man looked familiar and to confirm his suspicions he smelled his head. The barber looked around for his hat, and the girls, fearing trouble, ran from the house. The barber followed suit. Mr. Willis, throwing his hat and instrument after him, the barber picking them up on the run.
>
> The barber's friend gives him the laugh and the barber stops long enough to break his mandolin on the man's head. Then he dashes into the barber shop with nothing but the neck of the instrument in his hand. The barber's friend swears out a warrant for his arrest. Mr. Willis leaves the city next day and his wife sends the barber an invitation to call, feeling that he had been humiliated. On receiving this note the barber quit working on customers and dressed up again, although the boss tried to stop him. He was in such a rush that instead of paying the messenger he slapped him down and the boy to get even rushed to the depot and told Mr. Willis, who had missed his train, all about it.
>
> The police by this time had the warrant and were looking for the barber. Mrs. Willis greets him with an apology and he is entertaining her when she sees her husband coming. She hides the barber in a clothes press. Mr. Willis believed his wife's denial that the barber was in the house, but the latter couldn't stand the heat in the little clothes press and

came out. Through the window he went and the chase which follows in which the police take part ends in the barber's dive in the lake in which he upsets a boatload of fishermen.

Juli Jones, "The Barber," *Chicago Defender* 11, no. 32, August 5, 1916, n.p.

209. "The Barber," *Chicago Defender*, August 11, 1917, 4; "Among the Movies," *Chicago Defender*, August 11, 1917, 4. His 1917 film, *Mother*, was presumably not released that year in the city, if the date given is even correct.

210. "Screen Houses," *Chicago Defender*, December 22, 1917, n.p.

211. Richards, *African American Films through 1959*, 117.

212. Stewart, *Migrating to the Movies*, 210, 215–16.

213. Ibid., 211.

214. Foster's promotional copy cited in Richards, *African American Films through 1959*, 84.

215. Juli Jones, "Moving Pictures Offer the Greatest Opportunity to the American Negro in History of the Race from Every Point of View," *Chicago Defender* 10, no. 41, October 9, 1915. Also cited in Everett, *Returning the Gaze*, 54.

216. Jones, "Moving Pictures Offer the Greatest Opportunity to the American Negro in History of the Race from Every Point of View," 6.

217. "Foster the Moving Picture Man Returns," *Chicago Defender* 9, no. 25, June 20, 1914, 4.

218. Jones, "Moving Pictures Offer the Greatest Opportunity to the American Negro in History of the Race from Every Point of View," 6.

219. Ibid.

220. Pearl Bowser notes that community photographers were in some sense the true ancestors of black filmmaking, displaying the black community's efforts to represent itself and "establish a group identity." "Pioneers of Black Documentary Film," in *Struggles for Representation: African American Documentary Film and Video*, ed. Phyllis Rautch Klotman and Janet K. Cutler (Bloomington: Indiana University Press, 1999), 2–3.

221. "Peter P. Jones Heads Moving Picture Company," *Chicago Defender* 9, no. 24, June 13, 1914, 6.

222. Everett, *Returning the Gaze*, 113–14. Also see Bowser, "Pioneers of Black Documentary Film," 6.

223. Other players were Ethel Fletcher, Tom Lemonier, Effie Riddley, and Earl Watson. "Peter P. Jones Heads Moving Picture Company," *Chicago Defender* 9, no. 24, June 13, 1914, 6.

224. Everett, *Returning the Gaze*, 115.

225. Larry Richards states the film features "a dress parade, being reviewed by Governor Dunne . . . marching in Cuba during the Spanish-American War; being attacked and later repulsing the enemy on a bridge in Cuba

with 1,000 soldiers engaged in battle; taking a block horse on San Juan Hill; firing cannons; and their victory celebration." *African American Films through 1959*, 62.

226. Cited in Richards, *African American Films through 1959*, 88–89.
227. Richards, *African American Films through 1959*, 31, 124.
228. Ibid., 136.
229. Bowser, "Pioneers of Black Documentary Film," 11–13.
230. Richards, *African American Films through 1959*, 156.
231. Ibid., 155.

Notes to Chapter 7

1. Ideas about the "universal language" myth were widespread, envisioning the movies' popularity could recast their spectacles, drama and affect—even their violence and sexuality—into some greater, semimystical sense of belonging.

2. Lissak, *Pluralism and Progressives*, 2.

3. Ibid., 3–4; Lee Grieveson, "Fighting Films: Race, Morality and the Governing of Cinema, 1912–1915," in Grieveson and Krämer, *Silent Cinema Reader*, 170–78.

4. See, for example, Andrew Higson, *Waving the Flag: Constructing a National Cinema in Britain* (Oxford: Oxford University Press, 1997); Andrew Higson, "The Instability of the National," in *British Cinema: Past and Present*, ed. Andrew Higson and Justine Ashby (London: Routledge, 2000), 35–48; Andrew Higson, "The Concept of National Cinema," in *Film and Nationalism*, ed. Alan Williams (New Brunswick, NJ: Rutgers University Press, 2002), 52–67; Abel, *Americanizing the Movies*; Abel, *Red Rooster Scare*; Richard Abel, Giorgio Bertellini, and Rob King, eds., *Early Cinema and the "National"* (London: John Libbey, 2008); Paul Willemen, *Looks and Frictions: Essays in Cultural Studies and Film Theory* (London: BFI, 1994); Valentina Vitali and Paul Willemen, eds., *Theorising National Cinema* (London: BFI, 2006); Sabine Hake, *German National Cinema* (London: Routledge, 2008), esp. 1–25; Stephen Crofts, "Reconceptualizing National Cinemas," in *Theorizing National Cinema*, ed. Valentina Vitali and Paul Willeman (London: BFI, 2008); Mette Hjort and Scott MacKenzie, *Cinema and Nation* (London: BFI, 2000).

5. Crofts, "Reconceptualizing National Cinemas," in Vitali and Willemen, *Theorising National Cinema*, 44–57.

6. Andrew Higson, "The Limiting Imagination of National Cinema," in Hjort and MacKenzie, *Cinema and Nation*, 63. Also see Philip Schlesinger, "The Sociological Scope of National Cinema," in Hjort and MacKenzie, *Cinema and Nation*, 19–31.

7. Philip Rosen, "History, Textuality, Nation: Kracauer, Burch and Some Problems in the Study of National Cinema," in Vitali and Willemen, *Theorising National Cinema*, 18.

8. Eric Hobsbawm, *Nations and Nationalism since 1780: Programme, Myth, Reality* (Cambridge: Cambridge University Press, 1990), 88–93, 129–33. Also see Benedict Anderson, *Imagined Communities: Reflections on the Origins and Spread of Nationalism* (London: Verso, 1991, 1996), 109–10.

9. Hobsbawm, *Nations and Nationalism since 1780*, 18–23.

10. David A. Gerstner, *Manly Arts: Masculinity and Nation in Early American Cinema* (Durham, NC: Duke University Press, 2006), 66–67, 72–73.

11. "Making Good" (editorial), *Chicago Defender*, November 3, 1917, n.p. Also see Stewart, *Migrating to the Movies*, 210–18.

12. Leslie Midkiff DeBauche, *Reel Patriotism: The Movies and World War I* (Madison: University of Wisconsin Press, 1997), 3–5, 35–41.

13. During summer 1914, only one non-American film played Loop theaters (*Cabiria*), although it was a huge hit, playing eleven weeks at the Illinois (tickets 25¢–$1) then six weeks at the Ziegfeld at 25¢. The other eighteen features were American productions. *Neptune's Daughter* ran the longest (twenty-three weeks at the Fine Arts, a relatively small theater). *The Spoilers* (Colin Campbell, 1914, Selig) was next, running for eleven weeks at the much larger Studebaker. *Traffic in Souls* followed with five weeks at the Princess and two at the Comedy, then *The Christian* with seven weeks at the Olympic and *The Littlest Rebel* with five weeks at the Studebaker. All information from advertisements in the *Chicago Sunday Herald*, June–September 1914.

14. Loop audiences could choose from westerns like *Where the Trail Divides* (James Neill, Jesse Lasky–Paramount, 1914); *Salomy Jane* (Lucius Henderson and William Nigh, California Motion Picture Company–Alco, 1914); and *Rose of the Rancho* (Cecil B. DeMille, Famous Players–Lasky–Paramount, 1914) and small-town Americana like *The County Chairman* (Allan Dwan, Famous Players–Lasky, 1914) and *The Country Mouse* (Hobart Bosworth, Hobart Bosworth Inc.–Paramount, 1914). Although all these productions played for just one week, the emphasis on material of strong national interest is remarkable. During the fall, most of these theaters reverted to the live stage, leaving only two establishments playing films by November—the Studebaker and Fine Arts.

15. As Abel notes, Civil War narratives attempted to reconcile this through offering "romance[s] of reunion" between North and South, often played out literally through the central couple. Here it is played out in another form of family romance—between brothers. Abel, *Americanizing the Movies*, 61–62, 116–17, 141–43, 158–65.

16. Ibid., 163.

NOTES TO CHAPTER 7

17. It would have been familiar to many audiences: before it was a film, it was a best-selling book and a Broadway play (at the Liberty Theater, November 1911–January 1912, then a national tour) starring Dustin Farnum and Mary Miles Minter. It was also loosely based on *Uncle Tom's Cabin*, the most popular novel and then play of its time.

18. Abel, *Americanizing the Movies*, 142, 142–65.

19. "News of Photoplay Houses and Films to Be Seen There," *Chicago Sunday Herald*, August 2, 1914, sec. 2, 4. Quotation slightly altered to fit the syntax.

20. Advertisement, *Chicago Sunday Herald*, July 26, 1914, sec. 2, 3.

21. Advertisement, *Chicago Sunday Herald*, August 2, 1914, sec. 2, 3.

22. Advertisement, *Chicago Sunday Herald*, August 9, 1914, sec. 2, 3.

23. Andrew Kelly, *Cinema and the Great War* (New York: Routledge, 1997), 15.

24. "Universal Backs Wilson in Neutrality," *Motion Picture News* 10, no. 10, September 19, 1914, 57.

25. "National Board Makes Neutrality Move: Asks Exhibitors to Run Captions before War Films, Requesting Spectators to Refrain from Making Any Sympathetic Demonstration," *Motion Picture News* 10, no. 10, September 12, 1914, 28.

26. "In the Picture Playhouses: Reel Facts," *Chicago Herald*, September 25, 1914, 9.

27. "In the Picture Playhouses: Reel Facts," *Chicago Herald*, September 18, 1914, 11.

28. Kelly, *Cinema and the Great War*, 4.

29. Craig W. Campbell, *Reel America and World War I* (Jefferson, NC: McFarland, 1985), 33; Louella O. Parsons, "Seen on the Screen," *Chicago Herald*, November 25, 1915, 10.

30. "What to See This Week in Photoplays," *Chicago Sunday Herald*, June 24, 1917, part 6, 1.

31. "*Herald* war bulletins, *Herald* movies and verbal announcements from the stages of various loop theaters, in conjunction with the regular bills, have served to keep them crowded during the last week." "News of Photoplay Theaters and Films to Be Seen There," *Chicago Sunday Herald*, August 9, 1914, sec. 2, 4.

32. "Herald Adds to Scope of War News Service," *Chicago Herald*, August 5, 1914, 7.

33. Campbell, *Reel America and World War I*, 27.

34. "Herald Adds to Scope of War News Service," 7.

35. In August, they screened four reels of "European War Pictures" alongside the Marguerite Clark feature, *Helene of the North* (J. Searle Dawley, Famous Players–Paramount, 1915).

36. Campbell, *Reel America and World War I*, 27–35.

37. Ibid., 27–28.

38. "In the Picture Playhouses: Crowds Watch War Pictures," *Chicago Sunday Herald*, November 22, 1914, sec. 5, 6.

39. "In the Picture Playhouses: Belgian War Pictures Draw Big Crowds to Studebaker," *Chicago Herald*, November 16, 1914, 12.

40. Campbell, *Reel America and World War I*, 32–33.

41. Other nationalistic shorts toured the Loop, including a documentary series about the departments of the US government, *Uncle Sam at Work* (Henry Savage, Warner-Powers Co.–Universal, 1915), which played the Auditorium for two weeks in April and one week (at the Ziegfeld) in August. It is possible that *Uncle Sam at Work* was shown as a feature—it was a series of one-reel films, but some theaters showed all the episodes at once. Another nationalistic film was the historical drama *The Martyrs of the Alamo* (Christy Cabanne, Fine Arts–Triangle, 1915), which played the Studebaker for a week in October 1915.

42. "Editor of *Staats Zeitung* Replies to *New York Sun*," *Chicago Herald*, February 1, 1915, 2.

43. "Programs at the Moving Picture Theater: Select the Features That Appeal to You," *Chicago Herald*, February 20, 1915, 11.

44. Kelly, *Cinema and the Great War*, 17.

45. Campbell, *Reel America and World War I*, 32–34.

46. Ibid., 36.

47. Kelly, *Cinema and the Great War*, 16.

48. "Germany's Loss on the Lusitania" (editorial), *Chicago Sunday Herald*, May 16, 1915, 6.

49. Louella O. Parsons, "Seen on the Screen," *Chicago Herald*, November 12, 1915, 10; advertisement, *Chicago Sunday Herald*, October 24, 1915, sec. 6, 3. Also see Gerstner, *Manly Arts*, 56–58.

50. The juxtaposition of these films indicates how national identity was splintered according to regional cultures and their different perspectives. The New York–set *Battle Cry of Peace* evoked the European war to remind American viewers of possible threats to domestic security.

51. Louella O. Parsons, "Seen on the Screen," *Chicago Herald*, March 29, 1916, 7; advertisement, *Chicago Sunday Herald*, October 17, 195, sec. 1, 8.

52. Gerstner, *Manly Arts*, 54–60.

53. Kelly, *Cinema and the Great War*, 18.

54. *New York Times* review of *The Battle Cry of Peace*, August 7, 1915, part 8, 3.

55. Ibid.

56. Plot description from period sources and reviews, including Fred's *Variety* review, August 13, 1915, n.p.

57. Campbell, *Reel America and World War I*, 38.

58. *New York Times* review of *The Battle Cry of Peace*, 3.

NOTES TO CHAPTER 7

59. "Thompson Will View Film and Discuss Preparedness," *Chicago Herald*, October 22, 1915, 16 (back page or the "second front page").

60. Kogan and Wendt, *Chicago: A Pictorial History*, 199. In June 1919, for example, he hosted Irish patriot, Eamon De Valeria, and introduced him to the city council as "president of the Irish Republic." Lindberg, *Chicago by Gaslight*, 187. He later "promised to rid the city's schools and public library of British propaganda [and, in 1927] oust[ed] school superintendent William McAndrew for being a 'stool pigeon of King George V.'" Sawyers, *Chicago Sketches*, 161.

61. Gerstner, *Manly Arts*, 55.

62. Louella O. Parsons, "Seen on the Screen," *Chicago Herald*, March 29, 1916, 7.

63. Anthony Slide, *Early American Cinema*, rev. ed. (Metuchen, NJ: Scarecrow, 1994), 207.

64. Campbell, *Reel America and World War I*, 228.

65. Kelly, *Cinema and the Great War*, 18.

66. "Do Chicago Folk Lack Patriotism?" *Chicago Herald*, August 9, 1915, 1.

67. Wilson probably knew about Villa's plans to attack Columbus, but he let him go ahead. By this time, the antiwar, propeace president knew the United States would have to enter the war. He was also up for reelection so he let the raid go ahead, hoping it would heighten patriotism and prowar sentiment. It not only did this, it even increased the number of men signing up for the US armed forces. After all, Villa's attack reminded Americans of the permeability of their boundaries and the need to maintain sufficient military defenses to ensure national peace—the very message at the heart of *The Battle Cry of Peace* and other preparedness discourses. Kelly, *Cinema and the Great War*, 16.

68. Kelly, *Cinema and the Great War*, 16.

69. Louella O. Parsons, "It's Coming!" *Chicago Herald*, March 31, 1916, 8.

70. "*Getting Villa* on View Today," *Chicago Herald*, April 1, 1916, 2.

71. Louella O. Parsons, "Seen on the Screen," *Chicago Herald*, April 3, 1916, 9.

72. "*Getting Villa* Stirs Audience," *Chicago Sunday Herald*, April 2, 1916, 3. Clark was a Pickford-esque star, a very popular symbol of American innocence and grace who only appeared in a few war films in 1918 and 1919. The second most popular female star behind Pickford, Clark was associated with (often historical and usually European) romances and impersonated children. She was one of the biggest fund-raisers for the war effort after the United States entered World War I. As Sue Collins notes, she made a two-day appearance in her hometown of Cincinnati in November 1917 and was credited with more than $14 million in Liberty bond sales. A well-known stage actress before she was a screen favorite, Clark was signed to Famous Players, one of the companies associated with the highest levels of screen art. She also made short films

supporting the war, for which she was not paid. These included *The Biggest and the Littlest Lady in the World* (Liberty Loan Special, Paramount Famous Lasky, 1918) and *A Lesson in Saving Food by Marguerite Clark* (1918). Parsons's reference to Clark thus indicates something of the star's association with a particular articulation of nation that emphasized innocence, duty, and the reasons why men fight, while suggesting something about the level of skill and production values in this locally produced work of nonfiction. Sue Collins, "Emerging Political Authority and Cultural Policy in the Propaganda Campaign of World War I" (PhD diss., New York University, 2008); *Motion Picture News*, November 10, 1917, 3252; *Motion Picture World*, November 10, 1917, 845, 898. Also see DeBauche, *Reel Patriotism*, 115, 119–20; Campbell, *Reel America and World War I*, 89–90, 255.

73. Louella O. Parsons, "Seen on the Screen," *Chicago Herald*, March 29, 1916, 7.

74. "Chicago German Editor Predicts Defeat of U.S.," *Chicago Herald*, April 21, 1916, 3.

75. "Illinois Germans Plead for Peace," *Chicago Herald*, April 26, 1916, 7.

76. "*Twenty Thousand Leagues* Is Shown in Chicago," *Motion Picture News* 14, no. 7, October 28, 1916, 2658.

77. Louella O. Parsons, "Seen on the Screen," *Chicago Herald*, November 30, 1916, 6.

78. Ibid. She added that "Captain F. E. Kleinschmidt, born in Austria but a naturalized American citizen, through his influence in army circles and with the nobility, was enabled [sic] to get these scenes from the vanguard of the German army."

79. Campbell, *Reel America and World War I*, 139n13, 56.

80. *War Brides* played the Studebaker in early December 1916, Vitagraph's *The Girl Phillipa* was at the Ziegfeld in February 1917, *Joan the Woman* played the Colonial in April 1917, and *Womanhood* was at the Ziegfeld, also in April 1917. Advertisement, *Chicago Sunday Herald*, December 3, 1916, part 6, 4; "What's What and Who's Who in the Big Photodrama Theaters This Coming Week," *Chicago Sunday Herald*, February 11, 1917, part 7, 8; "A Display of Acumen," *Motion Picture News* 15, no. 18, May 5, 1917, 2821; advertisement, *Chicago Herald*, April 20, 1917, 7.

81. Campbell, *Reel America and World War I*, 52.

82. The Social Secretary, "Sale of Seats Begins for Showing of War Film," *Chicago Herald*, March 10, 1917, 14; Campbell, *Reel America and World War I*, 56.

83. "Patriotic Display at Showing of *Heroic France*," *Motion Picture News* 15, no. 15, April 14, 1917, 2328.

84. Advertisements, *Chicago Herald*, April 20, 1917, 3.

85. Anthony Slide, ed. and compiler, *Robert Goldstein and "The Spirit of '76"* (Metuchen, NJ: Scarecrow Press, 1993), xv.

86. "Joan of Arc Helps Get Recruits in Chicago," *Motion Picture News* 15, no. 17, April 28, 1917, 2649.

87. According to the *Herald*, "The *Chicago Evening Post* considered the event worthy of an editorial. The *Examiner*, the *Herald* through Richard Henry Little, dramatic editor, and Louella O. Parsons, and the *Tribune* all gave lengthy space to the exhibition." "Chicago Pays $10,000 at Single War Film Showing," *Motion Picture News* 15, no. 19, May 12, 1917, 3004.

88. "Picture Marines Work," *Chicago Herald*, April 19, 1917, 1.

89. "Navy Films to Spur Chicago Recruiting Will Be Shown Every Night during Week in Grant Park as Band Plays," *Chicago Sunday Herald*, April 22, 1917, part 1, 4; "Selig and Kleine Aid Women in Enlisting Efforts," *Motion Picture News* 15, no. 19, May 12, 1917, 3004.

90. "Joan of Arc Helps Get Recruits in Chicago," *Motion Picture News* 15, no. 17, April 28, 1917, 2649.

91. "A Display of Acumen," *Motion Picture News* 15, no. 18, May 5, 1917, 2821.

92. Chicagoan Bryant Washburn was one of Essanay's most popular young stars whose image combined romantic hero and outdoorsman. He appeared in several World War I films with Essanay and later for Artcraft under Cecil B. DeMille.

93. The casting of this film was particularly interesting in the light of later events. As Leslie Midkiff DeBauche notes, in 1918 Washburn was suspected of being a draft dodger, although this turned out to be a false rumor spread by an assistant director at Essanay who resented Washburn and had a crush on his wife. After a Secret Service investigation, he was fully exonerated and received an official apology. In the meantime, a tipster had passed the story on to the *Chicago Tribune*. DeBauche, *Reel Patriotism*, 32–33.

94. "Boom Recruiting with *The Man Who Was Afraid*," *Motion Picture News* 16, no. 2, July 14, 1917, 254.

95. Ibid.; Campbell, *Reel America and World War I*, 62.

96. "Chicago Notes and Comment: Leaks in the Loop," *Motion Picture News* 15, no. 18, May 5, 1917, 2846; advertisement, *Chicago Sunday Herald*, June 17, 1917, part 6, 5; William J. McGrath, "Chicago News and Comment: Leaks in the Loop," *Motion Picture News* 16, no. 1, July 7, 1917, 106.

97. DeBauche, *Reel Patriotism*, 36.

98. Ibid., 35.

99. Ibid., 38.

100. Ibid., 40–41, 45–48.

101. Ibid., 41.

102. "*Do Children Count?* Breaks House Policies," *Motion Picture News* 16, no. 2, July 14, 1917, 239.

103. *Is Marriage Sacred?* (1916–17) was so popular, it was extended twice. "Essanay's February Releases on General Program," *Motion Picture News* 15, no. 6, February 10, 1917, 891; "Added Subjects in Essanay's Marriage Series," *Motion Picture News* 15, no. 7, February 17, 1917, 1057; "New Essanay Series, *Do Children Count?*," *Motion Picture News* 15, no. 9, March 3, 1917, 1399; "*Do Children Count?* Breaks House Policies," *Motion Picture News* 16, no. 2, July 14, 1917, 239.

104. Titles of various installments included *The Guiding Hand* (episode 1), *Steps to Somewhere* (2), *The Wonderful Event* (3), *The Yellow Umbrella* (4), *A Place in the Sun* (5), *Where Is My Mother?* (6), *When Sorrow Weeps* (7), *The Uneven Road* (8), *The Season of Childhood* (9), *The Little White Girl* (10), *The Kingdom of Hope* (12).

105. Advertisement, *Motion Picture News* 16, no. 2, July 14, 1917, 214.

106. Delight Evans, "Bobo's Billie," *Photoplay* 13, no. 1, December 1917, 52.

107. "Essanay Offers Only Light Subjects during War," *Motion Picture News* 15, no. 23, June 9, 1917, 3597.

108. "Make Cheerful Pictures to Counteract War's Tragedy!," *Motion Picture News* 16, no. 10, September 8, 1917, 1629.

109. Ibid.

110. Essanay's George Spoor played a significant role in the war effort, so all his films could effectively be promoted as part of the company's broader patriotic mission. He helped fund Food Director Hoover's food economy campaign and was appointed chairman of the Motion Picture Bureau of Food Administration of Illinois. He produced 200-feet food economy films that were released weekly, providing theaters with six-color posters and paying for newspaper advertising. Addressed primarily at female patrons in neighborhood theaters, these films dealt with such issues as minimizing food waste and cooking with less meat. "Four minute men" accompanied these films, giving four-minute lectures on food economy and the war effort. DeBauche describes how these men were mouthpieces for government policy: to prevent confusion, they all delivered the same message at the same time in movie theaters nationwide. But as she notes, it may not have been confusion that prevented these messages from being heard in Chicago but dissent. "Spoor Organizes Exhibitors in Food Economy," *Motion Picture News* 16, no. 18, November 3, 1917, 3070; DeBauche, *Reel Patriotism*, 80–81.

111. Samantha Barbas, *First Lady of Hollywood: A Biography of Louella O. Parsons* (Berkeley: University of California Press, 2005), 38–39.

112. "At Film Theaters," *Chicago Sunday Herald*, April 29, 1917, part 6, 2.

113. Gordon Seagrove, "'Off Duty' at the Movies," *Photoplay* 13, no. 1, December 1917, 89–90 (all quotes from 90).

114. "The National Anthem in Picture Theatres" (editorial), *Motion Picture News* 16, no. 9, September 1, 1917, 1424.

115. DeBauche, *Reel Patriotism*, 21.

116. L. P., "Is the Future of the Movies Bright or Dark? Here's an Experts Opinion," *Chicago Sunday Herald*, June 10, 1917, part 5, 4.

117. "What's What and Who's Who in the Big Photodrama Theaters This Coming Week," *Chicago Sunday Herald*, April 15, 1917, part 6, 10.

118. "Hot Fight on Censor Who Bars Mary Pickford's Play," *Motion Picture News* 16, no. 3, July 21, 1917, 383; "Our Country versus Funkhouser" (editorial), *Motion Picture News* 16, no. 3, July 21, 1917, 370.

119. DeBauche, *Reel Patriotism*, 61.

120. Funkhouser quoted in Mae Tinée, "Proceeding to Censor the Censor," *Chicago Daily Tribune*, July 3, 1917, cited in DeBauche, *Reel Patriotism*, 63.

121. "Hot Fight on Censor Who Bars Mary Pickford's Play," 383.

122. Ibid.

123. John deBartolo, Review of *The Little American*, The Silents Majority website, http://www.silentsmajority.com, 1997. This website is no longer available as of 2012.

124. "Defenders Rally to Aid *Little American* Movie," *Chicago Herald*, July 14, 1917, 2. The popularity of *The Little American* in nearby cities demonstrated the censor's limited powers. Hundreds of Chicagoans traveled to see the film in Evanston and nearby Hammond, Indiana. Its positive reception in heavily German American Hammond was used to undermine Funkhouser's claims: "If any were offended by the film, no complaint was made by them." DeBauche, *Reel Patriotism*, 64–66; "Row with Censor Did *The Little American* No Harm," *Motion Picture News* 16, no. 7, August 18, 1917, 1120.

125. "Among those who saw the picture, praised it and decried Funkhouser's action in banning it were Paul Shorey, professor of Greek at the University of Chicago; Bishop Samuel Fallows, Mrs. Benjamin Carpenter, Mrs. A. C. Tenney, Miss Florence Temple, Alderman George Iliff and others." William J. McGrath, "Educators at Variance with Censor—He Remains Firm," *Motion Picture News* 16, no. 4, July 28, 1917, 580.

126. "Our Country versus Funkhouser" (editorial), *Motion Picture News* 16, no. 3, July 21, 1917, 370.

127. As the *Motion Picture News* noted, "All the papers in the United States carried stories about the 'Funkhouser Problem,'" "Row with Censor Did *The Little American* No Harm," *Motion Picture News* 16, no. 7, August 18, 1917, 1120. Shortly after the case was resolved in Artcraft's favor, the *News* opined: "Major Funkhouser's ridiculously frequent rulings affect the distribution of films in Chicago only. It therefore often happens that the interdicted pictures are being shown nightly to thousands of people in all the towns around Chicago, while Major Funkhouser is vainly charging at windmills in an attempt to prove

that the films would be harmful to Chicago morals" ("Court Reverses Major 'Funkie,' Who Is Twice Sued," *Motion Picture News* 16, no. 11, September 15, 1917, 1799).

128. Funkhouser cited in William J. McGrath, "Chicago Courts Overrule Censor on Pickford Film," *Motion Picture News* 16, no. 6, August 11, 1917, 1006.

129. "Funkhouser Again Opines That Film Morals Are Punk," *Motion Picture News* 16, no. 21, November 24, 1917, 3653.

130. William J. McGrath, "Chicago Courts Overrule Censor on Pickford Film," *Motion Picture News* 16, no. 6, August 11, 1917, 1006; "Row with Censor Did *The Little American* No Harm," *Motion Picture News* 16, no. 7, August 18, 1917, 1120.

131. "Notes of the Screen," *Chicago Herald*, August 6, 1917, 12.

132. "Have You $100 to Throw Away?" *Motion Picture News* 10, no. 15, October 17, 1914, 17.

133. Louella O. Parsons, "Big Picture Men Ready for Sacrifices If War Comes," *Chicago Sunday Herald*, February 11, 1917, part 7, 2.

134. Ibid.

135. "Chicago News and Comment: Patriotism among Film Manufacturers," *Motion Picture News* 15, no. 8, February 24, 1917, 1219.

136. Parsons, "Big Picture Men Ready for Sacrifices If War Comes," 2.

137. "Film Advertising Men Unite to 'Mobilize the Movies': Publicity and Advertising Managers Join Hands in Broad Campaign for Recruiting in Case of War—Screen, Poster, Newspaper Cooperation—President Wilson Notified—Corporations Express Their Willingness to Help," *Motion Picture News* 15, no. 13, March 31, 1917, 1993.

138. "'Our Boys at the Front' to Be Supplied with Cigarettes," *Motion Picture News* 16, no. 9, September 1, 1917, 1426.

139. Ibid.

140. "Red Cross to Distribute Smokes in American Training Camps," *Motion Picture News* 16, no. 12, September 22, 1917, 1978; "What to Do with Cigarettes and Pennies," *Motion Picture News* 16, no. 12, September 22, 1917, 1979.

141. "Mutual Releases Tobacco Film in Chicago," *Motion Picture News* 16, no. 22, December 1, 1917, 3848.

142. "Film Business Conditions Reported from All Sections: Chicago Outlook Is Sanguine," *Motion Picture News* 16, no. 4, July 28, 1917, 635.

143. Ibid.

144. "American Exhibitors Face Big Problems in War Crisis," *Motion Picture News* 15, no. 19, May 12, 1917, 2967.

145. "Theatre Men in Arms against Proposed War Tax," *Motion Picture News* 15, no. 18, May 5, 1917, 2844.

146. "All Chicago Exhibitors May Close Their Theatres," *Motion Picture News* 15, no. 22, June 2, 1917, 3421.

NOTES TO CHAPTER 7

147. William J. McGrath, "Picture Taxation Change to be Fought Out," *Motion Picture News* 15, no. 22, June 2, 1917, 3449.

148. "Higher Theater License Opposed by 'Movie' Men," *Chicago Herald*, June 2, 1917, 12 (back page).

149. William J. McGrath, "Planned Revision of Theatre Taxes Worries Exhibitors," *Motion Picture News* 15, no. 25, June 23, 1917, 3938. They suspended a decision until January 1918, but announced that they would be increasing theater taxes because the city needed the revenue (they wanted to gross $100,000, up from the current $84,000). Until then, all theaters charging under twenty cents admission would have to pay $200 per year, infuriating small exhibitors—those with 300- to 1,000-seat theaters. More protests and negotiations ensued, irritating the city council, which took steps to clamp down on exhibitors. By mid-September, the city had refused to renew licenses for twenty-four theaters, which the police finally closed. In one case, police entered the Little Majestic at 14 Division Street during a crowded performance, forced the audience to leave, turned out lights, and locked the doors. Manager Pedorr then had to return admissions to all patrons, with the city blaming the exhibitor for not renewing his license—even though Pedorr had paid the $100 fee two days earlier. A city clerk had refused his money, telling him to pay after the license had been approved. Evidently, all exhibitors whose theaters had been closed had had similar experiences. "New Tax Schedule Drawn Up—Exhibitors Protest," *Motion Picture News* 15, no. 26, June 30, 1917, 4099; "Shelve License Revision Plan," *Motion Picture News* 16, no. 2, July 14, 1917, 227.

150. "Washington Wants Facts" (editorial), *Motion Picture News* 15, no. 24, June 16, 1917, 3739.

151. "What the New War Tax Bill Means to You," *Motion Picture News* 16, no. 16, October 20, 1917, 2705.

152. "Tax to Collect over Fifty-Three Million from Pictures," *Motion Picture News* 16, no. 16, October 20, 1917, 2705.

153. "Exhibitors Protest at the Revenue on Admission Charge," *Motion Picture News* 16, no. 16, October 20, 1917, 2704.

154. "Second *Motion Picture News* Chart of National Film Trade Conditions," *Motion Picture News* 11, no. 10, March 13, 1915, 32–33. As early as October 1911, the *MPW*'s James McQuade noted that while the costs of film services, film rental, and theater operation had increased substantially since 1908, admissions were still pegged at five cents in Chicago (and New York City), while in smaller towns, ten cents had become the norm—higher on the West Coast. Even then, he warned: "Such a policy means retrogression." James S. McQuade, "Chicago Letter," *Moving Picture World* 10, no. 4, October 28, 1911, 281.

155. James S. McQuade, "Chicago League Annual Dutch Lunch," *Moving Picture World* 11, no. 8, February 24, 1912, 662.

156. "Why This Difference at the 'Movies'?" *Chicago Defender* 9, no. 49, December 5, 1914, 7.

157. William A. Johnston, "The Tax and Higher Admissions" (editor's letter), *Motion Picture News* 16, no. 16, October 20, 1917, 2702.

158. Ibid.

159. William A. Johnston "The Seventy Per Cent Man" (editorial), *Motion Picture News* 16, no. 19, November 10, 1917, 3240.

160. "War Tax and Operating Costs Boost Many More Admissions," *Motion Picture News* 16, no. 16, October 20, 1917, 2703.

161. Ibid.

162. "Varying Reports from Firing Line on First Effects of Tax," *Motion Picture News* 16, no. 20, November 17, 1917, 3420.

163. Johnston, "The Seventy Per Cent Man," 3240.

164. "The Reader Has His Say," *Motion Picture News* 16, no. 19, November 10, 1917, 3241.

165. "Some Questions Answered in Brief," *Motion Picture News* 16, no. 19, November 10, 1917, 3243.

166. "Chicago Exhibitors Divided on Exhibition Tax," *Motion Picture News* 16, no. 18, November 3, 1917, 3072.

167. William A. Johnston, "Watch Your Step" (editorial), *Motion Picture News* 16, no. 21, November 24, 1917, 3589.

168. "Chicago Public Meets Tax in Agreeable Mood," *Motion Picture News* 16, no. 21, November 24, 1917, 3592–93.

169. "Chicago Exhibitors Vary on Effect of Tax," *Motion Picture News* 16, no. 23, December 8, 1917, 3966.

170. Ibid.

171. "Come Through! It's Up to You—Do Your Bit, Movie Fan!" *Photoplay* 13, no. 3, February 1918, 37.

172. William J. McGrath, "Leaks in the Loop," *Motion Picture News* 16, no. 19, November 10, 1917, 3302.

173. Louella O. Parsons, "Seen on the Screen," *Chicago Sunday Herald*, September 23, 1917, part 6, 10.

174. "Aaron Jones Optimistic over the Coming Year," *Motion Picture News* 16, no. 21, November 24, 1917, 3652.

175. "Chicago Notes and Comment: Leaks in the Loop," *Motion Picture News* 15, no. 18, May 5, 1917, 2846.

Notes to Conclusion

1. Neil A. Wynn, *From Progressivism to Prosperity: World War I and American Society* (New York: Holmes and Meier, 1987), xvi–xvii.

2. Ibid., xx.

3. Jennifer Bean, "Introduction: Stardom in the 1910s," in *Flickers of Desire: Movie Stars of the 1910s*, ed. Jennifer Bean (New Brunswick, NJ: Rutgers University Press, 2011), 13–15.

4. Lea Jacobs, *The Decline of Sentimental: American Film in the 1920s* (Berkeley: University of California Press, 2008).

INDEX

Abbott, Edith, 18
Abel, Richard, 16, 103, 129, 180, 228, 229, 230, 255, 259, 311n54, 387n15
Ablschlager, Walter W., 343n55
Academy of Music theater, Chicago, 135
Addams, Jane, 40, 47, 97, 171, 180, 189, 307n75
Addams, Kate, 191
Addams, Minnie, 217, 372n41
adult-only films, popularity with black audiences, 234
Adult Ordinance of 1914, 352n169
advertising, film, 10
African American Chicago. *See* black community, Chicago
Alcazar theater, Chicago, 125, 164
Alhambra theater, Chicago, 135
allegories, 254; in films that aspired to national cinema, 52; and multiple diegesis films, 80–83, 87–88
Allen, Robert C., 17
Allison, May, 111
Altenloh, Emilie, 308n9
America, 259
American exceptionalism, 206, 228, 257, 261
American Fund for the French Wounded, 274
"the American Idea," 206
Americanization movements, 7
American Music Hall, Chicago, 223
amusement districts, Chicago, 3, 135
Amusement Protection League, 196

amusements, commercial, 8, 11
Anderson, "Broncho" Billy, 55
Anderson, Robert, 224
Arizona, 220
Aronson, Michael, 306n68
Artcraft, 280
Ascher, Max, 290
Ascher, Nathan, 150, 284
Ascher Brothers, 148, 150, 151, 284
Associated Motion Picture Advertisers, 285
athletic leagues, 8
Atlas Theater, Chicago, 214, 218, 232, 234
audience study, 11
avant-garde cinema, 45, 88
Avenue Theater, Chicago, 144, 224

Balaban and Katz Theater Corporation, 131, 148
Balides, Constance, 10
Ball, Charles B., 136
Bambi, 120
Bandbox theater, Chicago, 155, 157
Bara, Theda, 203, 234, 236–37, 378n144
The Barber, 247–48, 384n208
Bartlett, Adolphus, 305n67
Battle Cry of Peace, 389n41
The Battle Cry of Peace, 52, 80, 204, 227, 253, 254, 259, 263, 266–69, 270
Battle of Celaya, 271
Bayne, Beverly, 126
Beale, Mrs. W. G., 274
Bean, Jennifer, 15, 51, 104, 112

INDEX

"Beauty and Brains" star-search contest, 23n1, 93–94, 330n75
Beban, George, 67, 75
Beery, Wallace, 119
Behan, George, 75
Belasco, David, 46
Belgian War Pictures, 265
Bell, J. T., 249
Bell, John, 145
Bell, Marshall, 249
Bell Theater, Chicago, 145
Be Neutral, 262
Benjamin, Walter, 87
Bernhardt, Sarah, 112
Beware of Strangers, 56
big business, curbing of, 5
Bijou Dream theater, Chicago, 135, 154
Billboard, 42
Binet, Alfred, 39–40
Biograph, 237
Birmington, Katherine A., 193
The Birth of a Nation, 48, 162, 170, 201, 204, 225, 227, 234, 254, 267, 347n123; response of black community to, 207–8
Bishop, Seth, 36
Bison-101, 229
black actors, in mainstream films, 238–39, 378n149
Black Cat magazine, 55
black civil rights, centrality of military service to, 248
black comedies, insider parodies and laughter of recognition, 240–41
black community, Chicago: concentration on South Side, 211–12; concerns of Progressive Era, 208; concerns related to migrants from south, 209, 212; full citizenship as primary concern, 208; military contributions erased in all-white history, 258; popularity of cinema, 217–18; population in 1914, 211
black elites: favored middle-class values of uplift and propriety, 212–13; low social standing of cinema among, 216; participation in social reform, 213

black film audiences: and all-black seating areas, 226; craving for black stars, 237; dangers of attending films in white areas, 222; interest in feature films, 227–28; interest in longer films, 220; preference for sensational dramas and adult-only films, 234–36; preference for serials and sensation, 231–36; preference for westerns, 228–31; and race films, 242; reaction to racist films, 225–26; readings that challenged dominant white culture, 226; responses to *The Birth of a Nation*, 207–8; reworked white films into black culture, 209–10, 211; sharing of information about welcoming theaters, 225; sought access to theaters throughout city, 210–11; and stardom, 236–39; and white vision of nation, 205
black filmmaking, 24, 239–43; all films lost, 239; and *Birth of a Nation*, 370n5, 371n7; centered in Chicago, 210; and community photographers, 385n220; connections with black newspapers, 243; early comedies, 240–41; films as important social statements, 240; limited funding and distribution, 210; marginal and rare, 209; newsreel/actuality/documentary, 241; stereotypical black comedies, 241; used to assert black citizenship, 209
black films, stereotype-filled productions for white audiences, 210, 242–43, 380n171
Black Narcissus, 381n178
black press: bias against cinema as white form, 215; critique of cultural practices that confirmed white stereotypes, 212; drama as preferred film genre, 240; on importance of access to all types of entertainment for full citizenship, 222; interest in movies as texts, 227; opposition to comedy when used by black filmmakers, 241

black theaters, Chicago, 8, 213–22, *214–15*, 219; all-black staff, 220–21; black projectionists, 221; diverse identities, 219–20; exhibition and promotional strategies used in, 24; located in Chicago's Black Belt, 213; located in South State Street area, 213; promotions, 219; refuge from exclusion and discrimination, 218–19; role of music, 219. *See also* Stroll

Blackton, J. Stuart, 266, 267, 268, 269, 329n65

black vaudeville and musical comedy, 210, 371n10; stereotypical portrayal of blacks in white productions, 237–38

Blackwell, Carlyle, 126

Blanchard, Mrs. Guy, 200

Block, James, 356n58

Block, Samuel, 193

Block v. the City of Chicago, 179–80, 183, 356n58

Bob Cole's All Star Stock Company, 246

Bogle, Donald, 370n5

Boissevain, Inez Milholland, 97, 104, 327n38

Books Made to Balance, 122

Boorstein, Daniel, 102

Bordwell, David, 14

Boston theater, Chicago, 163, 164

Bosworth, Hobart, 74

Bow, Clara, 102

Bowen, Louise de Koven, 20, 97, 184, 192, 194, 200, 307n75

Bowles, George, 270

Bowles, J., 142, 143

Bowser, Eileen, 57, 66, 160, 320n37

Bowser, Pearl, 231, 240, 385n220

Boynton, M. P., 202

Brady, Alice, 126

Brady, William A., 93, 191

Brantlinger, Patrick, 32, 309n13

Braudy, Leo, 102

Breckenridge, Sophonisba P., 18, 200

Brewster, Ben, 51, 57, 78, 321n46

Brill, Lesley, 48

The British Tanks at the Battle of Ancre, 263

Britton, Gertrude Howe, 192, 194, 307n75

Broncho Billy Pictures, 228, 229

Brother, 247, 248, 249

Brown, Kid, 244, 383n197

Brownie camera, 98

Burkhardt, William, 199

Burnett, Frances Hodgson, 89

Burnham, Daniel, 7, 165–66, 337n15

Burnstein, Daniel Eli, 8

Burt and Grant, 383n197

Burton-Huyrain, Marie, 383n197

Bush, W. Stephen, 304n61

Bushman, Francis X., 126

Busse, Fred A., 171, 173, 175–85, 182

Buszek, Maria, 94

Butler, Nathaniel, 305n67

C. L. Chester Company, 271

Cabanne, Christy, 271

Cabiria, 156, 253, 348n129, 387n13

Calhoun, William, 68

Callaghan, J. F., 182

Camille, 235

Campbell, Craig W., 264

Canfield, Mary Cass, 328n46

The Caravan, 238

Carbine, Mary, 24, 209, 213, 219

Carey, Archibald J., 193, 225

Carmen, 161, 321n45, 347n112

Carnegie, Andrew, 104, 327n38

Carrizal Incident, 229, 376n115

Carson, Daniel, 68

The Case of Becky, 46

Cashman, Dennis, 7

Casino theater, Chicago, 163

Castle, Vernon and Irene, 326n37

Cattle Thieves of 62, 228

celebrity: aspiring to, 111–16; association with leisure and consumption, 329n65; emphasis on distinctive individuals, 102–3; films about, 96; and self-awareness, 127–29; and separation of accomplishment from renown, 102–3; and social mobility, 102; and transcending cultural boundaries, 100;

INDEX

celebrity (continued)
  and upward mobility, 102; vs. stardom, 99–100, 101
celebrity culture, 22, 50, 67, 92; and cultural narcissism, 127; and fascination with private lives of famous, 102; in Progressive Era, 94–95, 96, 98–104, 127
celebrity profile, 99
censorship, of films, 5, 9; and association of films with crime, 36–37, 38, 205; and authority of cinema to address matters of political significance, 169–70, 204, 353n7; and defining of cinema as important cultural institution, 174; demands for with emergence of features and multireel films, 41; Progressive Era phenomenon, 12, 171. See also Chicago film censorship
Central Vaudeville Circuit, 371n10
Chambers, John Whiteclay, II, 3, 4–5, 7, 299n8
character, concept based on self-mastery, 103
The Cheat, use of prologue to introduce principal characters, 69, 71–72, 321n45
Chicago: center of urban reform, 17; Class IV zoning restrictions, 137; crime wave of 1906-1907, 174; most Progressive of all American cities, 17–18; pro-German/anti-British sentiments during World War I, 25, 258, 273, 291–92; public works program, 18; rapid development, 18
Chicago City Club, 175, 352n3
Chicago City Plan of 1909, 7, 165, 337n15
Chicago Commons Settlement, 18
Chicago Daily Tribune, anticinema editorial, 177–78
Chicago Defender: concern about respectability of commercial amusements, 213; coverage of cinema, 213; coverage of the States Theater, 373n49; on Foster, 246, 247; on The Grafter, 246; on higher theater prices in black theaters, 288; and issue of citizenship in relation to cinema, 208, 223; on Jones, 250; praise for employment practices of black theaters, 220–21; protest of theater segregation, 222–23, 224; reticence of entertainment writers to discuss cinema, 217; story set in movie theater, 216–17; on Theda Bara, 378n144; troubled by black audiences' liking for comedies with negative black stereotypes, 241
Chicago Examiner, anti-cinema, 172, 188
Chicago film censorship, 19, 169–73; concern about effect of cinema on children, 175; history of, 173–75; Morals Court, 185, 189, 203, 359n72; most punitive regime (1913-1917), 171, 172–73, 187–98 (See also Funkhouser, M. L. C.); as political issue, 205; and urban clean-up campaigns, 173–74, 175, 200; Vice Commission, 12n57, 185, 186, 198–99, 312n57
Chicago film censorship (1907-1911, Busse), 19, 23–24, 173, 175–85; attacks on foreign films, 180–81; Busse's appointment of moderate figures to censorship board, 182; censorship board as part of uplift program, 178; challenge from National Board of Censorship of Motion Pictures, 183; initial support from film industry, 170–71, 172, 180; legal challenges to censorship, 179–80; licensing of theaters, 136–39; mandatory censorship of all films, 179; reformers' complains of laxity, 180; regulations on nickelodeons, 135–37, 176, 177; sermons against cinema by clergy, 181–82; support for American film, 172; theater surveillance by police, 176–77
Chicago film censorship (1911-1915, Harrison): Adult Ordinance of 1914, 352n169; all films censored from perspective of child, 194; appointment of Funkhouser as second deputy,

189–98; censorship board under jurisdiction of Morals Court, 185, 189, 203; censorship of classics, 197; Funkhouser appointees to board, 191–94; legal challenges to, 195, 197, 198; punitive censorship out of touch with public perceptions, 187–88, 190–91; second deputy of police as head of board, 188; severely punitive censorship code, 187–88; undercover "raids" of theaters, 196. *See also* Funkhouser, M. L. C.

Chicago film censorship (1915-1923, Thompson), 173; censorship out of touch with community standards, 204; censorship removed from Morals Court and police jurisdiction, 203–4; challenges to, 198–204; Thompson's investigation of city's censorship, 199; verdicts of censorship board on war films, 274

Chicago Herald: and cinema, 20, 171; editorial on *Lusitania*, 267; ridicule of film censorship process under Funkhouser, 195

Chicago Herald star-search contests, 96, 107; decrease in movie coverage after contests, 125; designed to sell subscriptions, 116; nationwide beauty contest sponsored by Universal, 120; "People's Movie Star Contest," 120–25; "Sue" contest, 117–20, 122

Chicago Historical Society, 20

Chicago Motion Picture Exhibitors' Association, 139

Chicago Motion Picture Theater Owners' Association, 290

Chicago Movie Exposition of 1917, star-search contest, 125–27

Chicago Political Equity League, 200

Chicago press: among most hostile to cinema in nation, 178; pro-German war films, 258; used Villa films to deflect sentiments away from Germany, 272

Chicago Sunday Herald, 157

Chicago theaters: and conflicting definitions of national identity in wartime, 25; daily attendance in 1914, 35; discrimination against African Americans, 22, 211, 223–25; disrespect of national anthem in war years, 270–71, 279; downtown theaters, 153–58, 348n129; entertainment district theaters, 162–68, 351n156; ethnic theaters, 166–67; first-run Loop houses, 23; licensing fees, 340n32; neighborhood theaters (*See* neighborhood theaters, Chicago); number of theaters in 1910, 35; racist films, 225; and self-presentation and self-display, 324n63; theater chains, 23, 147–53

Chicago Tribune: anti-cinema campaign, 172, 174, 175, 176, 181, 188; and Chicago's censorship board, 171; ridicule of film censorship process under Funkhouser, 195

Chicago Women's Club, 152

child care, in neighborhood theaters, 143

Children in the House, 89; multiple diegesis, 79; unobtrusive narration, 86–87

Childs, Robert W., 364n125

Chinese Exclusion Act, 255

cinema, 1907-1917, 302n50; adaptations of literary and dramatic texts, 313n7; and celebrity discourse, 96; community-centered neighborhood theater, 2; distinctive aesthetic properties, 2; emergence as national form, 208, 253–58, 282, 387n14; expanded the medium but did not introduce a new standard, 13; formal characteristics of, 22; and heightened identification with stars, 104; influenced by ideal of uplift, 12; influence of modernity, 14; linking of community appeal of cinema to citizenship and national identity, 24; and modern American national ideal, 207; as national cinema, 253–58;

403

INDEX

cinema (continued)
  non-inclusive vision of nation, 207; and Progressivism, 1, 2, 3–4, 10–12, 12–16, 21; relation to crowd consciousness, 27; universal language, 254; vehicle for thinking about staging of self, 95
cinema in Chicago, 16–26. See also Chicago theaters
cinema of attraction, 2–3, 41, 86; devices associated with, 70, 75; and Progressivism, 3
City Beautiful Movement, 7, 355n31
Civilization, 85, 87, 88, 204, 253
Civil War anniversary films, 226, 294
Civil War films, 258, 259–60, 387n15; used to comment on WWI, 261
Clark, Marguerite, 111, 204, 354n22, 390n72
Clark Theater, Chicago, 141
Classic, 113
Class IV zoning restrictions, Chicago, 137
clean-up campaigns, Chicago: and film censorship, 173–74, 175; launched by women's groups in 1916, 200
Cleopatra, 52, 203
clergy, Chicago: sermons against cinema, 181–82; use of cinema to increase congregations, 356n53
closed diegesis, 49
close-up (CU), 71
Cocks, Orrin G., 183
Cole, Bob, All Star Stock Company, 246
Coles, Bell, 244
Colgate, 120
Collier, John, 183
Collins, Sue, 390n72
Colonial theater, Chicago, 161–62, 223
The Colored Championship Base Ball Game, 244, 381n178, 382n183
Colored Soldiers Fighting in Mexico, 250
Columbia theater, Chicago, 135
Comedy theater, Chicago, 156
The Coming of Columbus, 161, 253
community, 47–49; association with uplift, 4, 5, 8; emphasis of film industry on, 2; as panacea for dangers of urban life, 8; social ideal of Progressive culture, 4, 5, 8, 28, 47–48, 65. See also neighborhood theaters, Chicago
Comte, Auguste, 33
Condon, Mabel, 189
Conor, Liz, 101
consumer economy, 10
Continental Theater Corporation, 151
Cooper, Kinky, 383n197
Cort theater, New York, 68
Cottage Grove Theater, Chicago, 138
cowboy girl westerns, 231
The Cowboy Millionaire, 228
Creel, George, 280–81, 296
crime, association of films with, 36–37, 38, 205
The Crimson Stain Mystery (series), 46, 232
Criterion theater, Chicago, 135
Crofts, Stephen, 255
Cronon, William, 337n15
Crosman, Henrietta, 109
crowd psychology, linked to hypnotism and psychological regression, 21
crowd theory, 11, 21; application to film audiences, baseball attendees, and customers of cheap amusements, 29–30; and association of films with crime, 36–37; feature films more suggestive and hypnotic than earlier cinema, 41; influence on film regulatory discourses and exhibition practices, 26, 28, 30; pseudoscientific accounts of changed subjectivity, 32; and spectatorship as collective social and psychic phenomena, 27–28, 30, 31–42; suggestion theory, 30; widely accepted response to modernity, 28
Cunard, Grace, 120

Daily Calumet, 20
Damaged Goods, 234
Damon and Pythias, 156
Dana, Viola, 126

404

INDEX

Daniels, Hubert, 136
Dankowski, John S., 193
Darktown Blues, 381n178
The Darktown Fire Brigade, 242–43
Dark Town Follies, 381n178
Daughter of the Gods, 52
Daughters of the American Revolution, 152
The Dawn of Truth, 251
Dean, Jack, 126
Dean, Julia, 109
DeBauche, Leslie Midkiff, 277, 280, 392n93
Deerfield-Shields High School, 275
Delano, Frederic, 305n67
De Luxe staging, 44, 67, 153, 158–62, 167, 168, 348n132
DeMille, Cecil B., 161, 321n45
depth staging, 58–59
Dewey, John, 18, 47
Diall, Gideon H.: *The Psychology of the Aggregate Mind of an Audience*, 12
The Diamond from the Sky (series), 232
dictagraph, 60, 61
Dictaphone, 60
Dimples, 200
Diner, Steven J., 3, 8
discrimination, in Chicago entertainment venues, 22, 223–24
Ditrichstein, Leo, 109
Divine, E. C., 162
Do Children Count?, 55–56, 277–78
Donaldson, Frank D., 223
Donnelley, Thomas, 305n67
Dooley, J., 241
The Double Cross (series), 232
Doubleday and Sons, 120
Downey (Chicago building commissioner), 136
downtown theaters, Chicago, 153–58, 348n129; less amenable than neighborhood theaters to feature films, 51, 157–58; size, 154
Drexel Theater, Chicago, 150
Du Bois, W. E. B., 249
Dunbar, Olivia, 40–41, 41, 44

E. T. Welch Grape Juice Company, 120
Easterly Theater, Chicago, 151
Eaton, Walter Prichard, 134
Eberts, Fred, 270
Ebony Company, 241, 380n171
Edeson, Robert, 109
Edison, Thomas, 100
educational reform, 7
Edwards, Richard Henry, 38, 134
Elba Theater, Chicago, 214
Ellison, Edgar, 244
Eltinge, Julian, 109, 110
entertainment district theaters, Chicago, 162–68, *165*, 351n156; adult-only pictures, 167; catered to thrill-seekers, 167; objects of reformers' attention, 164; short film programs, 167; South Halsted entertainment district, 162, 164–67; South State Street theaters, 164; West Madison Street theaters, 163–164; working-class, ethnic, and immigrant audiences, 163
The Escape, scientific filmed prologue, 68
Essanay, 17, 22, 52, 55, 277–78, 284; Black Cat features, 55, 56; films of local interest, 117; joined with First Illinois Regiment for recruitment drive, 276; partnered with *Herald* on star-search contests, 117; production of comedy during wartime, 278–79; superfeatures, 56; use of brands to market short features, 56; war films, 56
ethnic theaters, 166–67
Ettleson (Chicago city counsel), 198, 199
Evening American: attacks on cinema, 188; and Chicago's censorship board, 171
Everett, Anna, 209, 215, 226, 247, 370n5
Ewart, C. T., 361n98
exchanges: replaced excised footage in prints for out-of-town exhibition, 183; "Wisconsin Copies," 196
exhibition, 15, 22–23; influence of crowd theory on, 26, 28, 30; strategies of, and spectatorial self-awareness, 92; strategies used in black theaters, 24

INDEX

extras, 113
The Eyes of the World, 291

Fagin, Pete, 124, 125
Fairbanks, Douglas, 103, 219, 317n27
fallen woman films, 231
Faller, Sigmund, 290
The Fall Guy, 246
Famous Players Film Company, 196, 280, 390n72
fan magazines, 93, 101, 111, 112, 113, 329n65
Farrar, Geraldine, 80, 104, 347n112
fashion, calls for restrictions on in Chicago, 189, 361n98
feature, meaning of as headlining attraction in diverse program, 55
feature films (ca. 1909-1913), 53–56
feature films (1913-1917), 50; coexisted with shorts for at least four years (1912-1916), 15, 16; considered by critics to be more suggestive and hypnotic than earlier cinema, 41; depth staging, 58–59; did not displace but added to range of cinema, 51; and differentiation, 51; formal self-awareness, 66; formal strategies of, 57–59; four reels as industry standard for, 303n53; less popular in downtown first-run theaters than in neighborhood theaters, 51, 157–58; limited rate of film survival, 52; on matters of national interest, 259; and overseeing gaze, 59–66; repeated set-ups, 58; textual features, 51, 90, 91; tiers, 54
feminine subjectivity, increasingly visual, 101. *See also* women
feminism, and self-actualization, 106
Feuer, Jane, 77, 78
Field, Christine, 193
Fighting for France, 270
Film D'Art, 43
film industry, 1907-1917: alignment with Progressive values, 2, 9, 172; attempts to limit stars' salaries, 96; deglamorized stardom to retain power over business, 112–13; efforts to hire stage stars, 326n37; endorsed Wilson's neutrality policy, 262; focus on short films, 15, 52; informal regulatory efforts, 170; initial acceptance of Chicago's censorship regime, 170–71, 172, 180; marketed itself as American, 128–29; opposition to oppressive censorship, 172, 191; problems caused by fans' desire for screen fame, 113. *See also* World War I, and film industry
film service, 15–16, 53
Film Service Association, 355n41
film survival, low rates of, 69
film theory, contemporary, 31
Fine Arts theater, Chicago, 132, 151–52, 152, 156, 158
Five and Ten Cent Theaters: Two Investigations (Bowen), 20
five-reel film, 53, 54
The Flag Didn't Rise, 228
Florida Crackers, 381n178
Following the Flag in Mexico, 271
Fool and Fire, 247, 248
A Fool There Was, 62, 69, 71; prologue, 68
Foraan, Mrs. David R., 274
foreign films, 335n131; attacks on by American censors, 180–81
Foreman, Milton J., 272
Formes, Carl, 74
For the Honor of the 8th Illinois Regiment, 250
Fortnightly Club, 152
Foster, William, 24, 220, 234, 239, 382n179, 383n197; actualities films, 243–44; balance of uplift and comedy, 241; *The Barber,* 247–48, 384n208; *Black Narcissus,* 381n178; *Brother,* 247, 248, 249; *The Colored Championship Base Ball Game,* 244, 381n178, 382n183; *Darktown Blues,* 381n178; *Dark Town Follies,* 381n178; *The Fall Guy,* 247; as father of black films, 381n172; fictional world, 245–46; fiction films shot in Chicago Black Metropolis, 244; film of YMCA commemoration,

244; filmography, 381n178; films focused on black middle-class, 240; *Florida Crackers*, 381n178; *Fool and Fire*, 247, 248; *Fowl Play*, 381n178; *The Grafter and the Maid*, 247; *High Toned*, 381n178; *Honest Crooks*, 381n178; loss of all films by, 243; manager of Star Theater, 247; *Mother*, 247, 248; "Moving Pictures Offer the Greatest Opportunity to the Race," 248–49; *In and Out*, 381n178; *The Railroad Porter*, 243, 244–46, 381n172, 381n176; self-distributed films, 247; ties with *Chicago Defender*, 243; *A Woman's Worst Enemy*, 247, 248; writings for the black press, 247

Foster Film Company, 24, 242

Foster Photoplay Company, 210, 243–49

Fountain Theater, Chicago, 214, 219; adults-only films, 234

Fowler, Catherine, 78, 89

Fowl Play, 381n178

Fox, William, 203

Franke, Julius E., 289

Frankfurt School, 32, 49, 91

Franklin Theater, Chicago, 214

Freeman, Mrs. Halsted, 274

Freud, Sigmund, 28, 47

Freund, Ernst, 305n67

Funkhouser, M. L. C., 172, 173, 179, 189–98, 257, 365n142, 369n176, 394n127; appointees to censorship board, 191–94; belief in rigorous policing and prosecution of wrongdoing, 189–90; campaign against popular culture and fashion, 189; censorship of *The Little American*, 280–83; demise of, 198–204; inability to distinguish between classic films and exploitation, 197; popular with conservative reformers, 190; punitive film censorship out of touch with public perceptions, 190–91; undercover "raids" of theaters, 196

Gail, Jane, 60

Gaines, Al, 220

Gamson, Joshua, 102, 326n27

Gassaway, Gordon, 330n70, 330n71

Gates, Henry Louis, 241

Gault, Robert, 305n67

General Film Company (GFC), 53, 117, 196, 380n171; Special Feature Service, 54; *War Series*, 156

German heritage, and American identity, 257

German-language publications, Chicago, 257, 265

German war propaganda, 263

Gerstner, David A., 257, 267

Getting Villa, 271, 390n72

Ghosts, 74

The Girl from Frisco (series), 232

The Girl Philippa, 80, 274

A Girl's Folly, 111

Gish, Dorothy, 58

Gish, Lillian, 80

Glenn, Susan A., 100, 101

Globe Theater, Chicago, 161

Gold Rooster brand film, 238

Goldwyn, 53

Gorky, the Dragon, 195

Grady, Lottie, 244–45, 246, 383n197

The Grafter and the Maid, 244, 246

Grandin, Ethel, 46, 60

Grand Theater, Chicago, 214

Grau, Robert, 18–19, 147

Gray, John, 305n67

Great Fire of 1871, Chicago, 337n15

Great Migration, 211

The Great Secret (series), 232

The Green Cloak, 46

Gregg, Katherine, 37

Grieveson, Lee, 19, 29, 37, 39, 105, 170, 174, 178, 183, 301n35, 327n40, 353n7

Griffith, D. W., 5, 48, 51, 58, 68, 85, 122

Guggenheim, Eli, 201

Gunning, Tom, 15, 77, 86, 302n50

H. & H. Film Service, 195

Haag, Jack, 155

Hackett, Francis, 41, 44–45

Hake, Sabine, 255

INDEX

Hall, Luther, 224
Halsted Street Institutional Church Settlement, 165
Hamburger, Alfred, 130, 146, 147–53, 156, 158, 284, 342n46; admission discounts, 152; application of neighborhood theater strategies to downtown, 152; concern for audience tastes, 153; Hamburger theaters, Chicago, *149–50*
Hamlin theater, Chicago, 139–40, 143
Hansen, Miriam, 44, 49, 86, 229–30; analysis of *Intolerance*, 83–85, 86, 87; discussion of allegory, 87–88; discussion of feature films, 90–91
Harper, William, 305n67
Harris, Abraham, 305n67
Harrison, Carter, III, 24, 172, 173, 184, 198, 331n78, 365n146; hostility toward cinema, 186; vice crusader, 187. *See also* Chicago film censorship (1911-1915, Harrison)
Harrison, Louis Reeves, 57
Harrison, Mrs. Carter, 117
Harrison, Richard B., 383n197
Hart, William S., 219
Haymarket theater, Chicago, 135, 139
The Hazards of Helen, 233
Healey (Chicago police chief), 198, 199, 200
Heckman, Wallace, 305n67
Heffron, T. N., 54
Hell's Hinges, 321n45
Helming, Oscar C., 356n53
Henderson, Charles, 305n67
Herald Movies, 118, 263
Herald's German War Pictures, 265, 266
Herald War Movies, 265
Her Hour, 235
Heroic France: The Allies in Action, 274, 275
The Hero of Submarine D-2, 272
Her Temptation, 46
Hewlett, LaVeta, 381n178, 382n181
Higashi, Sumiko, 321n45
High Toned, 381n178
Higson, Andrew, 205, 255, 256

Hinckley, William, 79
Hitler, Adolph, 32
Hoben, Allan, 18, 170, 305n67, 361n98
Hodgson, John H., 146
Hodkins, W., 160
Hoffman, Maximillian A., 118
Hofstadter, Richard, 3, 6
Hollywood musical, 78
Holmes, Taylor, 56
Holt, Anna, 247
The Holy Land, 160
Home, Sweet Home, 51, 69, 83; allegory, 88; epilogue, 80; multiple diegesis, 78, 79
The Homesteader, 246
Home Theater, collapse of, 341n39
Honest Crooks, 381n178
Hopp, Joseph, 196
Horner, Henry, 139
Horowitz, Tony, 259
Hotchkiss, William, 305n67
housing conditions, 7, 166, 357n69
Howard, George Elliott, 37–39
Howard, June, 5
How Molly Made Good, 96, 328n51, 328n52; discourse on female professionalism, 108; showing of famous stars in their homes, 109
Hull House, 18, 165, 178
Hunsaker, Ogden K., 242
Hurley, E. F., 242
Hutchinson, Charles, 305n67
Hyde Park, 211
hypnosis: comparison with suggestive force of movies on audiences, 36, 38, 45; feature film plots dealing with, 45–46; used in comedies, 46
Hypocrites, allegory structured around multiple diegesis, 81–83

Igle, Harry, 199
Illinois, civil rights ordinance, 222
Illinois Federation of Women's Clubs, 135
Illinois Staats Zeitung, 265
Illinois Theater, Chicago, 156
immigrants, 128; campaigns to limit, 255; and entertainment district theaters of

INDEX

Chicago, 163; and national identity, 7, 206; Progressive assimilationist interventions, 7, 209, 254; and western films, 229
Immigrants Protective League, 305n67
Immigration Restriction League, 255
In and Out, 381n178
incense, burned during early feature films, 44, 84, 92
Independent films, 350n146
Infidelity, 46
The Inner Mind, 45
International Handkerchief Company, 120
Inter-Ocean, 178
interracial marriage, efforts to prevent, 255
Intolerance, 51, 204, 228, 254; and allegory, 85, 87; multiple diegesis, 78, 83–85; obtrusive narration, 86; parallelism, 86; publicity, 85
investigative journalism, 7
Iola theater, Chicago, 139
Is Marriage Sacred?, 55, 278, 393n103
The Italian, prologue, 75

Jacobson, Louis F., 202
Jacoby, "P.A.", 148
The James Boys in Missouri, 356n58
Jefferson theater, Chicago, 141
Jesselson, Max, 290
Joan the Woman, 274, 275–76, 278, 279, 321n45, 391n80; multiple diegesis, 78–79, 88; political allegory, 80–81, 85; scenes of World War I, 88; use of display, 86
Johnson, George, 241, 379n154
Johnson, Jack, 255
Johnson, Julian, 129
Johnson, Noble, 229, 238–39, 241, 379n154
Johnson, William A., 288–89
Jones, Aaron J., 147, 148, 284, 290
Jones, Henry "Teenan," 220, 228, 247, 374n68
Jones, Linick and Schaefer (JLS), 147, 148, 154, 162, 275, 284, 286, 291
Jones, Peter P., 24–25, 241, 248, 249–52

Jordan, Edwin O., 305n67
Jordan, Joe, and Pekin Orchestra, 219
Judson, Harry, 305n67
juvenile delinquency, 357n69
Juvenile Protective Association, 20, 165, 170, 174, 178, 184, 200, 305n67

Kalem, 52
Kandy Kids, 383n197
Karr, Mrs. G. F., 193
Kedzie Annex, Chicago, 141
Keil, Charlie, 1, 10, 12, 13–14, 301n32; *Early American Cinema in Transition*, 58, 302n40, 318n31
Kellerman, Annette, 152, 326n37
Kelly, Howard, 247
Kenney, F. R., 275, 278
Kenyon, Doris, 126
KESE (Kleine Edison Selig Essanay), 54, 55
Kimball Young, Clara, 234, 236
Kincaid—Gambler, 238
kinematographic grocery, 146–47
King, Mollie, 75
King Kong, 238
Kingsley, Sherman C., 174, 176, 177
Kirby, Lynn, 243
Kirk, Florence B., 193
The Kiss of Judas, 43
Klafter, David Saul, 341n39
Kleine, George, 52, 56, 175, 275
Knickerbocker, New York, 160
Kodak, 98
Kohlsaat, Herman, 305n67
Kolker, Henry, 109

Ladies' World, 120
The Lady from the Sea, 238
The Lady of the Snows, 117
Laemmle, Carl, 126, 264
Laemmle Film Service, 196
Lafayette Theater, New York, 243
Lakeside Classified, 20
Landauer, Mrs. Herman, 192
Langley Hippodrome, 150
Langston, Tony, 217, 219, 220, 221

INDEX

Lasky, 2
The Lass of the Lumberlands (series), 232
Lay Down Your Arms, 262–63
Lears, Jackson, 3
Le Bon, Gustave: *The Crowd: A Study of Popular Mind*, 21, 28–30, 33, 34, 39; influence on period social thought, 32–33, 34
Lee, Gerald Stanley: *Crowds: A Moving-Picture of Democracy*, 28, 31, 48
Lee, Lois, 323n1, 330n75
Lee, Mildred, 323n1, 330n75
leisure: association of celebrity with, 329n65; association of personality with, 103–4; disassociation from religious and secular holidays, 133; importance of in Progressive Era, 8, 10, 23, 133, 326n28, 336n9; public, 10; rise and expansion of, 3
leisure professionals, 336n9
Lenn, Elsa, 124
Les Misérables, 155, 253
Levée, Chicago, 174, 189, 337n15
Levinsky's Holiday, 225
Liberty Bonds, 296
Liberty (series), 232
Lieutenant Saring, 195
The Life of General Villa, 271
Life of Villa, 271
lighting, on screen during early feature films, 84, 92, 312n60
Lillison, Edgar, 247
Lincoln Jubilee celebration, 250
Lincoln Motion Picture Company, 238, 248
Lincoln Theater, Chicago, 214, 218, 227, 232, 373n49
Linder, Max, 125
Lindsay, Vachel: *The Art of the Moving Picture*, 31, 48, 85
Lindsey, Ben B., 37, 104, 327n38
Linick, Adolph, 147
Lissak, Rivka Shpak, 4, 47, 299n8
Literary Digest, 36
literary naturalism, 5
The Little American, 170, 197, 234, 259, 278; banning of in Chicago, 280–83;

394n124, 394n125, 394n127; prologue, 69, 71
The Little Girl Next Door, 198–99
The Little Princess, 89–90
The Littlest Rebel, 258, 259–61, 387n13
Loeb, Eva, 193
Loew-Victor Company, 118
Lola, 236
long shot (LS), 71
Loop theaters, Chicago, 23, 56, 153–54, 154–55, 159, 347n123; films played during February and March 1916, 367n168; high-end screenings, 155–57; two categories of first-run theaters, 158
Louise Amusement Company, 150
Love Aflame, 238
The Love Girl, 46
Low, Minnie, 192
Lubliner, H., 284
Lubliner and Trinz, 148, 290
Lucille Love: The Girl of Mystery, 231
Lusitania, 266
Lux Theater, Chicago, 218, 219, 227
Lyric theater, Chicago, 154, 155, 160, 162
Lyric theater, Minneapolis, 160

Macbeth, censorship of, 180–81
MacKay, Charles, 33
MacLane, Mary, 97, 328n46; *Men Who Have Made Love to Me*, 105–6; *The Story of Mary MacLane*, 105
Maeterlinck, Maurice, 188
The Magic Veil, 195
Majestic Theater, Chicago, 223, 371n10
Manhattan Madness, 317n27
manifest destiny, 206, 228
Mann Act, 255
Mantle, Burns, 109
The Man Who Was Afraid, 56, 276
Marlowe theater, Chicago, 135
Marsh, Mae, 111, 122, 126
Marshall, Matt, 250
Marshall, P. David, 28
The Martyrs of the Alamo, 389n41
mass culture: and homogeneity, 32; and self-made individual, 103

mass media, and celebrity culture, 99
mass psychology, 311n49
mattes, 86
Max Wants a Divorce, 125
May, Lary, 9–10
McAlister, Little Mary, 56, 278
McChesney, Alice, 122
McCormick, Mrs. L. Hamilton, 274
McCormicks, 172
McDonald, Alexander, 176, 177, 180
McDonald, Jack F., 322n50
McDonnell, John C., 340n37
McDowell, Claire, 238
McLane, Mary, 56
McQuade, James S., 106, 188, 312n60, 341n39, 342n46, 396n154
McVeagh, Franklin, 305n67
McVicker's Theater, Chicago, 68, 371n10
McWeeny (Chicago police chief), 224
Mead, George H., 18, 305n67
medium long shot (MLS), 58
medium shot (MS), 71
Meeker, Mrs. Arthur, 274
Mendel Beilis, 195
Men Who Have Made Love to Me, 56, 96, 105–6
The Merchant of Venice, 197
Merit Theater, Chicago, 214, 218; attack on black patron by white projectionist, 223–24; western films, 228
Merriam, Charles Edward, 18, 199, 305n67
Merriweather, Albert W., 223
Mersereau, Violet, 126–27
Metz, Christian, 86
Micheaux, Oscar, 229, 240, 246, 379n158
Miller, H. C., 163
Mills, Jerry, 246, 383n197
minstrel make-up, 238
Minter, Mary Miles, 200, 204
The Miracle, 188
Mitchell, Abbie, 223
modernist movements, post-World War I, 45
modernity, and early cinema, 14, 25
modernity thesis, 14
Moir, Harry, Jr., 125, 163

Monarch Theater, Chicago, 224
Monroe, Day, 304n63
Montgomery, Frank, 380n171
Moore, George, 290
Moore, Judy, 383n197
Morals Court, Chicago, 185, 189, 203, 359n72
Morse theaters, Rogers Park, Chicago, 142–43
Morville, Guy, 350n146
Mother, 247, 248
Motion Picture Bureau of Food Administration of Illinois, 393n110
Motion Picture Classic, 101
Motion Picture Exhibitors' League of America, 125–27
Motion Picture News, 17, 232, 285
Motion Picture Supplement, 329n65
Motion Picture World, 42, 136
Motography, 17, 196
Motts, Robert, 374n74
Mound Bayon, Mississippi, 251
Moving Picture World, 3–4, 20, 45, 46, 57, 116, 144–45, 163, 184, 286–87, 380n171
muckraking journalism, 7
Mueller, Paul, 272
multiple diegesis, 21, 22, 51–52, 53, 57, 77–90; and allegory, 80–83, 87–88; combination of old and new, 86; construction of separate narrative worlds existing independently within a single film, 78; devices used in cinema of attraction, 86; and idea of film as universal language, 85; juxtaposition of different temporalities, fantasies, and allegories, 51, 78–80; knowledge of narrator and spectators greater than that of characters, 87; portmanteau films, 78; pragmatic use of, 89; in prologues and epilogues, 51, 70, 73–74, 78; shift between different registers of reception, 84; use of in minor ways, 79; use of one- or two-reel film within feature, 89; *The Wishing Ring*, 73
Munson, Audrey, 104

INDEX

Münsterberg, Hugo: *The Photoplay: A Psychological Study*, 9, 12, 31, 85
Murphy, Ben, 380n171
Murray, Mae, 326n37
Musser, Charles, 306n69
Mutual Film Corporation, 2, 183, 195, 196, 285
Mutual v. Ohio, 170, 195
Myers, Johnston, 356n53
The Mystery of the Double Cross, prologue, 75–76

narrative films, and shifts in spectatorship, 27, 255
narrative frames, 73, 78
National Board of Censorship of Motion Pictures (later the National Board of Review), 183
National Board of Review, 9
national cinema, 253–58. *See also* cinema, 1907-1917
National German-American Alliance, 272
national identity: and City Beautiful movement, 355n31; divided according to regional cultures, 389n50; immigrants, and anxieties over, 7, 206; impact of World War I on, 257–58; linking of cinema to, 24; in Progressive Era, 106, 206, 253; and stardom, 129
National Security League, 266
Native Americans, ambivalent position of in films, 229, 378n149
A Natural Born Gambler, 237–38
The Ne'er Do Well, 152
Negro League Championship, 244
Negro Soldiers Fighting for Uncle Sam, 250
neighborhood theaters, Chicago, 8, 22–23, 134, 139–47, 342n46; architecture, 343n55; audience interaction, 131, 140; child care, 143; and cinema as respectable form of entertainment, 48; civic duties of, 23; as community oriented recreation, 2, 132, 140–41, 144, 335n1; decor, 141, 142, 344n61; dominant form of exhibition from 1907-1917, 11, 130–31, 167–68; *versus* entertainment district theaters, 167; exhibitors' involvement in community events, 145–47; idealized private sphere, 131, 132–33, 134, 143–44; kinematographic grocery, 146–47; names and characteristics of as of October 1914, *141–42*; patriotic appeals during WWI, 258; patrons, 133–34; patrons' reluctance to pay more than a nickel, 138; textually inscribed model of spectatorship, 133
Neptune's Daughter, 52, 151, 152, 348n129, 387n13
Nesbit, Evelyn, 104–5, 327n38, 327n40
The New Governor, 153, 225
New Negro, 212, 216
newsreels and documentaries, World War I, 263–66
New Star Theater, Chicago's only black-owned and operated movie theater, 219–20
New York, 202
New York, and early cinema, 17
New York Age, 382n185
nickelodeons, 17, 306n68, 339n30; in Chicago, 19, 23; Pittsburgh's claims as birthplace of, 18; regulations on between 1907 and 1911 in Chicago, 135–37, 176, 177
Night Riders, 356n58
Northwestern Military and Naval Academy, Lake Geneva, Wisconsin, 274–75
Northwestern University, 305n67

Oak Park Theater, Chicago, 146
O'Connor, Jeremiah, 187, 188–89, 361n93
O'Donnell, Charles E., 182–83
Official British War Films, 275
O'Hara Vice Commission. *See* Vice Commission, Chicago
Old Heidelberg, 58
Olerich, Henry: *A Cityless and Countryless World: An Outline of Practical Co-Operative Individualism*, 309n18
Olympic Theater, 263

412

one-reel film, 15
On the Fighting Lines with the Germans, 269–70
open booking, 54, 315n6
opening credit montage sequences, 67
Orchestra Hall, Chicago, 156, 157, 160
Orpheum theater, Chicago, 154
Osbourne, Baby Marie, 204, 238
Our Boys at Camp Grant, 285
Our Boys in France Tobacco Fund, Motion Picture Division, 285
Our Mutual Girl, 147, 327n38
Our Mutual Girl's Magazine, 147
overseeing gaze, 56, 57, 59–66
oversight, 22, 50, 106; and dissolution of privacy and role of family in urban space, 62; and performance, 64; and power, 65–66; in Progressive Era, 57, 60, 69–70, 171; and realignment of public and private, 171; and structuring of serials, 319n33
Owl Theater, Chicago, 214, 218, 219, 236, 373n49

pacifist films, 262–63
Palette, Eugene, 79
The Panama Exposition, 197
Panorama Theater, Chicago, 151
Paramount, 53
paranoia, 65–66
Park, Robert, 34–36, 40, 311n49
Parsons, Louella, 141, 157, 199, 269, 284, 348n129; on Alfred Hamburger, 148; on *The Battle Cry of Peace,* 269; on the Colonial Theater, 161, 162; on *Joan the Woman,* 279; on "People's Movie Star Contest," 122, 123, 124; on "Sue" contest, 119; on Villa films, 272; on *War on Three Fronts,* 273
The Passion Play, 160
Pastime theater, Chicago, 56, 125, 163
Pathé, 180, 202, 335n131, 355n41, 356n43
Patria (series), 232–33, 319n33
Pavlova, Anna, 104
Peiss, Kathy, 17
Pekin Stock Company, 246, 250

Pekin Theater, Chicago, 218, 374n74
The Penalty of Treason (series), 232
Pennington, Ann, 326n37
People's Institute, 183
Peple, Edward, 259
Perfection Pictures, 56
The Perils of Pauline, 319n33
personality: association with leisure and performance, 103–4; culture of, 8
Peter P. Jones Photoplay Company, 210, 242, 249–52; *Colored Soliders Fighting in Mexico,* 250; *The Dawn of Truth,* 251; filming of Lincoln Jubilee celebration, 250; *For the Honor of the 8th Illinois Regiment,* 250; *Negro Soldiers Fighting for Uncle Sam,* 250; origin in comedy, 250; *Progress of a Negro,* 251; *Re-Birth of a Nation,* 250; serious films about black history, culture, and military accomplishments, 249, 250–52; *The Slacker,* 251; *The Slaver,* 251; *The Troubles of Sambo and Dinah,* 250
Phoenix Theater, Chicago, 214, 217, 218, 219, 234; adults-only films, 234; Broncho Billy Pictures, 228; employment of blacks in senior positions, 220; feature of western films, 228
photographs, printed as postcards, 325n15
photography: and erosion of public and private, 98; and self-staging, 97–98
photo machines, in movie theaters, 94
Photoplay, 17, 101, 110, 111, 112–13, 279, 291, 320n36; "Beauty and Brains" star-search contest, 23n1, 93–94, 330n75
Photoplay Company, 24–25
Pickford, Jack, 74, 204
Pickford, Mary, 89, 103, 197, 200, 281, 323n72, 354n22
Pickford Theater, Chicago, 215, 219; adults-only films, 234; song and dance contests, 219
picture palaces, 301n32
Pierce, Carl, 280–81
Pittsburgh, claim as birthplace of nickelodeon, 18, 306n68

INDEX

Playground and Recreation Association of America, 336n9
The Playground (journal), 9, 336n9
Plimpton, Horace, 132
Poe, Edgar Allan: "The Man of the Crowd," 309n18
Pollard, Luther, 380n171
Ponce de Leon, Charles, 100
Poor Little Peppina, 200
popular culture theory, 21
portmanteau films, 51, 78, 79–80
Power, Tyrone, 54
Powers, John W., 181–82
precinema, 3
preparedness movement, World War I, 266–71
President Theater, Chicago, 150, 151
prestige pictures, 24, 55, 67
Prichard, Walter, 35
Princess theater, Chicago, 156
print media, and film audiences, 11–12
The Prisoner of Zenda, 320n37
professional sports, 3
Progressive Era: association between oversight and performance, 64; celebrity culture in, 22, 93, 94–95, 98–104, 126–27, 326n28, 326n31; changed relationships between public and private, 57, 62; dated from 1890 to 1917, 3; and early feature films (1913-1917), 50; efforts to stabilize modernity, 3, 5, 9, 87, 104, 127; emphasis on collective nature of spectatorship, 48–49; emphasis on communities, 8, 65, 85; four dimensions of, 5; ideals of uplift and community, 4, 5, 9, 12, 50; idea of temporary state of diversity, 254–55; and immigrant assimilation, 7, 209, 254; importance of oversight, 57, 60, 171; investigations into public amusements, 174; as later phase of modernity, 14; and leisure-centered lifestyle, 8, 10, 23, 133, 326n28, 336n9; loss of momentum after WWI, 292, 294–95, 295–96; and national identity, 106, 206, 253; and new collective social formations, 103; and public monitoring, 59, 95, 171; regulatory efforts, 5–6, 355n31; self-examination and oversight, 69–70; self-presentation in, 94; stress on integration of different aspects of culture while maintaining diversity, 92; and surveys, reports, and studies, 106; tension between modernity and tradition, 319n33; and transitional cinema (1907-1917), 2, 3–4, 10–12, 12–16, 21; as way of seeing, 4–10
Progressive Party, 17
Progress of a Negro, 251
prologues, 22, 56, 57, 68, 78, 320n38, 321n45, 321n46; acknowledgement of audiences' participation in other cinematic activities, 76; author prologue, 74–75; breaking of character by performers, 72; and consumption, 75; and differences of early features from later films, 67; direct engagement with audience and narration, 66; in features from 1913, 68–69; and films as self-aware texts, 69–70; forms of, 69; as mini stage plays, 67–68; moderation of hypnotic force of cinema, 77; and multiple diegesis, 51, 70, 73–74, 78; origination around 1912-12 as exhibition strategy, 67; and power of celebrity, 71; and self-aware spectator, 66–67, 69, 73, 76, 77, 91–92; as separate films, 68; undermine coherence of story world, 70; use of stage or performance frame, 68, 69; widespread use of, 69
public recreation, 9, 133
Pullman porters, 245

Quinn, Michael, 51, 56
Quo Vadis?, 52, 68, 152, 155, 227, 253

Rabinovitz, Lauren, 17, 174
race and cinema, 24. *See also* black film audiences; black filmmaking

414

The Railroad Managers, 228
The Railroad Porter, 243, 244–46, 381n172, 381n176
Ranch Girls on the Rampage, 231
Range Pals, 228
The Raven, author prologue, 74–75
Re-Birth of a Nation, 250
reconstructive spectatorship, 209–10, 211
Record-Herald, Chicago, 136–37, 178, 181
recreation, 9, 133
recreation departments, 336n9
Redemption, 105, 327n40
Red Feather releases, 238
reformers, on Chicago censorship board, 192–93
Regeneration, 62–66; association between oversight and performance, 64; inscription of power onto look, 64–65; juxtaposition of roles of management in law enforcement and crime, 64; narrative discourse of people watching others' actions, 63–64; overseeing gaze and loss of privacy, 63; prologue, 69
Regent Theater, New York, 68
regulation of films, Chicago: and balanced programs, 43–44; and industry reactions, 43–44; regulation of length of shows and theater lighting, 42; targeted longer shows and films, 42–43. *See also* Chicago film censorship
Reid, Mark A., 381n172, 381n176
Reid, Wallace, 58, 78, 81
Reinhardt, Max, 188
Relief and Aid Society, 178
Rice, Wallace, 193
Richards, J. R., 336n9
Richards, Larry, 370n5, 381n172, 385n225
The Right to Live, 198
Riley, W. J., 219
RKO, 67
Robson, May, 109
Roe, Clifford, 201
Romains, Jules: "The Crowd at the Cinematograph," 311n54
The Romantic Journey, 46

room-to-room/space-to-space cutting, 58
Roosevelt, Franklin Delano, 267
Roosevelt, Theodore, 266, 267
Rose, Mrs. N. S., 282
Rosen, Philip, 255
Rosenwald, Julius, 305n67
Rose theater, Chicago, 163, 164
Rosher, Charles G., 264
Ross, Charles J., 109
Ross, Edward Alsworth, 9, 34, 38–39, 307n75
Rothacker, 126, 274
Rothapfel, Samuel "Roxy," 67–68, 160, 161, 162, 349n138
Royal theater, Chicago, 132, 145
The Ruling Passion, 46
Russell, Lillian, 100
Russell, Sylvester, 215, 217, 219, 221, 228

Safeguards for City Youth at Work and Play (Bowen), 20
Saint Malachy's Roman Catholic Church, 182
Santa Claus and the Miner's Child, 184
Sargent, Epes Winthrop, 145
Saros, Daniel Earl, 3
Satana, 227
Saved by the Juvenile Court, 327n38
The Scarlet Letter, 197
Schaefer, Peter J., 147
Schiller, Sam, 288
Schlesinger, Philip, 256
Schoendstadt, Henry, 148
Schwartz, Samuel, 177
Scott, Cyril, 109
Scott, Lulu, 109
Screenland, 111
The Sea Wolf, 74
segregation. *See* Chicago theaters, discrimination against African Americans
self-awareness, 50; celebrity and, 127–29; as heightened consciousness of oneself as seen by others, 106–7; spectatorial, 66–67, 69, 73, 76, 77, 91–92, 92
self-creation, 106

INDEX

self-display, and cinema, 100–101, 324n63
self-help manual, 103
self-improvement, consumerist forms of, 103
self-monitoring, 8, 11, 12
self-presentation, 94
Selig, William, 15, 17, 45, 52, 53, 161, 253, 275, 304n61
Selig-Polyscope, 284; Diamond Specials, 54; Red Seal plays, 54–55; Spectacular Specials, 54
Selznick, Louis, 274
sensational films, appeal to black audiences, 234
serials: addressed collective social audience, 301n35; appeal to groups without social capital, 231, 234; dialectic of entrapment and freedom, 233; representations of white male villainy, 377n135; sensational melodramas, 377n137
settlement houses, 8, 18
Shadowland, 101
Sheldon, Edward, 153, 225
Sherman Antitrust Act, 6
The Shielding Shadow (series), 232
Shipp, Jesse, 383n197
Shippy (police chief), 176, 177
Shirk, Mrs. George M., 191
Shoecraft, Joe, 382n179
short films: film industry focus on, 1907-1917, 15, 52; programs of, 90, 167; still viable in 1916, 53
short program services, 54
Sid Euson's theater, Chicago, 135
Siedenburg, Frederic, 174, 192
Siegell, Ludwig, 150
Sienkiewicz, Henry, 68
signifying, 241
The Sign of the Rose/The Alien, 67
Silas Marner, 200
Simmel, Georg: "The Metropolis and Mental Life," 33–34
Sinclair, Upton: *The Jungle*, 7
Singer, Ben, 1, 15, 17, 51, 231, 234, 301n35, 302n49, 319n33

The Sins of the Sons, 201
Sittner's Criterion, Chicago, 139
Sklar, Robert, 301n35
The Slacker, 251
Slaughter, Cassie Burch, 244
The Slaver, 251
Slaves of Morphine, 195
Slide, Anthony, 269–70
Slonaker, James, 223–24
Small, Albion, 305n67
Smith, J. Hockley, 218
Smith, Joel, 180–81
Snow, Mrs. Charles G., 191
Snow White, 320n38; prologue, 69, 76–77, 78
social work, 7
sociology, origin in Chicago, 17
Some Legislative Needs in Illinois (Bowen), 20
Soundies Distributing Company, 246, 383n197, 383n200
South Halsted entertainment district, 162, 164–67; ethnic theaters, 166–67
South State Street theaters, Chicago, 164
Spanish-American War, 250, 254
Spear, Allan H., 221, 374n68
"spectatoritis," 38
spectatorship/spectatorship theory, 12, 21, 27; association of prolonged viewing and increased suggestion, 43; belief that identification with film threatened individuality, 43; collective nature of spectatorship, 12, 31, 37, 48–49, 84, 301n35; linked to utopian view of society, 48; narrative films and shifts in spectatorship, 27, 255; reconstructive spectatorship, 209–10, 211; and self-awareness, 66–67, 69, 73, 76, 77, 91–92; spectatorship linked with hypnosis and suggestion, 39, 40–41, 43
Speedway Theater, Chicago, 151
Spence, Louise, 240
The Spirit of '76, 263
The Spoilers, 69, 387n13; prologue, 72
Spoor, George, 55, 258, 276, 278–79, 284, 393n110

Stacy, Jack, 326n36
stage prologues, 68, 97
Stamp, Shelley, 12, 13–14, 75–76, 95, 113, 233, 301n35, 319n33, 324n6, 331n76, 376n122
stardom: and Americanization, 129; associated by public with chance and self-assertion, 112–13; and importance of work and talent, 101–2; mania of in 1910s, 93; rise of, 93
star endorsements, 330n68
stars: mostly women in 1910s, 99, 101, 335n129; personal appearances in local theaters, 326n36; qualities of, 330n70
star-search contests, 102, 127–28, 129, 326n31; *Chicago Herald* "Sue" contest, 117–20, 122, 129, 331n81, 331n82, 331n83, 332n92; Chicago Movie Exposition 1917 contest, 125–27; and creation of persona and marketing of, 102; and frustration of audiences with unfulfilled ambitions, 128; and illusion of opportunity, 95, 116; and local celebrity, 116–25; and photography, 97–98; *Photoplay's* "Beauty and Brains" contest, 23n1, 93–94, 330n75; and public appetite for film-related celebrity, 120; sponsors' promotion of products and building of circulation, 116; by Universal, 96, 333n96
star system, 16, 50, 51, 90, 104, 108
Star Theater, Chicago, 146, 202, 215, 217, 232; adults-only films, 234; all-professional song reviews, 219
States Theater, Chicago, 215, 219, 227, 234; adults-only films, 234; feature films, 227; sensational films, 235
Steffin, Walter P., 203
Steiner, "Big Bill," 18–19
Stewart, Anita, 122
Stewart, Jacqueline Najuma, 24, 209, 211, 212, 213, 215, 216, 220, 224, 226, 229, 231, 233, 240, 248, 370n5; on black theaters providing refuge, 218–19; on comedic treatment of black characters in Ebony films, 241; on *The Railroad Porter*, 245
The Stolen Play, 46
Stonehouse, Ruth, 238
"store room theater," 339n30
Storey, Edith, 126
Strand Theater Company, 160
Stroll: first- and second-run movie houses, 217; new movie theaters competing with older live theaters, 218; popularity of serials, 232; white-owned vaudeville and stock theaters, 221
Studebaker Theater, Chicago, 68, 152, 156, 157
Sue, 117–20, 121, 122, 123, 129
suggestion: associated with prolonged viewing, 43; as attraction, 45–46; and crowd theory, 30; described in electrical, telegraphic, or photographic metaphors, 39–40; described in terms of sickness and contagion, 39–40; as force that creates aggregate mind, 39; and hypnotism, 31, 39; and identification, 44; as visual force, 40
The Sunshine Line, 121, 124, 125
superfeatures, 50, 54, 56
superimposition, 86
The Survey of Conditions Demoralizing to Women and Girls in the Saloons of Chicago, 353n11
Susman, Warren, 93, 103
Swanson's Moving Picture Theater, 340n34, 340n35
Sweiter, Robert A., 365n146

Talmadge, Norma, 79, 111
tango, banning of, 189, 361n97
Tanner, Henry O., 249
Tarde, Gabriel, 33, 35, 39, 40, 47, 311n49
Taylor, Clyde R., 207
Taylor, Graham, 18, 192
telegraph, 60
telephone, 60
Thaw-White murder, 105, 327n40

theater chains, 23, 147–53
Theater De Luxe, 158–62
theaters, Chicago. *See* Chicago theaters
Thomas, Olive, 326n37
Thompson, William Hale, 171, 173, 198, 257, 269, 365n147; crackdown on public entertainment, 201; investigation of city's censorship, 199; investigation of Funkhouser's conduct, 198. *See also* Chicago film censorship (1915-1923, Thompson)
tinfoil sound recordings, 3
Told at Twilight, 238
Tom Sawyer, prologue, 73–74, 78
Toner, David K., 191
Toner, Henry J., 191
Tourneur, Maurice, 93
trade press, 3, 14, 22, 48, 131, 138
Traffic in Souls, 170, 197, 319n33, 321n46, 324n10, 387n13; and correct use of modern technology, 60; endorsement of Progressive methods of social control, 60; and overseeing gaze, 57, 59–62; prologue and epilogue, 57, 69, 321n46; references to both modernity and Progressivism, 60; reflection of societal concerns about white slavery, 59–62; reliance on oversight, overhearing, and use of surveillance technologies, 60, 61
transitional cinema, 1907-1917. *See* cinema, 1907-1917
Trans-Oceanic Film Company, 195
Triangle News, 146
Triangle Theater, Chicago, 2, 53, 54, 145, 146
Trilby, 45, 236
Trinz, J., 284
The Trooper of Troop K, 229–31
Tropical Film Company, 271
Trotter, Wilfred, 47, 308n1
The Troubles of Sambo and Dinah, 250
Trykay Film Company, 242
Tufts, James Hayden, 305n67
Tuskegee Institute, 251

20,000 Leagues Under the Sea, 75, 76, 78, 273
The Two Orphans, 237
Tyson, Mrs. Russell, 274

Uhlir, John Z., 178
The Unborn, 155, 235
Uncle Sam at Work, 389n41
Uneasy Money, 56
Unicorn Film Service, 53
United Film Service Protective Association, 355n41
United Photoplays, 198
Universal, 22, 126, 183; 1915 movie game, 147; star-search contests, 96
universal language theory, 48, 85, 386n1
University of Chicago, 18
University of Chicago settlement house, 305n67
Unwritten Law, 355n42
uplift, Progressive ideals of, 4, 5, 9, 12, 50, 212–13
urban clean-up campaigns, 8, 173–75, 200
urbanization, 6, 103
urban planners, Chicago, 337n15
urban poor, 5, 7
ushers, costumed, 92

vamp films, 231
The Vampires (series), 232
Vaudette theater, Chicago, 145
vaudeville theaters, 302n49; converted to neighborhood movie theaters, 139; white-owned on Stroll, 221
Veiller, Bayard, 235
Vendome Theater, Chicago, 213, 215
Verne, Jules, 322n54
Vice Commission, Chicago, 12n57, 185, 186, 198–99, 312n57
Villa, Pancho, 104, 254, 267, 271–73, 327n38, 376n115, 390n67
Vitagraph, 202, 253, 275; appeal of Funkhouser's ban of *Within the Law*, 202, 203; one-reelers, 58
Vittum, Harriet, 192, 200

VLSE (Vitagraph Lubin Selig Essanay), 54
The Voice on the Wire (series), 232
Von Suttner, Bertha, 263
Vorse, Mary Heaton, 40, 41, 308n9

Wade, Edward T., 224
Walker, George, 243
Walker, Lillian, 126
Walker, William, 207
"Walkin' the Dog" nights, 219
Waller, Gregory, 30, 371n10
Walthall, Henry, 74
War Brides, 80, 274, 278, 391n80
Ward, Fannie, 126
war documentaries and newsreels, 263–66
Warner Bros., 67
Warner Feature Film Company, 53, 196, 246
War on Three Fronts, 273
War Pictures, 265
The Warring Millions, 263, 265, 269
Warshauer, Dorothy, 119
Washburn, Bryant, 126, 276, 392n92, 392n93
Washburn, Mrs. Virginia Brooks, 193
Washington, Booker T., 249, 251
Washington Theater, Chicago, 215, 218, 232; adults-only films, 234; feature films, 227; western films, 228
Weigle, Edwin F., 265
Weinberg, Louis, 144
Wells, H. G., 309n18
westerns, 387n14; drew on discourses of nation and citizenship, 228–29; favored by black film audiences, 228–31; Native Americans in, 229
Whalan, Mark, 97
What Happened to Mary?, 233, 324n10
Where Are My Children?, 62, 155; allegory, 87, 88; prologue, 79; superimposition, 86
White, Pearl, 111, 126
white slavery films, 231, 235
Who Is Your Neighbor?, 235

Wigmore, John, 305n67
Wild Birds in Their Haunts, 160
Willemen, Paul, 255
Williams, Bert, 237–38, 243
Williams, Kathlyn, 322n50
Williams, Linda, 207–8
Williams, Peggy, 238
Williamson Brothers, 75
Willis, Wilbur F., 199
Wilson, Woodrow, 261, 266–67, 271, 286, 294–95, 390n67
"Wisconsin Copies," 196
The Wishing Ring, 320n38; multiple diegesis, 73; prologue, 70–71, 72–73
The Witch, 46
Within the Law, 202, 235
Wollen, Peter, 77–78, 88
The Woman God Forgot, 235
Womanhood: The Glory of the Nation, 253, 274
A Woman's Worst Enemy, 247, 248
women: cinema as hope for transformation, self-improvement, and luxury, 96, 104, 324n10; increased enrollment of in higher education, 97; increase in number working outside home, 96; interest in self-display, 100–101; Progressive Era as period of transition for, 97; turn to cinema for self-advancement blocked elsewhere, 96–97, 100
workplace legislation, 5, 7, 133
World Pictures, 2, 53, 93, 191; Special Film Corporation, 195
World theater, Chicago, 156–57
World War I, and film industry: army recruitment drives sponsored by film companies, 275–76; Chicago theaters accused of disrespecting national anthem, 270–71, 279; Chicago theaters at center of antitax movement, 289; class differences among Chicagoans in support of, 274; displacement of Progressivism's tenets, 25; impact on American national identity,

INDEX

World War I, and film industry (*continued*) 257–58; increased distrust in national government, 256; industry endorsement of Wilson's neutrality policy, 262; industry's lack of unity in approach to war, 258; labor shortages due to drafting of employees, 291; linking of cinema to patriotism, 284–86, 292; and nationalism and redefinition of boundaries, 25, 257; and neutrality, 261–63; patriotism and protests in theaters, 275–80; patrons' reception of war tax affected by demographics, 290–91; preparedness movement, 266–71; price cuts, 289–90; reduction in number of films, 277, 296; support for troops and resistance to war, 283–93; theater benefits for armed forces, 276; use of war to reposition, 292; views of how films should handle war, 277–78; war taxes on movie theaters, 25, 53, 283–84, 286–91

World War I films, 259–83; censorship of *The Little American,* 280–83; *Getting Villa,* 271–72; newsreels and documentaries, 263–66, 292; production not dominated by war and war themes, 277; pro-German films, 265, 269–70, 283; surge in pro-Allies films at outbreak of war, 275; unpopularity of war films, 279; upswing in war films as war became imminent, 273–74; verdicts of censorship board on war films, 274

Wyatt, Edith, 166

Wynn, Neil, 295

Yiddish vaudeville, 167
YMCA, 8, 244
Young, C., 167
Young, Clara Kimball, 329n65
Young, James, 236, 329n65
Young Romance, 324n10

Ziegfeld Theater, Chicago, 56, 151, 152, 156, 157, 158, 162
Zilligen, August, 195
Zimmerman, Louis, 224
Zintheo, Lucille, 330n75
Zueblin, Charles, 305n67
Zukor, Adolf, 326n37

www.ingramcontent.com/pod-product-compliance
Lightning Source LLC
Chambersburg PA
CBHW070257240426
43661CB00057B/2576